2006

IMPORTANT

W9-ABL-309

HERE IS YOUR REGISTRATION CODE TO ACCESS MCGRAW-HILL
PREMIUM CONTENT AND MCGRAW-HILL ONLINE RESOURCES

For key premium online resources you need THIS CODE to
gain access. Once the code is entered, you will be able to
use the web resources for the length of your course.

Access is provided only if you have purchased a new book.

If the registration code is missing from this book, the registration screen on our
website, and within your WebCT or Blackboard course will tell you how to obtain
your new code. Your registration code can be used only once to establish
access. It is not transferable.

To gain access to these online resources

1. **USE** your web browser to go to: **mhhe.com/chapin1**

2. **CLICK** on "First Time User"

3. **ENTER** the Registration Code printed on the tear-off bookmark on the right

4. After you have entered your registration code, click on "Register"

5. **FOLLOW** the instructions to setup your personal UserID and Password

6. **WRITE** your UserID and Password down for future reference. Keep it in a safe place.

If your course is using WebCT or Blackboard, you'll be able to use this code to
access the McGraw-Hill content within your instructor's online course.

To gain access to the McGraw-Hill content in your instructor's WebCT or
Blackboard course simply log into the course with the user ID and Password
provided by your instructor. Enter the registration code exactly as it appears to
the right when prompted by the system. You will only need to use this code the
first time you click on McGraw-Hill content.

These instructions are specifically for student access. Instructors are not required
to register via the above instructions.

The McGraw-Hill Companies

Mc Graw Hill **Higher Education**

Thank you, and welcome to your
McGraw-Hill Online Resources.

0-07-319387-9 t/a
Chapin
Social Policy for Effective Practice

REGISTRATION CODE
REGISTRATION CODE

6FB7-QAG8-WHCC-ACCW-EQ33

The McGraw-Hill Companies
Mc Graw Hill **Higher Education**

This is a much-needed series for social work education and the social work profession...one of the best I have seen in decades!

–Mildred C. Joyner, *West Chester University*

Each title is the first of its kind to offer instructors and their students a multidimensional understanding and experience of the world of social work:

- **Each book in the series is accompanied by a custom Web site, updated weekly,** that allows students to examine events in the news and to think about and discuss those events in the context of what they are reading. The Web site also links students to a wealth of carefully selected Internet resources that are constantly updated and refreshed.

- **A specially designed online reader, *The Social Work Library,* is also available to students,** with over 100 articles and book chapters linked to the key ideas and principles covered in each volume in the series.

- ***Practicing Social Work™,* a CD-ROM packaged with each volume in the series,** offers complex, richly populated case exercises, with multiple options in text and video for analysis and intervention. The CD gives students a real-world sense of how social workers approach cases from micro, mezzo, and macro perspectives and trains them in the use of social work tools they will likely encounter in their professional lives.

- **A free booklet on social work ethics accompanies each text** in recognition of CSWE recommendations, and is authored by Kim Strom-Gottfried, University of North Carolina, who is nationally recognized for her educational workshops on the subject.

New Directions in Social Work is a comprehensive effort by a team of accomplished social work educators to move social work education forward. We want to help you enrich and deepen your students' learning experiences. And we want to know what you think! Please e-mail us with your feedback. In the meantime, we welcome your students to a most gratifying, heartbreaking, edifying profession: social work.

Alice A. Lieberman, Series Editor
University of Kansas
e-mail: alicel@ku.edu

Rosemary K. Chapin
University of Kansas
e-mail: rchapin@ku.edu

Social Policy for
Effective Practice

NEW DIRECTIONS IN SOCIAL WORK: A McGRAW-HILL SERIES

Consulting editor, Alice A. Lieberman, University of Kansas
Technical consultant, Jerry Finn, Temple University

New Directions in Social Work is an innovative series of texts, software, and custom electronic content for the *foundations* courses in the Social Work curriculum. Each title is the first of its kind to offer instructors and their students a multidimensional experience and understanding of the world of social work. Each volume in the series includes a custom Web site, online reader, and *Practicing Social Work*, a unique collection of virtual case studies.

Books in the Series

Social Work and Social Welfare: An Invitation by Marla Berg-Weger

Contemporary Social Work Practice by Marty Dewees

Human Behavior in the Social Environment by Anissa Taun Rogers

Social Policy for Effective Practice: A Strengths Approach by Rosemary K. Chapin

Research for Effective Social Work Practice by Judy L. Krysik

Also from McGraw-Hill

Social Work Practice with a Difference: Stories, Essays, Cases, and Commentaries by Alice A. Lieberman and Cheryl B. Lester

The Social Work Experience: An Introduction to Social Work and Social Welfare, Fourth Edition by Mary Ann Suppes and Carolyn Cressy Wells

Social Policy for Effective Practice

A STRENGTHS APPROACH

Rosemary Kennedy Chapin

University of Kansas

Boston   Burr Ridge, IL   Dubuque, IA   Madison, WI   New York
San Francisco   St. Louis   Bangkok   Bogotá   Caracas   Kuala Lumpur
Lisbon   London   Madrid   Mexico City   Milan   Montreal   New Delhi
Santiago   Seoul   Singapore   Sydney   Taipei   Toronto

Higher Education

Published by McGraw-Hill, an imprint of The McGraw-Hill Companies, Inc., 1221 Avenue of the Americas, New York, NY 10020. Copyright © 2007 by The McGraw-Hill Companies. All rights reserved. No part of this publication may be reproduced or distributed in any form or by any means, or stored in a database or retrieval system, without the prior written consent of The McGraw-Hill Companies, Inc., including, but not limited to, in any network or other electronic storage or transmission, or broadcast for distance learning.

This book is printed on acid-free paper.

1 2 3 4 5 6 7 8 9 0 FGR/FGR 0 9 8 7 6

ISBN–10: 0-07-284582-1
ISBN–13: 978-0-07-284582-2

Editor in Chief: *Emily Barrosse*
Publisher and Sponsoring Editor: *Beth Mejia*
Special Projects Editor: *Rebecca Smith*
Developmental Editor: *Robert Smith*
Editorial Coordinator: *Ann Helgerson*
Marketing Manager: *Dean Karampelas*
Permissions Coordinator: *Sue Ewing*
Media Project Manager: *Sean Crowley*
Production Editor: *Leslie LaDow*

Manuscript Editor: *Laura Iwasaki*
Designer: *Kim Menning*
Interior Designer: *Glenda King*
Cover Designer: *Marianna Kinigakis*
Photo Research Coordinator: *Brian J. Pecko*
Production Supervisor: *Randy Hurst*
Composition: 9.5/13 Stone Serif by
    Interactive Composition Corporation, India
Printing: 45# New Era Plus by Quebecor

Cover image: © Photodisc

Produced in association with NASW Press, a division of the National Association of Social Workers.

NASW PRESS

Library of Congress Cataloging-in-Publication Data

Chapin, Rosemary Kennedy.
   Social policy for effective practice : a strengths approach / Rosemary Chapin.
      p. cm.
   Includes bibliographical references and index.
   ISBN-13: 978-0-07-284582-2 (alk. paper)
   ISBN-10: 0-07-284582-1 (alk. paper)
    1. Social service—United States. 2. United States—Social policy. 3. Public
welfare—United States. 4. Human services—United States. I. Title.

HV95.C416 2007
361.973—dc22

                                   2005057663

The Internet addresses listed in the text were accurate at the time of publication. The inclusion of a Web site does not indicate an endorsement by the authors or McGraw-Hill, and McGraw-Hill does not guarantee the accuracy of the information presented at these sites.

www.mhhe.com

361.973
C463

This book is dedicated to my husband, Barry,
and my children, Brett, Bridgett, and Ben, who
have unfailingly encouraged and supported
my work. It is also dedicated to my father,
Willie B. Kennedy, and to my mother,
Dorothy Konovalski Kennedy, who understood
the wisdom of building on people's strengths
and worked to do just that every day of her life.

DR. ROSEMARY KENNEDY CHAPIN is an award-winning teacher and researcher, possessing extensive program development experience in the social policy arena. After receiving her PhD, she worked as a Research/Policy Analyst for the Minnesota Department of Human Services, where she was involved in crafting numerous long-term care reform initiatives. In 1989, she joined the faculty at the University of Kansas, where she established and now directs the Office of Aging and Long Term Care (OALTC), which was created to improve social service practice and policy for older adults, particularly low-income elders. Her social policy research and strengths-based training initiatives can be viewed at www.oaltc.ku.edu. Dr. Chapin has been recognized at both the state and the federal level for her social policy research and advocacy. In addition to numerous articles and book chapters on social policy, she has also co-authored a text and various book chapters on the use of the strengths approach in social work practice with older adults. She teaches social policy and social work and aging courses at the University of Kansas.

Rosemary Chapin lives in Lawrence, Kansas, with her husband, Barry; cairn terrier, Smokey (think Toto); and the youngest of her three children.

BRIEF CONTENTS

CONTENTS

PREFACE

Welcome to the exploration of how social policy will shape your future practice. *Social Policy for Effective Practice: A Strengths Approach* is written for students who will become human services practitioners. It is designed to equip you to understand the processes of defining need, analyzing existing social policy, and influencing new policy. Moreover, the book presents each of these elements using a strengths approach. The premise of *Social Policy for Effective Practice* is that a greater focus on the strengths and resources of people and their environments rather than on their problems and pathologies should be integrated into the social policy development process.

Many social policy textbooks present a fragmented approach to understanding social policy. First, they discuss a variety of social problems. They then present frameworks for policy analysis. Finally, they conclude by reviewing some major social policies and programs. It has been my experience that students come away from a class using such a textbook with a beginning understanding of a variety of social problems and programs but with little idea of how to use what they have learned to understand or shape social policy when they become social workers. In contrast, *Social Policy for Effective Practice* provides an integrated approach to the policymaking process. A clear philosophical base and a common theoretical framework underlie the discussion of each component of the policy process. The focus is on how understanding social policy can contribute to effective social work practice on a day-to-day basis across the gamut of social work settings.

Whether you are in an undergraduate or graduate school of social work or in another helping profession, you will find this book useful as you attempt both to understand and to shape social policy. In my years of work in analyzing, making, and teaching social policy, I have been surprised at the hesitancy of many human service professionals to engage in the policymaking process at either the agency or the governmental level. The very people who are on the front line and therefore could provide valuable perspectives often don't recognize the resources they can bring to the policymaking arena. Just as unsettling, they have little idea of how they might influence social policy. My intent in writing this book is to provide you with clear and concise frameworks for understanding the elements of the policy process that incorporate a strengths approach and to equip you to use these tools to influence social policy.

My aim is to spark your desire to understand and influence social policy. In order to help reach this outcome, I have interwoven four essential themes throughout this book: (1) the importance of thinking critically about social policy, (2) the benefits of using the strengths perspective in policy analysis and development, (3) the vital role social policy plays in all areas of practice, and (4) the absolute responsibility of every social worker to engage in policy practice.

Take a look at the table of contents for this book. The chapter titles reflect content on social policy that is deemed basic for effective social work practice. In Chapters 1–6, we will examine different frameworks for understanding social policy as well as basic tools for analyzing and influencing social policy. We will also consider the influence of history and economics on social policy. Chapters 7–11 will then provide you with a chance to build your skills using basic tools to analyze policies affecting major client groups in a variety of fields of practice. Moreover, each chapter incorporates a strengths approach so that you can begin to consider clients' strengths and resources as well as their needs when evaluating relevant policies. In Chapter 12 the book concludes by looking to the future and considering ideas about how social workers can effectively respond to projected changes in the new century.

Social Policy for Effective Practice is supported by a CD-ROM, *Practicing Social Work,* which includes two interactive case studies. The book is also supported by *The Social Work Library*, which is comprised of online, full-text articles that relate to specific chapters. The *SWL* can be accessed at www.mhhe.com/chapin1. Additional margin links will guide you to the latest Web resources on the topics discussed. These margin links will give you and your clients access to the most current information about the major policies and programs we discuss.

End-of-chapter exercises will draw on the case studies to illustrate how the information provided in the chapter is directly applicable to social work practice. You can also expand your knowledge of the topics covered in the book through use of *The Social Work Library*.

The rich variety of resources and links provided as part of *Social Policy for Effective Practice* makes it possible to expand or contract the content to fit the variety of timeframes and levels in which social policy courses are taught. No matter what point in your education you are introduced to my text, I hope you will use the range of resources provided here not only as course material, but also as tools with which you will help to shape policy and programs in your chosen practice setting.

ACKNOWLEDGMENTS

Many people helped shape this book. Dr. Charles Rapp and Dr. Dennis Saleebey, who have been integral to the development of the strengths perspective, generously reviewed book drafts. Dr. Ann Weick's scholarship on reconceptualizing social work practice using a strengths approach has also informed my work. Beth Baca, originally an MSW student in my social policy classes, did a great deal of background research that helped in crafting *The Social Work Library* as well as many tables, graphs, and other resources that are part of each chapter. Beth Baca, Theresa Gordon, and Becky Fast all graciously reviewed and critiqued early versions of this book.

Steve Rutter, Dr. Alice Lieberman, Becky Smith, Dr. Robert Weiss, and Ann Helgerson were part of the inventive editorial team that helped make this integrative series a reality. The other authors of the book series, Anissa Rogers, Marty Dewees, Marla Berg-Weger, Judy Krysik, and Jerry Finn, have helped craft a new, integrated way of introducing core content to social work students. Kameri Christy McMullin developed the Instructor's Manual that makes it easy to create a first-rate course syllabus to accompany my text.

Thank you all for your help and encouragement.

C H A P T E R 1

Social Work and Social Policy: A Strengths Perspective

I'm working with the Thompsons, a homeless family in which the mom works full-time. She is struggling to take care of her two small children, but there is just no housing available in our area that she can afford.

I have an 85-year-old client, Rosalie Pachta, who can still live in the community but needs some help with bathing and dressing. Her children live in other states, and she can't afford formal home and community-based care service (HCBS). All of the publicly funded HCBS programs have long waiting lists. She may end up in a nursing facility because she can't continue to live in the community without services.

Andy, a 21-year-old who suffered a permanent disability in a motorcycle accident, wants me to help him find work. However, many jobs do not provide health insurance, and he is fearful that if he earns more than the allowable income, he will lose his Medicaid benefits.

SOCIAL WORK STUDENTS WHO ARE INVOLVED IN FIELDWORK FACE these kinds of dilemmas every day. Some students may become so overwhelmed that they decide social work is just "too hard," and they leave the field. Even worse, other students decide they can't fight "the system," so they tell their clients "There is nothing to be done." However, you can make a different choice. You can choose to understand and influence the social policies that will shape your practice and your clients' lives. **Social policies** are the laws, rules, and regulations that govern the benefits and services provided by governmental and private organizations to assist people in meeting their needs. Although the term *needs* can mean different things to different people, social workers define needs as the gaps between existing conditions and some societal standard or required condition. For example, our society has developed standards of adequate nutrition for children. When children do not have access to a sufficient variety of foods to meet those standards, then their nutritional needs are not being met.

My purpose in writing this book is to provide you with clear and concise frameworks as well as the knowledge, skills, and, most importantly, the desire to become involved in developing social policies that incorporate the strengths perspective. The **strengths perspective** is a philosophical approach to social work that posits that the goals, strengths, and resources of people and their environment rather than their problems and pathologies should be the central focus of the helping process (Saleebey, 1992). In this text, both the terms *strengths perspective* and *strengths approach* are used to refer to this philosophical approach. I believe that a greater focus on people's strengths and resources, a strengths approach, should be integrated into the social policy development process. To begin this learning process, this chapter introduces and critiques some of the basic concepts and frameworks that will be the building blocks of your understanding of policy making. In addition, it explains how the ways in which we define and understand social problems shape the social policies and programs that we develop to address those problems. **Social problems** are concerns about the quality of life for large groups of people that are either held as a broad consensus among a population and/or voiced by social and economic elites (Chambers, 2000). Examples of social problems are drug abuse, juvenile delinquency, and homelessness. Subsequent chapters—particularly Chapters 5 and 6—present detailed information on how social workers can help analyze and develop social policies designed to address these problems. In future chapters, you will also learn about the historical, political, and economic contexts that shape social policy, and about the major social policies that affect our clients.

SOCIAL WORK AND SOCIAL POLICY

Social policies shape the social welfare system of the United States. The term **social welfare** refers to a nation's system of programs, benefits, and services that help people meet those social, economic, educational, and health needs that are fundamental to the maintenance of society. Social policies make it possible for clients to receive benefits and services they may desperately need. When I use the term **client,** I am referring to the recipient of the direct service or benefit provided by the social worker rather than to the taxpayer or policy maker. Taxpayers and policy makers are important constituents, but clients are the social worker's main concern. The terms *client group* and *target group* also refer to the population that is the primary focus of a social policy or program. Therefore, these terms are used interchangeably throughout this book. In this text, we focus primarily on social policies that shape benefits and services for our clients.

Social work can be defined as "the professional activity of helping individuals, groups or communities to enhance or restore their capacity for social functioning and creating societal conditions favorable to this goal" (National Association of Social Workers, 1973, p. 4). Social workers clearly have an essential role to play in helping to shape the social policies that underlie our social welfare system. Social workers deliver social welfare services. Social services are provided to meet social needs. They include adoption services, child protection services, mental health counseling, case management, services for older adults, for people in the corrections systems, and for people with disabilities. The effectiveness of these social services will be influenced by the social policies that govern their delivery. Therefore social workers interested in increasing service effectiveness need to become involved in developing social policy.

The Relationship between Social Policy and Social Work Practice

In order to help you understand the relationship between social policy and social work practice more clearly, we can examine policies, programs, and practice in the area of child abuse and neglect. Social policies determine who may remove children from their homes, where the children can be placed, whether they can receive specialized counseling services, who can provide those services, and how much providers will be paid. Social policies create the social programs that shape social work. Social workers serving children as well as other client groups cannot hope to help their clients unless they understand these crucial parameters that shape how they practice.

The child in foster care, the older adult in a nursing facility, and the incarcerated teenager have all powerfully experienced the results of social policy. Social workers, whether in private practice, in public child welfare, in health care, or in any other setting, also experience the consequences of social policy. You can become a much more effective social worker if you have a basic understanding of how policy influences practice in your agency and in your community. These insights can also help you move beyond understanding how policies work and coping with the aftermath of social policy to become proactive in helping to shape policies.

Social policies can be developed by both the public and the private sector. Public social policies are those policies created by federal, state, and local governments. Public social policy constitutes the preponderance of social policy in the United States. Nevertheless, private entities such as religious organizations may also develop social policies and programs, such as funding a free preschool program for low-income families, that helps these families reach their goal of seeing their children succeed in school.

Social policies can benefit clients in many ways. Very importantly, they can assist clients in achieving their life goals. As one example, they can assist single mothers in securing well-paying jobs by mandating equal opportunity in employment. Social policies can also help clients by creating **social programs,** defined as the specified set of activities that are designed to solve social

EXHIBIT 1.1

Relationship of Social Welfare System, Social Policy, and Social Workers

SOCIAL WELFARE SYSTEM

Our social welfare system includes benefits and services for families who have incomes that are insufficient to adequately nourish children.

SOCIAL POLICY

The Child Nutrition Act created the Special Supplemental Nutrition Program for Women, Infants, and Children (WIC).

SOCIAL WORKERS

WIC Program provides food benefits as well as nutrition and health education and referrals to health and other social services when needed. Social workers deliver some of these services.

problems and/or meet basic human needs. For example, public social policies that create childhood nutrition programs make it possible for children to be adequately fed. Social workers are often involved in delivering the services that are part of these programs.

Exhibit 1.1 illustrates the relationships among the social welfare system, social policy, and social workers. Our social welfare system includes benefits and services for families who have incomes that are insufficient to adequately nourish children. The Child Nutrition Act is the social policy that created the Special Supplemental Nutrition Program for Women, Infants, and Children (WIC). Clients who qualify receive food benefits as well as nutrition and health education and referrals to health and other social services when needed. Significantly, social workers deliver some of these services. Note that the arrows between the boxes in Exhibit 1.1 go in both directions. Social workers are influenced by social policy, but they can also influence what social policy is made.

Although social policies and programs are often created to assist people, they can also be a means of oppression. For example, in the past, the United States enacted public social policies that mandated separate schools for people of color and denied them the right to vote. As a professional social worker, you will see firsthand the results of both failed and effective social policies. However, you will be expected to do more than simply complain about unjust and ineffective policies. You will be expected to engage in policy practice. **Policy practice** is defined as the "effort to influence the development, enactment, implementation, or assessment of social policies" (Jansson, 1994, p. 8). Engaging in policy practice will enable you to help craft policies that support effective work with clients. This book begins and ends with a challenge to use the tools provided in these chapters to engage in policy practice that benefits our clients.

Social Work Values, Social Policy, and Policy Practice

The *Code of Ethics,* developed by the National Association of Social Workers (NASW, 1999) to help guide our practice, requires us to implement core social work values into our practice. Two fundamental values that can guide our efforts to shape more effective policy are self-determination and social justice. **Self-determination** refers to people's control of their own destiny. As we shall see, this concept is essential to the strengths perspective, which argues that clients possess resources that can help them achieve their goals. **Social justice** involves the fair distribution of societal resources to all people. It focuses on the means by which societies allocate their resources, which consist of material goods and social benefits, rights, and protections. These values reinforce the proposition that people who are disadvantaged by the current social order should have equal access to resources and opportunities to meet their common human needs. Therefore, social workers are expected to campaign for societal action on behalf of disadvantaged groups, regardless of gender, race, age, disability, or other characteristics that have been the basis for denying access to resources.

Practicing Social Work

You can examine the codes developed by the NASW as well as by other professional groups on the Practicing Social Work CD-ROM.

The Social Worker's Responsibility for Policy Practice Like the NASW, the Council on Social Work Education (CSWE) has developed standards that reinforce the responsibility of social workers to become proficient in the policy arena and to engage in policy practice. For example, CSWE Accreditation Standards for social work programs in colleges and universities require that the curriculum contains content on policy practice. Nevertheless, many social workers remain hesitant to engage in the policy-making process at either the agency or the governmental level. Social workers who are on the front lines working daily with clients can provide valuable perspectives on the consequences of social policies. However, they often don't recognize the resources they can bring to the policy-making arena, and they have little idea of how they can influence social policy.

Web Link

Visit www.mhhe.com/ chapin1, to find links to the National Association of Social Workers and the Council on Social Work Education's Web site.

You can be a different type of social worker. Whether you are already involved in a field placement or are still preparing for field placement, this book can help you build the skills necessary to use what you will hear and see to understand current policies and advocate for more effective policies. You will learn to be a "listening post" for the stories that could help policy makers more clearly understand the impact of their decisions. This book will show you how to make your voice and your clients' voices heard in the policy arena and how to be innovative in guiding the policy process.

Often, interest in social work grows from a basic desire to "help people." However, interest in how policy practice can help clients typically must be developed. You are preparing for a career that focuses on people in their environments. People and their environments are interdependent. Social policies shape our clients' environment and thus influence our ability to help them. Social work courses will help you sort out what it means to assist people and will provide conceptual tools to guide your efforts. The next section of this chapter will explain how to begin connecting what you learn about policy to your interest in helping people.

Getting Started   Regardless of whether you are currently in field placement, you will most easily master the content of this text if you use it immediately and try to connect it with your personal experience. To help make those connections, let's reflect on a situation in which you tried to help another person. When you were working with that person, did you give any thought to how social policies may have influenced your ability to help? Even if you never considered this question, social policies undoubtedly affected your efforts. For example, if you were working for a social service agency, then the agency's policies determined who could receive what kinds of services, who could offer those services, and how those services would be financed. Even if you were trying to offer assistance on a less formal level, such as when friends were getting a divorce or a grandparent was injured, it is likely that policies governing marriage and divorce, child custody, or long-term care significantly influenced your ability to help secure resources for the person in need. If you learn how to analyze social policies and advocate for needed change, then your efforts to help people can become more effective.

You can begin practicing the skills you've learned here in your own life. Social policies shape your life and the lives of your friends and family. Therefore, if you take the time to examine which policies irritate you and which ones actually work well, you will develop your capacity to successfully negotiate a path to your goals. At the same time, you will be building the necessary skills to support your clients in attaining their goals.

SOCIAL WORK AND THE STRENGTHS PERSPECTIVE

At the direct interpersonal level, methods of developing social policies, like methods of social work intervention, typically have been problem-focused and generally were designed to detect deficiency or pathology in the person experiencing the problem. The understanding of problems as originating in individual pathology has its roots in the medical model in which identifying the individual's problem or pathology is basic to treatment. For example, a medical practitioner diagnoses a patient as having a pathological condition such as influenza or diabetes and then prescribes treatment.

Traditionally, many policy makers have employed a similar approach to understanding needs or problems. Like medical practitioners, they have focused on defining and assessing "problems" that characterize individuals and institutions within their community. This approach is not necessarily inappropriate. In fact, a careful analysis of core social problems needs to be done in order to craft and implement effective social policy. The problem is that this approach has seldom been coupled with similar attention to identifying the strengths of the people and their environments that the policy targets (Chapin, 1995). Further, social problem analysis that focuses on the pathology of the person experiencing the problem often leads to policy strategies that blame the victim of the problem for its existence. For example, a homeless mother may be deemed unfit and thus lose custody of her children, even though there is no available housing in the community that she can afford.

Think for a moment about problems in your community such as teenage pregnancy and homelessness. When people assess these programs, they frequently focus immediately and solely on possible deficits, or shortcomings, of the people involved. Thus, homeless people are homeless because of drug addiction or laziness, and teenagers become pregnant because they lack self-control. Our understanding of a social problem is sometimes so negative that we are led to believe the problem is impossible to resolve. For example, some cities and towns feel there is little they can do to significantly diminish the size of their homeless community. In such cases, our perception of the problem needs to be reexamined. We may be asking the wrong questions. Perceiving people's needs in new ways may lead us to new answers.

In contrast to the medical model, the strengths perspective examines the strengths, goals, and resources of individuals and their communities as well as the barriers to meeting need that exist in the broader environment in which social problems develop. For example, social workers who examine homelessness from the strengths perspective would begin by looking carefully at the variety of people who are homeless and exploring their strengths and goals as well as resources in the community. They would also consider broader elements such as current economic conditions, the availability of affordable housing, the possibility of mental health problems among the homeless population, and the availability of government programs to assist people with inadequate financial resources due to such factors as low wages and serious or chronic illness. Identifying and acquiring the resources necessary for homeless people to meet their goals are central to the strengths perspective. Similarly, viewing teenage pregnancy through this lens requires us to focus from the beginning not only on

The Social Work Library

If you are unfamiliar with the strengths perspective or would like more detailed information, The Social Work Library, found at www.mhhe.com/chapin1, provides a comprehensive background on this topic.

the problem but on the teenagers, their strengths and goals, and the resources they need. The strengths perspective asserts that homeless people and teenagers possess or have access to personal and environmental resources (or strengths) that can help them deal with and perhaps overcome these problems. Chapters 5 and 6 present a more detailed account of how social workers can use the strengths perspective to redefine social problems and devise more effective policies to address these problems.

The strengths perspective, which underpins the strengths approach, can be used to reformulate problem-centered approaches to understanding need and creating social policies. Consider, for example, a population that historically was marginalized in U.S. society—people with disabilities. Based on the deficits approach, this population was labeled as "handicapped," and their capacity to perform a constructive role in society was minimized. However, employing a strengths-based strategy, people with disabilities and their advocates insisted that these individuals could be employed and utilize community resources if access to jobs and facilities rather than their disabilities became the central focus of relevant social policies. Their activism led to passage of the Americans with Disabilities Act (ADA), a 1990 law that bans discrimination against people with physical or mental disabilities in such areas as employment and transportation. Clearly, this type of result could not have been achieved until policy makers were convinced to abandon the traditional deficits approach in favor of a more positive focus on strengths and resources.

Policy Practice Infused with the Strengths Perspective

When we understand there are alternatives to the view that social problems are rooted in individual or environmental pathology, we can explore new possibilities. In this section, we will consider how policy development could reflect a strengths-based approach. We will begin with the initial stage in the policy-making process, which is defining needs, strengths, and goals. We will then focus on reconceptualizing social problems, involving clients in the policy development process, and convincing decision makers to allocate resources to meet those clients' needs.

Recasting Human Needs and Social Problems   It is possible to recast the social problems foundation of the policy development process and reconnect with the basic human needs tradition promoted by social workers such as Charlotte Towle (1945/1987). Towle's most famous publication is *Common Human Needs*, a manual written for the Bureau of Public Assistance of the U.S. Social Security Board, which was originally published in 1945. Developed for public assistance workers, the manual is based on the premise that all people have common human needs. Building on this premise, we can view social policy as a tool for helping people meet these common needs. Using this perspective enables us to define social problems not in terms of human and environmental deficits but in terms of barriers that disadvantaged groups confront in attempting to satisfy such basic needs as food, shelter, and positive community participation. Further, the strengths perspective argues that many of these barriers result from discrimination and exclusion in educational, political, and economic spheres based on demographic characteristics such as race, gender, and socioeconomic status (SES) rather than on individual attributes (Rappaport, Davidson, Wilson, & Mitchell, 1975).

An essential task of effective policy making, then, is to identify individual and community resources that can be used to remove these barriers and to create opportunities for people who have been excluded from full community participation so that they can meet their goals. For example, when working with people with mental illness, it is important to understand not only their disability but also their strengths as well as any available environmental resources that may contribute to their recovery. What brings joy to their lives? What are their goals? What policies hamper their recovery? How might these policies be reformulated to build on their strengths? The strengths and goals of the client are legitimate starting places in developing social policy. Problems and deficits should not be given center stage. When problems or needs are presented without any consideration of individual and community strengths and resources, policy makers are left to make decisions based on biases and prejudices.

What types of resources might be available to disadvantaged groups? Perhaps the most fundamental are neighborhood and community institutions such as schools, community centers, health facilities, and self-help organizations. Appropriate social policies can both enhance these resources and increase the access of disadvantaged groups to them.

Expanding the Client's Role   Approaching policy development from a strengths-based rather than a problem-centered perspective leads to an expanded role for clients and a corresponding shift in the role of the social worker. According to the strengths approach, the role of the professional helper, including the social worker, is not that of policy expert who informs the public and develops policy goals on her or his own. Rather, the social worker's roles are to ensure that policy makers take clients' perspectives into account, to act as a resource person, and to collaborate with clients throughout the policy development process.

At the same time, a strengths-based strategy calls for a more active role on the part of the groups that are the target of the proposed policy. The strengths perspective recognizes that the definition of a need or problem shapes the policy options that are considered. In turn, social policy essentially determines the allocation of scarce resources. Therefore, it is crucial that clients be included in the processes whereby needs are identified, problems are defined, and policies are developed.

A fundamental belief of the social work profession is that policy makers must understand the programs and policies they create from the viewpoint of the target population (Marsh, 2002). For example, policy makers need to understand that homelessness has many causes, and hearing about or talking to a homeless mother who works hard but cannot find affordable housing can help them see the issue in a new light. Social workers know that any initiative that does not start "where the client is" will more likely fail.

Temporary Aid to Needy Families (TANF), the federal program that provides financial assistance to low-income parents, is an example of how the failure to focus on clients' perspectives can produce inappropriate policy. TANF has strict work requirements, but it has inadequate provisions for expanding existing day care programs. This type of flaw highlights the need for policy makers to understand clients' perceptions and community strengths. Had more policy makers believed that most clients who are single mothers relied on public assistance not because they were unwilling to work but because they had to care for their young children, they might have incorporated less-stringent work stipulations into the law. In addition, they might have provided greater funding for day care centers, schools, and other community institutions that could care for children while their mothers worked. Providing their children with proper day care is a goal for many parents, and existing high-quality care is a community strength. When policy makers consider client goals and community strengths, as well as needs, more effective policies can be crafted.

Giving voice to the realities of service recipients can help policy makers who see recipients as the "other" to perceive the common human needs that they and the recipients share (Banerjee, 2002). Policy makers as well as TANF recipients are parents and recognize that children need care. Of course, there will not be consensus about needs among all recipients and policy makers. Such consensus is unnecessary. A variety of opinions and views typically are expressed when a policy is being formulated. However, consensus around broad goals, such as providing adequate care for children, can often be developed.

Claimsmaking   Recognizing needs, strengths, and goals from the client's perspective creates a base for policy making. However, for social policy to be enacted, concerned individuals must make a successful claim that resources should be allocated to meet a recognized need. This process is known as **claimsmaking.** Claims are often influenced by values and are intended to establish rights to resources. For example, social workers make social justice claims for people with disabilities based on their strong belief that these individuals have the same right as other citizens to access community services. Claimsmaking that asserts the right to equal opportunity for all citizens is consistent with the strengths perspective. Moreover, the strengths approach requires that clients themselves be involved in the claimsmaking process. We examine claimsmaking in greater detail in Chapter 6. For now, you need to be aware that simply recognizing a need will not result in the enactment of social policies to address that need. Rather, concerned parties have to make a successful claim that the need deserves attention at the policy level in order to gain support for policy formulation.

When social workers attempt to engage in claimsmaking and influence policy formulation, there will be groups that oppose their ideas as well as groups that agree with them. Potential economic gain and loss and political ideology will influence their views. Chapter 4 examines this economic and political context, as well as the conflictive nature of policy making, in greater detail. In addition, the policy practice sections in Chapter 6 explore strategies and tactics for dealing with conflict and negotiating consensus. Working to resolve conflict and consensus building are essential parts of policy practice and, in fact, can be a great way to develop your own strengths. Involving clients in this work helps them increase their power, that is, to become **empowered.** The strengths approach, like other empowerment-based helping strategies, seeks to help client groups build skills that can lead to achieving more power over their lives.

Principles of Strengths Perspective Policy Practice

As we have observed, the strengths perspective, which underpins the strengths approach, is rooted in a number of basic concepts and principles. The most important policy-focused strengths perspectives principles are listed below. These principles are discussed in depth in Chapter 5. Many of these principles are not unique to the strengths perspective. Social workers have discussed and used many of these principles to guide effective social work practice in the policy arena in the past. These strengths policy principles build on the work of Rapp, Pettus, and Goscha as well as other social workers who are searching for ways to incorporate social work values into the policy development process (Rapp, Pettus, & Goscha, in press). The strengths perspective is a stance that puts social work values into action.

- The strengths and goals of your clients are legitimate starting places in developing social policy. Problems and deficits should not be given center stage.

- Given that the definitions of social problems that typically guide policy and program development are socially constructed, our clients' perspectives concerning their problems, needs, strengths, and goals should be part of the social construction of need for policy development.

- Structural barriers that disadvantage our clients in meeting their needs and create unequal opportunities should be emphasized when claims for the right to benefits and services are made.

- The strengths perspective is premised on social work values of self-determination and social justice. Claims for benefits and services that allow people to overcome these additional barriers are made based on the right to equal access to resources and opportunities to meet needs and reach goals for citizens regardless of gender, race, age, disability, or other characteristics that have been the basis for denying access.

- Social policies and programs should build on individual and community strengths and resources and remove structural barriers that disadvantage the target group.

- The role of the social worker is not that of the expert who helps shape policy for hapless victims. Rather, it is that of the collaborator and resource person who helps gain attention for the perspectives of the target group.

- Social policy goals and design should focus on access, choice, and opportunity that can help empower the target group in meeting its needs and goals. The target group should be involved in all phases of policy development.

- Evaluation of the efficacy of social policy should include evaluation of outcomes for clients.

Frameworks for Policy Development

The Social Work Library

If you would like to compare these as well as other frameworks, explore the resources available at www.mhhe.com/chapin1. Explanations of the strengths perspective presented here build on the work of many authors (Rapp, 1998; Rapp & Chamberlain, 1985; Rapp, Pettus, & Goscha, in press; Saleebey, 2002; Tice & Perkins, 2002; Weick, Rapp, Sullivan, & Kisthardt, 1989). Several of these resources are available at The Social Work Library.

Now that we have examined basic concepts and principles, we can explore how the strengths perspective can be integrated into a framework for policy development. Note that I emphasize what the strengths perspective can add rather than claiming that other policy development frameworks should be abandoned. Approaches to policy development on which this book is based incorporate frameworks developed by a variety of authors, including Gilbert and Terrell (1998) and Chambers (2000).

Box 1.1 compares a problem-centered framework with one infused with the strengths perspective. This comparison can help you explore the ways in which social problems are defined and social policies are developed. This box summarizes many of the ideas previously discussed in this chapter and illustrates how those ideas inform the various stages of policy development. Although the strengths perspective shifts the focus away from individual problems, it does not require that we deny deficit or misery. However, it does demand that we shift our perspective, attitude, and language to focus on possibility and opportunity and the potential of the individual, who has strengths as well as needs.

The point of Box 1.1 is not to propose that only one of the formulations of the policy development process is correct or presents truth. Indeed, the problem-focused approach may more clearly reflect how policies have been and are

PROBLEM-CENTERED APPROACH	STRENGTHS-BASED APPROACH
Define problem.	Define needs, goals, and barriers.
• A situation is labeled a problem to be corrected.	• Identify basic needs and barriers to meeting needs.
	• Identify client goals.
Analyze problem, causes, and consequences.	Formulate policy alternatives.
	• Identify ways that barriers to reaching goals are currently overcome by clients (strengths) and through programs (best practice).
Inform the public. Engage in claimsmaking.	Claimsmaking is based on right to self-determination and social justice.
Develop policy goals.	Identify opportunities and resources necessary for people to meet their goals.
	Formulate policy goals informed by consumer collaboration.
Legitimize policy goals by building consensus.	Legitimize policy goals by negotiating consensus.
Develop and implement policy/program.	Develop and implement policy/program.
	• Program design informed by consumer collaboration.
	• Implementation informed by consumer involvement.
Evaluate and assess policy/program effectiveness.	Evaluate outcomes.
	• Evaluation and assessment emphasizes client outcomes and client feedback to improve policy.

BOX 1.1

Comparison of the Problem-Centered and Strengths-Based Approaches to Policy Development

Source: Adapted from "Social policy development: The strengths perspective," by R. Chapin. Social Work, 40, 4, pp. 506–514. Copyright © 1995 by National Association of Social Workers, Inc. Used with permission of NASW. Based on the work of Chambers, 2000; Gilbert and Terrell, 1998; and Tice & Perkins, 2002.

currently being made. Rather, the presentation of the strengths-infused framework highlights the values that underlie this approach, the outcomes you can expect when you use this approach, and the direction this approach provides for understanding and developing social policy. It focuses on discovering strategies that people who are confronted with barriers to meeting their identified needs can use effectively.

Further, attention to the process of negotiating the definitions of problems and policy goals as a component of the policy-making process reinforces the responsibility of social workers to help clients negotiate a consensus that reflects their view of reality. For example, more policy makers need to understand that many single mothers work full-time at a minimum wage job and are still unable to provide adequate food, shelter, and health care for their children because the minimum wage is so low and they don't have access to the education needed to secure a better-paying job. Hearing about or talking to these single mothers can help policy makers see issues in a new light. When social workers help initiate such an interaction, they are helping to negotiate an expanded understanding of the truth.

Moreover, once the policy has been negotiated and formulated, the strengths perspective mandates that clients be involved in implementing and evaluating the policy and programs that are enacted. This statement suggests that benefits and services, financing, and the service delivery system should be evaluated primarily on their effectiveness in helping clients achieve their goals rather than on cost, ease of administration, or potential for creating profit in the private sector. In summary, then, the policy-making process that includes the strengths approach strongly emphasizes that clients must be involved throughout all of its phases. It also recasts claimsmaking and the role of the social worker, and it stresses the importance of focusing on client outcomes in evaluating policy effectiveness.

IDENTIFYING AND DEVELOPING YOUR POLICY PRACTICE ABILITIES

The Social Work Library

Go to www.mhhe.com/ chapin1 to complete a strengths assessment on yourself.

A good place to start to apply the strengths perspective is with yourself. Take a good look at yourself and identify your strengths, resources, and areas of expertise. Exploring your own strengths lays the groundwork for discovering your client's strengths. Recognizing that your clients possess expertise and can share stories of strength and resilience will enable you to examine policy from an expanded perspective.

Consider becoming involved with grassroots efforts to develop services. Students in my policy classes often take me up on this challenge. For example, one group of students met with elder advocates and decided to help develop a home-sharing program for older adults and students. The older adults indicated they had large homes and needed someone to help with upkeep. They were willing to have someone live with them for reduced rent if that individual would help out. The students knew many other students who needed housing and would be willing to help older adults with upkeep. Class members were encouraged to see themselves as competent, to look for strengths in the person and the environment, and to become involved in developing policies and programs in the community. Their project culminated with the presentation of a model program that was then modified and implemented with the support of the local senior center. The students also helped the center develop policies governing home sharing. Their work provided the class with a hands-on example of policy and program development that included careful attention to the older adult population's perceptions of its needs and goals, recognition of strengths and resources within the community, and a search for "best practices" models in other communities. Opportunities to get involved in such efforts exist in every community.

Such involvement will also give you a chance to learn firsthand about the economic and political considerations and conflicts that influence policy. If you have some personal experience dealing with such conflicts, then you will find the content in coming chapters on such considerations and conflicts much easier to apply.

No doubt, there are many people in your community who can help you build policy practice skills. Think about the people you know. Is there someone who you believe is particularly savvy about how to shape social policy? The individual you identify might be the person in your agency or college who interprets the rules and regulations when there is a question. Typically, there is latitude in interpretation, and this person understands what discretion is possible and, we hope, uses it to the benefit of clients or students. This person is shaping social policy. Your agency or college may also have a staff person who is assigned to lobby at the legislature or make presentations at public hearings.

If you can't identify anyone you currently know who you feel is particularly savvy, get to know someone who is effectively engaged in policy practice. This task is not difficult. Begin by considering your interest area. For example, if your primary interest is working with older adults or children, there are advocacy groups in your area that are led by people who are working to influence policy every day. Call them up. Take them to lunch. If you have time, volunteer to help with one of their initiatives. Then, observe what they do. Ask questions. If you develop an ongoing relationship, see if they will talk with you about the ideas presented in this book, how these ideas might apply to their work, and how you might implement some of these ideas. As a volunteer, you can contribute a fresh perspective, help translate theories you are learning into practice, conduct background research, and help build coalitions among students, practitioners, and advocates (Sherraden, Slosar, & Sherraden, 2002).

Volunteering even a little time to a policy advocacy effort is a great way to network. Effective networking underlies effective policy practice. In Chapter 6, in the sections on policy development, we will examine networking and many other specific strategies and tactics that are useful in influencing policy. However, if you are not already involved with people who are role models of effective policy practice, then begin now to build your network. You will learn to apply the content of this book much more easily if you know the specifics of actual policy practice efforts.

As students and later as practitioners, you will likely lead very busy lives. Some of you will have jobs in which lobbying and client advocacy are primary job functions. Many of you will provide counseling and case management. However, in all social work roles, a practitioner who is alert to policy implications will be able to carve out some time to help shape policy. There are numerous ways that you can do so. For example, you can begin reshaping the views of fellow voters simply by speaking up when your clients are stereotyped. You can also call or e-mail your state legislator when you feel that policies aren't working for your clients. If you brainstorm with other students, all sorts of ideas for influencing policy that don't require great amounts of time or expertise will emerge. You aren't expected to craft new laws and get them passed single-handedly. Rather, most policy changes happen incrementally, and anything you can do is important for your clients. Many social workers feel as powerless as their clients. Effective involvement by a wider group of social workers can change that dynamic.

Integrating a Strengths Perspective: Benefits and Cautions

A major goal of social work education is to foster critical thinking skills. With this precept in mind, you should adopt a healthy skepticism concerning the advantages of integrating a strengths perspective into your policy practice. I encourage you to weigh the potential benefits and drawbacks of the strengths perspective. I hope there will be time for just such a discussion in your class. The following discussion of benefits and cautions can serve as a starting point for your critique.

Benefits of the Strengths Perspective   When thinking about the merits of integrating a strengths perspective into social policy courses, I see many positive results, including the following benefits.

First, as previously discussed, the strengths perspective offers an antidote to victim blaming. Clients are not seen as problems. Problem admiration is not the order of the day. As we have seen, the strengths perspective requires workers to assertively look for strengths and resources in their clients as well as the clients' families and environment. Often, students are reluctant to ask people about their strengths and goals. It is instructive to note that asking clients about their capacity to go to the toilet or bathe is easier for students initially than asking about hopes, goals, and dreams. Fortunately, however, even students who were trained in the pathology-centered approach typically develop skills in identifying strengths rather quickly.

Second, the strengths perspective provides a voice to populations whose views previously were ignored. Listening to traditionally oppressed groups, including people of color, women, gays and lesbians, and people with disabilities, explain how they have managed to survive and even thrive can help students put into practice such basic social work values as social justice and respect for the individual. The emphasis on exploring strengths in the context of unique life experiences is appropriate across ethnic, cultural, and income groups (Chapin, 2001). Further, the insights gained from this approach can inform claimsmaking based on rights to equal access.

Third, once students move beyond the model of a professional who hears about deficits and lays out a solution, they generally become enthusiastic from listening to ideas that emerge from client groups and uncovering resources in the community. Students become energized and shrug off the sense of hopelessness that I have observed too many times in students who focus primarily on what often appear to be overwhelming problems in oppressed communities. Indeed, after recognizing that clients frequently can identify solutions to their own problems, students become enthusiastic about working collaboratively to make whatever headway is possible.

Students from historically oppressed groups particularly seem to warm to the strengths approach. For example, a Native American student who was also a tribal leader on her reservation developed a strategy for using gambling proceeds to build a health and social services infrastructure based on the strengths perspective. She began by educating tribal leadership on how to use a strengths perspective to determine where tribal resources should be targeted. She then conducted an assessment of strengths and needs on the reservation. Healthy children and older adults were identified as major strengths. She then advocated for a change in tribal policy. She pressed for the use of gambling proceeds to build an infrastructure on the reservation to help maintain healthy children and older adults. This infrastructure included day care facilities and assisted living. She also collaborated with parents and older adults who were potential consumers of these services as well as with other tribal policy makers to influence policy.

Social workers who are committed to supporting client autonomy should seriously consider adopting an approach based on collaborating with consumers of services in trying to influence policy making. In summary, then, some of the benefits of using a strengths perspective are (1) it moves us away from victim blaming, (2) it reflects basic social work values, (3) it provides fresh ideas, and (4) it involves consumers of services in policy making.

Cautions Regarding the Strengths Perspective Despite all of the benefits we have just discussed, there are some concerns we need to consider when applying the strengths perspective to social policy. First, when we downplay clients' needs, we can also lose the sense of urgency to address these needs. Conversely, if we focus exclusively on the hungry child, the homeless family, or the bereft older person, then policy makers and taxpayers may be more likely to agree to spend tax dollars to help these people than if client strengths are emphasized as well. Social workers and clients must find ways to present needs effectively so that sufficient resources are provided to build on strengths. Surely it is possible to portray strengths as well as needs in a manner that can garner resources while avoiding victim blaming.

A second concern is that once students understand the strengths perspective, they may come to believe that it is the only appropriate approach, no matter what the policy issue. The strengths approach adds a useful perspective, but it is not the only conceptual tool that social workers need to be effective at policy practice. Instead, successful policy practice requires mastery of a variety of concepts and skills, including a comprehensive understanding of how social problems are constructed and how to analyze need. This book focuses on building those skills.

Third, empirical research on the effectiveness of social work practice based on the strengths perspective is limited (Staudt, Howard, & Drake, 2001). Although there is extensive anecdotal evidence that the strengths perspective is a useful tool, little formal research has been conducted to provide empirical evidence of the specific mechanisms by which practice grounded in the strengths perspective influences client outcomes. Research is needed to delineate more clearly how the strengths approach operates in comparison to other strategies.

For all of these reasons, it is critical that you carefully scrutinize the benefits and drawbacks of all the conceptual tools you will be exposed to in the course of your social work education, including those that integrate a strengths perspective. Every conceptual tool serves to illuminate some aspects of a situation and blind us to others. Think about what you might miss using a strengths perspective, as well as what you might see that was formerly overlooked.

Connecting Social Work Values to Policy Practice

In this chapter, we have considered how the strengths perspective builds on social work values and how a strengths approach can be incorporated into policy practice. We have also examined the pros and cons of doing so. Now, I want to challenge you to consider how you can incorporate social work values such as client self-determination, commitment to social justice, and a nonjudgmental approach into your policy practice work with clients. Remember, social policies don't always help to meet clients' needs. In some cases, they create need, reinforce oppression, and undermine strengths.

As long as clients are disadvantaged by policies and resulting programs that do not reflect social work values, social workers must strive to lessen those effects, to modify offensive policies, and to craft effective policy at the agency and legislative levels. So, here is a chance to try your hand at putting social work values into practice. What kinds of policy practice initiatives could help the Thompsons, Rosalie Pachta, and Andy, whose cases we considered at the beginning of this chapter? Remember, Rosalie has informed her social worker that she may have to go to a nursing facility because she has no way to pay for the services she needs if she remains in the community. Similarly, Mrs. Thompson has explained that there is no housing in her community that she can afford. Finally, Andy is fearful because government policies prohibit many people in need from receiving public health insurance. Look back at the list of principles on page 11 for ideas about how social work values can be put into action with these clients. What actions could you and these clients take to improve the policies that govern housing and health care?

CONCLUSION

Social workers today are facing a most challenging policy arena. As students and future social workers, your commitment to help shape policies and programs that can provide the resources, supports, and opportunities necessary for clients is vital. Integration of the strengths perspective into your understanding of social policy can help clarify your crucial role in shaping social policy, provide concrete guidance in how you can proceed in helping to craft effective policy, and can reinforce your responsibility to view the people with whom you work as collaborators and sources of expertise. The following chapters are designed to equip you with new tools for conceptualizing social needs or problems, a more inclusive approach to policy formulation, and an expanded array of policy options. You will learn how to analyze policy and programs and how they are developed. You will discover how the historical, political, and economic context affect social policy. You will learn about specific policies and programs in areas including child welfare, mental health, and work with older adults and how these policies and programs influence social work practice. We will explore your role in policy practice. The text closes with a focus on the future. I invite you to share in the excitement of learning to understand and help shape social policies and programs that can potentially help thousands, and in some cases, millions, of clients.

MAIN POINTS

- Social workers need to engage in policy practice in order to be effective practitioners. Students can and should choose to develop their policy practice skills.

- Social work values are the foundation for policy practice.

- Problem-focused models for defining problems and developing policy can limit the social worker's ability to craft effective policies that build on clients' strengths.

- The strengths perspective can be used to reconceptualize the policy-making process.

- The role of a social worker using the strengths perspective shifts from that of expert to that of collaborator and resource person.

- There are benefits to integrating a strength perspective as well as cautions that critical thinkers should consider.

- Begin now to build your policy practice skills. Becoming involved in policy practice in your community will enable you to try out the ideas that are presented in this book and begin to translate theory into practice.

EXERCISES: PRACTICING SOCIAL WORK

Meet the Sanchez Family

Insert the CD in your disk drive and click on the Sanchez family icon. Spend some time exploring the elements available in the case dossier.

After exploring the Sanchez family case, respond to the following questions:

1. Identify three social policies that influence social work practice with the Sanchez family. Try to identify one federal, one state, and one agency policy if possible. What are the policies, and how do they influence practice?

2. Do you think Mr. and Mrs. Sanchez would consider the policies you have identified effective? What improvements can you suggest?

3. What persons or groups do you think made these policies. If you could talk to these people, what would you like to tell them about the results of their decisions to implement the policies? How might you ensure that the voices of the people affected by these policies, such as the Sanchezes, are taken into consideration by policy makers in ways that do not harm the service recipients?

Meet the Black Feather Community

You can begin to develop policy practice skills by completing the exercises that introduce you to the Black Feather interactive case presented on the CD-ROM enclosed with your text. Although this case vignette contains information focused on doing research, that same information is also useful for understanding social policy and engaging in policy practice. In fact, the use of research is an important component of policy practice.

Explore how the program works by experimenting with the options; then open the Meet the Community segment. Familiarize yourself with the Systems Perspective tool in the Tools segment. Click on the Engage tab. Read the Opening Copy and then click on Black Feather (start here). Imagine you are a social worker in this community. You might be a social worker in the mental health center, the schools, the public health department, or with Indian Health Services.

Become familiar with the key actors and the agencies and their programs that provide services to this community.

Once you have explored the basic facts, respond to these questions:

1. After considering your strengths as suggested in the text, what assets do you feel you bring to work with the Black Feather community? What particular knowledge, values, and skills do you believe you will need to work effectively in this community? Use the Values Inventory under Professional Value in the Tools section of the interactive case study to help inform your thinking. Do you feel have beginning cultural competency in working with the Native American community? If not, how can you build that competency in the context of your university and home community?

2. Begin to identify issues that may become the focus of policy practice. Of course, you will want to find out from community members what issues they believe are important before beginning to plan a policy or program change initiative with them. However, at this point, what gaps or overlaps can you identify in the services provided in this community?

3. Considering the different approaches to policy practice discussed in the text, how do you think social workers using the strengths approach would differ from those using a problem-centered approach in their work to craft more effective policies and programs in this community? How would the strengths-based social worker approach the community and what would the relationship and focus look like? What social work values could guide their work? Be as specific as possible.

EXERCISES: THE SOCIAL WORK LIBRARY

Read "The strengths perspective: Possibilities and problems" (Saleebey, 2002), and respond to the following:

1. Based on the content in Saleebey's chapter and the first chapter of this policy text, identify benefits as well as critiques and cautions that should be considered when using the strengths perspective in policy practice.

2. Can you identify any other benefits or cautions that need to be considered?

CHAPTER 2

The Historical Context: Basic Concepts and Early Influences

Private churches and charities do a much better job of ministering to the needs of the poor. Government should get out of the business of charity and leave that work to the churches and nonprofit organizations.

What our elected officials need to do is to return to the policies that supported rugged individualism and didn't coddle the poor.

Every person born in this country should be guaranteed a minimum income and health care as a right of citizenship.

I HAVE HEARD ALL OF THESE ASSERTIONS IN THE COURSE OF POLICY debates. All the speakers were convinced they were speaking the truth. You probably have heard some of these comments yourself. By the time you finish reading this chapter and thinking about how you will use the information you learn in your future practice, you should be able to enter into the debate concerning each of these issues. This ability to shape opinion is basic to policy practice. In order to understand current social policies and to discuss options for change, however, you need to become familiar with the historical developments that have shaped our current approaches. This chapter will provide historical background on social policies, the social welfare system, and the profession of social work.

Although many people might take our current social welfare policies for granted, they are actually the product of centuries of change, debate, and struggle. Your study of this historical context as part of your social work education will be much more useful for practice if you explicitly link what you are learning about history to the policies that shape contemporary social work practice. History is not merely a prologue to the present. Rather, the ways in which historical social policy approaches are understood and reinterpreted directly and immediately affect the social policy decisions made today. For example, religious teachings introduced thousands of years ago have immediate influence on moral choices that policy makers now face. It is my hope that the historical overview provided in this text will spark your curiosity and lead you to delve more deeply into the sources referenced in this chapter as you complete your course assignments and embark on your future social work practice.

THE GENESIS OF SOCIAL WELFARE POLICY

Because the social worker's clients often are people living in poverty, this chapter initially explores cultural practices in preindustrial societies that gave rise to current programs for people who have low incomes. The major religions of these early cultures required their adherents to care for people who were poor. Although some people worked unceasingly to relieve the immediate poverty surrounding them, powerful members of the ruling elites were careful to maintain the social and economic barriers that oppressed the poorest people. Thus, the social welfare structures that evolved to address poverty also served as a means of social control and supported the society's dominant economic structures. This relationship between social welfare and the economy, which applies to current social policy as well, is examined in greater detail in Chapter 4.

Religious Traditions

We will begin our discussion of the early historical mandates that shaped social policy for the poorest people in ancient societies and that continue to shape social policy in your community today by examining selected religious traditions from around the world. You can build on these examples to begin exploring other religious traditions that are influential in your community.

Judaism Basic Jewish teaching and law, known as the Torah, contains numerous mandates to provide for people living in poverty within the context of the agrarian society of the time. For example, Leviticus 19:9–10 instructs: "And when ye reap the harvest of your land, thou shalt not wholly reap the corners of thy field, neither shalt thou gather the gleanings of thy harvest. And thou shalt not glean thy vineyard, neither shalt thou gather the fallen fruit of thy vineyard; thou shalt leave them for the poor and for the stranger: I am the Lord your God." Overall, the Torah instructs that justice be extended even to the most vulnerable members of society (Anderson, 1986).

Islam Similarly, all branches of Islam accept the fundamental tenet that the faithful are required to provide charity to people in need. The Koran (Qur'an) teaches that the faithful are to give up part of their wealth for the benefit of poor people and persons with disabilities. This annual almsgiving is called *zakat*. According to the Koran, when you give away part of your possessions, whatever is left will be blessed. "Piety does not lie in turning your face East or West. Piety lies in . . . disbursing your wealth . . . among your kin and the orphans, the way-farers and mendicants, freeing the slaves . . . and in paying zakat" (Qur'an 2:177).

Buddhism In India, in the 6th century BC, Siddhartha Gautama, the Buddha, instructed the faithful to seek a "middle way" between human desires and a completely meditative life. The teachings of the Buddha, known as the *dharma*, maintain that people are reborn into successive lives until they attain complete wisdom. Further, good deeds toward others may help lead to rebirth as a more prosperous and wiser individual. Each person is expected to feel compassion for and to assist those whose burdens in life are the hardest. The focus is on the individual doer of good, and the belief is that giving will enrich the giver. From the beginning of the establishment of Buddhist monasteries, Buddhist monks have helped needy individuals and families in the surrounding community by giving food and alms. This work is considered an example to others of how they should behave. One of the teachings in the *Dhammapada* (The *dharma*) is: "They are true disciples who have trained their hands, feet, and speech to serve others" (Hays, 1989, p. 195).

Confucianism Although more of a moral philosophy than a religion, Confucianism, which developed around 500 BC and is based on the teachings of the philosopher Confucius, has been highly influential in China. Confucianism is an extensive guide to living that stresses the individual's duty to society and the natural compassion of the human heart. It requires its adherents to care for the needs of their extended families, even if doing so requires self-sacrifice. In addition, the development of natural compassion is expected to lead an individual to help wherever she or he perceives need. Confucianism stresses individual development and does not address the role of the lord, state, or government in helping people in need. However, the emphasis on moral and decent behavior for individuals includes a duty to be helpful to others.

American Indian Religions The diverse religious traditions of American Indians also emphasize the importance of caring for one's neighbor. (The terms *American Indian* and *Native American* are used interchangeably throughout this text.) Indeed, the basic social structure of Native American groups often reflected a collective approach to the use of the tribe's resources. Sharing with your neighbors was necessary for the survival of the tribe. For example, Puritan Edward Winslow, who recorded many of his observations of Wampanoag behavior in 1675, wrote that "every sachem (tribal leader) taketh care for the widow and fatherless, also for such as are aged and any way maimed, if their friends be dead, or not able to provide for them" (Segal & Stineback, 1977, p. 83). Native Americans as well as other ancient cultures recognized that the ability to work together as a group conferred a competitive advantage in the struggle for survival. Care by group members, one for another, strengthened the willingness to work together as a group.

Christianity   Christian religious teachings instruct that people serve God by caring for one another. Jesus told a parable about people entering the kingdom of God. "Then the righteous will answer him, saying, 'Lord, when did we see you hungry and feed you, or thirsty and give you drink?' And the King will answer them, 'Truly, I say to you, as you did it to one of the least of these my brothers, you did it to me'" (Matthew 25:37, 40). The apostle Paul wrote, "Faith, hope, and love [charity] are all important, but love is the greatest" (I Corinthians 13:13). Elevation of the importance of charity and the portrayal of poor people as just as worthy as rich people—or perhaps worthier—in the eyes of God to enter the kingdom of heaven, are themes reflected in early Christian biblical teachings.

Current Implications

Several important elements of these early religious teachings and practices clearly have implications for the current U.S. social welfare system. First, each culture developed a system or an institutionalized method to provide for the social welfare of less-fortunate people; that is, the system was mandated in writing and implemented in practice. Second, charity was defined as a religious duty, and the righteous person shared at least a portion of her or his wealth with people in need. Third, charitable actions were directed primarily toward people in the local area. Finally, accepting charity was relatively non-stigmatizing; that is, the recipient was not criticized or considered inferior. Of course, in all societies, the ideal and the actual practice vary widely for many reasons, including the generosity of the almsgiver, community attitudes toward the specific people in need, and the economic conditions of the day. However, examining the written documents and the historical records of practices at the time provides insight into the guiding principles of the period.

The themes that characterized earlier cultures continue to influence social welfare to this day. For example, advocates for policies that redistribute resources often contrast the great wealth and conspicuous consumption of some U.S. citizens with the poverty of many children and elders. Watch for messages in the media that are based on the assumption that their audience does or should believe that people in need are worthy of help and that charity is important for both the giver and the receiver. I encourage you to examine the early religious writings discussed above as well as other religious teachings for additional examples of attitudes and practices related to social welfare and to consider how they do or do not relate to current social welfare practice.

Conflicting Views regarding Social Welfare

Other, conflicting themes also emerge when we examine the history of social welfare. For example, although ancient Greek and Roman societies developed social welfare systems, Greek and Roman philosophers warned against rewarding paupers for begging rather than working. Similarly, by the 13th century, Christians were clearly differentiating between the "worthy poor" and people who were considered to be poor simply because they were unwilling to work. They were also questioning the appropriateness of help for strangers. Parallel tensions between the mandate to help all poor people versus willingness to help only those people of the same religious background are clearly reflected in the social policies and social programs that determine how religious organizations distribute charity today.

In the United States in the 1800s, the wedding of Social Darwinism and the Protestant work ethic created further support for stigmatizing the poor as somehow different, unworthy, and even less fit to survive. **Social Darwinism** is a social philosophy that applies Darwin's theory of evolution based on natural selection to human societies (Reid, 1995). Social Darwinists such as sociologists Herbert Spencer and William Graham Sumner proposed that poverty was part of natural selection: In a competitive society, those who were most capable and worked hardest would succeed, and others would fail. Therefore, helping people in poverty would only perpetuate laziness and benefit people who were unfit to survive. People who amassed great wealth were seen as living testaments to the correctness of these beliefs. Everyone was responsible for her or his own fate.

Not all Americans, however, embraced this harsh philosophy. Rather, countervailing beliefs developed within the religious communities themselves. For example, proponents of the "Social Gospel" that called for social justice for people in poverty were present in Protestant and Catholic denominations in the late 1800s and 1900s. They preached that just wages and profit sharing were necessary to alleviate the ills of poverty, overwork, and underpayment, and they spoke out against laissez-faire capitalism, concentration of wealth, and unrestrained competition (Swatos, 1998; Trattner, 1999). **Laissez-faire** is a doctrine that proposes minimal or no government regulation of economic activities.

It is clear that human societies have attempted to deal with poverty and inequality since the earliest times. Our examination of history indicates that people in many societies have called for social justice. Unfortunately, it also demonstrates that these calls were often disregarded and that societies throughout history have justified inequality and poverty. As you read about historic and current social welfare practices, consider what future students might identify as the guiding principles of our current programs for assisting people in poverty.

- How do historical policy approaches shape current policy?
- What was the cultural milieu at the time this historical approach was taken? Is the current milieu the same or different?
- What were the group interests, and who were the key players involved in these policies?
- Is there any reason to think the approach would work better or worse today?
- Did this policy approach build on the strengths of the target population? Alternatively, was it predicated on a pathology or deficit view of the people to be helped?

BOX 2.1

A Framework for Linking History and Current Social Policy

A FRAMEWORK FOR UNDERSTANDING HOW HISTORICAL APPROACHES INFLUENCE CURRENT POLICY

Consider the questions in Box 2.1 as we examine the history of social welfare. These questions are designed to help you understand the implications of historical events for current social policy and social work practice. They have been raised by a number of social policy academicians (Chambers, 2000; Chapin, 1995; Spano, 2000). You can ask and answer these questions for yourself as you build your historical knowledge base. The answers below focus on using the framework and information previously provided to consider current faith-based policy initiatives at the federal level. The intent of these initiatives is to give public funds to religious organizations so they can provide public social services. Proponents of faith-based initiatives hope that churches and religious institutions can assume more of the burden of providing public welfare. Some proponents assert that if this shift occurs, then private funding of social welfare programs may begin to replace public monies, thereby reducing the government's welfare role. Be aware that the answers presented below are not intended to be exhaustive but rather are meant to start you on your way.

- **How do these historical policy approaches shape current policy?** Religious and faith-based approaches to poverty have influenced social policy historically and continue to do so today. Support for social justice and aid to people in poverty, differentiation between the worthy and unworthy poor, and ambivalence toward strangers and immigrants are all historical themes that are reflected in current social policy. Today, religious organizations continue to minister to the needs of people in poverty, and policy proposals to fund more faith-based organizations to provide public social services have many supporters.

- **What was the cultural milieu at the time this historical approach was taken, and is the current milieu the same or**

different? Early approaches to social welfare developed in largely agrarian societies with rather homogeneous populations. Also, religious institutions typically played a major role in providing social welfare. As societies became more diverse, the issue of how to treat people who were not perceived as similar to oneself became highly divisive. This is even truer today, given that the United States is made up of people from a great variety of ethnic and cultural backgrounds. People with different religious backgrounds may be wary of faith-based social services because of past experiences of intolerance and attempts to proselytize them. The challenge we have yet to meet in our society is to recognize similarities while respecting differences.

- **What were the group interests, and who were the key players involved in developing these policies?** In very early cultures, particularly in desert societies in which many of the major religions first developed, it was clear that even those members who had relatively more resources would not survive without the help of the group. People were tied together through "status relationships" such as family member, lord, or serf. Powerful people such as tribal leaders, lords, and family heads had greater status and thus could develop systems that favored and maintained their positions. These leaders often influenced the systems of charity developed by religious institutions. Maintenance of social control by powerful elites as well as mutual aid motivated social welfare in these societies.

- **Is there any reason to think the approach would work better or worse today?** Contemporary U.S. society is highly complex, diverse, industrialized, and technologically advanced rather than primarily agrarian. Although religious institutions still play an important role in providing social welfare, many people do not belong to organized religious groups. Additionally, many church-based welfare services already receive large amounts of funding from federal and state governments and don't have sufficient private funds to take on more roles. For example, religiously affiliated nursing facilities often receive more than half of their income from Medicaid, a program jointly funded by the federal and state governments.

- **Did this policy approach build on the strengths of the target population? Alternatively, was it predicated primarily on a pathology or deficit view of the people to be helped?** In societies in which many people were living at subsistence levels, it appears that poverty held little stigma, and people provided help through religious organizations with the knowledge that they themselves could become needy if poor crops or sickness depleted their resources. Such societies viewed community members as having strengths as well as vulnerabilities. However, as the gap between rich and poor members of the society widened, the belief that people in poverty were somehow different or unwilling to work became more widely accepted. It is easier to see strengths in people you perceive as similar to yourself and to magnify the deficits of people you see as very different. Although religiously affiliated organizations may do an excellent job of caring for members of their own faith community, critics of this policy express concern that people of differing cultural and religious backgrounds will not receive culturally competent service.

You can apply this same framework to what you learn about social policy as you read through the remaining sections of this chapter. By using the framework questions, you will be able to look at historical information in new ways and will develop new ideas about policies that might be more effective for your clients.

This short exploration of how earlier cultures and religions influenced current thinking about social welfare illustrates the impact of a wide variety of cultures from around the world on social policy today. We now turn to specific historical governmental approaches to caring for people in poverty that are generally recognized as having direct impact on current U.S. social policy. Because many specific elements of current U.S. policy can be traced to social policies developed initially in England during the Middle Ages, this examination will begin with the English Poor Laws.

ENGLISH POOR LAWS

Trends and major social welfare events that took place in England from the Middle Ages to the enactment of the Poor Law of 1601 have greatly influenced U.S. social policy. The feudal system of the Early Middle Ages was based on a hierarchy in which the lord owned the land and the serfs farmed the land and received the protection of the lord. In return, the serfs owed their labor and portions of their agricultural product to the lord. This agrarian economy produced very little surplus, and famine was common. Nevertheless, poor people were not considered criminal. In fact, Canon Law—law directing church activities— demanded that each parish provide for the poor. Anyone who had extra resources was exhorted to share with the poor. However, the "willfully idle" were not to be assisted (Quigley, 1996a).

In general, treatment of serfs and peasants was at the discretion of the lord, and it varied greatly based on available resources and the lord's temperament. Prior to the Middle Ages, begging and giving had long been supported by Church teachings; however, after the 13th century, the Church began to view begging more negatively (Quigley, 1996a). During the Middle Ages, guilds, foundations, and hospitals contributed to the welfare infrastructure. **Guilds** were associations of merchants and artisans that provided mutual aid and disaster insurance for their members. Private foundations and churches played a major role in this society.

Background of the Poor Law

By 1500, however, English society was experiencing a dramatic economic, political, and social transformation. The feudal system had declined, and feudal relationships that bound serf and lord were giving way (Reid, 1995). At the same time, although the majority of the population continued to make their living in agriculture, many small industries, particularly textiles, were beginning to develop. In addition, a stratum of society made up of tradesmen and merchants was emerging in which position was based on profession rather than birth. Contracts that specified number of hours to be worked or product to be delivered, rather than status such as that of a lord or serf, increasingly defined the relationships among parties. Unlike farming, which was located primarily in small villages, the emerging industries were concentrated in the growing numbers of towns situated throughout the country. In that sense, England was undergoing the initial stages of the industrialization movement that reached its fruition in later centuries.

Population Growth and Migration   At the same time that the growth of towns and industries was remaking English society, the country was experiencing a major population increase. Beginning in 1348, a series of outbreaks of plague known as the Black Death claimed the lives of between one-third and one-half of England's overall population. As these epidemics subsided, however, the population began to rebound. During the period 1500–1700, the number of inhabitants nearly doubled (Clark & Slack, 1976). Unfortunately, in many agricultural villages, the number of residents was increasing at the same time that land was becoming scarcer. One reason for this dilemma was that landowners were enclosing lands that formerly were accessible to the community for raising sheep to supply wool for the expanding textile industry. In addition, many agricultural families continued to practice *primogeniture,* which meant the eldest son inherited the entire estate. As a result, many villagers had to acquire land or seek employment elsewhere (Cannon, 1997; Clark & Slack, 1976).

Perhaps the major result of rural overpopulation was a massive migration to the towns. People from farming villages moved to towns in large numbers hoping to find work or—if work was unavailable—some type of charitable relief. Unfortunately, despite the growth of industry during this period, the towns also lacked sufficient jobs and housing for this migratory population. One result was *subsistence migration,* in which poor migrants moved from town to town, looking for work or begging for charity. By 1600, the number of vagrants and beggars may have been as high as 20,000. More serious than begging were the growing complaints of criminal behavior by these groups. Many concerned people began to associate vagrancy with an "underworld culture" that threatened the social and economic order (quote from Singman, 1995, p. 17; see also Cannon, 1997; Clark & Slack, 1976).

Poverty   Compounding the problems of crime and vagrancy were the increasing poverty rates of the 16th century. As we have already seen, the towns could not provide jobs and housing for all new arrivals. In addition, many workers who found jobs became victims of seasonal unemployment. They also lost their jobs during periods of economic downturn, which unfortunately were common throughout this period. Moreover, a series of poor harvests that culminated during the years 1594–1597 led to shortages of grain and higher grain prices, which in turn generated popular discontent. In many towns, at least 20 percent of the residents were unable to meet their basic needs (Singman, 1995, p. 17). As poverty and unemployment increased, the demand for relief increased accordingly (Clark & Slack, 1976; Rowse, 1950).

The English government implemented some policies during the 16th century to address the poverty issue. The Poor Law of 1536 required wealthier families to contribute money to assist people in need. Significantly, these efforts distinguished between the "deserving" poor, who were worthy of assistance, and the "able-bodied" poor, who were not. The "deserving" poor consisted of individuals who were poor through no fault of their own and could not work for a living. Included in this group were orphans, elderly people (especially widows), and women with children who had been abandoned by their husbands. In contrast, individuals who were capable of supporting themselves if they could find work were considered able-bodied. This category included workers who lost their jobs due to seasonal employment and men who were returning from service in the army and navy. The Poor Law denied direct monetary assistance people who were able-bodied but poor, although monies collected under the law could be used to create jobs for this group.

The Poor Law of 1601

As poverty increased over the course of the 16th century, however, towns were unable to meet the growing demands for assistance. In addition, the taxes assessed to the wealthier people for the care of poor people became a burden to many taxpayers. Thus, by 1600, "poverty was the major concern of all urban governors" (Clark & Slack, 1976, p. 121). Consequently, local officials looked to the central government in London for support. Finally, in 1597, Parliament agreed to consider the issue. In 1601, the government passed the Act for the Relief of the Poor, more commonly called the Poor Law of 1601. This law created a uniform system for addressing the issues of poverty and unemployment by empowering justices of the peace in every parish to appoint officials known as overseers of the poor, who supervised the relief programs. The law further authorized the justices to levy a tax to raise funds for relief.

Analyzing the Poor Law   Although the Poor Law attempted to address the entire spectrum of poverty, it retained the distinction between "worthy" and "unworthy" poor people. Regarding the "worthy poor," the law instructed the towns to raise "competent sums of money for and towards the necessary relief of the lame, impotent, old, blind, and such other among them, being poor and not able to work" (quoted in Axinn & Stern, 2001, p. 10). Tax monies also could be used to assist unemployed people who were capable of working, but only by "setting to work all such persons" (quoted in Axinn & Stern, 2001, p. 10). Included in this group were children whose parents were unable to support them. These children either could be required to work or could be assigned as apprentices to learn a craft.

Relief took different forms. Many needy people, particularly in agricultural villages, continued to receive **outdoor relief,** that is, aid provided to them in their homes or other noninstitutional settings. In contrast, other recipients were required to enter workhouses and almshouses. **Workhouses** were publicly funded establishments in which large numbers of laborers were brought together to perform some type of work and sometimes to receive job training. Although workhouse residents were better off than unemployed workers and beggars, conditions were sufficiently harsh so that people looking for work would consider private employment of any type before applying for public charity. In contrast, **almshouses** were supported by private funds, and they were reserved for the "worthy poor," particularly elders. In reality, however, the distinctions became blurred, and many elderly people and unmarried mothers eventually sought refuge in workhouses.

This system provided the foundation for poor relief in England for several centuries. A subsequent law, the Act of Settlement of 1662, attempted to resolve the vagrancy problem by restricting assistance to people who had been born in the parish or were longtime residents. This law embodied the principle of **local responsibility,** which mandated that each locality was responsible for helping only its own residents. Needy people who were not long-term residents had to return to the parish in which they were born in order to receive aid (Cannon, 1997; Clark & Slack, 1976; Olsen, 1999; and Rowse, 1950).

Influence of the Poor Laws on U.S. Social Policy   Because the United States based many of its laws on the systems in place in England, it is not surprising that our policies dealing with poor people reflect many of the elements found in the Poor Laws. For example, consider the designation of elders, people with disabilities, widows, and orphans as the "worthy poor," and the designation of other groups as "unworthy." We can see similar philosophies at work today if we contrast benefits provided by two current social welfare programs: Old Age, Survivors, and

Disability Insurance (OASDI), popularly known as Social Security, and Temporary Aid for Needy Families (TANF). Social Security is intended for "worthy" recipients such as retired workers and families of deceased and disabled workers. In contrast, TANF provides assistance to low-income families with children. Their parents are often depicted as unworthy of help. Does it surprise you to learn that the average monthly benefit for a retired worker covered by OASDI exceeds $900 compared to approximately $400 for a family receiving TANF? In addition, the legislation that instituted TANF contains strict work requirements.

Think about how these principles continue to be played out as you progress through the rest of this chapter and also Chapter 3, which trace the development of social policies and social welfare systems in the United States from colonial times until the present. Additionally, you can consider how these principles and philosophies influenced the history of the profession of social work, which is also presented in this chapter.

SOCIAL WELFARE POLICY IN THE UNITED STATES

Having examined the history of social welfare policy in England, we now shift our focus to the history of social welfare policies in the United States. The remainder of this chapter traces the development of U.S. social policies through the early years of the 20th century. Chapter 3 then begins with World War I and continues through the administration of George W. Bush. You will see that, as our population grew and became more diverse, our economy became more industrialized, and our society became more urban, some of the responsibility for helping people in need gradually shifted from private institutions and state and local governments to the federal government. At the same time, social work emerged as a profession that applied both personal experience and scholarship in the social sciences to the task of assisting poor people and other marginalized groups. However, in recent decades, a conservative political philosophy has emerged that is challenging many of the social welfare policies established throughout the course of the 20th century.

The Colonial Era: Adapting the English System, 1600–1775

Native Americans living in North America when the colonists arrived were the first people to provide European immigrants with charity—the donation of goods and services to people in need—in what would become the United States. However, the struggle for control of the land by white settlers was marked by bloodshed, broken treaties, and oppression of Indian peoples. Colonialism began along the eastern shore in the 1600s when both Dutch and English settlers and merchants started the process of supplanting established Native

American communities. In the Southwest, Spanish invaders were accompanied by Catholic missionaries, who numbered 3,000 by the 1600s (Day, 1999). Native Americans, who were suffering the brunt of the invaders' demands for tribute, were tended in missions. The missions became a major welfare system that provided hospitals and shelters for homeless people, elders, and people with disabilities. They also provided hospice care and alms for poor people.

Social Welfare in the English Colonies   The English colonies that developed along the Eastern seaboard categorized poor people in much the same way that England did, distinguishing between the "worthy" and the "unworthy" poor. Poor people frequently were expected to move in with relatives. In fact, the colonies passed laws that required families to "take in" their impoverished and disabled relatives and to post bond for immigrating relatives to ensure their support. Local government, churches, and private philanthropy offered support only when families could not provide for their relatives.

Public relief at the time was based strictly on a **residual approach,** that is, relief was provided only if the marketplace or family was unable to provide for a person's needs. Residual approaches are often contrasted with an **institutional approach,** which asserts that government should assure basic food, housing, health, income, employment, and education needs as a right of citizenship in advanced economies. These approaches to welfare provisions are discussed in more depth in Chapter 4. A residual approach reflected the values and culture of colonial society. Further, the fledgling colonies had neither the money nor the infrastructure to sustain an institutional approach.

Towns in the colonies developed their own policies toward helping poor people. Whatever assistance was provided had to be funded through local resources. Reflecting the philosophy that underlay the English Act of Settlement, some towns instituted eligibility rules that restricted poor relief to people who owned property or had been residents for a specified number of years.

Almshouses and Workhouses   In 1658, the first workhouse was opened in Plymouth Colony (Quigley, 1996b). As the numbers of people needing care increased, the quest to find less costly means of providing help and the need to share fixed costs among a larger number of people or communities fueled the growth of institutions for the poor (Quigley, 1996a). Workhouses were also called *houses of corrections* because their philosophy required people to work and they housed people who violated colonial laws (Quigley, 1996b). Many times, these institutions were not segregated by gender, age, or infirmity. All residents were expected to work when they could. Mortality rates were high. Almshouses and workhouses were the forerunners of hospitals, mental institutions, penitentiaries, and reform schools (Day, 2000). Some almshouses began to segregate people with mental illness from other residents. These institutions were the forerunners of asylums for people with mental illness.

It is clear that in the United States, as in England, policies governing the treatment of poor people were designed to ensure that everyone who could potentially work would be motivated to do so even for meager or no wages. These policies helped provide a continuous supply of human labor for farms and industry. However, they also indicated that governments were assuming more responsibility for people in need. At the same time, ongoing efforts were made to find ways to reduce the costs of providing for poor people, and citizens expressed continual dissatisfaction with whatever system was being used to provide such assistance (Quigley, 1996b). The emphasis on work remains a central tenet of many of our policies for poor people. Although support of economic independence can be characterized as building on strengths, many policies that reinforced the necessity of work were not designed to support or promote economic independence.

Slavery and Indentured Servitude   Slavery is the most extreme example of the control of human labor to benefit and profit the ruling class. In the colonies, slaves were defined as property by law.

Additionally, colonial societies contained a large population of indentured servants, people who were required to work for someone to pay off a debt. In fact, almost half of white immigrants were indentured when they arrived in America. The typical term of indenture was five to seven years, although it doubled for political dissenters (Faragher, 1990). Many people agreed to be indentured in order to pay for their passage to America. In addition, England sent paupers, dependent children, beggars, and political dissenters to the colonies as indentured servants (Hymowitz & Weissman, 1980). Overall, approximately 350,000 indentured people came to America prior to 1775, predominantly boys and young men between the ages of 15 to 25. Although indentured servants were supposed to receive remuneration such as land or money when they completed their indenture, such remuneration was often meager, if it was provided at all.

When opportunities to own land, vote, receive an adequate education, share in the profits that result from your labor, and earn a living wage are denied, then policies with work requirements become oppressive tools that keep poor people locked in poverty. Underlying most of these policies was the assumption that poverty was a result of individual failure or misfortune, not of economic or societal change. Therefore, policy reforms based on these assumptions could be instituted without disturbing the economic or societal status quo (Quigley, 1996b).

The American Revolution: Civil Rights in the New Nation, 1775–1800

The American Revolution ushered in a new system of government in the colonies. The writings of European intellectuals such as John Locke and Adam Smith, as well as earlier Protestant reformers such as Martin Luther, John

Calvin, and John Wesley, contributed to the development of a basic "liberal" construct that stressed individualism, the moral importance of work, personal responsibility, and distrust of collectivism and centralized government, which was reflected in much of the social policy developed during this period (Leiby, 1978; Reid, 1995).

 Web Link

Go to the "Remember the Ladies" Web site, found at www.mhhe.com/chapin1, and read the letter that Abigail Adams sent to John Adams in 1776 imploring him to "remember the ladies." Be sure to read the rebuke John Adams sent in reply.

The Constitution and Civil Rights   The Constitution was intended to increase the power of our central government while continuing to protect state and individual rights. The democratic political system instituted by our new constitution specified that elected representatives would make policy decisions. Elections were to be decided by the majority of voters, and until the 20th century, voters were almost exclusively white men. Rights for women were ignored, despite pleas from influential women of the time, such as Abigail Adams, to "remember the ladies." White men also controlled most of the country's resources, and the social policies that the new nation developed reinforced this control.

Nevertheless, although the Constitution initially protected only the rights of white, landowning males, it established the basis for civil rights in the nation. Many framers of the Constitution believed that the ability of voters to choose their leaders would not be enough to protect their basic rights. Therefore, they appended a written bill of rights that outlined exactly which freedoms were guaranteed to U.S. citizens. The Bill of Rights comprises the first ten amendments to the Constitution, and it addresses such issues as freedom of speech and of the press, the right to trial by jury, and protection against unreasonable searches and seizures. Subsequent amendments as well as numerous judicial rulings have expanded and ensured constitutional rights that underpin the civil rights standard that we have today.

Civil rights protection for citizens is a cornerstone of social welfare. Without this protection, public benefits and opportunities can be withheld from certain groups, who are then left without legal recourse. Moreover, individuals and groups who are denied basic civil rights face substantial barriers to opportunities and limited access to society's resources. We will explore the relationship between civil rights and social welfare in greater detail in Chapter 7.

Although the newly established federal government was unwilling to address the plight of most categories of people in need, they were willing to provide assistance to men who had fought for their country. In 1790, Congress provided financial support for disabled veterans and widows and orphans of veterans (Axinn & Stern, 2001). Though small, these pensions continued to be provided with little debate for veterans of American wars.

Expanding Federal, State, and Private Assistance   The Constitution laid the groundwork for a system that held states primarily responsible for the social welfare of their citizens. However, in 1798, the federal government did establish the

U.S. Public Health Service (Barker, 1999). The Public Health Service was a federal system of health care and hospitals designed for U.S. merchant seamen. In the 19th century, the agency's responsibilities were expanded to include medical examination and quarantine of immigrants. Currently, this agency is charged with responsibility for public health and safety. However, as the 18th century drew to a close and the 19th century dawned, much of the assistance to individuals was still provided through voluntary, charitable giving.

In their analysis of U.S. social welfare from the strengths perspective, Tice and Perkins (2002) pointed out that this tradition of private philanthropy helped to support educational programs, libraries, and community organizations such as emergency services and firefighting. There was growing awareness in both the public and the private sector that lack of education and healthcare were linked to poverty and that communities needed to develop health and social service systems in order to thrive. The United States has a long tradition of creating private-public partnerships to address these community needs.

From Independence to Civil War: Racism, Expansion, and Immigration, 1800–1865

During the first half of the 19th century, the new nation expanded dramatically in size. Its population also grew as large numbers of immigrants arrived from Europe, especially Ireland, Germany, and the Scandinavian countries. The abundant natural resources in the United States provided many immigrants, including free African immigrants, with opportunities to escape poverty. However, for people in slavery and for Native Americans, this economic growth and development meant greater oppression. At the same time, the debate over slavery raised questions about the role of race in U.S. society, and the federal government systematically removed Native Americans from desirable lands in the east.

Treatment of African Americans   By the early 19th century, the South was relying on the labor of increasing numbers of slaves to build its economic infrastructure. Slaves were considered the property of slave owners and were therefore ignored by the formal service system. In 1857, the Supreme Court confirmed the lack of basic rights for African Americans. In *Dred Scott vs. Sanford*, it ruled that any person of African ancestry, whether slave or free, could not be granted citizenship in the United States and thus could not sue in the federal courts. Dred Scott was a slave who had sued for his freedom because he had moved from a slave state to a free state. The *Dred Scott* ruling undermined rights for African Americans because they were unable to use the courts to protect themselves.

Informal methods of self-help developed in this vacuum. Building on this tradition, strong self-help organizations developed and continue to flourish in black communities in the present day. Support for self-help organizations and continuing mistrust of the formal social service system in the black community today are legacies of slavery. Social workers and policy makers who are unaware of the ramifications of this history will not be as effective in attempting to develop and implement policies and programs in the black community.

During this period, many black and white abolitionists campaigned for an official end to slavery. Frederick Douglass, an escaped slave, was a very influential speaker and writer in the movement. Escaped slave Harriet Tubman joined the abolitionist movement and played a significant role in the Underground Railroad, which assisted slaves in escaping from the South, often to Canada.

The Plight of Native Americans   Native Americans were driven from their lands as growing numbers of white settlers made their way westward. In 1824, the government created the Bureau of Indian Affairs. The United States thus assumed legal responsibilities for Native Americans and promised material assistance, but oppression and decimation continued. Violations of treaties with Native Americans were commonplace. In the 1831 Supreme Court decision *Cherokee Nation vs. Georgia,* Chief Justice John Marshall denied a claim by the Cherokee Indians in Georgia that they constituted a sovereign foreign nation. Rather, Marshall characterized Indian nations as "domestic dependent nations." Although conceding that Native American peoples should exercise some control over their lands, Marshall ruled that all American Indians were "completely under the sovereignty and dominion of the United States." He compared their relationship to the U.S. government to "that of a ward to his guardian" (quoted in Commager, 1958, pp. 256–257).

During the period between the Revolutionary War and the Civil War, most Native American peoples living east of the Mississippi River were driven from their traditional homelands to areas farther west. In 1830, Congress passed the Indian Removal Act, which ultimately forced most tribes to abandon their traditional lands and settle on reservations located west of the Mississippi (Hine & Faragher, 2000). By 1850, the removal was basically complete, and white settlers had appropriated the lands that the Indians previously inhabited (Kutler, 2003). In 1851, Congress passed the Indian Appropriation Act, which declared the lands to which the Indians had relocated to be official reservations (Nabokov, 1993).

As white settlers began to move west of the Mississippi, the push to confiscate Native American lands continued. An 1871 act of Congress officially terminated the practice of entering into treaties with Native American peoples. Future dealings were to take the forms of "agreements" and special laws. The Dawes Act, passed in 1887, eliminated the traditional system of tribal ownership of land by allotting plots of land to Native American individuals and families. These allotments were restricted to 160 acres, thereby confining Native Americans to smaller and smaller regions and eroding their communal way of

www.loc.gov/exhibits/african/ afam006.html

You can learn more about these early abolitionists from the Library of Congress Resource Guide for the Study of Black History & Culture.

life. Excess land was sold to white settlers. These policies effectively controlled and limited all aspects of Native American life (Nabokov, 1993).

Hispanics or Latinos in the Southwest   To accommodate westward expansion, the United States focused on gaining new territory and securing borders, especially its border with Mexico. In 1845, the United States officially annexed Texas after it had achieved independence from Mexico. A resulting conflict regarding the Texas-Mexico border led to war between the United States and Mexico.

In 1848, after two years of fighting, the two countries signed the Treaty of Guadalupe Hidalgo. Under the treaty, Mexico ceded a vast territory to the United States, including present-day Arizona, California, and New Mexico and parts of Colorado, Nevada, and Utah. As a result, the Hispanic population of the United States increased dramatically. The treaty further specified that Mexican nationals living within the new border would be granted citizenship and protection of property and civil rights. However, conflicts between new, non-Hispanic settlers and Mexican landowners frequently resulted in the Mexicans losing their lands in legal disputes. The treatment of Mexican Americans and the presence of legal and undocumented Mexican workers in the United States would become a major source of controversy and a key issue in social welfare policy, as we shall see in the next chapter.

Discrimination against Immigrants   Six million people, mostly poor people from Europe, immigrated to the United States between 1820 and 1860 (Coll, 1972). A large number of these immigrants were unskilled and faced stereotyping and discrimination. Many immigrant families lived in crowded urban slums. When work was available, parents and children often toiled long hours under harsh working conditions. Immigrant families who managed to acquire the resources necessary to move west also faced a daunting struggle to establish new homesteads and find ways of making a living in an often hostile environment.

Prejudice toward these immigrants from groups who had themselves been immigrants during an earlier period made the transitions even more difficult. For example, some earlier immigrants claimed newly arrived Irish immigrants were lazy and Irish men could not be counted on to support their families. These derogatory stereotypes are similar to the prejudices faced by African Americans. Despite these obstacles, some immigrant families managed to succeed and make a better life for themselves, although many remained in poverty. However, the essential difference that made the trajectory to becoming part of the melting pot possible for Irish, but much more difficult for all people of color, is that Irish immigrants could change their names and lose their accents. However, people of color cannot blend into white culture because their skin color will continue to be a marker. As detailed in Chapter 7, a different path to the acquisition of a fair share of social resources is necessary for them (Basch, 1998).

Growth of Cities and Institutions   Cities on the east coast grew rapidly during this period as these waves of poor immigrants sought places to live and work. However, these cities failed to develop adequate sanitation or safety standards. Living conditions in the cities were deteriorating. Thus, by the 1820s, the United States was searching for its own version of reform (Reid, 1995). Some economists at the time argued that providing public welfare aid to poor people in their homes further impoverished them, made them feel even less capable, and decreased the standard of living for everyone (Trattner, 1999). People who considered poverty to be the result of individual failings tended to view poor communities as teeming with people who exerted negative influences that would continue to trap people in poverty. Urban slums were considered breeding grounds for criminals and slackers who might prey on upstanding citizens. Some influential people came to believe that poor and dependent people needed to be exposed to the "right environment" so that they could become "useful" (Reid, 1995). The institution began to be viewed as the best solution to all manner of social ills including misbehaving children, impoverished elders, people with disabilities, and unwanted infants. During this period, states began to enact social policies to regulate local government's provision of social services and institutions. However, the federal government continued to reject a more active role in social welfare.

The defeat of this reform effort is similar to the failure of the Mental Health Equitable Treatment Act of 2001, which sought to provide mental health insurance benefits at the same rate as medical insurance as well as coverage of the noninsured for mental health treatment. Both of these bills represented potential expansion of rights for people with mental illnesses, but defeat demonstrated the federal government's continuing reluctance to institute sweeping changes in the area of mental health. This topic is covered in greater detail in Chapter 10.

This reluctance can be seen in the federal response to efforts by Dorothea Dix to reform the nation's institutions. Dorothea Dix, a leader in the reform movement, was instrumental in the establishment of state mental health institutions, including New Jersey's first mental hospital in 1845. She also challenged the federal government to provide 5 million acres of public land on which to build institutions for people with mental illnesses (Axinn & Stern, 2001). In response, Congress passed a bill in 1854 providing for institutions not only for people with mental illnesses but also for people who were blind and deaf. President Franklin Pierce vetoed the bill, thus reaffirming that the states, and not the federal government, were responsible for providing social welfare. Pierce also feared that charitable provisions for the care of people who were mentally ill would imply that the government eventually had to care for all needy persons (Trattner, 1999).

The Civil War and Its Aftermath: Reconstruction, Segregation, and Homesteads, 1865–1900

The Civil War (1861–1865) was fought to preserve the Union and to delineate states rights. Following the northern victory, human slave labor was abolished, and changes were made to policies regarding the treatment of African Americans. The period immediately following the Civil War, known as Reconstruction, witnessed some real, if temporary, progress in African American civil rights. Also during this period, the federal government passed legislation to assist primarily white families in purchasing lands in the West.

Reconstruction   Perhaps the most significant development during this period was the ratification of three amendments to the Constitution, sometimes referred to as the "Reconstruction amendments." In 1865, the 13th Amendment, which prohibited slavery, was ratified. In 1868, the 14th Amendment was ratified. This amendment guaranteed citizenship for "all persons born or naturalized in the United States" and guaranteed all citizens the rights to "due process of law" and "equal protection of the laws."

Significantly, in 1884, the U.S. Supreme Court ruled in *Elk vs. Wilkins* that Americans Indians were not covered by the 14th Amendment because they were not citizens. Citing, among other cases, *Cherokee Nation vs. Georgia,* the court affirmed that the Indian tribes, although not technically "foreign states," nevertheless were "alien nations" whose members "owed immediate allegiance to their several tribes" and "were in a dependent condition" to the U.S. government. Because tribal members were not citizens by birth, they could achieve citizenship only by separating from their tribes and becoming naturalized, like other subjects of foreign governments. Only those Indians who completed the naturalization process were entitled to the protections of the 14th Amendment (*Elk vs. Wilkins*, 112 U.S. 94, 1884).

The 15th Amendment, which followed two years later, guaranteed voting rights for all male citizens, including the former slaves. Female abolitionists had hoped that women also would attain the right to vote. However, the 15th Amendment extended the suffrage to African American men but not to women.

Opposition to black suffrage quickly emerged. Vigilante groups such as the Ku Klux Klan, organized in Tennessee in 1866, resorted to violence and intimidation to prevent the newly enfranchised voters from exercising their rights. In response, the federal government issued a series of Force Acts during 1870–1871 that authorized the government to use military force if necessary to enforce the 15th Amendment. As a result of these enforcement efforts, the freedmen voted in large numbers, and African Americans filled many elected positions in the South and even won a handful of seats in the U.S. Congress. However, Reconstruction was ended when northern Republicans compromised with southern Democrats to elect their presidential candidate for 1876, Rutherford B. Hayes, in exchange for an end to the northern military presence in the South. As we shall see, after the northern military presence was removed, policies were enacted in the South to counteract the advances achieved during this period.

It was also during Reconstruction that the first federal welfare agency, the Freedmen's Bureau, was established. The Freedmen's Bureau was created to provide a variety of services to African Americans as they transitioned from slavery to freedom, such as establishing schools, providing food, educating former slaves regarding landownership, and acting as an employment agency. The Bureau lasted only seven years and did not accomplish all its intended goals.

Nevertheless, it assisted many displaced African Americans, and it helped to establish a new economic role for former slaves.

From Reconstruction to Jim Crow   After Reconstruction ended, conditions for African Americans in the South deteriorated. By imposing a system of poll taxes and literacy tests and simply blocking the voting booths, white southerners eventually denied African Americans their rights as citizens throughout the South.

This process whereby most of the racial reforms instituted during Reconstruction were overturned continued throughout the last decades of the 19th century. A critical step in this development occurred in 1896, when the Supreme Court ruled in *Plessy vs. Ferguson* that separate accommodations for African Americans were constitutional as long as they were judged to be "equal." In the wake of this decision, states and municipalities passed numerous Jim Crow laws that legally separated white people from black people in public areas and institutions, including schools, restaurants, theaters, hospitals, and parks (Knappman, Christianson, & Paddock, 2002). In addition to social and educational segregation, African Americans experienced discrimination in employment that often forced them into the least-skilled, lowest-paying jobs. In this way, the Jim Crow laws worked to keep African Americans in poverty and also allowed people in power to profit at their expense. Thus, the Jim Crow laws are a classic example of social policies that perpetuate rather than alleviate poverty and oppression. of the Black People

The Homestead Act   Although the federal government did not enable most of the former slaves to become landowners, it did help white settlers to acquire homesteads. In 1862, Congress passed the Homestead Act, which allowed families to assume ownership of land—generally in the West—after they lived on it for five years (Hine & Faragher, 2000). This act enabled thousands of Americans, including veterans and widows of veterans, to become landowners. Unfortunately for Native Americans, this policy continued the uprooting that had begun decades earlier. The land made available to settlers was originally communal Native land. So at the same time that the government sought to aid white settlers, it continued to ignore the plight of Native Americans.

The Origins of Modern Social Work

The years following the Civil War witnessed massive increases in immigration and urbanization, which magnified the need for social services. However, the federal government continued to leave social reform to the states, cities, counties, and private charities, and the job done by these entities was uneven. Programs for people in dire need were overburdening city, county, and state budgets. One response to these developments was the beginning of the modern social work profession. Pioneering foremothers of social work struggled during this period to change the way the needs of poor people were met. Social work traces its roots to the child-saving movement, the Charity Organizations Societies (COS), and the settlement house movement (Trattner, 1999).

The Child-Saving Movement   The child-saving movement developed in response to the growing numbers of children who were overcrowding institutions and living on the streets of the cities. Because there was very little assistance of any kind to maintain impoverished families, the children suffered. Although the belief that the family should not face interference from the state was widespread, there was also some popular support for child welfare initiatives because children had long been included among the "worthy poor" who were deemed deserving of assistance. At the same time, many citizens were also concerned that failing to intervene with poor children would lead to higher rates of crime, juvenile delinquency, and other social problems (Trattner, 1999).

In 1853, Charles Loring Brace, a Protestant minister, founded the first Children's Aid Society in New York. Similar child-saving societies were established in other cities and towns during this period (Axinn & Stern, 2001). Brace organized the famous "orphan trains" that carried thousands of children west to be placed with families across the United States between 1853 and 1929. Brace argued vehemently that children should be redeemed in a home environment that could provide for their needs and demonstrate adequate family life. This approach directly conflicted with the prevailing ideal of saving children through correctional or reformatory methods that were popular at that time. Some of the relocated children were treated well in their new homes, but others were abused and worked unmercifully. Further, these children were not necessarily orphans; some were children of single parents or immigrant families who were simply too poor to support them. The taking of these children from their communities, even when parents were unable to care for them, engendered anger and resentment, especially among Catholic immigrants.

 Web Link

To learn more about the fascinating history of the orphan trains and to read firsthand accounts of the children's lives in the West, click on the Orphan Train Web link, found at www.mhhe.com/chapin1.

This child-saving movement was the precursor of home foster care. Other children-saving efforts were also initiated during this period. The first Society for the Prevention of Cruelty to Children was founded in New York in 1875, and soon other cities established such organizations to prevent maltreatment of children. These organizations were the precursors of our current child protection system.

The Charity Organization Society and Social Darwinism   The Charity Organization Societies (COS) began to develop in the United States in the late 1870s. The COS tried to organize diverse philanthropic groups to reduce the possibility that people were receiving assistance from more than one group and to provide "friendly visitors" to people in need. The COS developed the idea of **"scientific charity,"** which involved the use of systematic procedures to assess who was in need and to determine the most effective and efficient strategies to address those needs. Early COS workers were influenced by the writings of Thomas Malthus, a British economist who predicted that populations would multiply faster than the production of goods to meet their needs. They were also influenced by the Social Darwinist philosophy espoused by Herbert Spencer and William Graham Sumner. This "science" of the day was used to support the belief that giving money and provisions to people in poverty could interfere with the process whereby the fittest people were naturally selected for survival and reproduction.

Reflecting these views, the early COS workers believed that poor people caused their own problems through spending thoughtlessly, neglecting responsibility, refusing to exert themselves, and drinking excessively. Therefore, providing direct financial assistance to these people would reinforce these negative behaviors rather than encourage initiative and self-help (Trattner, 1999). For this reason, early COS workers identified moral reform as the most effective antipoverty policy.

When Josephine Shaw Lowell, who was associated with the first COS, founded in 1877 in New York, was asked by a contributor how much money would go directly to people in poverty, she proudly replied, "Not one cent!" (Trattner, 1999, p. 90). However, as workers began to actually learn about the conditions of poor people firsthand, their understanding began to expand. The COS engaged in social research that broadened views of how science could inform charity, helped sustain and organize charitable giving during this period, organized record keeping, and developed training programs. Their emphasis was on the individual, not social reform, and they were pioneers in social casework. By the 1890s, the COS workers were interested in establishing themselves as a profession.

The Settlement House Movement   Social work also traces its roots to the settlement house movement. Although the first settlement house in the United States was not founded until 1886, we discuss this movement here to complete the discussion of the three major roots of social work.

Both scientific charity and the Progressive Era, discussed in the following section, influenced the settlement house movement (Reid, 1995). Stanton Coit started the first settlement house in the United States in New York in 1886 after he had resided at Toynbee Hall in England. Inspired by work at Toynbee Hall, well-known social reformers Jane Addams and Helen Gates Starr founded the famous Hull House in Chicago in 1889. Settlement houses were established in working-class neighborhoods in the areas where reformers wanted to implement changes. The workers resided in these homes on a permanent basis.

Significantly, settlement house workers put into practice many of the tenets that we identify with the strengths perspective. Work in the settlement houses was premised on the belief that need in impoverished communities arose from economic, educational, and political exclusion rather than from individual deficiencies. Consequently, in contrast to COS workers, settlement house workers focused much of their attention on social reform rather than individual casework. These early reformers sought to identify and marshal individual and community resources to find alternative ways to meet needs. They saw the common human needs of women, children, and laborers, and they were instrumental in starting preschools and the juvenile court system. Hull House settlement workers focused on helping immigrant families. However, the needs of African Americans were again largely ignored (Tice & Perkins, 2002). *racism play a role?*

Building the Social Work Profession   By the end of the 19th century, the social work profession was starting to gain public recognition as a profession and to offer training courses for friendly visitors and settlement house workers. In 1900, the term *social workers* was first used by educator Simon N. Patten to refer to both friendly visitors and settlement house workers (Barker, 2003). During the late 19th and early 20th centuries, Progressive Era reformers pushed for publicly financed social services, and social workers were needed to provide these services. The Progressive Era thus created an environment conducive to the growth of social work.

Despite early separation of the settlement house movement and charity organizations, both groups were beginning to cooperate and even merge by the turn of the century (Trattner, 1999). In 1909, Jane Addams was elected president of the National Conference of Charities and Correction, an organization that was instrumental in establishing casework as a distinct field within the social services. In 1917, Mary Richmond published *Social Diagnosis,* which became a primary text for social workers. Richmond applied the medical model to social work and prescribed investigation, diagnosis, prognosis, and treatment focused on the individual. Casework began to overshadow the social reform movement with roots in the settlement houses (Tice & Perkins, 2002). Also in 1917, the first organization for social workers was established; it currently is called the National Association of Social Workers (NASW).

By the 1920s, training programs established by the COS began to develop into schools of social work. Although these programs emphasized the individual, they recognized that human problems also arose from deficiencies in the social structure, communities, and families. However, in addressing these problems, they taught social workers to provide social services rather than to advocate social reform. *(changes in the community)*

African American Social Workers   African American pioneer social workers of this period recognized that racism was the major barrier that prevented African Americans from meeting their basic needs. Significantly, they focused on both helping individuals within their communities and addressing the larger societal issues. Racism was at the center of these larger issues, and African American social workers directed their practice toward community and organizational change.

The African American community developed its self-help efforts in the face of its exclusion from many services available in the white community. For example, women's clubs organized throughout the country and communicated with one another about their goals, including promoting education of women and children, improving family conditions, and promoting the civil rights of African Americans. The National Association of Colored Women's Clubs (NACWC) was formed in 1896 and enhanced solidarity. Many of these early social workers taught at "Colored" colleges and finishing schools, as part of the tradition of teaching the African American community to advocate for itself. By the first quarter of the 20th century, some courses of social work study specifically for and about African Americans had been implemented. These pioneer social workers played an important role in improving life for members of the African American community. Their work continues to be a model for service delivery, focusing on mutual aid, racial solidarity, and self-help efforts (Carlton-LaNey, 1999).

The Progressive Era and the Expansion of Social Welfare Policy, 1900–1920

The Progressive Era began in the late 1800s and continued through the first decades of the 1900s. The period leading up to the Progressive Era was one of strife between industrialists and labor. Progressive leaders believed that an activist, morally responsible government, rather than laissez-faire government, was needed to constrain the negative economic and environmental impacts of unrestrained industrial capitalism. Consequently, the government engaged in several cases of "trust busting," and Congress passed the Clayton Antitrust Act in 1914 to limit the size and power of large corporations. Progressive reformers also were interested in developing the concept of **social insurance,** whereby society recognized the normal risks of living, and people and the government pooled money to help out when misfortune, such as unemployment, injury, or sickness, struck.

During the Progressive Era, the federal government started to assume responsibility for child protection, consumer protection, and progressive taxation to finance reforms and social welfare policy. It encouraged reform of urban governments and pressed for laws regulating working conditions for women and children. During the administration of President Theodore Roosevelt, Congress passed the Meat Inspection Act and the Pure Food and Drug Act to protect consumers against unsafe products. Also during this period, African Americans and women organized to improve their political and economic status. Two organizations that emerged during the Progressive Era— the National Association for the Advancement of Colored People (NAACP) and the National Urban League (NUL)—played a major role in the struggle for African American civil rights and economic opportunities throughout the 20th century. In addition, women's suffrage advocates finally achieved their goal in 1920 with the ratification of the 19th Amendment, which extended the franchise to women.

Progressive reformers had also laid the foundation for increased federal involvement in social welfare by successfully pressing for the establishment of a federal income tax, which was authorized by the 16th Amendment and ratified in 1913. The income tax was a progressive tax; that is, people with higher incomes paid a greater percentage of their income than low-income people did. Later administrations would use tax revenues to fund programs for people in need.

Maternalistic Approaches and Mothers' Pensions   Women activists also pressed for public programs to provide cash assistance for poor mothers and children at the state level. Progressive pressure for mothers' pensions led to establishment of programs to support mothers and children in most states between 1911 and 1919 and set the stage for the assumption of funding of many social welfare programs by the federal government in the 1930s. Establishment of state programs meant that access to help for these families would no longer be based on rules developed by private philanthropic organizations and that assistance would no longer be doled out as charity by well-to-do individuals with an attitude of superiority (Reid, 1995).

Leaders of the mothers' pension movement asserted that bringing up children was a civic duty for mothers, who should be allowed to devote full-time efforts to child rearing (Tice & Perkins, 2002). Unfortunately, these programs were never adequately funded, and they reached only a small proportion of eligible women. Applicants had to pass a **means test,** that is, they had to demonstrate financial need. In addition, they had to pass a morals test. For the most part, only single mothers who were judged not to have violated the moral codes of the community received pensions. Therefore, most of the pensions were awarded to widows, while single mothers generally were unable to pass the morals test. Moreover, Hispanics, Native Americans, African Americans, and immigrant groups faced discrimination when applying for these benefits.

Overall, the proportion of women receiving pensions was minimal compared to the need in the minority and immigrant communities. Even for those mothers who did qualify, the pensions were so small that many recipients still had to work (Gordon, 1998). Then, as now, critics feared that a program that put money into the hands of poor women who were unattached to male breadwinners would encourage more men to abandon their families. Some critics even characterized the pensions as a downward slide toward state socialism (Tice & Perkins, 2002).

Historians such as Theda Skocpol (1993) have defined the mothers' pension movement as an effort to establish a maternalistic as opposed to a paternalistic approach to family support. That is, this initiative was developed around mothers, in contrast to the later Social Security program, which reflected the male breadwinner model. (We will examine the Social Security Act in the next chapter.) Supporters lauded this maternalistic approach to family support for recognizing the importance of helping women provide for their children in the absence of male breadwinners. However, the state mothers' pensions declined and eventually collapsed in the face of the Great Depression of the 1930s, when it became clear that only the federal government had a sufficient tax base to support impoverished families during economic downturns (Tice & Perkins, 2002).

Child Welfare   Another area in which the nation made progress during this period was child welfare. From the mid 19th through the early 20th century, reformers pressed vigorously for improved care for orphans, child labor laws, and programs to enhance children's health. Pioneer settlement house workers such as Jane Addams, Florence Kelley, and Lillian Wald were leaders in this effort (Tice & Perkins, 2002). Their efforts bore fruit as Congress passed a bill in 1912 establishing the Children's Bureau within the Department of Labor. Significantly, the Bureau was not allocated any regulatory authority. However, it was empowered to investigate and publicize the working and living conditions of the nation's children. As such, the Bureau represented the first agency within the federal government that focused exclusively on child welfare (Trattner, 1999).

One issue to which the Bureau's investigations drew attention was child labor. During this period, many very young children toiled long hours under appalling conditions. Congress enacted the Keating-Owen Child Labor Act in 1916 to regulate child labor. Although the bill was declared unconstitutional by the Supreme Court two years later and condemned in some quarters as a threat to family life, it served as a model for subsequent state regulations. By 1930, every state as well as Washington, D.C., had enacted child protection laws (Day, 1999; Link & Catton, 1967).

The New Immigration   Although Progressive Era advocates experienced some success in establishing more humane social welfare policies, racism and discrimination against certain groups actually increased during this period. In addition to racism and discrimination aimed toward African Americans, the late 19th and early 20th centuries witnessed increased discrimination and prejudice against immigrants. Immigration patterns began to change, as immigrants increasingly came from countries in southern and eastern Europe, including Italy, Russia, Poland, and Greece, rather than northern and western Europe. Whereas the majority of "old immigrants," such as Germans and Scandinavians, were

Protestant, many of the "new immigrants" were either Catholic, Orthodox, or Jewish. As in earlier periods, fears of greater competition for jobs combined with a general mistrust of people who spoke foreign languages and came from different cultural backgrounds to create barriers to integration into U.S. society. Though very limited, nascent social work initiatives such as the settlement house movement worked to ease this transition. Nevertheless, in the 1920s, the government passed legislation that severely curtailed immigration to the United States.

CONCLUSION

In this chapter, we have explored social welfare approaches from ancient cultures to the beginning of the 20th century. These approaches and historical events continue to influence social policy and programs today. If you take a few moments to reflect on the five questions listed in Box 2.1 when considering a given policy or program, you will see these connections. Understanding historical approaches will help you identify and critique the motivation, values, and ideologies that drive current policies and programs. It will also enable you to identify similar policies and programs that were implemented in the past and to evaluate their results. Look back at the three quotes at the beginning of this chapter. Take some time to consider what you have learned in this chapter that would help you speak up during discussions of the topics highlighted in those quotes. It is vital that social workers speak up when subjects critical to their clients' well-being are debated. The examination of historical policy initiatives can provide valuable insights that can help social workers as well as policy makers develop more-effective policies and programs.

MAIN POINTS

- History is not just a prologue to events of the day but rather has a direct influence on current social policies and programs.

- The five questions in the framework provided in this chapter (see Box 2.1) will help you explore the relationships between current social policies and programs and historical approaches.

- Poor Laws passed in the 1600s in England—which established public responsibility for paupers, categorized worthy and unworthy poor, and established residency rules—influence many of our current social policies and programs.

- Oppression of people of color throughout our history continues to influence social policies and programs.

- The social work profession traces its roots to the child-saving movement; the Charity Organization Society, which stressed casework and individual causality of poverty; and the settlement house movement, which advocated for structural change, including changes in sanitation laws and child labor laws.

EXERCISES: PRACTICING SOCIAL WORK

Working with the Black Feather Community

The tribes who live in the Black Feather region were part of the 19th century forced relocation known as the Trail of Tears. How do you think that history may affect the people of the Black Feather community currently? In what ways do you believe this history might have contributed to the conditions currently experienced in the Black Feather community?

EXERCISES: THE SOCIAL WORK LIBRARY

Read "How welfare became a dirty word" (Gordon, 1998), and respond to the following:

- What were the assumptions that drove the funding of mothers' aid pensions in the early 1900s?

- How were the assumptions of mothers' aid pensions and the subsequent AFDC program in the Social Security Act different from the assumptions guiding the approach of black women welfare advocates?

- After passage of AFDC, what factors increased the stigma associated with programs for women and children and equated AFDC with welfare?

OTHER EXERCISES

Take time to visit the Social Work History Station at the Boise State Web link found at www.mhhe.com/chapin1, and learn about the conditions in our country that led to the development of our earliest institutions. Try to imagine what it would have been like to have been a small child in one of the poorhouses (alms houses) in the United States in earlier centuries. Then imagine yourself as an old person living there. The strengths perspective insists that policies should be developed taking into account the point of view of the recipients. Considering the economic realities of the day, from your vantage point as a child or an old person in the poorhouse, can you imagine what types of policies or programs might have been more helpful to you?

CHAPTER 3

The Historical Context: Development of Our Current Welfare System

THIS CHAPTER CHRONICLES MAJOR POLICY INITIATIVES FROM World War I through the dawn of the 21st century. In many ways, the nation made great strides during this period in helping people meet their basic needs. Life expectancy increased dramatically, and poverty rates and child mortality rates decreased as improved public sanitation and health care, labor laws, and pensions provided increased protection for the citizenry. At the same time, as this chapter will show, basic needs, such as health insurance, still go unmet for millions of Americans.

EXPANDING THE WELFARE STATE IN WAR AND DEPRESSION: 1917–1945

As we saw in Chapter 2, Progressive reformers left a rich legacy of public sanitation, public health, child labor, and state-level mothers' pension laws. These reforms set the stage for a major expansion of the welfare state during the New Deal of the 1930s, a topic we discuss later in this chapter. However, U.S. entry into World War I in 1917 generally drew attention away from domestic reform efforts, though the nation did approve the 18th Amendment, which established Prohibition, and the 19th Amendment, which extended the vote to women, in 1919 and 1920, respectively. At the same time, the psychological problems experienced by many veterans of the war increased national attention on, and the allocation of resources for, mental health treatment provided by social workers. Mary Richmond and many of her colleagues were actively involved in efforts by the American Red Cross to provide casework services to displaced veterans and their families after World War I. However, Jane Addams, as well as other prominent social reformers of the day, had opposed World War I.

One major social policy reform took place shortly after the end of the war, when women finally achieved the right to vote in all elections. The struggle for women's voting rights was a long one. A major milestone took place in 1848, when Elizabeth Cady Stanton and Lucretia Mott organized the first women's rights conference at Seneca Falls, New York. In the ensuing years, a number of women's rights groups were formed, the most prominent being the National American Woman's Suffrage Association (NAWSA). As early as 1878, these groups called for a constitutional amendment to guarantee full voting rights for women. Although several states—particularly in the West—extended the franchise to women, many other states either restricted voting by women to certain elections or outlawed it completely.

During World War I, the NAWSA, under the leadership of Carrie Chapman Catt, led the final push for a women's suffrage amendment. This movement gained the support of President Woodrow Wilson, in part because of women's contributions to the war effort. Consequently, the 19th Amendment, which mandated that "the right of citizens of the United States to vote shall not be denied or abridged by the United States or by any State on account of sex," was finally ratified.

Having secured the right to vote, some women's groups struggled for a broader guarantee of rights and opportunities. In 1923, the Equal Rights Amendment (ERA) was introduced into Congress for the first time. It was defeated, but it was subsequently reintroduced every year until 1972, when it finally passed the Congress. However, it was not ratified by a sufficient number of states to become part of the Constitution.

The New Deal

The decade following World War I was a time of prosperity for many Americans, and the needs of those people who did not share in that prosperity were largely ignored. Voters elected three successive Republican presidents: Warren G. Harding, Calvin Coolidge, and Herbert Hoover. However, unlike Progressive Republicans such as Theodore Roosevelt, these presidents were unwilling to engage in large-scale social reform.

The reluctance of the federal government to provide aid to people in need lessened markedly in the face of the stock market crash of 1929 and the dire economic conditions of the Great Depression of the 1930s. The influence of the larger economic environment on millions of Americans who were now without jobs could not be denied. Franklin Roosevelt, a Democrat, was elected president in 1932 and held the office until his death in 1945. The Roosevelt administration implemented a series of economic policies that reflected the theories of British economist John Maynard Keynes. Keynes advocated increased government spending and manipulation of interest rates in order to dampen inflation and manage recessions. We will examine Keynesian economics in greater detail in Chapter 4.

During the Roosevelt administration, the federal government initiated work relief programs and other forms of aid to needy people. These policy and program innovations are referred to collectively as the **New Deal.** The Works Progress Administration (WPA), the Civilian Conservation Corps (CCC), and the Civil Works Administration (CWA) were among the most prominent New Deal programs. These programs employed millions of people in such diverse activities as building roads, bridges, and other public works; planting trees and preserving forests; and performing plays and painting murals. The Great Depression and the New Deal marked a fundamental change in the way many people thought about need and the responsibility of the government to address need. The conviction that the federal government must assume some responsibility for people who are in need through no fault of their own replaced the principle that social welfare was largely a local and state responsibility. States could no longer afford the pension programs that some of them had developed. Because the states had shown themselves to be incapable of meeting such widespread need, federal aid to the states was now considered vital.

Social workers were leaders in the development of several New Deal programs. For example, Harry Hopkins (director of the Federal Emergency Relief Administration [FERA]), Frances Perkins (Secretary of Labor), and Martha Eliot (U.S. Children's Bureau) as well as many other social workers helped develop and administer the new social policies of the era (Tice & Perkins, 2002). As discussed in Chapter 1, Charlotte Towle wrote *Common Human Needs,* a manual originally developed for the Bureau of Public Assistance of the U.S. Social Security Board (1945/1987). Towle's monograph was based on the premise that people have common human needs, and it helped articulate a more compassionate view of people who could not provide for themselves. Social work was distinguishing itself as a profession that addressed not only individual needs but also the need for policy reform at the state and national levels.

 Web Link

If you would like to read more about the New Deal and the work of these and other famous social workers, go to the New Deal Web link at www.mhhe.com/chaplin1.

The Townsend Movement   In the years leading up to the Depression, people were living longer, yet there were fewer and fewer jobs, particularly for older adults. Researchers estimated that three out of four persons over age 65 were unable to support themselves. Also, as a result of societal changes, many families did not or were not able to support their elder members in the way that was previously expected.

To address this issue, the Townsend Movement, a grassroots effort to provide more generous retirement benefits to senior citizens, arose in California. During the Depression, Dr. Francis Townsend developed a plan that called for the government to provide benefits for retired people over age 60. Retirees would receive a monthly benefit of $200, which they would be required to spend within the month. In this way, Townsend sought to stimulate the economy by providing money for consumption. At the same time, by encouraging people over 60 to retire, the Townsend plan would open up jobs for younger workers. Townsend advocated paying for the plan through a special sales tax.

Townsend outlined his plan in numerous letters to the editor of his local newspaper. He was associated with the Liberal Party, and his plan was popular in his native state, where its proponents supported those candidates who endorsed it. Nationally, the Townsend Movement had a strong following among elders, and it is credited with influencing President Roosevelt and Congress to pass the Social Security Act in 1935. The movement helped make clear that some sort of support for elders had become necessary.

The Social Security Act   Partially in response to the Townsend Movement, in 1935 Congress enacted a major piece of social policy legislation, the Social Security Act. This law encompassed both major social insurance and public assistance programs that have become integral to our social service system. The original act made provisions for old-age benefits; financial assistance for aged and blind persons and dependent and crippled children; maternal and child welfare; public health measures; and unemployment compensation. It provided benefits to retired workers through a system of social insurance, which replaced the more stigmatizing practice of public assistance. Policy makers realized that retired workers were people much like themselves who obviously needed and deserved income security in old age.

 Web Link

If you would like to learn more about the history of the Social Security Act, you can link to the Social Security Web site at www.mhhe.com/chapin1.

The Old Age, Survivors, and Disability Insurance program, established by the Social Security Act and subsequent amendments, is a social insurance program that is based on the proposition that "worthy" workers and their employers can pool money to provide for retirement, disability, and surviving family members after a worker's death. Linking worthiness to paid work in industries in which men were the primary employees reinforced the role of the male breadwinner. Because many jobs such as farmworker and housekeeper were not initially included in the program, it also meant that people of color, unmarried women, and children often were not covered and were segregated into separate, needs-based public assistance programs.

Perhaps the most important public assistance program established by the Social Security Act was Aid to Dependent Children (ADC), which provided cash assistance for needy children. The law defined a "dependent child" as "a child under the age of 16 who has been deprived of parental support or care by reason of the death, continued absence from the home, or physical or mental incapacity of a parent" and who is living with the other parent or another relative. Initially, payments were made only for the care of children, not for their parents or other caretakers. Later, caretaker grants for parents of dependent children were added, and the name of the program was changed to Aid to Families of Dependent Children (AFDC). Overall, public assistance programs have been much more controversial and less generously funded than benefits for "worthy" retirees.

Web Link

To see all of the areas of economic security covered in the original Social Security Act, go to the Web site link at www.mhhe.com/chapin1.

The provisions for retired workers contained in the Social Security Act were originally called Old-Age Insurance (OAI). As the name implies, benefits were restricted to the retired workers themselves. However, amendments adopted in 1939 extended coverage to two additional categories of people: (1) the spouse and children of a retired worker, and (2) the survivors of a deceased covered worker. It was at this point that the name was changed to Old-Age and Survivors' Insurance (OASI) (DeWitt, 2003). In 1956, disability insurance benefits were added for workers aged 50–64 and for adult children of retired or deceased workers with permanent and total disabilities. The program then became known as Old-Age, Survivors', and Disability Insurance (OASDI). In 1960, workers of all ages and their dependents were made eligible for disability insurance benefits (Social Security Administration, 2005).

In the Chapter 8 discussion on income support policies, we critique legislation such as the Social Security Act on many levels. For now, it is important to recognize that passage of the Social Security Act represents a milestone in the development of public support for people in need. Significantly, those parts of the act that provide social insurance were premised on the belief that people have common human needs rather than the idea that destitution is an indicator of individual deficits. The act therefore brought new resources into communities to aid citizens in meeting their needs. In this sense, these provisions reflect a strengths perspective. At the same time, however, the public assistance programs established by the act were means-tested and failed to address the structural barriers that keep people in poverty, such as lack of access to employment, adequate education, and health care.

The Impact of World War II

 Web Link

Take a look at the Rosie the Riveter link at www.mhhe.com/chapin1 and click on History *to find out how women were drawn into new kinds of jobs and the dilemmas they faced.*

Just as World War I had diverted the nation from the Progressive movement, the attack on Pearl Harbor in December 1941 drew national attention away from the social reforms of the New Deal. At the same time, the nation's entry into World War II had a profound effect on the economy. The federal government increased spending dramatically, creating jobs for millions of Americans in the armed services and in war-related industries. Consequently, the United States finally emerged from the Depression. As millions of men joined the military, women entered the workforce and often moved into nontraditional areas such as manufacturing jobs in shipyards and aircraft factories. When the war was over, however, the jobs and the supports such as work-site day care largely disappeared, and women were once again bombarded with messages extolling the virtues of traditional gender roles.

The horrors of the Holocaust led many Americans to begin to reexamine beliefs that supported prejudice and discrimination in the United States. The Holocaust illustrated that eugenics, which encourages the reproduction of people thought to have desirable genetic traits, has horrific consequences when

Images of strong women like Rosie the Riveter were used to recruit women into factory jobs during World War II.

Source: By Howard J. Miller. Produced for Westinghouse for the War Production Coordinating Committee, NARA Still Pictures Branch. Copyright © Corbis.

taken to its logical end. These lessons contributed to the civil rights movement of the 1950s and 1960s.

THE EVOLUTION OF THE MODERN WELFARE STATE: 1945–1970

With the end of World War II in 1945, the federal government developed programs to address the mental health needs of veterans and to provide support for returning veterans. In this section, we will trace the effects of these initiatives on the larger society. We will also explore the strides made in securing civil rights in the 1950s and 1960s, and we will consider the successes and failures of federal antipoverty programs during this period.

During the administration of Harry Truman (1945–1952), many people in the United States began to enjoy relative affluence in a period of prosperity. Significantly, the federal government played a vital role in promoting this prosperity. For example, in 1944, Congress passed the Servicemen's Readjustment Act, commonly referred to as the GI Bill of Rights, that helped returning soldiers build assets. The GI Bill provided loans for veterans to purchase a home or establish a business, and it provided money for tuition, which enabled many working-class and middle-class veterans to attend college. The rationale for the bill was that veterans should be returned to civilian status in a way that would restore the opportunities they lost by serving in the war.

If the GI Bill is considered in the larger political and economic context, the education and training that the veterans received upgraded the overall quality of the U.S. workforce. In addition, the GI Bill reflected a strengths perspective in that it focused not on individual deficits but rather on finding ways to overcome structural barriers by enhancing economic and educational opportunities and helping veterans build their assets. Proposals to provide a "GI Bill approach" to ameliorating poverty for single mothers with children and people with disabilities are discussed in later chapters.

In addition to focusing on the economic needs of returning veterans, the federal government addressed the mental health needs of World War II draftees by passing the Mental Health Act of 1946, which created the National Institute of Mental Health (NIMH) and ultimately helped move public treatment out of state institutions and into community-based programs (Reid, 1995). The GI Bill and the Mental Health Act were evidence of the federal government's more activist role in the area of social welfare. Although these efforts enjoyed some degree of success, many people did not benefit from these gains or participate in the nation's increasing affluence. For example, African Americans continued to struggle against Jim Crow laws, and poverty remained widespread for many traditionally oppressed groups.

Significantly, the social work profession continued to upgrade standards for social work education during the postwar period. The National Council on Social Work Education was established in 1946 to study differences and relationships between bachelor's-level and master's-level education in social work. This organization was later renamed the Council on Social Work Education (CSWE). The CSWE is the accrediting body for BSW and MSW programs today. This period also witnessed the consolidation of several social work associations to form the National Association of Social Workers (NASW), which took place in 1956. NASW remains social workers' major national professional association today.

The Struggle for African American Civil Rights

During the postwar years, individuals and institutions could legally discriminate against people based on skin color. Consequently, racial segregation in housing, education, employment, medical treatment, and even burial sites continued. Social reformers had not yet awakened mainstream America to the need for civil rights for African Americans. However, war experiences with the extremes of Nazi racism led some white Americans to question racist practices in their communities. White liberal groups began forming coalitions with black civil rights groups. In addition, throughout the 1940s and 1950s, the large-scale migration of African Americans to northern cities, where they could vote, increased their political power.

The Challenge to School Segregation   In a milestone event, the National Association for the Advancement of Colored People (NAACP) challenged the separate-but-equal doctrine via the court case *Brown vs. Board of Education of Topeka*. In 1954, the Supreme Court ruled that in "public education the doctrine of 'separate but equal' has no place." It further asserted that "separate educational facilities are inherently unequal" and therefore violated the 14th Amendment's guarantee of equal protection of the law (Knappman, Christianson, & Paddock, 1993). The *Brown* decision is an excellent example of how the judiciary generates social policy. This ruling, which overturned the 1896 *Plessy vs. Ferguson* ruling that separate but equal facilities are constitutional, helped bring an end to Jim Crow laws. For this reason, it is considered one of the most important civil rights rulings of the 20th century. However, 15 years after *Brown vs. Board of Education*, 80 percent of black schoolchildren were still being educated in segregated facilities (Day, 1999).

The Challenge to Jim Crow   Beginning in the 1950s, African American civil rights activists and their white allies initiated a campaign of direct action to challenge the nation's system of racial subordination. On December 1, 1955, an African American woman named Rosa Parks refused to surrender her seat on a Montgomery, Alabama, bus to a white person, in violation of local segregation laws. Black residents of Montgomery responded by boycotting the city's bus system. The boycott continued for almost a year until the Supreme Court ruled that Montgomery's segregation law violated the 14th Amendment. Not only was the boycott a landmark victory for advocates of social justice, but it brought attention to a new civil rights leader, Dr. Martin Luther King, Jr., and a new organization, the Southern Christian Leadership Conference (SCLC), that were willing to directly challenge the oppressive racial system of the South (Patterson, 1996).

Civil rights protests intensified in the 1960s. On February 1, 1960, four black college students in Greensboro, North Carolina, sat down at a lunch counter that was designated "Whites Only." They were not served, but their sit-in continued until closing time. Similar sit-ins to protest segregation in theaters, churches, swimming pools, and stores occurred across the South.

Black leadership in the South mobilized to press for civil rights. In May 1963, King and the SCLC led a major protest in Birmingham, Alabama, to demand an end to segregation and employment discrimination in the city. The Birmingham police eventually arrested hundreds of demonstrators and used water hoses and police dogs against them as a stunned nation followed these developments on television. Later that year, King delivered his famous "I Have a Dream" speech to a multiracial audience of 200,000 people in Washington, D.C. The following year, Mississippi segregationists murdered three civil rights workers: social worker Michael Schwerner, James Chaney, and Andrew Goodman.

Web Link

To learn more about Brown vs. Board of Education, *visit the Web site listed at www.mhhe.com/chapin1. Click on* History and Culture *to take an online tour of sites involved in this case. You can also explore a variety of detailed background information.*

Web Link

If you have never heard Dr. Martin Luther King Jr.'s "I Have a Dream" speech, find the Web site listed at www.mhhe.com/chapin1 and link to the speech.

Civil Rights Laws   One concrete goal for which most civil rights activists campaigned was the enactment of a comprehensive national law to protect the civil rights of African Americans. This objective was achieved with the passage of the Civil Rights Act of 1964, which prohibited employment discrimination on the basis of race, sex, or ethnicity; banned federal funding for institutions that practiced discrimination; and mandated equal access to public accommodations. (We will examine the specific features of this law in Chapter 7.) That same year, the 24th Amendment, which prohibited the use of poll taxes or any other taxes to deny voting rights in federal elections, was ratified. The following year, Congress passed the Voting Rights Act of 1965, which suspended literacy tests and assigned federal registrars to enroll voters. The Voting Rights Act essentially provided for enforcement of the 15th Amendment (see Chapter 2). Civil rights advocates used these laws and amendments to launch a successful assault on the Jim Crow system.

The Struggle for Mexican American Civil Rights

As discussed in Chapter 2, the annexation of Texas and the Treaty of Guadalupe Hidalgo that concluded the Mexican War significantly increased the Hispanic or Latino population of the United States. Throughout the Southwest, Hispanics as well as legal and undocumented Mexican immigrants were exploited to meet the demand for cheap farm labor. They received low wages and were forced to work and live under dangerous and unsanitary conditions. U.S. policy toward immigrant workers fluctuated greatly depending on economic conditions. During prosperous times, when the demand for labor rose, the government encouraged Mexican workers to enter the country, although only temporarily. In contrast, during the Depression, thousands of Mexican Americans were deported (Nash et al., 2004).

Responding to discrimination and exploitation, Hispanic migrant workers began to organize to demand decent wages and working conditions. In 1962, Cesar Chavez created the National Farm Workers Association, which pressed for fairer treatment of these workers. Three years later, that group evolved into the United Farm Workers (UFW) and initiated La Huelga, a major strike of agricultural workers in California (Patterson, 1996). The struggle to improve conditions for these workers continues today.

Mental Health and Mental Retardation Initiatives

Recall that in 1946 Congress passed the Mental Health Act, which focused increased attention on the treatment of people with mental illness. During the early 1960s, advocates for people with mental retardation and mental illness pressured the federal government to allocate greater resources for their treatment and to increase opportunities for community-based care. Significantly, they found a powerful ally in President John Kennedy, who had a sister with mental retardation. Their efforts culminated in the passage of the Mental Retardation Facilities and Community Mental Health Centers Act of 1963. This act provided money to construct and staff community mental health centers and mental retardation facilities nationwide. Although the mental health centers were never sufficiently funded to meet the need for community-based services, the act helped usher in an era of deinstitutionalization in which people with mental illness were reintegrated into the larger community rather than confined and treated in mental hospitals (Trattner, 1999).

The War on Poverty

Closely associated with the civil rights movement were a variety of initiatives by the federal government to address the problem of poverty. The administrations of presidents John Kennedy (1961–1963) and Lyndon Johnson (1963–1968) implemented a number of programs to create jobs, improve education, and provide financial assistance to people in need. Kennedy was influenced in particular by *The Other America,* published in 1962 by political scientist Michael Harrington. Harrington's book helped open the eyes of the American people to the reality of structural poverty that arose from unemployment and lack of opportunities rather than individual deficits. *The Other America* is often credited with ushering in another discovery of poverty, a problem that had been given less attention following the Depression. The book focused public attention on people in depressed areas who had not benefited from the relative affluence of the 1950s.

New Frontier Antipoverty Programs   Kennedy's domestic program, known as the New Frontier, included several measures to help move people out of poverty. For example, the Area Redevelopment Act of 1961 allocated federal monies to depressed areas such as Appalachia. The following year, Congress approved the Manpower Development Training Act (MDTA) to train or retrain workers who lacked the skills necessary to succeed in a changing economy. Further, the Equal Pay Act of 1963 attempted to address the issue of gender-based wage discrimination by promoting the concept that women should receive equal wages for performing the same work as men. Although these initiatives were limited in both their scope and their funding, they symbolized a growing belief that the federal government should take action against poverty even during relatively prosperous periods (Patterson, 1996).

Of special significance for social workers were the 1962 Public Welfare Amendments to the Social Security Act, referred to as the Social Service Amendments. These amendments allocated federal support to the states so that local welfare departments could provide recipients of public assistance with casework, job training and placement, and other social services. Social workers who

 Web Link

If you would like to learn more about the civil rights movement during the Kennedy presidency, go to John F. Kennedy Library and Museum (2002), Civil Rights Leaders and the President. *The link can be accessed at www.mhhe.com/chapin1.*

proposed ideas to the president for addressing the dependency of public welfare recipients and family breakdown indicated that these interventions would promote motivation and family unity, which in turn would reduce the welfare rolls significantly (Day, 1999). Instead, the welfare rolls increased by nearly 50 percent between 1962 and 1967.

There were a variety of reasons for this increase. One reason was that during the 1960s, large numbers of African American mothers began to claim AFDC benefits. Formerly reluctant to claim such benefits as a right of citizenship, black women were no longer willing to see their children go without health care, and they felt strongly that their children should stay in school rather than go to work to help support their families (Tice & Perkins, 2002). In addition, social workers and other activists engaged in outreach in order to help more people living in poverty. At the same time, eligibility rules were relaxed so that more people could receive help. However, the low levels of public assistance did not provide clients with sufficient support to take advantage of expanded educational and social services (Reisch, 2000). For example, people lacking sufficient funds for transportation and day care could not attend job training and parenting classes.

Because social workers had advocated for the Social Service Amendments, when these programs failed to reduce the welfare rolls, it contributed to increased skepticism about the effectiveness of social services. Poverty is essentially a lack of money and other resources; therefore, ameliorating poverty requires not only resolving the personal problems of poor people but also overcoming the structural barriers they confront and reforming the major social service systems. The idea that welfare rolls would be significantly reduced by offering social services to individuals to lift themselves out of poverty without addressing the social conditions that caused their poverty was contrary to what many social workers knew about the interactions of people and their environment. However, in order to secure funding for programs that can help in individual cases, advocates often promise unrealistic outcomes. Unfortunately, unkept promises accumulate and contribute to public cynicism regarding the efforts of both the government and social workers to assist low-income people.

The Great Society and the War on Poverty   The assassination of President Kennedy in November 1963 ushered in the presidency of Lyndon Johnson, who was able to work with Congress to pass civil rights, health, and antipoverty legislation. These policies and the programs they created were core initiatives of Johnson's Great Society, which included his War on Poverty. Like the Progressive Era and the New Deal period, the 1960s witnessed major social policy developments. As you read the following discussion of the Great Society and the War on Poverty, consider how these periods were both similar and different and identify the forces that helped bring all these periods of increased reform to an end.

The centerpiece of Johnson's War on Poverty was the Economic Opportunity Act of 1964. This landmark law focused on community organizing, social action, increasing economic opportunities, and empowering rather than "fixing" the poor. Among the programs and agencies established by the Economic Opportunity Act were:

- The Office of Economic Opportunity (OEO), which oversaw the administration's antipoverty activities

- Volunteers in Service to America (VISTA), a program in which volunteers directly assisted people in need, including migrant workers and individuals with mental illness or other disabilities

- A Job Corps to train young men who were unemployed and lacked adequate job skills

- Community action programs (CAPs), which provided services and resources such as education, housing, health care, and job training to impoverished communities while encouraging "maximum feasible participation" by the residents of those communities

- Head Start, a program administered by OEO that provided medical care, nutrition, school preparation, and parental education to aid poor preschoolers (Bernstein, 1996)

The Economic Opportunity Act reflected the belief that overcoming poverty would not be achieved by changing individual characteristics of poor people but instead would require major changes in the way opportunities for education and employment were provided. These changes, in turn, could take place only as people in poverty learned the power of the vote and people from traditionally oppressed groups such as inner-city African Americans and Hispanics or Latinos began to hold office and exercise political power. When viewed from this perspective, then, the Economic Opportunity Act reflected a strengths-based approach to combating poverty.

Antipoverty programs initially did not incorporate social workers because the intent was to rely less heavily on professionals and instead acknowledge that the target groups themselves were the experts on how to escape poverty. However, these groups soon brought in social workers to help with community organizing, administering antipoverty programs, and providing direct services (Popple, 1995).

Medicare and Medicaid   Another feature of the Great Society that was intended to combat poverty was federal legislation to assist older adults and low-income people in meeting their medical expenses. In 1965, three decades of lobbying for incorporating health care into the Social Security Act finally resulted in the passage of Title XVIII, which established Medicare, and Title XIX, which

 Web Link

Visit the Centers for Medicare and Medicaid Services (CMS), at www.mhhe.com/chapin1 and explore the Web site to learn more about the history of Medicare and Medicaid.

established Medicaid. Although these programs did not provide universal health care for all citizens—a goal we have still not achieved—they did ensure basic medical care for certain categories of citizens.

Medicare is a national health insurance program for people age 65 and older who are eligible for Social Security and for certain categories of younger people with disabilities. Medicare focuses primarily on acute care and provides little coverage for long-term care. Medicare Part A provides hospital insurance, and Medicare Part B is an optional program that allows people 65 and older to purchase coverage for Medicare-eligible physician services, outpatient hospital services, certain home health services, and durable medical equipment. The Medicare program is federally funded through payroll taxes.

Medicaid provides health care for certain categories of people with very low incomes as part of public assistance. It is a means-tested program that is financed jointly by federal and state dollars. Although typically thought of as the source of health care for poor families with children, Medicaid also pays more than half of nursing home costs nationally because many older people are impoverished by the costs of nursing home care and thus become eligible for Medicaid. Many younger people with disabilities also qualify for Medicaid. Although states can use Medicaid to make home- and community-based services available for some older adults and young people with severe disabilities, there are often long waiting lists for these services.

The War on Poverty: Successes and Failures   As we would expect from any major reform effort, the War on Poverty experienced both successes and failures. This observation is significant because many people have overlooked the actual benefits of policies and programs that were created in the 1960s. Instead, they remember the antipoverty efforts associated with this period only as failures rather than as programs that promised too much and were inadequately funded but nonetheless generated some positive outcomes for clients. Certainly, the civil rights legislation of this period attempted to address the structural problems created by discrimination. Significantly, the national poverty rate dropped from 22 percent in 1960 to 11 percent in 1974. Although the improving state of the economy was the major cause of this decline, the antipoverty programs contributed as well.

In addition, several of the antipoverty policies and programs implemented during this period survived and are still important today. In addition to Medicare and Medicaid, these initiatives include Head Start, the Food Stamp Act of 1964, and the Older Americans Act of 1965. Through the Food Stamp Act, low-income families were able to purchase additional food. The Older Americans Act contains a number of provisions designed to promote social interaction and enhance independent living for older adults. For example, funding for congregate meals and transportation helped community-dwelling older adults meet nutrition needs more adequately and lessened their social isolation. This law incorporated such strengths-based policy tenets as empowering clients, involving them in developing and providing services, and increasing opportunities for them. Take a moment to think about the lessons we can learn from examining the various policies and programs implemented during the 1960s and consider the implications for social policy reform today.

Unfortunately, the costs of the Vietnam War helped put an end to many of the Great Society antipoverty initiatives. Because it is difficult to afford both "guns and butter," the major antipoverty programs generally received inadequate funding. In addition, most of these programs failed to address the social, economic, and demographic forces that were causing the welfare rolls to rise. For example, increasing numbers of low-income families were migrating from the South to urban areas in the North, where they found insufficient job opportunities, inadequate housing, and ineffective transportation systems. However, critics who were not mindful of these underlying deficiencies classified the War on Poverty as a failure when welfare rolls increased and poverty continued.

In their book *Regulating the Poor*, Frances Piven and Richard Cloward, a social worker, examine historical periods of increase in economic assistance for low-income citizens through the 1960s. They contend that programs providing economic support to poor people expanded not in relation to need but rather as a tool for controlling unrest, particularly in U.S. cities (Piven & Cloward, 1971). Their analysis points to the outpouring of economic assistance during the period of civil unrest of the 1960s. They assert that the government provided temporary economic aid to regulate unrest rather than to address the structural problems of unemployment and discrimination that limited opportunity. Although their assertions are certainly open to debate, their critical analysis helped increase awareness of the multiple goals of antipoverty initiatives.

The cutback of funding for antipoverty programs led Martin Luther King, Jr. to wonder whether social and economic justice would ever become a reality for African Americans and poor people. Other black leaders, such as Malcolm X and Stokely Carmichael, openly rejected the premise that nonviolence and integration would produce racial equality. They rallied their followers with calls for "black power" and "black separatism." However, a coalition of white and black civil rights advocates opposed their ideas because they felt that black Americans did not control sufficient resources to establish a separate economy. Also, many people continued to believe that integration could succeed. However, a white backlash that emerged in response to the separatist rhetoric and to urban riots such as the one in the Watts section of Los Angeles in 1965 fueled a political turn to the right that contributed to the election of a Republican president, Richard Nixon, in 1968.

THE 1970s: CONTINUITY AND CHANGE

Richard Nixon presided over the tumultuous first years of the 1970s. Nixon's administration was marked by controversy that culminated in the president's resignation. However, his administration almost doubled spending on anti-poverty programs over that of the Kennedy and Johnson administrations (Tice & Perkins, 2002). Our discussion of the 1970s highlights experiments with a different approach to providing cash assistance to low-income people, the negative income tax. We will also consider the continuing push for greater civil rights. Building on the civil rights reforms of the 1960s, several marginalized groups struggled to improve their situation in the 1970s. We will focus on the struggles of two such groups—women and Native Americans—to achieve social justice. We will also consider social policies that were implemented to promote their civil rights and to enhance the resources available to them.

Family Assistance Experiments

Perhaps the major social welfare initiative of the Nixon administration was the Family Assistance Plan (FAP), proposed by presidential adviser Daniel Patrick Moynihan. The FAP would have established a minimum income for all families by providing cash assistance to families whose incomes fell below a certain level. This policy is sometimes referred to as a "negative income tax." Reflecting a philosophy that dates at least to the English Poor Laws, the FAP also would have required all able-bodied recipients to work or to participate in a job-training program. If enacted, this plan would have replaced AFDC.

However, the FAP quickly became the target of criticism from across the political spectrum. Liberals pointed out that the minimum income level was actually less than the established poverty level. Moreover, they objected to the work requirements, in part because the "able-bodied" poor included mothers with children over three years of age. Meanwhile, many conservatives argued that the FAP would significantly increase federal spending on welfare, especially if other assistance programs, such as food stamps, were not eliminated as part of the plan. Nixon himself, who was more concerned with foreign policy, eventually lost interest in the FAP, and it never passed the Congress (Moynihan, 1973; Trattner, 1989).

Although not implemented nationally, these negative income tax experiments heightened interest in providing income to low-income families through the tax system. Reflecting this interest, Congress passed legislation in 1975 that established the Earned Income Tax Credit (EITC), which provided a refundable tax credit to "families whose incomes fall below the federal poverty line even though they are supported by full-time workers" (Jouzaitis, 1993, p. 17). Although this tax credit was modest and did not significantly reduce poverty, it established the principle of using the tax system, administered through the

 Web Link

If you would like to learn more about early development of this less stigmatizing method of helping people in poverty, visit the Negative Income Tax Web site at www.mhhe.com/chapin1.

Internal Revenue Service, to provide resources to low-income citizens. This approach, similar to the tax incentives, mortgage deductions, and other welfare programs for wealthy and middle-class families, reduces the stigma of assistance and helps more people realize that the tax system is a method for providing welfare and that most people are likely welfare recipients themselves.

Social Service Reforms

Although the 1970s are not considered a period of major social service reform, several measures introduced during the administrations of Richard Nixon and his successor, Gerald Ford, contributed to the social welfare of people in need. One reform involved child welfare. Child welfare advocates lobbied intensely for a national standard for child protection and, in response, Congress passed the Child Abuse Prevention and Treatment Act of 1974. This law also enabled child advocates to document national trends in child abuse and to publicize the need for protective services for the first time.

Social Welfare and Tax Initiatives   Other initiatives sought to increase assistance to low-income groups. For example, in 1972, Congress enacted legislation creating the Supplementary Security Income (SSI) program. Prior to 1972, states had a patchwork of programs to provide assistance to elderly people, blind people, and people with disabilities who had limited or no income. SSI replaced this arrangement with a uniform national system. In addition, the Social Service Amendments of 1974, specifically Title XX, provided grants to states to provide social services to welfare recipients as well as people above the poverty line. Although the amount of money available for these programs was capped, states were given a great deal of latitude in determining how the services were to be provided. Social Security and SSI benefits were also indexed through an automatic cost-of-living adjustment (COLA) (Tice & Perkins, 2002).

Watergate and After   Despite these reforms, the Watergate scandal, which led to Nixon's resignation in August 1974, further undermined the public's belief in the positive power of government, thus mitigating against the expansion of social programs that had marked the 1960s and early 1970s. The next two presidents, Gerald Ford and Jimmy Carter, were focused on controlling the budget deficit and taming inflation. Carter did propose a guaranteed annual income plan that would have created an income safety net for all Americans, but it was not enacted (Tice & Perkins, 2002).

Women and Civil Rights

The women's movement increased its advocacy efforts during this period. In 1966, a group of activists founded the National Organization for Women

(NOW) to press for equal rights for women. Its first president, Betty Friedan, was the author of the landmark book *The Feminine Mystique.* This book helped increase awareness of societal stereotypes that limited women's roles and impeded their efforts to secure equal rights. Women's rights activists pressed for equal opportunities across a broad spectrum, including employment, education, and athletics.

As we saw earlier in the chapter, amendments to the U.S. Constitution to guarantee equal rights for women were introduced repeatedly in Congress beginning in 1923. Finally, in 1972, Congress passed the Equal Rights Amendment (ERA), mandating that "equality of rights under the law shall not be denied or abridged by the United States or by any State on account of sex." Supported by groups such as NOW, the amendment was passed by 21 states. However, opponents such as the Moral Majority raised fears of women and men using the same bathrooms and pregnant women and mothers being drafted in wartime. Consequently, the ERA never gained the approval of the 38 states needed for ratification.

The Social Work Library

To learn more about the impact of Title IX, read the U.S. Department of Labor Title IX, Education Amendments of 1972, which can be accessed at www.mhhe.com/chapin1.

However, other policy reforms influencing women's lives were more successful. For example, Title IX of the Education Amendments of 1972 banned discrimination and exclusion in schools on the basis of sex in both academic and sports arenas, thus opening wider the doors of opportunity for women (Title IX Education Amendments of 1972). The following year, the Supreme Court decision *Roe vs. Wade* legalized abortion. However, despite the activist environment of the time and the preponderance of women in the social work profession, the NASW did not elect a woman president until 1980 (Hooyman, 1994).

American Indians and Civil Rights

The 1970s also witnessed increased activism by American Indian groups. Many of these actions focused on the status of American Indians within the broader political system. Recall from Chapter 2 that the *Cherokee Nation vs. Georgia* ruling of 1831 placed the various Indian tribes under the jurisdiction of the U.S. government, denying them the status of sovereign nations. Decades later, the Dawes Act replaced the traditional tribal system of landownership with an individual and family system. In the 20th century, Native American activists and their advocates in the government began to challenge these arrangements. In 1934, as part of the New Deal, Congress passed the Indian Reorganization Act, which officially abolished the Dawes allotment policy and returned certain expropriated lands to various tribes. Moreover, it authorized the tribes to establish governments or councils that would exercise some degree of sovereignty (DeLoria, 1993).

Termination and Relocation   The New Deal reforms demonstrated greater sensitivity toward Native American autonomy and culture. However, in the more conservative political atmosphere of the 1950s, the government's focus shifted to incorporating Indian peoples into mainstream U.S. culture. To accomplish this objective, it pursued the policies of termination and relocation. Formally implemented by two congressional actions of 1953, *termination* involved abolishing the special status of tribes as wards of the federal government and authorizing the states to assume some of the functions of the tribal governments. One objective of this policy was "to cut off public aid to Indians and to get them to fend for themselves" (Patterson, 1996, p. 376). However, because the government failed to provide transition supports, many Native Americans suffered heavy financial and property losses. For example, when Native Americans were billed for property taxes they were unable to pay, they lost their homes, which in turn left them unable to support schools, sanitation systems, and highways in their communities.

Groups like the National Congress of American Indians (NCAI) vigorously opposed termination, characterizing it as just another form of oppression. The NCAI argued that Native Americans should exercise a dual identity as members of a tribe and as U.S. citizens. By the time President Nixon ended this policy in 1969, several dozen tribes had been terminated (DeLoria, 1993; Patterson, 1996; Tice & Perkins, 2002).

A related policy, *relocation*, encouraged Native Americans—primarily young people—to move from their reservations to cities. The purpose of this policy was not only to provide greater economic opportunity but to promote assimilation into "white" culture. Unfortunately, relocation "frequently involved nothing more than a trade of rural for urban poverty" (DeLoria, 1993, p. 427). Consequently, many disillusioned young people returned to the reservations, where they also faced myriad social problems.

Militancy and the Struggle for Sovereignty Like other marginalized groups, Native Americans adopted the direct-action strategies of the civil rights movement during the late 1960s and 1970s. In 1968, activists organized the American Indian Movement (AIM), which played a major role in many subsequent protests. The following year, a group of Indians from several tribes occupied Alcatraz island, California. In 1972, activists organized the "Trail of Broken Treaties" caravan to Washington, D.C., where a group of militants took over the headquarters of the Bureau of Indian Affairs (BIA).

Perhaps the most dramatic confrontation occurred in 1973 when an alliance of AIM members and Oglala Lakota (Sioux) people occupied several buildings in Wounded Knee, South Dakota, where many Lakota had been massacred by U.S. troops in 1890. Their objective was to publicize both the severe social problems that existed on the local reservation and the many treaties that the U.S. government had failed to honor over the years. Federal agents quickly encircled Wounded Knee, and shots were exchanged. The ensuing standoff lasted more than two months. The occupation finally ended when the government agreed to review its treaties with the Lakota (DeLoria, 1993; Nash et al., 2004; Patterson, 1996).

Activists also used the courts to press historical land claims that were supported by treaties but had never been honored. They used similar tactics to assert traditional water rights and fishing rights. These actions led to frequent confrontations with whites who claimed that Native Americans were receiving special treatment from the government (DeLoria, 1993; Nash et al., 2004).

Child Welfare   Another target of Native American activism was government policy regarding child welfare. During this period, Native American children were being removed from their homes and placed with white families, until almost 30 percent of Indian children were no longer being raised in Native American homes (Tice & Perkins, 2002). Child welfare policies and practices that were not culturally sensitive contributed to the wide-scale adoption and out-of-home placement of these children with little regard for preserving their Native heritage. In response to a coordinated effort by a number of tribes, Congress passed the Indian Child Welfare Act in 1978. This act reestablished tribal authority over the adoption of Native American children. The goal of the act was to strengthen and preserve Native American families and culture. In sum, then, Native American militancy was directed toward two objectives: (1) reasserting traditional sovereignty, identities, and cultures, and (2) alleviating social problems such as poverty, unemployment, and alcohol abuse that were common on the reservations.

 Web Link

You can learn more about the history of the Indian Child Welfare Act through the Web link at www.mhhe.com/chapin1.

American Indians continue to struggle to change conditions that lead to poverty and substance abuse. Approximately 23 percent of Native Americans and Alaskan Natives still live in poverty. In addition, the Substance Abuse and Mental Health Services Administration (SAMHSA) reports rates of substance abuse of 17 percent for American Indians, compared to 9 percent for the overall population (Substance Abuse and Mental Health Services Administration, 2004; DeNavas-Walt, Proctor, & Mills, 2004). American Indian leaders are working to identify and implement effective strategies to bring about structural as well as individual change to help alleviate these problems.

Affirmative Action

One major development that affected the economic status and opportunities of all of the groups we have just discussed was the transition from a policy of simple nondiscrimination to affirmative action. **Affirmative action** is a general term that refers to policies and programs designed to compensate for discrimination against marginalized groups such as women and people of color. In order to redress losses to people who have suffered discrimination and to their descendants, affirmative action policies establish criteria that give these groups preferential access to opportunities, most importantly in education and employment.

Affirmative Action and Employment   Title VII of the Civil Rights Act of 1964 prohibits employment discrimination based on race, color, religion, or national origin, and it empowers the federal courts to "order such affirmative action as may be appropriate" to remedy past injustices. However, at that point, affirmative action referred only to such actions as reinstating employees who had been terminated due to discrimination. In the ensuing years, however, the concept of affirmative action was broadened to include specific actions designed to attract and retain female and minority-group workers. For example, Executive Order 11246, issued September 24, 1965, required all government contractors to submit written "Compliance Reports" that specify the number and percentage of minority workers on their projects (Weiss, 1997).

In 1969, the so-called Philadelphia Plan went even further, mandating that government contractors submit numerical goals and timetables for hiring minority workers. It also empowered the government to cancel the contracts of employers who failed to comply with these regulations and to prohibit them from receiving future contracts. Numerical hiring targets became an essential feature of many subsequent affirmative action plans in both public and private employment. They also led to charges of fixed quotas and reverse discrimination by opponents of these policies (Weiss, 1997). **Reverse discrimination** is defined as discrimination against the majority group due to affirmative action policies designed to redress discrimination against minority groups.

Affirmative Action and Education   During the 1970s, affirmative action was extended to education as well as employment. In 1972, the federal government began to require colleges to prove that they were recruiting qualified women and minorities in order to keep federal funding. These policies also generated charges of reverse discrimination, as critics charged that white students were being denied admission in favor of minority students who were less qualified.

This conflict eventually found its way to the U.S. Supreme Court in the 1978 case of *The Regents of the University of California vs. Bakke.* Allan Bakke, a white male applicant, had been denied admission to the medical school at the University of California at Davis even though he had a higher grade point average than some minority candidates who were admitted. The court ruling in the *Bakke* case can be interpreted as a partial victory for both opponents and advocates of affirmative action. On the one hand, the court struck down the use of strict racial quotas in determining school admissions. Consequently, Bakke was admitted to the medical school. On the other hand, the ruling upheld the use of race as one determinant of admission to higher education. Affirmative action thus evolved into one of the most controversial issues in the country, and opposition to this policy became a fundamental feature of the emerging conservative movement that characterized the 1980s.

Changes in Social Work

Web Link

To learn more about state specific licensure laws, access the Web link for the Association of Social Work Boards, Licensing Requirements, *found at www.mhhe.com/chapin1.*

During the 1970s, the NASW developed a model licensure bill, and social workers lobbied for legislation that would require practitioners to be licensed at the state level. Proponents argued that licensure would protect the public, improve the status of the profession, protect social workers against competition from people without licenses, and enable social workers to be paid directly by health benefits programs for providing services. Most health benefits programs such as Medicaid will pay directly only for services provided by licensed professionals. However, licensure requirements can reduce the ability of low-income people and people of color, who often have limited access to the required education, to practice social work. Consequently, these requirements have led to charges that social work is an elitist profession. Despite these charges, today all 50 states plus the District of Columbia regulate the certification of social work practice and the use of the professional title (Bureau of Labor Statistics, 2002–2003).

Overall, the social service sector continued to grow during this period as the for-profit and voluntary sector expanded (Reid, 1995). However, some analysts have asserted that social work moved further away from involvement with social policy by the end of this period largely because of shrinking funding for public sector casework (Tice & Perkins, 2002). Although social workers became more focused on clientele who could pay for services, the profession's historic focus on collective responsibility for poor and oppressed populations was not extinguished. In fact, if you examine NASW policy statements and social work journals throughout that period and up until today, you will find evidence of that continuing commitment as well as a growing interest in private practice.

RETRENCHMENT: 1981 TO THE PRESENT

Ronald Reagan, who became president in 1981, ushered in an era of conservative politics. Reagan did not cut spending on all social programs. For example, Medicare expenditures actually increased. Rather, he targeted social welfare programs that were directed primarily toward low-income Americans. The conservative portrayal of the welfare state as a failed social experiment served to rationalize initiatives by the Reagan administration to curtail federal funding for these programs (Reid, 1995). Reagan adopted the policy of **devolution,** whereby responsibility for social welfare increasingly would be transferred from the federal government to the states. He also sought to increase reliance on the private sector to provide social welfare services. This approach involved **privatization,** a policy that transfers ownership or control from government to private enterprise. Typically, in the United States, privatization has meant allocating public funds to private for-profit or nonprofit entities that then provide the benefits or services. As a corollary to privatization, the administration sought to cut back some social programs so that tax dollars could be reinvested in the private sector in order to increase economic growth. These efforts, endorsed by both President Reagan and his successor, George H. W. Bush, will be examined in the following section.

Implementing a Conservative Agenda

In addition to curtailing spending on social programs for low-income Americans, Reagan successfully lobbied Congress to reduce taxes and increase defense spending. These policies in turn increased the federal deficit. Under these circumstances, curtailing social welfare spending could be justified as necessary to hold the deficit in check. It is important to note that endorsing tax cuts garners taxpayer support in a way that a direct attack on programs for older people and children living in poverty does not. However, tax cuts frequently translate into decreased services for vulnerable populations.

Reagan's approach, dubbed "supply-side economics," was supposed to dampen inflation and revive the sluggish economy. This approach sharply contrasted with Keynesian economics, which had informed the New Deal initiatives and endorsed increasing government spending and manipulating interest rates in order to combat inflation and manage recessions. The combination of tax cuts and reduced social welfare spending under Reagan's administration was also supposed to encourage wealthy recipients of the tax cuts to donate more money to charity. Thus, there would be much less need for the federal government to be involved in social welfare. In fact, traditional social programs provided by government could be privatized.

Under both the Reagan and the George H. W. Bush administration, federal policies placed less emphasis on structural change that would increase opportunities for traditionally oppressed groups. They ignored the following realities: (1) the minimum wage was so low that people working full-time for that wage could not lift their families out of poverty, and (2) many traditional manufacturing jobs were relocating to countries where wages and environmental standards were even lower. Instead, social policies reemphasized individual pathology as the reason that people could not provide for themselves. Even people with disabilities were not spared. Applications for federal disability claims were turned down in unprecedented numbers. People who were already on the disability rolls were afraid even to consider working or undertaking any sort of rehabilitation effort for fear that they would lose their benefits.

Many leaders from major religious and private charities, although interested in private/public partnerships, were aware that they never could garner sufficient private resources to replace major public social programs that serve millions of people. In reality, a major shift from public to private funding can lead to cutbacks in services and benefits for poor people under the guise of less government "interference."

New Federalism, OBRA, and Devolution

The Reagan administration also sought to restructure the relationship between the federal and state governments. The administration's policy, labeled the "New Federalism," transferred ever more responsibility to the states for the social welfare of their citizens. Specifically, Reagan proposed that the states assume all costs for the Food Stamp program, SSI, and AFDC. However, the federal government would take full responsibility for Medicaid. Reagan also encouraged religious institutions to take over programs for people in need.

OBRA and Block Grants   Although the Reagan administration was unable to convert this vision into reality, it did preside over the passage of the Omnibus Budget Reconciliation Act (OBRA) of 1981, which reduced funding for social programs. For example, funding for Food Stamps was reduced 19 percent, and AFDC was reduced 11 percent. In addition, eligibility requirements for AFDC were tightened.

The OBRA also transformed the nature of federal assistance to the states. Specifically, it consolidated dozens of **categorical grants**—in which the federal government strictly regulated how the monies were spent for programs such as community development services, mental health, alcohol and drug abuse, social services, and maternal and child health services—into a much smaller number of **block grants,** which allocated much of the decision-making authority to the states (Kenney, 1981). Under the changed funding structure, states no longer had to provide matching funds for any of the block grant programs in order to receive federal funds. The block grants allowed state and local governments greater latitude in directing federal funds toward specific social problems. On the negative side, however, the OBRA reduced federal funding for each block by 25 percent to 30 percent.

Theoretically, the reorganization was supposed to offset these cuts by reducing duplication and increasing flexibility. In reality, programs were cut back not only because federal funding was reduced but also because the states were no longer required to provide matching funds in order to receive the same amounts of federal monies as they had in the past. In many cases, funding declined by 50 percent. By 1984, the poverty rate had risen to 15 percent, higher than any period since the 1960s (Tice & Perkins, 2002).

Funding for community mental health centers was collapsed into block grants that could be used for a variety of mental health services. This development diminished the ability of community mental health centers to provide services necessary to enable people with serious mental illness to successfully live in the community. States were attempting to deinstitutionalize more people who had lived in state mental hospitals. Community mental health centers were unable to fulfill the promise of community treatment for people who were deinstitutionalized as state mental hospitals downsized and closed (Day, 1999; Haynes & Holmes, 1994).

Pressures to Reduce Social Service Spending   Pressures to reduce social welfare spending intensified in 1986 when Congress passed the Gramm-Rudman-Hollings Bill. The bill's intent was to help eliminate the federal debt by mandating across-the-board budget cuts if Congress and the president could not agree on how to balance the budget. The result was another budget cut affecting important health and social programs (Day, 1999). Congress and the president also made the biggest cuts ever to funding for children's social services. In 1988, Congress did pass the Family Support Act with the stated intent of providing education and job training programs for AFDC recipients. However, then as now, the lack of well-paying jobs combined with inadequate funding for day care prevented many female recipients from adequately supporting their children. This reality limited the effectiveness of the act.

Equal Opportunity Initiatives Stalled   During this period, efforts to secure equal employment opportunity made little headway. The Civil Rights Act of 1964 established the Equal Employment Opportunity Commission (EEOC) to combat employment discrimination. However, the fact that people of color continued to experience much higher unemployment rates than white workers and earn much lower average wages made it clear that equal employment opportunity was not being achieved. Women also made only limited progress toward achieving equal opportunities during these years. By 1970, more than 50 percent of all women ages 35–54 held jobs outside the home (Tice & Perkins, 2002). Although a major shift from service to white-collar jobs occurred for women between 1940 and 1981, women continued to be overrepresented in low-paying jobs such as beautician, food preparation staff, nurse's aide, housekeeper, and child care worker. In 1986, the National Commission on Working Women indicated that 77 percent of all employed women worked in low-pay occupations and industries. Nonetheless, by 1989, when conservatives achieved a majority, the Supreme Court backed away from its support of affirmative action (Axinn & Stern, 2001).

From Reagan to Bush   George H. W. Bush took office in 1989 vowing to follow in Reagan's footsteps by holding the line on domestic spending, avoiding a tax increase, promoting a conservative social agenda, and maintaining a strong national defense. However, circumstances and continued activism on the part of some marginalized groups sometimes pressured him to change course. For example, in 1991, mounting racial tension exploded into race riots in Los Angeles following the acquittal of four white officers who were videotaped beating Rodney King, an African American, after a high-speed chase. In November of that year, after two years of debates, vetoes, and threatened vetoes, President Bush reversed himself and signed the Civil Rights Act of 1991. This act strengthened existing civil rights laws and provided for damages in cases of intentional employment discrimination. Two years later, gay rights advocates organized one of the largest civil rights demonstrations in U.S. history. Almost 1 million people participated in the Third National March on Washington to demand equal rights for gays and lesbians and an end to discrimination based on sexual orientation. We will examine the struggle to end discrimination based on sexual orientation, from the development of gay and lesbian activist organizations in the 1950s until today, in Chapter 7.

One group that achieved a major breakthrough during the Bush years was people with physical and mental disabilities. In 1990, Congress passed the Americans with Disabilities Act (ADA), which prohibited discrimination against people with disabilities in employment, public accommodations, and transportation. The ADA provides a clear example of how legislation that builds on strengths can be passed in a conservative era. The act had determined support from the disability advocacy community. At the same time, its emphasis on work spoke to traditional American values and therefore attracted the endorsement of many conservatives. We will discuss the ADA in more detail in Chapter 7.

Advocates for people in need had hoped that with the collapse of the Soviet Union, defense spending would be reduced and domestic issues would receive more attention and funds. However, with the few exceptions discussed above, Bush generally maintained the policy priorities of the Reagan era and, in the face of a sluggish economy, was not reelected.

"New Democrats" and Social Welfare Policy

William Jefferson Clinton assumed office in 1993. He identified with the moderate wing of the Democratic Party. Clinton had helped cofound the Democratic Leadership Council (DLC) in 1985, which sought to establish middle ground between more traditional liberal Democrats, who favored income redistribution, civil rights legislation, and cutbacks in defense spending, and "new Democrats," who focused on a narrower range of economic reforms such as job training, infrastructure improvement, free trade, national standards in education, and balanced budgets. "New Democrats" focused more on the needs of the middle class, in part because they feared that the Democratic Party was losing voters who believed that the interests of low-income groups and racial minorities were more important to the party than their needs (Tice & Perkins, 2002).

Some of the social welfare policy initiatives of the Clinton administration provided much-needed help for diverse constituencies. In addition, the administration tried unsuccessfully to create a universal health care system for the United States. At the same time, however, the passage of legislation that replaced AFDC with Temporary Aid to Needy Families (TANF) represented a giant step backward in the effort to provide economic security for our nation's children.

Family Leave and People with Disabilities   The Clinton administration sponsored basic reform efforts that assisted families and people with disabilities.

Regarding families, in 1993, Congress passed the Family and Medical Leave Act (FMLA). This law required employers to guarantee unpaid leave for workers following births or adoptions or in the event that a dependent or family member became ill. In 1999, Congress passed the Ticket to Work and Work Incentives Improvement Act. This legislation allowed millions of Americans with disabilities to remain eligible for Medicaid or Medicare if they became employed. Prior to the passage of this law, many people with disabilities were reluctant to seek work out of fear of losing their health coverage. It also provided vouchers to pay for vocational rehabilitation. This law thus enabled more Americans with disabilities to work and thereby lessen their dependence on public benefits (Social Security Administration, 2000; Washburn, 1999).

Health Care: The Reform That Never Happened   In contrast, the administration experienced far less success in its efforts to reform health care. Many people hoped that the unfinished agenda of extending health care coverage beyond the categories of people covered by Medicare and Medicaid would be completed by instituting universal health care. In 1994, the Clinton administration supported a bill that would extend medical coverage to 95 percent of Americans by 2000 and establish a commission to devise a strategy to reach the remaining 5 percent. In many cases, employers would be required to assume some of the costs (Horton, 1994). However, the effort failed, and in November 1994, voters elected a Republican Congress, ushering in the Contract with America.

The Contract with America and the PRWORA   The Contract with America was a series of conservative proposals sponsored by Speaker of the House Newt Gingrich. It included reducing taxes on capital gains and imposing a "gag rule" that prohibited medical practitioners who receive Medicaid payments from discussing abortion as an option with their female patients (Drew, 1996). A major focus of the Contract was to further decrease the role of the federal government in providing for social welfare. This agenda was a legacy of the Reagan administration. Its supporters helped propel the passage of the Personal Responsibility and Work Opportunity Reconciliation Act of 1996 (PRWORA). This law replaced AFDC with Temporary Aid to Needy Families (TANF), thereby canceling the federal guarantee of support for poor children that had been established by the 1935 Social Security Act. The TANF legislation limited recipients to five years of support and required them to work. The TANF program can vary widely from state to state. If a state runs out of money, it can terminate all TANF payments.

Further, the PRWORA limited Food Stamps and SSI benefits for legal immigrants. It also left provision of Medicaid, TANF, and Title XX benefits for legal immigrants up to the discretion of each state's Department of Health and Human Services (DHHS). Echoes of colonial poor laws could be seen in the return to an emphasis on local responsibility and limiting aid to "strangers." Soon after PRWORA passed, benefits were reinstated for legal immigrants residing in the United States prior to the passage of the act. However, benefits were still denied to new immigrants entering the United States. These actions underscored the belief that it was inhumane and unjust to terminate benefits already in place for legal immigrants, but it also indicated reduced national responsibility for "strangers" entering the country. People feared that large-scale immigration would drive up the costs of public education and public aid. These economic concerns replaced earlier fears of immigrants' religious and political ideas. We will examine both TANF and Social Security as currently configured in greater detail in Chapter 8, where we focus on income-based social policy.

Because of increased economic prosperity during the second Clinton administration, more low-income people with children were able to find jobs. However, the safety net for low-income families had been greatly weakened. By this time, many of these families were headed by single women. In 2000, 33 percent of all births were to single mothers, almost double the rate of 18 percent in 1980 (Martin, Hamilton, Ventura, Menacker, & Park, 2002). Although many single mothers support their children without ever receiving TANF benefits, most families receiving TANF are headed by single women. The lack of adequate day care and the inability of many of these women to move beyond minimum wage jobs leave the children in these families at great risk of negative outcomes such as poor health and not completing their high school education.

Asset-Based Approaches to Poverty   During the Clinton years, federal and state policy makers explored ways to help low-income families acquire assets. Much of the impetus for this approach came from social workers. One popular strategy was to institute public and private matched savings plans. These initiatives allowed low-income people to save money to pursue their education, purchase homes, or start small businesses, and their savings would be matched through either public or foundation funds.

These policies reflect the strengths perspective in that they build on the goals of the person in need and help her or him acquire resources in a non-stigmatizing manner. In fact, these policies have helped families build assets they could then use to keep themselves and their children out of poverty throughout their lifetime. Recall that other asset-based programs, such as the Homestead Act and the GI Bill of Rights, benefited previous generations of Americans. It is to be hoped that asset-building programs will assist increasing numbers of low-income families to secure a higher standard of living. However, when we examine the rates of poverty experienced by the American family in the last half of the 20th century, it is clear that income inequality is increasing in our society and that existing policies are not adequately addressing the problems of children who are growing up in poverty.

Poverty and the American Family

When the Social Security Administration first began to track rates of poverty in 1959, it calculated that 22 percent of the population was poor. During the end of the 1960s, when the War on Poverty was initiated, and the 1970s, when spending on social services increased, the poverty rate was reduced approximately in half, to about 11–12 percent. It subsequently rose to 15 percent during the Reagan administration and then stabilized at around 13–14 percent. Following another peak of 15 percent in 1993, the poverty rate returned to 1970 rates of 11–12 percent from 1999 to 2001. However, rates have been increasing incrementally since 2001, with 12.5 percent of the population living in poverty in 2003 (DeNavas-Walt, Proctor, & Mills, 2004). Although approximately 45 percent of people in poverty are non-Hispanic whites, people of color are disproportionately bearing the burden of poverty.

Income inequality decreased from 1947 to 1968; however, since that point, it has been increasing. Household inequality grew slowly in the 1970s and then rapidly in the 1980s. This trend has continued through the early 2000s, though the yearly rate of growth is slower than was true of the 1980s. By 2003, the share of national income going to the lowest quintile (one-fifth) was only 3.4 percent, whereas the highest quintile received almost 50% (DeNavas-Walt, Proctor, & Mills, 2004).

During this period, the economy was transitioning from an industrial base to a service and informational base. As a result, it produced many well-paying jobs in such fields as computers and finance. At the same time, however, it generated many low-paying jobs in service areas such as fast-food restaurants and department stores. In addition, changes in the configuration of the American family also affected the income distribution of households. For example, divorce rates increased to 23 divorces per 1,000 married women by 1980 but then decreased slightly by 1995 (Axinn & Stern, 2001). In addition, the percentage of births to single white, African American, and Hispanic or Latino mothers also rose during this period. Single-parent households typically have lower incomes compared to two-parent households and, thus, a higher prevalence rate of poverty (DeNavas-Walt, Proctor, & Mills, 2004).

The New Century

George W. Bush was the first president of the 21st century. The second Bush administration ushered in a period of economic and political turmoil as the economy slumped and the United States went to war in the Middle East. Conservative proposals to turn over many social welfare services to religious organizations and to limit abortion rights occupied the political agenda of the day. With Republicans in control of the White House and both houses of Congress, resources and services for people in poverty, children, and elders were scaled back in many areas.

Web Link

Click on the NASW Web link at www.mhhe.com/chapin1 for a discussion of the implications of faith-based initiatives from a social work perspective.

Privatization and Faith-Based Initiatives   Like the Reagan and first Bush presidencies, the administration of George W. Bush sought to increase the private sector's responsibility for social programs, thereby decreasing government responsibility and reducing public expectations that government is responsible for the welfare of its people. Increased reliance on, and funding for, faith-based initiatives was a key component of the administration's privatization program. The assumption that the state, rather than religious institutions, could best provide social assistance was again under attack at a time when many citizens were not even affiliated with a religious denomination. Policy initiatives to strengthen faith-based social services received both support and criticism from religious institutions that were interested in expanding their ministry but were wary of assuming financial and organizational responsibilities they could not meet. State experiments with turning over adoption and foster care services to religiously based organizations had already driven some of these organizations into bankruptcy (Kansas Action for Children, 2001). As we saw in our examination of the Great Depression, relying on churches and nonprofit institutions for social services and benefits, particularly during economic downturns, is not economically viable social policy.

Tax Cuts and Reduced Benefits   By combining tax cuts with greatly increased defense spending, the Bush administration limited the amount of money available for maintaining social services without directly attacking popular programs that provided opportunities for poor children and elders. Today, hundreds of thousands of people across the nation who qualify for assistance are on waiting lists or are turned away when they apply for help with child care, meals, utility bills, and housing (Claxton & Hansen, 2004). Further, because federal and state tax codes are often linked, diminished tax revenues also generate cutbacks at the state level. In general, as federal and state support for education and social services declines, the private sector and local governments must increase support, or opportunities will disappear. Traditionally poor and oppressed communities have the least capacity to fill this funding gap, so poor schools and people become poorer yet. In turn, structural barriers that keep people in poverty are reinforced, and the distance between the haves and the have-nots increases.

Challenging Affirmative Action and Abortion Rights   The Bush administration also supported legislative and judicial actions against two major social welfare policies of the 1970s: affirmative action and abortion rights. Regarding the former, in 2003, the U.S. Supreme Court overturned an affirmative action program at the University of Michigan, but it upheld a more flexible program at the university's law school. In both cases, Bush had called for abolishing the programs (Greenhouse, 2003).

Bush also signed into law two controversial congressional initiatives relating to abortion rights. The first bill, passed in 2003, bans so-called partial birth abortions (Tanne, 2003). The second, passed the following year, in effect defined a violent federal crime against a pregnant woman as two crimes—one against the woman and one against the fetus. Critics charged that by affirming that a fetus has separate rights, Congress was contradicting the underlying philosophy of *Roe vs. Wade*. In addition, in 2001, Bush prohibited federal funding of any overseas programs that provide abortions or even counsel women regarding abortions (Goldstein, 2004).

Both the policies governing aid to poor families, such as TANF, and the policies designed to make small changes in the economic and societal status quo, such as minority preferences at colleges and universities, are being reconfigured under the conservative president, and their capacity to address social and economic inequities is being reduced. Because Bush was reelected for a second term, the Supreme Court, which has often been the champion of the oppressed, may become much more conservative with his appointment of Chief Justice John Roberts to replace Chief Justice William Rehnquist as well as his appointment of Justice Sandra Day O'Connor's replacement. It appears the modest gains made in lessening structural barriers to opportunity and full participation in the economy are in danger of being rolled back.

HISTORICAL IMPERATIVES FOR THE 21st CENTURY

As the needs of poor children continue to go unmet and the number of older adults grows with the aging of the baby boomers (people born between 1946 and 1964), we must take steps to ensure that young and old people are not pitted against each other in the struggle for necessary resources. Social welfare policy in the new millennium cannot ignore the graying of America. Social insurance programs for older adults must be reformed before the baby boomers begin to retire and collect Medicare and Social Security benefits. The Medicare Trust Fund is currently projected to run out of money in 2023. In contrast, Social Security is solvent for a much longer time, and it can be kept solvent for generations to come if some fairly modest changes in benefits, tax rates, and eligibility are made soon.

Unfortunately, if these modest changes are not made, large structural changes may undermine these very successful programs. As one example, these programs could be dismantled and replaced with means-tested programs. Indeed, many influential political groups initially fought the development of these programs, believing that family and religious institutions rather than government-administered social insurance programs should provide for the income and health care of elders.

People who still seek to reduce these programs have found allies by attempting to link poverty among children to spending on programs for elders, thus promoting intergenerational conflict. However, young versus old is a false dichotomy. If we are lucky, all of us will become old someday. Children are not poor because older adults receive Social Security; poor children disproportionately live in single-parent homes headed by women who receive lower wages than men do. Low wages result in poverty and contribute to inadequate income in old age because they severely limit workers' ability to save money and to contribute to a pension fund. In contrast to Social Security and Medicare, programs that helped support low-income families, such as AFDC, have already been dismantled. These programs were not abolished so that the Social Security retirement program could be funded; rather, the push to do away with the safety net for young families was fueled by many of the same forces that press to significantly scale back the benefits provided through the Social Security retirement fund.

We are entering a unique time in history when four and five generations of many families will be alive at the same time. Therefore, our social policies need to ensure that the generations continue to live in harmony. The moral obligation of one generation to another can be combined with enlightened self-interest in crafting viable policies.

Environmental concerns also will influence the development of social policy in the new millennium. For example, social policies in the area of housing subsidies that contribute to urban sprawl lead to increased fuel consumption for transportation and the destruction of natural habitats. Therefore, social policies that help low-income people live where they have easy access to jobs or public transportation will become even more critical. In general, a deteriorating environment will contribute to increased health problems, and careless use of our natural resources will lead to worldwide shortages of valuable resources. Environmental groups such as the Green Party can contribute a worldview that questions existing social policies and considers issues from a transgenerational perspective. That is, policies are considered not only for how they affect the environment today but also for what they mean for the environment our children and grandchildren will inherit. Although third-party groups have experienced limited success in the United States, environmental groups such as the Green Party have increased public awareness of environmental concerns and can also help conceive and develop policies that support the strengths of a diverse population. However, such policies will develop only if many people become involved.

Throughout U.S. history, social welfare policy has developed in the context of the culture of capitalism (Wilensky & Lebeaux, 1965). This culture has resulted in an uneven patchwork of programs that blend humanitarianism with an emphasis on self-reliance and competitiveness. The challenge is to build on this heritage to develop social welfare policies that assume the worthiness of all citizens and support all citizens in meeting their basic needs.

CONCLUSION

You can use what you have learned about analyzing history when you encounter new social policy. Now it is time to return to the framework for linking historical and current policy that was introduced in Chapter 2. This framework can guide your investigation of new policy. The framework components are:

- How did historical policy approaches shape current policy?

- What was the cultural milieu at the time this historical approach was adopted, and is it the same or different today?

- What were the group interests, and who were the key players?

- Is there any reason to think the approach would work better or worse today?

- Did this policy approach build on the strengths of the target population? Alternatively, was it predicated on a pathology or deficit view of the people to be helped?

As you confront new social policies in the field, take time to consider their historical precedents. History directly shapes social policy today. Armed with historical insight and knowledge of policy precedents that built on the strengths of target groups, you will be more capable of understanding the policy and advocating for needed changes.

MAIN POINTS

- The 20th century ushered in important social policy initiatives, including child labor laws, women's right to vote, antidiscrimination laws, Social Security, Medicaid and Medicare legislation, and public health and sanitation laws. However, many basic needs, such as health care, still go unmet for large numbers of Americans.

- The widespread poverty experienced during the Great Depression of the 1930s helped create a new consensus that supported establishment of many major health and social service policies and programs. However, support for such initiatives is now waning, and a new consensus must be forged if policies providing for universal health care and adequate income support for all children are to be enacted.

- Oppressed groups have struggled to eliminate discrimination on the basis of race, gender, and sexual orientation. Although they were successful in gaining passage of important policy initiatives such as the Civil Rights Act, Title IX of the Education Act, and the Indian Child Welfare Act, discrimination persists.

- The War on Poverty experienced both successes and failures.

- New Federalism is an initiative to return power to the states.

- The United States has a long history of public-private partnership in providing for people in need. The current push for privatization of social welfare reflects a growing reluctance on the part of the federal government to take responsibility for the welfare of its citizens.

- Certain policies, such as the GI Bill of Rights and the Americans with Disabilities Act, reflect the premise that people have strengths and will take advantage of opportunities if structural barriers are removed. Other policies, such as the Personal Responsibility and Work Opportunity Reconciliation Act of 1996, begin with the premise that people must be made to work and that social policy should therefore focus on strict work requirements and time limits rather than on removing structural barriers such as inadequate day care, health care, and transportation.

- The history of social policy in the United States has been shaped by a variety of complex factors and values. It is not a simple story, and simplistic explanations rob you of the understanding of the many and often conflicting factors and values needed to be an effective policy practitioner.

EXERCISES: PRACTICING SOCIAL WORK

Working with the Sanchez Family

1. Could members of the Sanchez family qualify for TANF or Medicaid in your state? If so, which members?

2. Where do you think Roberto could turn for medical care if he became seriously ill?

3. What are the historical precedents for denial of benefits based on residency or citizenship?

Working with the Black Feather Community

Take time to familiarize yourself with each segment of the Black Feather case study. Your text recounts the advocacy efforts of Native Americans during the 1970s and more recently.

1. What kind of advocacy efforts being led by Native Americans in the community can you identify in the Black Feather scenarios?

2. How did they influence social policy and social programs?

3. Were they successful or unsuccessful? Why?

EXERCISES: THE SOCIAL WORK LIBRARY

New Federalism and Social Justice

Read "Federalism and social justice: Implications for social work," (Linhorst, 2002) and respond to the following questions.

1. Identify approaches to policy change taken during the dual, cooperative, and New Federalism eras.

2. After reviewing this article and reviewing the policy changes from 1980 to the present outlined in this chapter, discuss how the cultural milieu of New Federalism influenced the passage or failure of various legislation.

3. In this article, federalism is discussed in terms of social justice and the federal government's provision of distributive justice. What are the implications for social work policy practice in an era of devolution?

Faith-based Initiatives

Read "Charitable choice and faith-based welfare: A call for social work," (Cnaan & Boddie, 2002) and respond to the following questions.

1. How do you think giving more public money to faith-based organizations to provide social services will affect the availability of non-faith-based social service alternatives?

2. What ethical issues need to be considered when developing policy to implement a faith-based approach to social service provision?

3. What ethical issues might arise for you as a social worker working at a faith-based organization?

OTHER EXERCISES

1. Interview someone who remembers the Great Depression of the 1930s, World War II, and/or the Civil Rights Movement. Ask her or his opinion on why these events happened and what it was like to experience them. Ask if this person thinks the social policies and programs that arose as a result of these events such as the New Deal policies, the GI Bill, and school desegregation were effective or not. Based on your study of history, do you agree or disagree with this person's opinion? Why or why not?

2. One of the lessons of history is the power of language. Examine current newspaper or magazine articles and note how the term *welfare* is used. How does the language surrounding the term lead readers to attach positive or negative connotations to it? Watch for other examples of how language is used to produce negative or positive portrayals of people, policies, and programs with which social workers are involved. What influence do you think this use of language has on efforts to develop strengths-based social welfare policies and programs?

CHAPTER 4

The Economic and Political Contexts

T HE PREVIOUS TWO CHAPTERS EXPLORED THE DEVELOPMENT OF social welfare policies in the United States. One theme that runs throughout these chapters is that economic fluctuations and political change interact with shifting social values to shape and reshape U.S. social policy. In order to understand how social policies and social programs are created and why they succeed or fail, you will need to become familiar with the economic and political contexts of social policy. The process whereby social policy is developed and implemented is not a technically oriented, politically neutral undertaking. Rather, it is strongly influenced by political and economic interests and ideologies. The **economic context** of social policy focuses on the production, distribution, and use of income, wealth, and resources. In contrast, the **political context** focuses on the pursuit and exercise of power in government or public affairs. Although these two terms have distinct meanings, they are typically enmeshed in the policy-making process. Competition and conflict, inherent in economic and political processes, influence how, when, and what types of social policies and programs are developed and implemented.

EFFECT ON SOCIAL POLICY

The economic and political contexts of social policy in the United States reflect the workings of a capitalist system. The United States has a **marketplace economy,** which means that citizens exchange goods and services, typically by working for a salary. Citizens may also possess assets such as stocks, property, and other investments that are sources of income. These income sources generate the money that is necessary for citizens to purchase goods and services. In a marketplace economy, this is how citizens are expected to meet their needs and wants. However, we know that many people in our society cannot work because of disability, discrimination, or sickness. Significantly, the market system contains no mechanisms to provide for their basic needs. Moreover, even for those who can work, jobs may be unavailable, or the compensation may be inadequate to meet the basic costs of food, shelter, and health care.

The question then arises, "How should our society respond to these people in need?" Not surprisingly, there is no overriding consensus on this question. As we saw in the previous chapters, individual responsibility and the work ethic are basic values that have influenced the development of social policy in the United States. At the same time, however, social responsibility is also a traditional U.S. value. Reflecting this value, the United States has developed a social welfare system to help balance the mandates of the marketplace with the realities that (1) some people are unable to work and (2) economic cycles inevitably lead to unemployment and to shifts in the types and location of jobs that are available.

Political support for government policies and programs to assist people who are unable to meet their needs through the marketplace has waxed and waned over time. In general, when the economy is doing well, people may place increased emphasis on individual responsibility, as more individuals become able to provide for their own needs. Conversely, when the economy is failing, people may be more likely to turn to the government for relief. However, with the shift in responsibility from federal to state and local governments since 1980, social programs have become tightly bound by budget constraints, a topic we will examine later in the chapter.

We have been focusing on social policies designed to assist people in need. However, social workers must be aware that social policy can also erect institutional barriers that discriminate against whole groups of people. Such policies are designed to create and maintain a labor force that is willing to work for very low wages. A historical example is the "separate but equal" policy that provided inadequate education for African American children. Although this policy was outlawed by the *Brown vs. Board of Education* decision, existing state school funding formulas that don't provide sufficient resources to adequately educate children "of color" in impoverished neighborhoods cause these children to face lifelong barriers in securing a job that pays an adequate wage. Additionally, the hereditary concentration of wealth and power can create an economic and political aristocracy who craft policies that support private wealth and opulence and ignore structural barriers to equal opportunity. Potential for economic gain and lower taxes for people in power shape social policy options and influence their support.

The Impetus for Social Programs

As shown in Chapter 1, two requirements generally must be met before a public social program develops in the United States. First, there must be a clear indication of a social problem, or what some economists have termed a "market failure." A **market failure** is a "circumstance in which the pursuit of private interest does not lead to an efficient use of society's resources or a fair distribution of society's goods" (Weimer & Vining, 1999, p. 41). That is, the free market, the family, and other private entities are not providing for a basic need like education, health care, or retirement income for a sizable segment of the population. Second, people in power and their constituencies must recognize the problem and support political intervention. They must be convinced that government action, as opposed to private intervention, will not do more harm than good (Waldfogel, 2000).

When determining whether government action is necessary, some economists posit that focusing on market failures does not sufficiently examine all costs involved in the pursuit of private interest or trade. These economists suggest that transaction costs should also be included in determining when the government should intervene in a situation once a market failure has been defined (Zerbe & McCurdy, 2000). **Transactions costs** refer to all costs incurred during government interventions, including financial, economic, personal, and environmental costs. For example, when a city develops publicly funded low-income housing, there may be a financial impact on people who own low-cost rentals because they may no longer be able to rent their properties as quickly. People who are concerned about a social problem should weigh the transaction costs against the expected benefits of intervention to determine whether intervention is appropriate or desirable.

Going further, groups and individuals who examine options for intervention generally consider both economic efficiency and equity. The principle of **economic efficiency** focuses on three interrelated issues: (1) the probable impact of the intervention on the overall economy, (2) the relative merits of spending on one social program rather than another, and (3) the ways in which the incentives and/or disincentives created by the program will likely influence individual behavior.

To understand how principles of economic efficiency can be applied to social policy, consider the debate over care for people with mental illness in institutions versus communities. Throughout much of our history, people with mental illness were generally treated in institutions such as poorhouses and mental hospitals. Eventually, however, the high costs associated with state institutions, coupled with a concern for economic efficiency, helped fuel a growing interest in community-based care. Further, programs to integrate people with serious mental illness into the community were expected to help create access to employment and other supports that make it possible for these individuals to change their lives for the better. In addition, it was hoped that community residents would change their attitudes and behavior as they became more personally involved with individuals with mental illness. These factors all helped generate growing support for the policy of deinstitutionalization, whereby patients of state mental hospitals were moved into the community.

Although the economy of the town where the mental hospital was located was often negatively affected as facilities downsized or closed and jobs were lost, the overall economic impact was mitigated because new jobs were created in the home communities of people with mental illness. If community-based care could be provided more economically and could achieve more positive outcomes for clients, then it would constitute a better use of society's resources and would be economically efficient.

The principle of **equity** revolves around an underlying question: Will the policy treat all people with a particular need equally, a concept referred to as **horizontal equity,** or will it redistribute resources to people in need who possess fewer resources and thus exhibit **vertical equity** (Waldfogel, 2000)? Referring back to the provision of services for people with mental illness, horizontal equity would extend equal access to services to all people with mental illness irrespective of ethnicity, location, socioeconomic status (SES), or age. In contrast, social policy based on vertical equity might provide services to people with low incomes at no charge while requiring people with higher incomes to pay a fee.

Institutional and Residual Approaches to Social Welfare

Determining the best approach to addressing a social problem requires us to negotiate between efficiency and equity. In the United States, two approaches to social welfare—institutional and residual—are continuously debated when social policy is formulated. Proponents of both approaches make claims about the efficiency and equity of their programs. Therefore, policy makers and social workers must evaluate these claims and determine which programs should be funded and implemented.

Institutional Approaches   The **institutional approach** to social welfare policy asserts that government should ensure that the basic needs of all citizens—particularly for food, housing, health, income, employment, and education—are adequately met. Advocates of the institutional approach focus on creating universal programs, funded through taxation, that address these common human needs. As their name suggests, **universal programs** provide services and benefits to all citizens in a broad category. For example, our public school system is a universal program because it makes education broadly available to all the country's children. Universal programs are generally considered more efficient than selective programs in determining eligibility. For example, when everyone in a broad category, such as children between the ages of 5 and 18, is automatically eligible, the eligibility determination process is greatly simplified, and administrative costs are significantly reduced. Consequently, more of the funding for the programs goes directly to beneficiaries. Because universal programs typically attempt to treat all aid recipients equally, they are identified with the concept of horizontal equity.

Residual Approaches   In contrast to the institutional approach, the residual approach posits that the government should intervene only when the family, religious institutions, the marketplace, and other private entities are unable to adequately meet the needs of certain populations. Therefore, public assistance should be offered only in cases of dire need when all other support systems have failed. Moreover, tax dollars collected from a broad spectrum of citizens should be used to provide assistance that is narrowly targeted to those individuals or groups who possess the fewest resources. Thus, the residual approach reflects the principle of vertical equity because it redistributes resources to people with the greatest need. Residual policies tend to create **selective programs,** defined as programs that provide benefits and services only to those segments of a population that meet specific eligibility requirements. For example, whereas public education is a universal program because it is available to all children, Head Start is a residual program because it is designed specifically for low-income students.

The residual approach uses means tests to target benefits to people in need. This process cuts down on overall spending because the program does not fund people who are able to assist themselves. With their differing eligibility requirements, the main intent of the programs is not to treat all people equally.

INFLUENCES ON THE SOCIAL WELFARE SYSTEM

When the United States was founded, independent farmers made up 80 percent of the labor force (Bell, 1987). The other 20 percent were primarily independent handicraftsmen and tradesmen. Today, the vast majority of the labor force is composed of wage and salary workers. Many of these workers are employed in service occupations, information technology, manufacturing, and white-collar, corporate work. In addition, the majority of working-age women participate in the labor force. Clearly, significant economic change has transformed our country.

Competing Explanations for the Development of the Welfare System

Over the centuries, our economy has evolved from an agricultural and small business base to a postindustrial base that encompasses service and information technology occupations. Many theorists argue that, in addition to transforming our way of life, the evolution of our economy gave rise to the modern social welfare system. We examine several of their theories and hypotheses below. This examination is informed by the work of James Midgley (1998), a scholar of international social policy.

The Industrialization-Welfare Hypothesis   One explanation of the origins and functions of the welfare system, termed the *industrialization-welfare hypothesis,* emphasizes industrialization as a significant factor in the development of the welfare state. This hypothesis proposes that the traditional welfare functions performed by the family, church, and community in a preindustrial society—for example, caring for elderly parents—are assumed by the government in industrial and postindustrial societies, not out of humanitarian motives, but because industrialization undermines these institutions. When families are uprooted as family members relocate in search of employment and opportunities, then poverty, deprivation, and social need increase. In response, the government establishes a variety of social programs designed to substitute for the traditional welfare system.

The Maintenance of Capitalism Hypothesis   A second explanation of the development of the welfare state, termed the *maintenance of capitalism hypothesis,* also emphasizes the role of capitalist industrialization in the creation of the welfare state. However, this theory highlights the role of the welfare state in encouraging capitalism (Piven & Cloward, 1971). More specifically, it postulates that a "power elite" made up of people from the government and private sector exerts great control on all policy making for the purpose of maintaining their positions and wealth.

One variation of this hypothesis argues that social welfare policy is used to control women's lives (Abramovitz, 1996). For example, the types of caring work that women traditionally have done for their children and families at home are not defined as "work" for the purpose of securing benefits such as retirement income through Social Security. Consequently, women must either marry a person eligible for Social Security or enter the paid workforce to secure retirement benefits. Further, when social programs are not in place to make it financially possible for young single mothers to stay at home and care for their children, they often must take minimum wage jobs, thus ensuring a ready supply of low-wage workers. Recall from Chapters 2 and 3 that social policies are instituted both to assist people in need and to promote social control.

The Accumulation and Legitimizing Hypothesis   Another explanation of the relationship between social welfare and industrial capitalism posits that the government introduced welfare programs to promote both accumulation of capital by businesses and popular acceptance of the capitalist system (O'Connor, 1973). Accumulation of capital and acceptance, or legitimizing, of capitalism are both necessary functions of the welfare state. The government's role is to introduce social programs that create an efficient yet inexpensive labor force. Public education is one example of a popularly accepted social program that leads to improvements in the capabilities of the workforce. Publicly financed health care also helps create a more productive workforce. When government assumes the cost of these programs, the result is lowered business costs and increased business profits. At the same time, programs such as Social Security, services for people with disabilities, and welfare payments can enhance social contentment and stability, thus creating an environment that is conducive to business growth. In this sense, the accumulation and legitimizing functions of welfare capitalism benefit both the recipients and the capitalist system. On the negative side, however, the state's ability to provide the services that maintain the system eventually becomes exhausted, thereby precipitating a crisis.

Social Conscience Hypotheses   Other popular explanations include the *social conscience* or *humanitarian impulse hypotheses*. According to these hypotheses, human beings have innate, altruistic concerns for other people. This natural drive in people has led to the creation of the modern welfare state. These explanations trace the roots of the modern welfare state to the charitable activities of ancient religious groups and early philanthropists. However, proponents of social conscience theory also argue that, due to industrialization, people are no longer as willing to assist others. People's desire to help others has been continually weakened by urbanization, the emphasis on individualism, and increased competitiveness. Moreover, these factors have created additional social problems that cannot be resolved simply by humanitarian aid. Therefore, it is now much harder to garner support for the expansion of the welfare state, even though modern societies are experiencing serious social problems that require immediate attention.

The Marshall and Titmuss Hypotheses   British theorists T. H. Marshall and Richard Titmuss cast additional light on conceptions of social welfare when they developed arguments focused on legitimizing the social welfare function. Marshall (1950) argued that ensuring rights to an adequate education, housing, and income was part of the evolution of citizenship rights. As citizenship was granted, civil, political, and social rights were extended beyond the aristocracy. People in a democracy are not as capable of fulfilling their responsibilities of citizenship without legal protection of all of these basic rights.

Richard Titmuss (1974), of the London School of Economics, had a profound influence on the development of social policy, particularly the institutional approach. Titmuss argued that government actions to provide for the social welfare of its citizens have desirable moral consequences such as institutionalizing altruism, increasing solidarity, and promoting reciprocity and social responsibility. Titmuss further maintained that, unlike economic goods, which are scarce services or items such as cars and televisions that have a price when sold, social goods such as public education and streets should not be bought and sold in an open market. Titmuss played a major role in promoting social welfare as a social right and in encouraging the study of social policy.

Economic and Social Conscience Hypotheses: A Critique   Scholars have examined international evidence to determine whether certain of the hypotheses we have just reviewed are useful interpretations of the dynamic of social welfare. Midgley pointed out that although some of these hypotheses have been posited as possible explanations for the U.S. welfare state, international evidence currently does not provide a great deal of support for any of them (1998). Looking for one overall explanation of the development of welfare states is most likely too simplistic. Instead, different hypotheses might cast light on the development of specific welfare policies and programs. For example, concern for quelling social unrest as embodied by the Townsend movement certainly influenced the passage of the Social Security Act of 1935. In addition, the political debate was greatly influenced by religious leaders. Similarly, the impulse to control women's lives is unquestionably reflected in the debate surrounding work requirements and marriage incentives for recipients of Temporary Assistance for Needy Families (TANF). All of these motivations as well as others are undoubtedly afoot in our society. If we can recognize these diverse motivations and do not insist on characterizing people involved in the debate simplistically, this understanding can help us craft and enact strengths-based legislation.

We cannot expect that all of the players involved in passing any legislation will be motivated by the same forces. For example, people favoring a residual approach to income-support programs, who generally champion free market strategies and downsizing the public sector, and people favoring an institutional approach to social welfare, may find common ground and support public investment to prepare a well-educated workforce, which contributes to a healthy marketplace economy. An understanding of the motivations of key actors is necessary if we are to craft support for policies and programs that benefit our clients.

Economic and Political Schools of Thought

In addition to the groups and ideologies we have just discussed, major political and economic schools of thought have shaped social welfare policy in the United States. The United States has a long history of pluralism. A **pluralistic process** of creating policy means that no one particular group holds all the power. Instead, many interest groups and citizens are actively involved in creating and implementing policies that they believe will benefit themselves and others. With any social policy, certain groups stand to gain or lose economically. A variety of interest groups and political parties have developed both public and private approaches and strategies at the federal, state, and local levels that contribute to our social welfare system. We begin our exploration of this topic by discussing three fundamental economic philosophies: Keynesian economics, supply-side economics, and democratic socialism. We will then shift our focus to the political arena and examine how different political philosophies and the three branches of government affect social welfare policy.

Keynesian Economics   The economic school of thought known as **Keynesian economics,** also referred to as *demand-side* or *consumer-side economics*, is based on the writings of John Maynard Keynes, an English economist who published the book *The General Theory of Employment, Interest, and Money* in 1936. Keynes rejected the traditional laissez-faire philosophy that free market competition would automatically facilitate full employment, making government intervention both unnecessary and undesirable. Instead, he posited that modern economies are not self-correcting; therefore, government stabilization efforts are necessary to keep a capitalist economy running smoothly. Specifically, Keynes argued that the government should stabilize the economy through the use of **fiscal policy,** that is, by increasing or decreasing spending and taxes in response to economic conditions. When individuals or private businesses don't consume or invest enough, then the government must intervene. Demand-side economics also emphasizes the importance of public investment in **human capital**—that is, programs such as education, health care, and job training that make people more productive—in order to increase national wealth.

Keynes's theory guided U.S. social policy during the Great Depression. His ideas clearly were reflected in the various New Deal programs that sought to increase demand for goods and services—and therefore create jobs—by providing income and work opportunities to people in need. Overall, Keynesian principles are integral to liberalism and its efforts to develop a comprehensive public welfare state. **Liberalism** is a political philosophy that endorses individual freedom and advocates government intervention to ensure an adequate minimum living condition for all people. The type of government activism on behalf of people in poverty that Keynes proposed is most typically supported by the liberal wing of the Democratic Party.

Supply-Side Economics   In contrast, **supply-side economics** guides the conservative political view of social welfare, which informs the conservative wing of the Republican Party. In contrast to liberals, conservatives oppose widespread change in the political sector and advocate a laissez-faire economy and a minimal welfare state. Supply-side economics was greatly influenced by the work of conservative economist Milton Friedman and his theories of **monetary policy** or **monetarism.** Friedman argued that Keynesian strategies of using fiscal policy to smooth out business cycles actually harm the economy and fuel economic instability. According to Friedman, government policy should be restricted to promoting steady growth in the nation's money supply, that is, the total amount of money that is circulating in the economy.

Influenced by Friedman, supply-side economics gained momentum in the 1980s. However, supply-side economists have increasingly rejected Friedman's idea of gradually increasing the money supply and instead have focused on tax cuts. They argue that tax cuts, particularly for wealthy people, will lead to large increases in investment, spending, and savings, which in turn will expand the economy and create jobs. Allowing people to retain a larger portion of their income after taxes will encourage them to work more hours and thereby increase the supply of goods and services available to consumers, hence the term "supply-side" (Roberts, 1988). Ultimately, some of these benefits will "trickle down" and improve economic conditions for low-income groups. Supply-side economics provided the rationale for the large-scale tax cuts enacted during the administrations of Ronald Reagan and George W. Bush.

Democratic Socialism   A third philosophy, **democratic socialism,** which was greatly influenced by Michael Harrington, adopts a dramatically different stance. Advocates of democratic socialism argue that because capitalism is predicated on the pursuit of individual self-interest and profit, it inevitably increases social inequality and therefore cannot be relied upon to advance the public good. Democratic socialists further posit that the expansion of government in the social welfare arena comes about, not through the actions of altruistic government officials, but rather through the struggle of the working class and its allies. As their name suggests, democratic socialists believe in the democratic process, and they work to bring about change in the economic system. Because they define social problems as stemming from an unjust society, they view the expansion of social welfare as a step toward social justice.

Neo-conservatism and Neo-liberalism   As we move from the economic to the political landscape, we now turn our attention to two political philosophies—neo-conservatism and neo-liberalism—that are currently vying for the power to shape social welfare policy. Although neo-conservatives and neo-liberals both support the same ideal of a just and decent society, they often disagree about what constitutes such a society and how to accomplish these goals. **Neo-conservatives** seek to restrict the government's role in promoting social welfare, and they advocate the transfer of welfare responsibility from the government to the private sector. Neo-conservatives insist that social welfare programs be compatible with traditional social values such as self-reliance and personal responsibility as well as with a market economy. Consequently, they don't necessarily perceive high unemployment and low wages as problematic.

   In contrast, **neo-liberals** support a more active government role in achieving economic growth and social justice. Nevertheless, neo-liberals differ from traditional liberals in their belief that institutions other than the government need to play a bigger role in achieving social justice. For example, they advocate investment by corporations in human capital and social welfare, and they do not believe that the accumulation of corporate profits necessarily conflicts with the advancement of the social good. Significantly, neo-liberals are beginning to reject the types of social welfare policy that were reflected in New Deal programs.

Other Political Influences   Communitarians, libertarians, and the Green Party are also part of our political landscape. **Communitarians** represent a mix of liberal and conservative traditions. They emphasize the need to rebuild communities, and they encourage two-parent families. Communitarians advocate for individual rights and equality; however, they also believe that communities and institutions need to build character and promote virtues of citizenship. This role can be more important than individual rights at any given time. They favor greater involvement of local government and communities in promoting social welfare. Another political group, **libertarians,** believes that government grows at the expense of individual freedom. Therefore, they are critical of taxation, and they reject the argument that government should be involved in social or economic activities. Instead, they seek to eliminate the entire welfare system and restore the roles of family, church, and other nongovernmental entities in assisting people in need.

Although they are widely portrayed as being primarily interested in ecological awareness, the **Green Party** represents a much broader range of values and political views. Regarding social welfare policy, the Green Party advocates social justice, nonviolence, personal and global responsibility, and respect for diversity. They actively support universal health care, civil and equal rights, and financial support for children, families, people with disabilities, caregivers not in the workforce, and other individuals who are vulnerable to poverty.

 Web Links

You can access brief overviews of some of these political groups by going to www.mhhe.com/chapin1 and clicking on the Libertarian and Green Party links.

We have briefly discussed major schools of economics and political ideologies. Given this political and economic context, how can we use this information to understand the development of a particular policy or program at a given time? To answer this question, think back to the historical context of the New Deal social policies of the 1930s. Economic instability and deflation experienced during the Great Depression fueled political initiatives informed by Keynesian economic thought. From a different perspective, the sluggish economic growth and high inflation of the 1970s ushered in the conservative supply-side economic and political policies of the 1980s. The influence of popular values and the interplay of the economic and political context of these two periods brought about two very different approaches.

At different periods in our history, various political parties have pressed for equality of opportunity, income redistribution, and civil rights. The political process is conflictual. The two major political parties, the Democrats and the Republicans, spend a great deal of money and time vying for media attention and ultimately citizens' votes. Each party wants to control the legislative, executive, and judicial branches of government at both the federal and the state level. We turn now to the influence of these three branches of government on our social welfare system.

The Three Branches of Government

There are three branches of government at both the federal and the state level: the legislative, executive, and judicial branches. In theory, each branch performs separate and distinct functions. Simply put, the legislative branch makes laws; the executive branch concurs in lawmaking, enforces the laws, and develops budgets; and the judicial branch interprets the laws. However, the reality is that all three branches create social policy and influence our social welfare system in complex and interrelated ways. Social workers who are aware that all three branches of government make social policy can craft strategies that are more effective for influencing social policy. Chapter 6 provides guidelines for this process.

 Web Links

If you do not know the structure of each branch, how a bill becomes law, or the relationships among the three branches, be sure to visit the Web sites listed at www.mhhe.com/chapin1.

At the federal level, the **executive branch** includes the president, the vice-president, the cabinet, the president's advisers, and all of the offices and agencies that serve the president and execute federal policy. At the state level, the governor, the cabinet, and all of the offices and agencies charged with executing state policy belong to the executive branch. When they develop budgets, champion legislation, and create the rules and regulations necessary to implement laws, they are making social policy. Congress, the major component of the **legislative branch,** is *bicameral;* that is, it consists of two chambers, the House of Representatives and the Senate. Both chambers are charged with passing legislation. They are independent of each other, but they must agree on proposed legislation for it to become law. Most states also have a bicameral legislature. The **judicial branch** comprises the court system. Both federal and state judiciaries include a supreme court, a court of appeals, and district courts. When the judicial branch interprets legislation, rules on legal intent, or determines whether legislation violates the Constitution, it is actually making social policy.

THE IMPACT OF FUNDING STRATEGIES

When considering the political context, it is important to remember that policy making is about rationing resources. Social policies determine who gets how much of the pie. You only have to observe one year's federal or state legislative session to learn that dollars are finite. Although social workers should support efforts to expand the pie and draw upon untapped strengths, they must never lose sight of this reality. The amount of funding allocated to implementing social policies and programs determines the extent to which their clients' needs can be met. If you examine the federal and state budgets and monitor the budgetary process, you can determine how different funding strategies shape outcomes for your clients.

Federal and State Budgets

Analysis of the federal budget provides insight into the priorities established and the values played out through the political process. In 2004, the federal

Source: Clay Bennett/ © 2002
The Christian Science Monitor
(www.csmonitor.com). All rights
reserved.

government spent nearly $2.3 trillion. This amount was equal to approximately 20 percent of the nation's gross domestic product (Congressional Budget Office, 2004). **Gross domestic product** (GDP) is the total monetary value of all goods and services produced in a country annually. Each year, the White House prepares a budget through the Office of Management and Budget (OMB). It then submits the budget to Congress for authorization and appropriation. For example, in February 2005, the administration of George W. Bush proposed a budget of $2.57 trillion for fiscal year (FY) 2006 (Office of Management and Budget, 2005). (The federal fiscal year runs from October 1 to September 30.) It is particularly important for social workers interested in shaping federal and state programs to track appropriations, because this is where the decisions are made concerning how much money will actually be spent on different programs.

Mandatory versus Discretionary Spending Although the size of the federal budget grows yearly, policy makers realistically can exercise control over only a part of it. The majority of the budget is earmarked for **mandatory spending,** which is government spending directed toward individuals and institutions that are legally entitled to it. Mandatory spending includes payment of the interest on the national debt and funding for entitlement programs. An **entitlement program** is one for which all citizens who meet the eligibility requirements legally qualify. Perhaps the most prominent examples are Social Security and Medicare. In theory, Congress possesses the power to limit or even reduce mandatory spending by modifying entitlement programs. For example, recall that Aid to Families with Dependent Children (AFDC) was an entitlement program; however, the legislation that replaced AFDC with TANF abolished this entitlement. Generally speaking, however, Congress is reluctant to tamper with

 Web Link

To view detailed information on the current federal budget, go to www.mhhe.com/chapin1 and refer to the White House Web site.

the major entitlement programs because they benefit a majority of Americans and therefore are very popular with voters.

Consequently, congressional decision making focuses on that portion of the federal budget (approximately one-third) that is termed **discretionary spending** (Wilson and DiIulio, 2004). Discretionary spending refers to all the spending authorized by the 13 appropriation bills that are passed each year by Congress and signed by the president. It includes funding for national defense, transportation, educational and social programs such as Head Start, and agriculture. Each year, Congress and the White House struggle to establish priorities concerning which programs to fund and how much money to allocate to them. One difference between discretionary and mandatory spending is that the government imposes a ceiling on discretionary spending. If that money is completely used, then the government has no obligation to allocate an additional amount.

All discretionary spending and some mandatory spending such as payment of interest on the national debt are funded through general tax revenues. General tax revenues include individual income taxes, corporate taxes, and excise taxes. Taxes are either regressive or progressive. **Regressive taxes** require people with lower incomes to pay higher rates or proportions of their income. For example, sales taxes on food and clothing are regressive because low-income people spend a higher percentage of their income on these necessities. In contrast, **progressive taxes** require people with higher incomes to pay higher rates or proportions of their income. The federal government runs a surplus when the amount of all tax revenue exceeds the cost of mandatory and discretionary spending in a given year. Conversely, it runs a deficit when spending exceeds tax revenues. In FY 2004, the federal deficit totaled $412 billion; for FY 2005, it was projected to increase to $427 billion (Office of Management and Budget, 2005).

There is a great deal of confusion surrounding the funding of Social Security and Medicare, two entitlement programs that require mandatory spending. Although these programs are included in the overall budget, they are designed in part on an insurance model and are funded through payroll taxes that flow into the Social Security Trust Fund and the Medicare Hospital Insurance Trust Fund. Although many critics complain about the percentage of the federal budget that is devoted to these programs, the current level of payment of payroll taxes is more than sufficient to fund these programs today. In fact, current contributions are creating a large surplus in the Social Security Trust Fund rather than contributing to the deficit. We will examine the funding of Social Security in detail in Chapter 8.

Federal Spending   The federal budget exerts a powerful influence on social welfare policy. It represents the priorities of our lawmakers. The federal government can raise funds across the country and provide funding for social and health programs in every state, even when problems like a prolonged drought

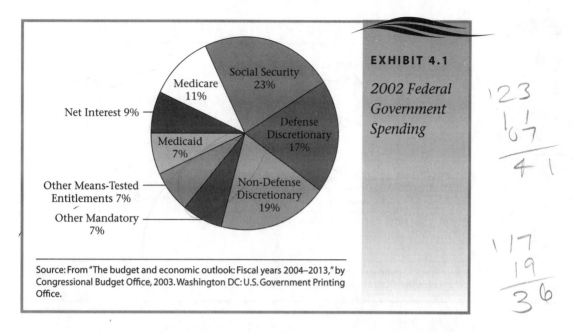

EXHIBIT 4.1

2002 Federal Government Spending

Source: From "The budget and economic outlook: Fiscal years 2004–2013," by Congressional Budget Office, 2003. Washington DC: U.S. Government Printing Office.

or the bankruptcy of major industries compromise the economic base of particular states. Look at Exhibit 4.1 to see how federal dollars were being spent in 2002. Conflicts over the allocation of our tax dollars revolve around three basic issues: (1) who should pay, (2) who should benefit, and (3) which programs should grow and which ones should shrink (Schick, 2000). Government spending is a **redistributive process,** meaning that some people gain and other people lose. As an obvious example, when expenditures for defense escalate, fewer dollars are available for social programs unless lawmakers are willing to let the federal deficit grow unchecked. The result typically is loss of benefits and services for clients and loss of health, education, and social service jobs in both the public and the private sector. Political differences over these three issues must be resolved—at least temporarily—before the budget can be approved.

A careful examination of the types and percentages of expenditures from year to year discloses clear shifts in spending. Exhibit 4.2 shows the shift in government spending as a proportion of GDP. Overall, government spending in the past 40 years has decreased slightly as a percentage of GDP. During this period, spending for discretionary expenses has decreased, while spending on mandatory and entitlement expenses has increased. In terms of actual expenditures, between 1962 and 2003, discretionary spending decreased from 12.7 percent to 7.6 percent of GDP, whereas mandatory and entitlement spending increased from 4.9 percent to 10.9 percent. Significantly, the increase in mandatory spending is due largely to increased costs for the Medicaid and Medicare programs. Because health care costs are expected to rise and millions of baby boomers will become eligible for these programs in the near future, this trend will likely continue in the coming decades (Congressional Budget Office, 2004).

EXHIBIT 4.2

Major Components of Spending, 1962–2003

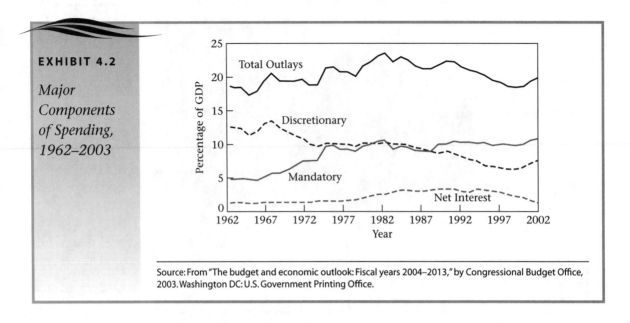

Source: From "The budget and economic outlook: Fiscal years 2004–2013," by Congressional Budget Office, 2003. Washington DC: U.S. Government Printing Office.

Beyond direct service spending, the government promotes social welfare through many other policies such as tax incentives that encourage savings for retirement, educational policies and expenditures, and antidiscrimination laws. At the same time, however, when the government offers a tax incentive, then tax dollars that normally would have been collected are not. As a result, a smaller amount of general tax revenue is available for other programs. Uncollected tax dollars leave fewer dollars available to pay for benefits and services without increasing the federal deficit.

State Spending Policies   State budgets also have important ramifications for social welfare policy. As discussed in Chapter 3, beginning with the Reagan administration, the federal government has increasingly shifted responsibilities for social welfare programs to the states. Federal and state budgets are linked in that the states receive financial support and incentives for certain programs such as Medicaid for which they are required to provide matching funds. States that fail to provide these funds lose the federal monies. The amount of the match differs by state and is determined by a formula that takes into consideration the state's poverty rate.

As we saw in Chapter 3, for some programs, such as TANF, federal support takes the form of block grants, which allow the state more discretion over how federal monies will be spent. Block grants typically are capped, so that if the need for services increases, the federal government will not provide additional funding. Unfortunately, need often increases because the state or local economy declines. When this occurs, corporate profits fall, and workers are laid off.

Consequently, the state tax base shrinks, and tax revenues decline. Because federal funds are capped, the federal government will not compensate for the loss of state revenues. Moreover, most state governments are required by law to balance their budgets, unlike the federal government. Consequently, states must adopt some combination of the following policies: increase taxes, reduce spending, and find new sources of revenue. Unfortunately, spending cuts often target social welfare programs, regardless of their effectiveness. Consequently, during economic downturns, discretionary programs are subject to cutbacks and elimination at the very time when people need them most.

In general, a state's economic resources and political climate determine which programs will be cut and how drastically. As we would expect, the political power of interest groups at the state level strongly influences these decisions. Take a moment to think about what happens in your state in terms of the representation and influence of low-income people, particularly women and people of color. Because these groups are generally underrepresented in state legislatures, their interests often are not protected during economic hard times. Thus, the social programs designed to assist them are especially vulnerable to the pressures to reduce spending. To compound these difficulties, state governments are particularly vulnerable to business threats to downsize or relocate if the state raises taxes, even if the tax revenues would be used to finance necessary social programs.

For all of these reasons, the ability of individual states to help their citizens meet their basic needs is more limited than the federal government's ability to do so. Not surprisingly, then, the federal government has assumed the responsibility to protect the interests of U.S. citizens—particularly women and other minorities—at times when the states were struggling (Gordon, 1998). Overall, the federal government is more stable and can provide more substantial benefits to a larger number of people in need.

The Role of the Private Sector

Of course, not all social welfare programs are funded or administered by the government. Rather, many programs operate through the private, or nongovernmental sector. In fact, as discussed in Chapter 3, privatization has emerged as a major political trend since the 1980s. The private sector is composed of many for-profit organizations such as hospitals, nursing homes, substance abuse centers, and counseling centers. It also includes the not-for-profit sector: religious institutions, foundations, and other charitable organizations. Private sector initiatives can be very flexible, and they employ a variety of funding strategies. They often have a mix of clients who pay privately for their services and clients who receive federal or state funding. For example, in a for-profit nursing home, it is not uncommon for more than half the residents to have their bills paid by taxpayers through Medicaid. Such for-profit facilities are able to serve private-pay clients more affordably and still make a profit because infrastructure and fixed costs are financed largely by public funding for clients who qualify for government programs in both for-profit and not-for-profit facilities.

Because the private sector does not simply draw on public funds to provide social services, the assets of these organizations typically increase in value when the economy is growing, so that private funding for social services can be enhanced. Even so, a relatively small proportion of funding for many not-for-profit agencies comes from charitable contributions. In addition, people are more able to pay privately for services when the economy is growing. During economic downturns, the amount of services such organizations can provide is often constricted. As with state governments, then, as need increases, the available resources decline.

Benefits and Drawbacks of Different Combinations of Funding Strategies

In our pluralistic system, both public and private funding contribute to the provision of social welfare services, and creative use of both sources is often necessary to meet our clients' needs. Private funding and provision of services can be particularly important for innovative or controversial services from which public funding might be withheld, such as abortion counseling and shelters for gay and lesbian victims of domestic abuse. At the same time, however, private supporters can exclude people they consider "unworthy," and they can attach conditions many people might find objectionable. In pursuing these policies, they are not subject to the same public scrutiny or oversight as public programs are. For these reasons, public funding and provision of services may be preferable when the service is either particularly important or not profitable or when the population it serves is especially vulnerable. Protection against child and elder abuse is an example of such services. In such cases, public scrutiny and accountability become very important.

Public and private funds can also be combined to fund benefits and services. Your college or university may provide a good example of such a combination. For example, if you are attending a public university, it is likely that private contributors financed many of the buildings, private donors funded many scholarships, and even some of your professors may be partially paid through private endowments. If you are attending a private college, it is likely that public funds are being used to provide student loans to low-income students and that your professors are conducting research funded by the federal or state government.

In considering the benefits and drawbacks of different funding combinations for social programs, many analysts emphasize that taxation can generate very large amounts of public funds, thereby ensuring more year-to-year stability. Indeed, it is the public sector that can realistically provide sufficient funds to mount major social welfare programs nationwide, although the private sector might provide the actual services. Private funding is generally much more limited. Also, it can be either restricted or very flexible, depending on the wishes of the people who control the funds. Private and public funding both have their advantages and disadvantages, and social workers need to consider both when attempting to develop funding strategies for needed services.

SOCIAL WELFARE EXPENDITURES IN THE UNITED STATES

The United States is often described as a welfare state. Nevertheless, the adequacy of the nation's social policies and programs is often debated. To evaluate social policy in the United States, we must carefully consider the definition of social welfare expenditures. Typically, the term **social welfare expenditures** refers to all spending necessary to sustain the core federal and state social welfare programs. The core federal programs include TANF, Social Security, Medicaid, Medicare, Supplemental Security Income (SSI), Food Stamps, Head Start, various housing programs, job training programs, educational grants, veterans' benefits, and unemployment benefits. State and local programs include education, programs for people with mental illness, health and social services for children and older adults, corrections programs, and workers' compensation. Although these programs are administered on a state or local level, they are often subsidized by the federal government.

In this country, about 20 cents of every dollar of the GDP is spent on social welfare. Contrary to popular opinion, most social welfare spending in the United States is not for cash payments or other forms of assistance for poor people. In fact, this type of aid makes up only 16 percent of social welfare expenditures, and it represents only 3.5 percent of GDP (Waldfogel, 2000). Rather, the largest and most rapidly growing component of social welfare spending is social insurance, which amounts to about 10 percent of GDP. Significantly, most of the recipients of social insurance benefits are not poor, although many of them would fall into poverty were it not for these programs.

The Nature of U.S. Social Welfare Spending

Recall from Chapter 3 that, beginning in the 1980s, there has been growing pressure for changes in the social welfare system, including curtailing welfare benefits, reconfiguring universal programs based on the insurance principle, and instituting strict means-tested programs that the majority of citizens do not expect to ever use (Karger & Stoesz, 2002). Support for cutbacks was fueled by a sluggish economy, increased mistrust of government, and growing pressure from globalization, a phenomenon we discuss later in the chapter. The conservative political philosophy that emerged during this period favored privatization of a variety of social welfare activities and the devolution of many fundamental services to the state and local levels.

The success of the various initiatives that evolved from this philosophy has been mixed at best. On the negative side, increased fragmentation in a welfare system already notorious for its lack of cohesion has been widely documented. As one example, piecemeal, uncoordinated public and private initiatives to feed and house adults and children who are no longer eligible for public financial assistance are being cobbled together at the local level to provide needed assistance. Signs such as long lines at food pantries and growing numbers of Americans who lack health insurance, contrasted with yet more tax cuts for the wealthiest Americans, indicate that we are in a period of private opulence and underfunded social programs. Though some programs were cut drastically, for the most part, overall funding for social welfare programs has been increasing on an annual basis. Yet, this trend of increased funding has not been able to adequately address need.

Total federal spending has increased since George W. Bush took office in January 2001. This increase includes both mandatory spending on programs such as Social Security and Medicare and discretionary spending for defense, homeland security, and social welfare programs. Social welfare spending increased as a percentage of GDP from 3.1 percent in 2001 to 3.4 percent in 2004 (Shapiro & Kamin, 2004). Yet, the Bush administration has pressed for slower growth of total discretionary spending. In order to achieve a goal of 3.9 percent growth of total domestic spending, priorities have been set for defense, homeland security, and other discretionary funding. The "enhanced security, restraint elsewhere" policies have directly influenced non-defense, non–homeland security discretionary spending (hereafter called *non-security discretionary spending*), including funding for social welfare programs.

In 2001, the Clinton administration's final budget showed a 15 percent growth of non-security discretionary spending. The Bush administration subsequently cut growth to 6 percent in 2002 and continued to reduce the rate of growth every year through 2005. At that point, the increase in non-security spending had declined to 1 percent, which was below the rate of inflation (Office of Management and Budget, 2005). Bush's strategy did not allow for adequate growth of programs that meet the needs of poor children and elders.

Then, in 2005, the Bush administration went even further. Rather than calling for a smaller increase in non-security discretionary spending, the White House submitted a budget for FY 2006 that proposed reducing such spending, in part by cutting or eliminating funding for more than 150 programs (Office of Management and Budget, 2005). Almost one-third of these programs involved education, including vocational training, educational technology, Grants for Incarcerated Youth, and Even Start, a literacy program for low-income students. Also targeted for elimination were job-training programs, an EPA program that helped finance water-treatment projects in low-income neighborhoods, and the Community Development Block Grant (CDBG) program, which helped fund agencies that provide employment, education, and housing services to low-income people (House Budget Committee, 2005; Pear, 2005; Stevenson, 2005).

Moreover, this funding trend would continue into the future. In fact, according to the Center on Budget and Policy Priorities, if the president's spending targets for defense, homeland security, and foreign affairs through 2010 are to be met, then non-security discretionary spending will have to be reduced by $214 billion during that period, including $66 billion in 2010 alone, which would leave such spending 16 percent below the level of 2005 (Kogan & Kamin, 2004). In addition, the budget proposed changes in certain entitlement programs, including Medicaid and food stamps, that would save an additional $137 billion over 10 years (Horney, Greenstein, & Kogan, 2005; Office of Management and Budget, 2005). Although budget proposals may not be enacted in their entirety, they are beneficial for understanding priorities and potential future needs that may be addressed through legislative advocacy.

It is clear that government has long been used to promote social welfare and will continue to be used that way. What is less clear is whether public resources will be spent primarily to enhance the social welfare of the middle and upper classes or will go to support basic, universal benefits for all citizens. For example, some critics contend that many middle- and upper-income citizens receive substantially more government support through the tax system than low-income citizens receive via social welfare programs targeted at specific needs such as poverty and unemployment.

Social Welfare and Tax Expenditures When social welfare is defined broadly, it is clear that most social welfare expenditures are not targeted toward low-income people. However, social welfare often is popularly defined as including assistance for people categorized as needy or deficient but excluding policies that benefit people with higher incomes. For example, definitions of social welfare expenditures inevitably include funding for public housing for low-income families, but they often overlook tax deductions for home mortgages. This practice is common despite the fact that both policies help families obtain housing they otherwise could not afford. Further, tax deductions for medical care, special tax breaks for large corporations, and tax deductions for college tuition all could be considered public social welfare expenditures. In fact, defining them as such helps draw attention to what has been termed *the upside-down welfare state.*

Economists apply the term **tax expenditures** to tax deductions that the government extends to particular groups in order to assist them in obtaining social services such as housing, health care, and education. Although tax expenditures typically are analyzed separately from social welfare expenditures,

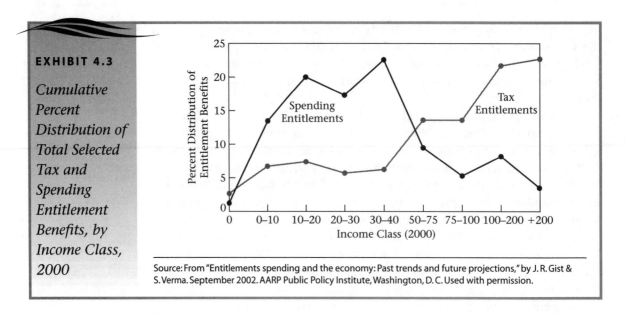

Source: From "Entitlements spending and the economy: Past trends and future projections," by J. R. Gist & S. Verma. September 2002. AARP Public Policy Institute, Washington, D. C. Used with permission.

EXHIBIT 4.3

Cumulative Percent Distribution of Total Selected Tax and Spending Entitlement Benefits, by Income Class, 2000

they represent lost revenue that the government is not able to use for other purposes, such as paying down the debt, providing more military funding, or increasing social welfare expenditures. The government determines that this money will remain with the person filing her or his taxes instead of being collected for other purposes.

Exhibit 4.3 illustrates the impact of major social welfare and tax expenditures on different income classes. This graph reflects expenditures on the following programs: SSI, veterans' benefits, unemployment insurance, federal pensions, Medicaid, Medicare, Social Security, and military pensions. The tax expenditures include mortgage interest, child tax credit, untaxed Social Security, childcare credit, charitable contributions, income property tax, real estate tax, and medical expenses. A clear, class-based pattern emerges from this analysis. On the one hand, the majority of the social welfare expenditures assist those people or families with low or middle incomes, except in the case of military pensions, which are distributed primarily to people with higher incomes. On the other hand, tax expenditures largely affect people or families with incomes above $50,000. The major exception is the Earned Income Tax Credit (EITC), which generally benefits low-income taxpayers (Gist & Verma, 2002).

Overall, then, when we analyze both social welfare and tax expenditures, we discover that expenditures going to middle- and upper-income families in non-stigmatizing ways often exceed the amounts going to low-income families (Gist & Verma, 2002). This policy is sometimes justified by the argument that expenditures targeted to upper-income citizens will improve the economy. However, it is clear that expenditures for low-income people also provide economic stimulation because these people must spend most of the money immediately on necessities.

Adequacy of Current Expenditures for Social Programs

Earlier in this chapter, the principles of economic efficiency and equity were discussed in terms of evaluating interventions. Another important principle for social workers to consider is the adequacy of social welfare programs, including those provided by the tax system. **Adequacy** refers to the ability of social welfare programs to address and sufficiently meet the needs of the general public. Determining whether public expenditures on social welfare are adequate is a complex task. One way to assess social welfare programs in the United States is to look at the equality, equity, and adequacy of income distribution.

Income distribution in the United States is highly unequal. In 2003, median household income in the United States was $43,318. However, the highest quintile (one-fifth) of the population was earning at least $86,867 at the same time that the lowest quintile was earning less than $17,984. Income includes earned income, social welfare benefits, and capital gains, but it does not include tax deductions. The U.S. Census Bureau reports that the percentage of the nation's overall income received by households in the lowest quintile decreased from 4.3 percent in 1980 to 3.4 percent in 2003, while at the same time the highest quintile experienced an increase from 43.7 percent to 49.8 percent (DeNavas-Walt, Proctor, & Mills, 2004).

Equitable income distribution can be achieved by redistributing income through social welfare programs and tax strategies. Income inequality can be reduced by redistributing income from those with high incomes to those in poverty. Determining the need for redistribution of income can be understood by evaluating the adequacy of income for those with low to moderate incomes. The actual income level of the lowest quintile (after inflation adjustments) has increased since 1970, although their share of national income has decreased. Exhibit 4.4 illustrates the growth of income for both the lowest and highest quintiles as well as the median household income from 1970 to 2001. Growth in income provides households with more money to meet basic needs such as housing and food. However, this increase does not guarantee adequacy, because low-income households might not have been able to meet their needs prior to the increase. In addition, the cost of living escalated during this time period. Also, as the chart indicates, income levels for the lowest quintile have increased less than either the median household income or incomes for the upper quintile. Consequently, the gap between the income classes has increased.

In order to determine adequacy of income and social welfare programs in the United States, it is also important to look at how much it actually costs a

EXHIBIT 4.4

Income Distribution by Group, 2001

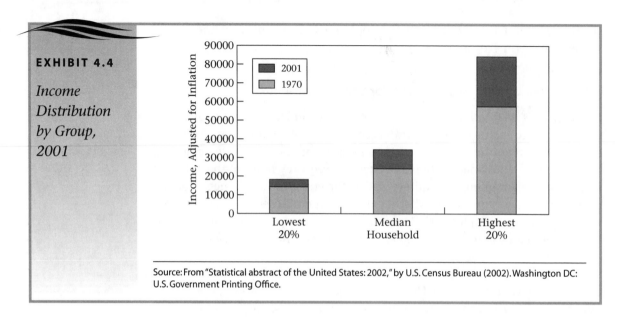

Source: From "Statistical abstract of the United States: 2002," by U.S. Census Bureau (2002). Washington DC: U.S. Government Printing Office.

household to live. However, this is a complicated process, because the cost of living in New York might be much different than it is in Missouri. Also, different people might define basic needs and their costs in different ways. Understanding adequacy, equity, and equality in terms of income distribution and social welfare programs is important for evaluating policies. Another way to evaluate the adequacy of expenditures on social welfare programs in the United States is to examine social welfare expenditures and outcomes in other countries, a topic to which we now turn.

U.S. Expenditures Compared to Those of Other Countries   Although some critics contend that the problem with the U.S. economy is the high level of spending on social welfare, the reality is that by international standards, social welfare spending in comparison to the size of the U.S. economy is not high. In fact, the United States has never provided the full array of social welfare protections, especially universal health care, that most Western governments do.

The Organisation for Economic Co-operation and Development (OECD), an international organization devoted to promoting economic growth and world trade, has collected data on the social spending of various countries from 1980 to 1998. The social expenditures fall into three broad categories: (1) pension payments such as old-age cash benefits, including survivors' benefits; (2) income-based support for working-age people who are experiencing need due to illness, disability, or loss of earnings; and (3) health and other expenditures for children, older adults, and people with disabilities, as well as active programs that focus on training people to return to work. Not included in these

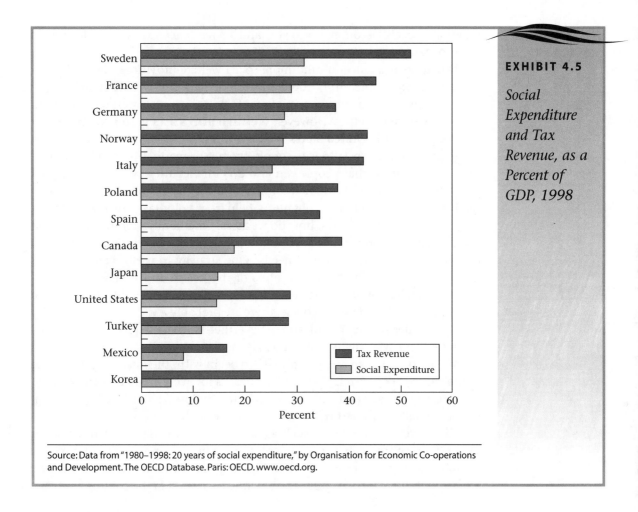

Source: Data from "1980–1998: 20 years of social expenditure," by Organisation for Economic Co-operations and Development. The OECD Database. Paris: OECD. www.oecd.org.

EXHIBIT 4.5

Social Expenditure and Tax Revenue, as a Percent of GDP, 1998

data are tax expenditures, non-mandatory private social expenditures, and educational expenditures. The OECD also was unable to include an accurate representation of expenditures by all the many levels of government such as towns and counties (Organisation for Economic Co-operation and Development, 2001). In addition, the OECD collected information about tax rates of different countries.

Exhibit 4.5 compares the United States to other countries in terms of social welfare expenditures and tax revenues as a proportion of GDP. The chart clearly illustrates that the United States devotes less of its overall wealth to social welfare spending than most of the other countries do. Moreover, it does not tax its citizens as heavily, compared to the countries that provide more extensive social welfare benefits. These trends remain true despite the fact that in recent decades, most Western governments, like the United States, have either cut social programs or arrested their growth in response to high rates of unemployment and inflation, sluggish economic growth, and increasing pressure to reduce what were considered to be excessive levels of taxation.

Due to its hesitance to fund more social welfare provisions, Wilensky and Lebeaux (1965) defined the United States as a "reluctant welfare state." Proponents of this position continue to advocate policies similar to those offered in other developed countries. However, **welfare pluralists** in this country reject the notion that the United States is a laggard in the social welfare arena. They do not believe that social needs should be met primarily by the government. Instead, they argue that people can and do enhance their well-being through their own efforts or with the help of neighbors or their families by purchasing services on the market, or by obtaining help from voluntary organizations.

The question thus arises, how do we assess whether the approaches used in the United States are as effective as the publicly financed programs in other countries at addressing citizens' needs? One strategy to use in answering this question is to examine basic indicators of the health and welfare of the citizenry, including infant mortality, childhood poverty, mental and physical health, and elder welfare. Of course, there are probably a variety of reasons why countries differ on these indicators. Nevertheless, the adequacy of the social welfare system certainly is one of them.

What does such an analysis reveal? To begin with, the infant mortality rate in the United States is relatively high: 7 deaths for every 1,000 live births, compared to 5 in Canada and 3 in Sweden (United Nations, 2004). The U.S. rate undoubtedly reflects in part the absence of universal health care that is available in other developed countries such as Sweden and Canada. The United States also has one of the highest rates of childhood poverty among developed countries. Focus on policy outcomes is an integral part of the strengths perspective, and we will spend time examining outcomes for clients in the coming chapters.

The Ramifications of Globalization

A final factor we will consider that affects social welfare policy in the United States is globalization. **Globalization** refers to the international economic, political, and social integration of the world's nations. This process of integration is transforming the economic and political context in the United States. Globalization influences trade and labor markets. The increased ease of shipping, traveling, and communication means that goods, services, information, and currency can be moved around the world with more frequency. This movement allows companies to look for workers in other countries to perform jobs for wages lower than those paid in the United States. In turn, this process exerts pressure on wages in the United States to remain low (Blau, 2004).

The economic status of our citizenry is greatly influenced by decisions made by corporate policy makers. Many of these corporations operate globally, which means they are largely outside the control of any single government.

Moreover, when governments are unable to agree on regulations, such as international wage or pollution standards or the protection of basic human rights, the power of these corporations is enhanced. In fact, concentration of wealth and power in the hands of giant multinational corporations enables them to exert great influence over the operations of governments worldwide.

Globalization is exerting a significant impact on the health and well-being of our citizens. A global economy influences the growth and development of public social programs. All Western nations, including ours, are experiencing an increasing need to become competitive or stay competitive in the new global economy. One strategy to become more competitive is to reduce government spending so that tax burdens can be reduced.

At the same time, however, as more and more workers become dislocated due to global economic change, the need for social services is increasing. As governments reduce spending on social programs in an attempt to make their economies more globally competitive, people in need suffer. In the current environment, the prospects for direct financial assistance for these people are becoming more remote. It is possible, however, that strategies that focus on the role of government in promoting social investment in people so that they can more effectively participate in the productive economy and provide for their own social needs can garner sufficient support to be enacted in the global economy as well as in the United States (Midgley, 2000).

The social development approach is such a strategy. Developed by social workers, the **social development approach** seeks to harmonize economic development with social welfare policy by redistributing wealth and resources in ways that also promote economic growth (Midgley, 1999). Social development also seeks new ways of removing barriers to economic participation so that resources are returned to the economy and human capital is developed to its fullest potential. This approach involves government intervention, but primarily in the form of social investment with positive rates of return. Among other things, government funds can be used to (1) train jobless people and persons with disabilities for real jobs within their communities, (2) enhance community-held assets such as social infrastructure by encouraging local people to work with public agencies to build clinics and parks, (3) support micro-level enterprise development, and (4) encourage recipients to maintain savings accounts, which are matched by the government. Significantly, the outcomes of social programs based on this approach can be carefully evaluated, which can then increase their effectiveness.

Perhaps because the social development approach was shaped by social workers, it is not surprising that this strategy reflects the strengths principles of starting from common human needs, providing opportunities and garnering resources so that people can build on their strengths, identifying and removing barriers to self-sufficiency, and focusing on outcomes. If social investment in human capital enables people currently in poverty to train for real jobs, save

Web Link

*If you would like to learn
more about how the social
development approach has
been used in this country and
around the world, visit the
Center for Social Development's Web site at
www.mhhe.com/chapin1.*

money, own even a small share of community assets, and become productive
and creative in their own businesses, then these people will become part of the
functioning economy. So far, this approach has been adopted by several developing countries and is widely supported by the United Nations.

THE ECONOMY OF THE AGENCY

It is important to apply the theories and concepts you learn in class to day-to-
day social work practice. In this chapter, we have discussed the economic and
political context of social welfare policy. In terms of your actual practice, you
should be aware that social work agencies also have an economic context. In
order for an agency to provide benefits or services, it must have sufficient
financial resources to pay staff salaries and benefits and to meet such basic costs
as office space and supplies. These costs are beyond the actual tangible benefit
that goes to the clients such as the TANF payments, housing subsidy, or foster
care payment.

Every social service agency employs administrators who are responsible for
ensuring that there are sufficient financial resources to meet these needs. In
most agencies, these administrators also have the authority to make decisions
that influence service or benefit delivery. For example, if an agency is funded
primarily by private donations and private payments from clients, the administrators realize that clients who cannot afford to pay can be served only if the
agency attracts sufficient donations and clients who pay privately. Similarly, in
public and private agencies that are reimbursed on the basis of client diagnoses,
administrators know they must carefully plan staffing and services so that they
can meet their financial obligations based on these diagnoses. If they want to
raise the rate of reimbursement, they will need to serve people with more severe
diagnoses. This particular reality has led to the phenomenon of "charting for
dollars," in which the diagnosis is made with an eye to which particular diagnosis will bring in sufficient funds to serve the client adequately. For example,
a young person who may need family counseling could also be diagnosed as
having a mental illness such as depression because of the greater reimbursement available to serve someone so diagnosed.

So, you may be asking yourself, what does all of this have to do with social
policy? When you are having a difficult time grasping the logic of either a
national, state, or agency policy, one useful piece of advice is to "follow the
money." Many agency programs and policies are heavily influenced by the
financial ramifications of the policy that regulates how they are funded. Like
many of the ideas presented in an initial social policy class, entire books could
be written on this subject. However, you can begin to educate yourself in the
area where you will practice social work. Ask how agencies you are involved

with are funded. Are they publicly or privately funded, or do they receive both public and private funds? Is the agency public, private for-profit, not-for-profit, or volunteer? Think about how funding may be driving policy decisions. What incentives or disincentives are created for clients and workers by the way the agency is funded? Ask to see the agency budget. Ask questions about funding and financing. This can be done in the spirit of student inquiry. In fact, as a student, you are in the perfect position because you are expected to ask questions, and no question should be considered dumb. Of course, you will need to use the well-developed interpersonal skills you hopefully already have or are learning in your social work classes to make these inquiries in a respectful and non-threatening way. If you begin to consider the economic context and to ask these questions, you will understand much more readily and be able to anticipate policy changes in your agency.

CONCLUSION

Policy makers as well as the citizenry are faced with the task of restructuring the U.S. welfare state so it can respond more effectively to the changing political, economic, and social forces facing the United States. Increased public wariness of new initiatives, fed by the successful effort to defeat health care reform, clearly must be considered by policy makers attempting to develop programs that address the new economic and political realities connected to globalization. We need programs that increase economic productivity and human capital rather than restrict it. The values of reciprocity, responsibility, productivity, social integration, family and community cohesion, and social choice can be reflected in public social policy that also increases social justice. Advocates of social justice need to make clear to the public how social programs contribute to the overall well-being of society. Social responsibility is not the obligation solely of the poor.

It is too simplistic to believe that one type of program or the same incentives will work for all people. There is no reason to believe that all poor people, disabled people, or elders will respond to incentives or opportunities in the same way. It is to be expected that people in poverty differ as do people who are not poor. It is naive to think any one public welfare policy would make it possible for most people in poverty to become self-sufficient. People have different strengths, needs, and resources. In charting new welfare policy, it is important to couple opportunities and incentives for self-sufficiency with a realistic assessment of the labor market's capacity to provide a sufficient number of jobs that allow families to live above the poverty level. Initiatives should also be evaluated in terms of their effect on environmental resources so that they continue to be sources of strength rather than problems. Valid outcome benchmarks are needed to measure the success of strategies that are touted as alternatives to traditional publicly sponsored social welfare approaches, and influential organizations need to regularly monitor those outcomes and widely publicize the results. Kids Count, a nationwide initiative to track the well-being of children in this country, sponsored by the Annie E. Casey Foundation, is an example of such an effort (Annie E. Casey Foundation, 2004). Strategies that combine concerns about economic productivity and social welfare may appeal to a wider political spectrum. Social workers can help craft such policies by doing research and advocacy work that highlight the strengths and capacities of their clients. In a pluralistic society such as ours, where many groups vie to influence public social policy, strategies around which consensus can be built are key.

MAIN POINTS

- Social workers cannot adequately understand the social policies that determine how they will practice and what benefits and services their clients will receive unless they examine the economic and political contexts.

- The economic context focuses on the production, distribution, and use of income, wealth, and resources. The political context focuses on power seeking in government or public affairs. Both exert powerful influences on social welfare policy.

- The United States is a capitalist system with a market economy.

- Explanations of how the economic and political contexts have influenced the development of social welfare policy include hypotheses that focus on the use of welfare policy to even out economic cycles, control workers, and maintain capitalism. "Humanitarian impulses and social conscience" as well as activism by the working class also influenced social welfare policy.

- The legislative, executive, and judicial branches of government all create social policy.

- The size of the federal budget, the size of the federal debt, compulsory spending required for entitlement programs, and interest on the federal debt all limit discretionary spending whereby the priorities of the current president and Congress can be reflected.

- Social welfare policy and tax policy are contributing to the widening gap between rich and poor in the United States.

- Globalization influences social policy and must be taken into account in developing a new consensus to support a more effective, pluralistic welfare system. Strength principles can be useful in evaluating new options.

EXERCISES: PRACTICING SOCIAL WORK

Working with the Sanchez Family

1. Can you identify a federal and a state social policy that influences the services or benefits for which members of the Sanchez family may be eligible? How would these benefits be affected by a growing federal deficit or state budget shortfalls?

2. Go to the Web link that identifies conservative and liberal publications and Web sites. Pick one of the policies you identified to answer the question above and compare how the policy is depicted in a conservative and in a liberal publication. How do you account for the differences?

3. Review background information about the Sanchez family. How do you think globalization influences their success in meeting their basic needs?

Working with the Black Feather Community

1. It is clear that economic factors as well as cultural factors are influencing the willingness of some of the members of the Black Feather community to support the anti-smoking campaign. Identify and discuss the economic and cultural factors that influence the community in regard to policy changes aimed at reducing smoking among adolescents.

2. Just as in the Black Feather community, casino gambling is providing a source of assets for many Native American tribes. Identify some of the advantages and drawbacks of growing economic dependence on casino gambling on some reservations.

EXERCISES: THE SOCIAL WORK LIBRARY

Supreme Court's Influence on Social Policy

Read "Social work and the Supreme Court: A clash of values; a time of action" (Lens, 2004), and then respond to the following:

1. Why is it important for social workers to understand how the Supreme Court influences social policy?

2. Discuss the distinction between legislative and constitutional court decisions and explain how and when implementation of decisions can be stopped.

Social, Fiscal, and Corporate Welfare

Read "Everyone is still on welfare: The role of redistribution in social policy" (Abramovitz, 2001), and respond to the following:

1. What are fiscal and corporate welfare?

2. Write down three welfare benefits that you or your family have received.

3. Discuss whether there was any stigma attached to the benefits and the reason for its presence or lack of presence for you or your family.

CHAPTER 5

Tools for Determining Need and Analyzing Social Policy

I finally grasped why social workers study social policy! I was able to help my clients reach their goals because I understood the social policies and programs that could assist them.

—A SOCIAL WORK STUDENT

NOW THAT WE HAVE CONSIDERED THE HISTORICAL, SOCIAL, political, and economic contexts that shape social policy, it is time to delve into policy analysis in more depth. As new content on the policy analysis process is introduced, you can build your policy practice skills by applying what you learned about the context of social policy. The purpose of this chapter is to explain the steps involved in analyzing existing social policies and programs so that you can understand them and evaluate their effectiveness. The chapter initially explores needs determination, because needs determination is the foundation on which a policy is built. We will examine traditional problem analysis methods, and we will also explore how examining strengths, goals, and needs can build a foundation for more effective policy and programs. We will then link needs determination to other steps in the policy analysis process. This chapter also demonstrates how policies can be analyzed based on the strengths perspective.

We discussed some of the steps in policy analysis in Chapter 1. This chapter examines these steps in greater detail and presents a framework for analyzing social policy. Chapter 6 then builds on your understanding of policy analysis to consider the policy development process and policy practice in more depth.

POLICY ANALYSIS FUNDAMENTALS

As we have seen in previous chapters, social policies are designed both to meet the needs of the citizenry and to support the social order. Thus, they often have the dual purposes of alleviating social problems and maintaining social control.

Although social policy may address individual needs, it also benefits the host society. In fact, efforts to meet societal goals may cause the social welfare policy to be less effective in meeting your clients' goals. For example, a city may be willing to fund a homeless shelter not only to provide a haven for the homeless population but also to clear homeless people from around businesses. Therefore, it often establishes the shelter away from the business hub, where job possibilities are greatest. It is important to realize that social welfare policies are not a one-way street whereby taxpayers' hard-earned dollars flow to people in need with no hope of offering benefit to the society at large. In fact, just the opposite is typically the case.

You can identify the societal needs that are being met by examining how need is being defined. Consider the case described above. If we define the problem as homeless people discouraging shoppers and needing shelter, then establishing a policy to fund a homeless shelter away from the business hub is an obvious solution. In contrast, if we view the homeless population as people with strengths who face barriers to resources, then we are more likely to formulate policies for constructing shelters that provide easy access to jobs and other resources.

Social Conditions and Social Problems

Indeed, the way that the public and policy makers view a situation determines whether any social policy is developed at all. For example, for years in our society, discrimination in employment was considered a social condition, simply "the way things are." When a woman or a person of color could not get a job that paid a living wage, that was just a personal problem. Whereas a personal problem negatively affects an individual in a unique way, a social problem negatively influences a large group of people. Therefore, a social problem generally requires a structural or systemic solution rather than a primarily personal solution. A systemic solution affects the prevailing structure of society. Policies that prohibit discrimination in employment are examples of solutions that aim to bring about societal change.

Before such social policies develop, it is usually necessary to convince at least a sizable segment of the public that a problem or need exists that warrants intervention. Very often, the people affected by the problem have played an active role in achieving this public recognition. For example, as we saw in Chapter 3, focusing public attention and outrage on the problem of discrimination was—and continues to be—a long and arduous struggle. The efforts of people of color and women, who were the targets of discrimination, were central to the struggle to change public perceptions.

Advocates have used a variety of strategies for increasing public recognition of a social problem, including (1) conducting research and collecting supporting data, (2) identifying the barriers that the problem creates, and, most importantly, (3) attracting media attention. Advocates have also increased public recognition through litigation, direct action in the form of education (teach-ins, media events), physical confrontation and mass mobilization (rallies, marches, picketing, sit-ins), and economic tactics such as sanctions and boycotts. Once they gained recognition of the condition as a problem, they could garner public support for programs and services to alleviate the problem by publicizing the harmful effects of the problem for both the individual and society as a whole.

Many of the social policies that govern agencies where social workers are employed are designed to ration resources targeted to alleviate a condition that has been labeled a social problem. Social policies structure the services and ration the amount of funding and resources that go to agencies that address these problems. Social policies are necessary because human needs and wants are unlimited, whereas most resources are not. Existing social policies designed to address society's most pressing needs were created because these needs or problems were defined in a way that resources to help alleviate the need were mobilized.

Alternative Views

When analyzing existing policy, it is vital that you examine how policy makers and the public understood the social problem or need at the time the policy was made. At the same time, you should consider whether there are alternative ways of understanding those needs that might lead to more effective policy making.

When you are thinking about alternative understandings of need, carefully consider the questions to be asked rather than quickly moving to gather facts or seek answers. For example, many of the policies we will study have been designed to address the problem of poverty. In considering poverty, the question that first comes to mind is, "Why are people poor?"

There are a variety of explanations for the causes of poverty. Some authors on the subject have argued that people are poor because they lack a work ethic or are intellectually inferior. These authors ignore the structural causes of unemployment, such as inadequate educational systems in poor neighborhoods, lack of jobs, and discrimination. It is true that some people have intellectual limitations, drug and alcohol addiction, and other personal challenges that work to keep them impoverished. Social workers know these challenges must be addressed and that policies designed to provide individual services are crucial. However, they also know that many of the structural causes of unemployment and poverty are not effectively addressed and therefore contribute to the development of, and lack of adequate treatment for, personal problems. For example, the lack of jobs that pay a living wage and provide health benefits in a community will increase the number of families who don't receive preventive health care and don't have access to treatment for mental health and substance abuse problems. Part of the preparation for being a social services professional is exposure to a wide variety of ways of understanding conditions in our society. Later in this chapter, we will explore how to apply the strengths perspective in reframing the questions used to examine poverty and find alternatives to existing policies.

Defining Needs and Problems: The Social Constructionist Approach

In this chapter, you will learn how to integrate the strengths perspective into the process whereby we define needs and social problems. To do this effectively, you will need some background information on the conceptual underpinnings of this perspective. The strengths perspective reflects a **social constructionist approach** to reality, which posits that our explanations of all human interactions—including social problems—are based on socially and personally constructed views of reality (Geertz, 1973; Gergen, 1999). The term "socially and personally constructed" suggests that personal beliefs and group consensus shape what a group of people consider to be real at a given time.

To comprehend the social construction of reality more easily, consider historical periods when the majority of people were convinced that witchcraft and personal sin caused both natural disasters and personal suffering. Over time, careful and more objective observations dispelled many of these beliefs. Even when we attempt to be objective, however, our observations are shaped by our preconceptions. Leaders in the natural sciences and in the social sciences acknowledge that the observer shapes all observations and the meanings she or he attaches to those observations. Thus, all observations regarding human situations that are classified as social problems are fundamentally shaped by who the observer is. Meaning is socially constructed.

For the purpose of integrating the strengths perspective into social policy, it is entirely unnecessary to enter into a lengthy debate about the existence of objective reality. However, it is important for you to understand how reality has been constructed and reconstructed in relation to core social policy issues basic to social work. Many factors, including values, ideology, and past experience, influence our interpretations of reality. The following discussion illustrates how different people interpret the same reality from very different perspectives based on these factors.

The Social Construction of Teen Pregnancy   The policy debate concerning teen pregnancy provides an example of how reality is constructed based on the values and beliefs of the observer. Recall from Chapter 1 that different people identify different causes for this problem. For example, some people define teen pregnancy in terms of moral failure; based on this construction of the problem, they are more likely to argue that abstinence is the only viable solution. In contrast, other people perceive the problem as a failure by our schools to provide adequate sex education; their proposed solution would be to provide teenagers with information about and access to contraceptives. Advocates for the right to abortion might define a pregnancy in terms of lack of access to abortion facilities. For the teen mother herself, the pregnancy may represent a rite of passage to womanhood.

Clearly, our society has not achieved a consensus on the causes of teen pregnancy. Consequently, we have developed often conflicting social policies related to sex education, adoption, child support, and public welfare based on differing views of why teenagers become pregnant. Ultimately, the inability to understand that there is more than one correct way to view this issue limits our capacity to work effectively on behalf of the mother and her child.

The Social Construction of Family Violence   Although there are always differing beliefs within a society, at any given time there can also be widespread agreement, a consensus, about social issues. That consensus in turn shapes the society's responses to those issues. Significantly, however, this consensus also can change over time. As an example of shifting consensus, let's consider an issue of vital concern to social work: domestic violence. Until relatively recent times, violence against family members was widely perceived as the father's prerogative. Indeed, it was the father's duty to keep order in the home, and violence was an acceptable tool with which to accomplish that duty. Over time, however, that consensus changed. Today, a husband who beats his wife is guilty of committing a criminal act.

In many states, however, parents are still allowed to administer the same discipline to a wayward child. In fact, there are undoubtedly a sizable number of people in many U.S. communities whose view of reality supports physical punishment as an essential ingredient of successful child rearing. "Spare the rod and spoil the child" is a maxim many people still live by. Thus, the consensus regarding the physical punishment of children has not changed as dramatically as the consensus regarding the physical punishment of a spouse.

Understanding Different Views of Reality   If you understand that views of reality differ over time as well as among people at any given time, you can begin to see definitions of needs and problems in a new light. People have different perspectives depending on their place in society and therefore interpret the same problem in fundamentally different and often conflicting ways. Defining a problem in a certain way may prevent a person from considering many possible policy alternatives. Armed with these insights, you can ask what motivates particular groups to define needs or problems in a certain way. You can also consider how that definition may shape social policy and lead to positive or negative outcomes for your clients.

Furthermore, certain conceptions of social problems are privileged. Our society gives experts the power to define reality for people. Groups empowered to define social problems in the policy arena because of their positions include political officeholders, religious leaders, lobbyists, media personalities, foundations, and university researchers. Because their opinions are widely circulated, these opinions frequently become accepted by a large segment of the public, including members of the target population themselves. Conversely, the people in need generally are not privileged, and their opinions are often not taken into account when the problem is defined in the policy arena.

Understanding how social problems have been constructed will also help us identify the prevailing causal theories underpinning those definitions of the problems. Policies are supposed to result in intervention either to eliminate the cause or to lessen the consequences of a social problem. However, many times, little or no research has been conducted to support the supposed causal relationship, an issue we will discuss in more detail later in the chapter.

USING STRENGTHS PERSPECTIVE PRINCIPLES TO CONSIDER NEEDS DETERMINATION

In Chapter 1, we discussed strengths perspective principles that you can use as tools to gain a broader perspective on need and to guide your social policy analysis. These principles are presented for your review in Box 5.1. The primary focus of this chapter is on analysis of existing policy so that you can evaluate its merits. We will also discuss how strengths principles can be applied to help you consider alternative and perhaps more effective policy approaches. In this section of the chapter, we will consider how to apply the first two principles. Ways to use the other principles are discussed in subsequent sections.

Strengths perspective principles 1 and 2 assert that (a) social policies should be developed based primarily on analysis of client strengths and goals rather than problems and deficits, and (b) the definition of need should incorporate clients' perspectives. You can apply these principles directly when you analyze the way in which a given policy defined need. Moreover, after you explore the definition of need, these principles can help you consider alternative definitions.

Policies that created high-rise public housing projects are excellent examples of how policy makers addressed a social problem—inadequate housing for low-income people—without considering the way members of the target population understood their needs and goals. If anyone had bothered to ask the low-income families who were inadequately housed, very few would have responded that they want to live on the ninth floor of a high-rise building surrounded by concrete and thousands of other low-income people. However, because policy makers, who likely did not want poor people in their neighborhoods, focused

BOX 5.1

*Principles of
Strengths
Perspective
Policy*

1. The strengths and goals of your clients are legitimate starting places in developing social policy. Problems and deficits should not be given center stage.
2. Given that the definitions of social problems that typically guide policy and program development are socially constructed, our clients' perspectives concerning their problems, needs, strengths, and goals should be part of the social construction of need for policy development.
3. Structural barriers that disadvantage our clients in meeting their needs and create unequal opportunities should be emphasized when claims for the right to benefits and services are made.
4. The strengths perspective is premised on social work values of self-determination and social justice. Claims for benefits and services that allow people to overcome these additional barriers are made based on the right to equal access to resources and opportunities to meet needs and reach goals for citizens regardless of gender, race, age, disability, or other characteristics that have been the basis for denying access.
5. Social policies and programs should build on individual and community strengths and resources and remove structural barriers that disadvantage the target group.
6. The role of the social worker is not that of the expert who helps shape policy for hapless victims. Rather, it is that of the collaborator and resource who helps gain attention for the perspectives of the target group.
7. Social policy goals and design should focus on access, choice, and opportunity that can help empower the target group in meeting its needs and goals. The target group should be involved in all phases of policy development.
8. Evaluation of the efficacy of social policy should include evaluation of outcomes for clients.

Note: These strengths policy principles build on the work of Rapp, Petus, and Goscha, as well as other social workers who are searching for ways to incorporate social work values into the policy development process (Rapp, Petus, & Goscha, in press).

only on the problem, they crafted ineffective, even inhumane, solutions. Although many of the policies we will analyze do not reflect a strengths approach, we can still use a strengths lens to evaluate the policy and determine its merits.

Social workers who utilize a strengths perspective perceive the client group or target population that is the subject of social policy as an interdependent component of the general population (Rapp, Pettus, & Goscha, in press). That is, they focus on how members of the larger society influence and in turn are influenced by the target group. Rather than placing our initial focus on the social problem, we should consider the needs, strengths, and goals of the target population as well as potential community resources.

As you analyze existing policy, you will uncover a variety of interpretations of social needs. However, if you take the time to also think about these strengths principles as part of that analysis, you can begin to recognize instances in which the experiences of the people in need have been distorted due to the historical emphasis on their alleged deficits or pathology. For example, when you analyze existing policies to reduce poverty, you can use these principles to reframe the questions about the causes of poverty. You could ask, "What resources or opportunities are necessary for people in our society to prepare and compete for jobs that will support a family above the poverty level? How many people don't have these opportunities? Why does this happen?"

The answers to these questions and the policy options that they suggest are very different from those that arise from a deficits approach. They require people to consider why people are powerless and to examine which pathways to power are (and are not) available to various groups. Typically, people who are unable to meet their needs do not have access to the same resources and environment as other people. Just as a pathology- and deficits-based approach provides policy makers with an understanding of need that does not lend itself to building on strengths, so a strengths approach provides a focus that does not dwell on individual deficits.

I believe that the past intense focus on deficits has not produced effective solutions for many clients. Therefore, it is time to experiment with a different approach. However, lest we fall into the same mistakes that characterize the deficit-focused approach, it is important to remember that seeking a single cause or truth to explain complex problems such as poverty is too simplistic an approach.

ANALYZING SOCIAL PROBLEMS FROM AN EXPANDED VIEWPOINT

Previous content on defining need and using strengths principles has prepared you to analyze social problems from an expanded viewpoint. Examining the definitions of problems that laid the foundation for policy will help you uncover the assumptions that were made about the people the policy is designed to serve. This section examines social problem analysis and discusses how the strengths principles outlined above can be integrated into that analysis. The problem analysis approach discussed here builds on the work of a number of policy analysts (Chambers, 2000; Gilbert, Specht, & Terrell, 1998; McInnis-Dittrich, 1994).

In order to understand the definition of social problems or needs that shaped a social policy, you need to:

- Examine how the problem or need was defined and documented
- Consider how values and self-interest shaped the definition and documentation

• Determine which causal theories have been developed based on the definition of social problems and what consequences are ascribed to the problem so defined

Defining and Documenting Problems or Needs

To illustrate how a social problem is defined and documented, we will use the example of the Stewart B. McKinney Homeless Assistance Act (P.L. 100-77). This act, sometimes referred to as the McKinney-Vento Homeless Assistance Act, was originally passed in 1987. For brevity, it will be referred to hereafter as the Homeless Assistance Act. If you are not very experienced with legislation, I urge you to take time to examine this act, which you can find at the Web site listed in the margin. I will use elements of this act to illustrate the policy analysis process throughout the chapter, and being familiar with the act will help you understand the policy analysis framework. The Homeless Assistance Act was the first major piece of federal legislation designed to respond to homelessness. Some towns and cities were experiencing difficulties coping with the growing homeless population, had documented the need, and were exerting pressure to have homelessness defined as a national problem.

The Social Work Library

You can review the full text of this legislation and practice using Thomas, a widely used link to legislation, by looking this act up under Public Law 100-77.

To identify the official definition of the need that motivated the legislation, look first at the legislation itself. Sometimes, the legislation contains a section called "general provisions," "legislative intent," or "findings" that provides this information. In the Homeless Assistance Act, you will find information about needs and definitions of homelessness in the first section, General Provisions. This section contains findings that homelessness is a national crisis and that states and localities need federal assistance to deal effectively with this crisis. Because homelessness previously had been considered largely a local problem, redefining it as a national problem was critical to garnering federal resources for local initiatives.

The General Provisions section defines a homeless person as "an individual who lacks a fixed, regular, and adequate nighttime residence; and an individual who has a primary nighttime residence that is a private or public place not designed for, or ordinarily used as, sleeping accommodation for human beings; an institution that provides a temporary residence for individuals intended to be institutionalized; or a supervised publicly or privately operated shelter designed to provide temporary living accommodations (including welfare hotels, congregate shelters, and transitional housing for the mentally ill)" (McKinney-Vento Homeless Assistance Act, 1987). As you can see, the definition of need and the target population can be quite general and open to interpretation at the level at which the legislation is actually implemented.

Of course, as with the other social problems we have discussed, there are alternative definitions of homelessness. The professional literature as well as sources such as homeless shelters and advocacy organizations might define

The Social Work Library

You can view fact sheets from the National Coalition on the Homeless at www.mhhe.com/chapin1. Visit Legislation and Policy.

Web Links

Access the Web site for the National Coalition for the Homeless through the link at www.mhhe.com/chapin1.

homelessness in different ways. For example, the National Coalition for the Homeless provides fact sheets with alternative definitions, and many other resources that are helpful in understanding homelessness.

Once we have defined homelessness, we can count cases in order to document need. However, because different researchers will define the problem in diverse ways, research studies sometimes provide wildly divergent estimates of the size of the homeless population. For example, should a person who has been sleeping on her relative's couch for the last month because her home was destroyed by fire be classified as "homeless"? Obviously, studies that include such cases will generate different numbers compared to studies that exclude such cases. Clearly, then, agreeing on a definition and then counting or documenting the number of homeless people in a given area is not an easy task. However, understanding how the problem or need was defined and documented is a key step in policy analysis.

This analysis of the diverse definitions of homelessness highlights the central point that all social policies—whether their overriding objective is social welfare, social control, or both—are based on socially constructed beliefs concerning people and social conditions (Loeske, 1995). Significantly, need often is not systematically documented until a condition is socially constructed as a problem. In the case of homelessness, for example, until the homeless population began to infringe on the business community, city officials seldom documented the numbers of homeless people. At that point, however, officials became more planful in controlling homeless people, thus initiating the process whereby homelessness was defined as a national problem worthy of federal intervention.

Further, a social condition sometimes goes largely unnoticed by the larger society until it is identified as a problem. For example, emergency room staff can log the number of women injured by their spouses and the police can record the number of domestic violence calls to which they respond, but these numbers will not even be collected and analyzed until the social condition of battered women is labeled and identified as an indication of deviant behavior.

Defining the problem helps in identifying the number of people who have need and can help convince policy makers that they should take action. Focusing on negative outcomes for groups of people, such as higher rates of homelessness for veterans and former foster children or higher rates of poverty and lower life expectancy for people of color, calls attention to social justice issues without depicting the target population as pathological. Information on differential outcomes can often be accessed from statistical reports compiled by the U.S. Census Bureau, from professional literature, and from many Web sites. When analyzing social policies, it is important to have an understanding of the problem that includes the dominant view as well as divergent views.

You also need to question whether the problem or need has been identified in ways that will make it possible to evaluate how outcomes for the target group have changed after policies were implemented. In the Homeless Assistance Act, the defined problem is homelessness. Using a strengths perspective, we can evaluate the effectiveness of this policy in terms of clients' accomplishments in reaching goals. For example, how many formerly homeless people have now acquired adequate permanent housing? However, a second problem identified in the Homeless Assistance Act is lack of coordination of service providers. Outcomes in terms of improved coordination will be harder to document.

Values, Ideologies, and Self-Interest

Examining the values that define a condition as a social problem provides insight into the "should statement" that underlies the perception of that problem. Individualism, self-reliance, and equality are basic values in our culture. Our belief in self-reliance is reflected in the statement that people *should* work and meet their own needs. Should statements are implicit in most descriptions of social problems and in the resulting policies. Parents *should* care for their children. Children *should* have adequate food, clothing, and shelter. Teenagers *should* abstain from sex. Women *should* have equal rights. Look for the should statements in the information you read depicting social problems and social policies. For example, the purpose statement of the Homeless Assistance Act places special emphasis on homeless programs that serve families with children, elderly people, and veterans. These groups historically have been considered the worthy poor who should receive help.

Sometimes an entire body of belief or ideology develops in support of specific values. An ideology may guide a social movement. For example, members of the women's movement work hard to gain widespread acceptance of the should statement that women should have equal rights. They have generated large quantities of research and theory designed to support equal rights for women. Social movements can do a great deal to shape the definition of a problem and to document the problem in ways that reflect their values and ideologies. Self-interest is a strong motivator for people to take part in social movements. Altruism also motivates activism. By examining who wins or loses when a problem is defined in a specific way and the size of the gain or loss, you can often gain insight into which group was able to dominate the problem-definition process.

To draw on an example from the disabilities field, people with disabilities who are living in the community need social services as well as medical services. However, their medical needs garner the vast majority of attention and funding. Physicians' groups, whose members provide that medical care, are very influential in determining which needs receive attention. Social services providers are not as influential. This power imbalance helps explain why medical needs, not social service needs, receive greater attention and funding.

Professional groups, corporations, and myriad advocacy groups all lobby to promote a definition of the need or problem that is in their self-interest. In the case of the Homeless Assistance Act, it was in the interest of states and localities that homelessness be defined as a federal issue, and they lobbied for that outcome. Similarly, social workers themselves often define needs for the target population that can be met by their services. For example, social workers have helped point out the special needs of homeless people who have mental illness and have pressed for policies that provide for outreach and case management services for homeless people who are mentally ill.

Causal Theories

It is necessary to understand the causes and consequences that policy makers attribute to a social problem because the policy is supposed to eliminate the causes or lessen the consequences of that problem. The findings section of the Homeless Assistance Act acknowledged the complex and varying causes of homelessness and the consequences of lack of shelter for different groups, including people with disabilities, families with children, American Indians, elderly people, and veterans.

Further examination of our earlier example of teen pregnancy provides another view of the complex nature of causes and consequences associated with a social problem. Lack of self-control on the part of adolescents, absence of parental supervision, the media, birth control, and the women's movement have all been identified as causes of this problem. The consequences include sexually transmitted diseases, unwanted pregnancies, and abortions. Children who were unwanted and are not well cared for are more likely to become teen parents themselves. Thus, causes and consequences are linked in a circular fashion by which the consequence becomes a cause.

However, consider that, historically, many women have been wives and mothers in their teens. Indeed, in many cultures, this was the expectation, not something to be abhorred. If you are mindful of this history, you can reconsider whether the problem is primarily teen sexuality and how and why societal and familial support of teen sexuality has changed. You can see that the business of determining cause and consequences is difficult, often circular, and can lead to redefinition of the social problem. Further, social policies based on some formulations of cause may create or exacerbate social problems rather than alleviate them. Policies that force schools to begin to exclude information on birth control from sex education efforts may lead to increases in teen pregnancy.

Although a variety of causes and related interventions for a social problem may have been identified, adequate research to support the supposed causal chain and interventions frequently has not been conducted. Acknowledging this deficiency, researchers are now working hard to develop connections among problem, intervention, and outcome. Significantly, groups who are the subject of research are increasingly being actively engaged in the research process. As one example, researchers are asking people who have successfully overcome a problem such as substance abuse how they did so and how other people can best be supported in these efforts. Other researchers are asking people who are still addicted to help identify the barriers to recovery. Involving the target population in the research is consistent with the strengths principle that people are experts on their own needs and goals, and this approach helps focus attention on successful strategies, even at the point of needs determination.

Some policies you will analyze reflect strengths-based thinking more clearly than others but may have elements that are not strengths-based and may have unintended negative consequences. However, when the goals of the target group are ignored and the primary emphasis is on meeting societal goals that continue to keep target members powerless, a policy is clearly not strengths-based. Remember, social polices can change. The voices of people in need can lead to revision of policies. You will learn how you can help encourage this process in Chapter 6.

Claimsmaking

We now move our focus from analysis of problems and needs to the claims-making process. Claimsmaking connects the social problem or needs assessment and the resulting social policy. Even if policy makers agree that a need exists, they may not necessarily agree that the need deserves to be met. Instead, a compelling claim for resources must be made. Recall from Chapter 1 that claimsmaking is the process that promotes recognition of a social condition as deserving of action by policy makers. Examples of claimsmaking are holding a demonstration to demand equal rights for Latinos or lobbying a member of Congress to provide prescription drugs for older adults.

The Various Bases of Claimsmaking Claims can be made on a variety of bases. In some cases, claims are based on rights. For example, women could make a claim of domestic violence only after they won the right to be considered more than the property of their husbands. The claim of domestic violence is based on the assumption that spouses do not have the right to batter each other.

Other bases for claims include comparative disadvantage and, more broadly, an appeal for social justice. The claim may be made that public schools should provide free breakfasts for children from low-income families because these children are at a disadvantage when trying to learn on empty stomachs. Further, consider how claims are made on behalf of elders and children in general. Advocates for both groups claim that we should help elders and children because they are a part of our community and we are responsible for their well-being. This claim reflects our belief in social justice. In addition, we can make a further claim for children based on utility. Specifically, if we don't invest in our children, they won't be competent to take on important roles in our society, and we will all suffer. For elders, we can make a claim based on reciprocity. This population worked hard, fought our wars, and raised children. Now, they deserve to rest and receive our care. It is not only the need that propels action. It is the claim that the policy-making entity has a responsibility to meet the need based on values held in common or, more typically, based on claims of utility in combination with appeals based on values.

Returning to the Homeless Assistance Act, it is clear from the findings section that successful claims for federal involvement on behalf of homeless children and elders as well as other groups were made in order to get the law passed. For legislation in general, information concerning the bases for claims-making often can be found in the initial sections of the law. Articles in journals around the time legislation was being developed as well as current publications that discuss the legislation are also good sources for this information.

Assumptions Embedded in Claimsmaking   Claimsmaking is complex and nuanced. When you are considering claimsmaking, it is important for you to be aware of the assumptions embedded in the claim. For example, a claim for spending on older adults based on their deserving rest and care for past contributions will likely promote policies that increase funding for nursing homes rather than encourage employment opportunities. Keep in mind, however, that the population of adults ages 65 to 74 will bulge in the coming years. These individuals are often healthy enough to work and may need to work to pay their bills. Therefore, they will have a greater need for policies that support older workers and lessen age discrimination than for more retirement facilities. Consequently, advocates will have to craft a new claim that identifies the structural barriers confronting older workers and emphasizes the importance of removing those barriers.

We observed earlier that claimsmaking is often based on rights. Significantly, successful claimsmaking can also result in the establishment of rights. For example, eligible older adults now have the right to health care through Medicare and can take legal action if Medicare refuses to pay for covered care. Examining how such successful claims were structured, limited, and promoted helps us understand current policy and enact future policies.

When a claim is made that a need deserves to be met, it must compete for resources with other claims that may be more compelling. For example, since the terrorist attacks of 9/11, claims for increased spending on defense have been much more successful than claims for greater social spending. In earlier chapters, we examined key factors that influence whether claimsmaking succeeds and social policy is enacted. For example, the economy influences the definition of social problems and also the amount of resources available to address these problems. Similarly, history provides precedents and sets the stage for policies to emerge. Of course, politics influences who has power and who does not. Values and ideologies fuel social movements that press claims for certain policies. The interplay among these factors shapes both the claimsmaking process and the social policy that is developed.

As an example, recall our discussion of the Social Security Act of 1935 in Chapter 3, which explained how economic conditions during the Depression increased public acceptance of an expanded federal role in promoting social welfare. In addition, policy makers felt pressure to reduce the chance of the political upheaval that might be fueled by emerging social movements such as the Townsend Movement. Members of the Townsend Movement pressed the claim that people who had worked all their lives should not become paupers in their old age. In addition, people were living longer, which meant that they needed greater financial support in their post-retirement years. Finally, there were historical precedents for such intervention in the form of government-funded pensions for war veterans. The interplay among all these factors propelled passage of the landmark Social Security Act.

As you analyze the development of the major social policies that shape your practice, consider how the interplay of these key factors shaped the original policies and continues to shape efforts at reform. Articles in social work journals related to your area of practice often provide this background.

Using Strengths Perspective Principles to Consider the Claimsmaking Process
After you explore the claimsmaking process for a particular policy, use strengths perspective principles 3 and 4 (see Box 5.1) to help you evaluate the extent to which claims are strengths-focused. The principles essentially state that claims should (a) emphasize the structural barriers that prevent clients from meeting their needs and (b) reflect the basic social work values of self-determination and social justice. If you determine that a claim does not meet these criteria, then you should consider alternative claimsmaking approaches that incorporate a strengths perspective.

A FRAMEWORK FOR POLICY ANALYSIS

In the previous section, we explored how the processes of need analysis and claimsmaking shape existing policy. You will need to keep the link between these processes in mind as we continue our exploration of the steps in policy analysis. These steps can be thought of as a framework made up of specific elements to help structure our analysis. Examining policies and programs using a policy and program analysis framework will help you determine why a policy is effective or ineffective.

Scholars have developed a variety of frameworks for the purpose of policy analysis (Chambers, 2000; Dobelstein, 1996; Gilbert & Terrell, 2001; Popple & Leighninger, 1998). These frameworks as well as others vary extensively in terms of their length, focus, and intent. Some focus on key policy elements, others on the historical context of the policy, and still others on understanding the problem. When you are analyzing a policy or program, it is easy to become overwhelmed by the vast quantity of information that you can access. The framework presented here is an excellent and relatively simple way to begin analyzing policy. It draws on common elements shared by many of the frameworks. These elements focus on the essentials of policies and programs. They include:

- Policy goals

- Benefits and services

- Eligibility rules

- Service delivery systems

- Financing

 **The Social Work Library**

If you would like to examine and compare different frameworks, you can go to www.mhhe.com/chapin1, where various frameworks are outlined.

Most frameworks focus at least in part on certain elements needed to implement and evaluate a policy such as those presented by Chambers (2000) and discussed in more detail in this section. Frameworks vary greatly in their emphasis on strengths, but as a social worker with a general understanding of the strengths perspective, you can use these frameworks and the strengths perspective to analyze both social policies and programs.

The following section will familiarize you with the policy elements listed above. The discussion of factors to consider when analyzing each element also builds on selected portions of Chambers's analytical framework, which can be viewed at the link provided in the margin note (Chambers, 2000).

After you become proficient at using the basic framework presented here, you may want to consider a variety of frameworks in more detail and begin to determine for yourself which elements and aspects of policy are most important when you are analyzing policies. For now, the framework presented here is easy to remember and will serve you well as a starting point.

Also, as you utilize this framework, you can use strengths perspective principles 5, 7, and 8, from Box 5.1, to evaluate the extent to which policy and program goals, benefits and services, eligibility rules, service delivery systems, and financing reflect attention to client and community strengths. In regard to policy analysis, these principles affirm that social policies should (a) help remove structural barriers that limit your clients' full participation in the life of the community; (b) emphasize access, choice, and opportunities for clients that can lead to empowerment; and (c) be evaluated in terms of client outcomes. Note that principle 5 builds on principle 3, which focuses on claimsmaking based on structural disadvantages your clients face, in that principle 5 asserts that social policies should help remove these structural barriers.

Policy Goals and Objectives

When analyzing a policy, it is essential to examine its goal and how the policy might alleviate the identified need or problem or achieve a desired condition. A **policy goal** is a statement of the desired human condition or social environment that is expected to result from implementation of the policy. A goal helps you understand what a policy is supposed to accomplish. For example, a goal of the legislation that established the Special Supplemental Nutrition Program for Women, Infants, and Children (WIC) is to safeguard the health of low-income women, infants, and children up to age five who are at risk of poor nutrition (Food and Nutrition Service, 2003).

Goals may be stated in general or abstract terms. In contrast, objectives spell out in more detail what is to be accomplished. Social policies often establish social programs. Objectives provide more specific detail about services and outcomes on which programs are evaluated so that program administrators can determine how to proceed. They are specific statements that operationalize desired outcomes. Several different objectives may be developed for the same goal. For example, one objective for the WIC policy discussed above is to increase the birth weight of infants in low-income families. Another objective is to increase breast-feeding among the mothers enrolled in the program. In the latter case, if the objective specifies a desired percentage of increase, then it provides a specific statement of expected outcome by which to evaluate the program's effectiveness.

Locating Goals and Objectives   As with claims and the definition of needs, the goals and objectives for a particular policy are often found in the preamble or general provisions of the enabling legislation. You can also look into the legislative history that contains the background material legislative committees use in framing the legislation. Law school libraries and the public document centers of university libraries have copies of legislative background information and well-versed librarians who will guide you to specific sources. In the case of state legislation, state legislative libraries are good sources of background information. In addition, many states have legislative library hotlines staffed by knowledgeable librarians who can help you find this material. Descriptions of programs, available from agencies that administer the programs created by the policy, also provide information on policy goals, and legislation is now easily accessed online.

Referring once again to the Homeless Assistance Act, you will find the goals in the General Provisions section under Purpose. The goals are to create the Interagency Council on the Homeless, to allocate funds and public resources, and to institute programs for meeting the needs of the homeless population in a more coordinated manner.

Manifest and Latent Goals   Goals can be both manifest and latent. **Manifest goals** typically are publicly stated, whereas **latent goals** are not. Latent goals may be intended by some of the policy makers, but they are often goals on which it would be difficult to achieve consensus or that would not be considered socially acceptable. Consequently, it is easier not to state them explicitly. For example, a manifest goal of the Homeless Assistance Act is to provide funding for services for homeless people; a latent goal may be social control of homeless people so that they don't interfere with shoppers.

When you examine the goals and objectives of a policy or program, you need to determine whether the goal is clearly stated, measurable, and concerned with ends rather than means. The goal of increased coordination in the Homeless Assistance Act is concerned with the means of meeting the needs of the homeless population rather than the end of reducing homelessness. Although increased coordination may lead to a reduction of homelessness, when the stated goal is concerned with the means of reaching a goal, people can lose sight of the end goal and instead evaluate outcomes in terms of how many coordinating meetings were held rather than how many citizens are no longer homeless. Measuring and documenting increased coordination may also be difficult. However, the Purpose section of the legislation also contains the stated goal of meeting the needs of the homeless.

In addition, you should consider whether the goals can be accomplished by the activities prescribed by the policy. For example, one possible manifest goal of a program that promotes adequate nutrition for pregnant mothers is to improve the health status of their babies. Activities designed to achieve that goal, which could be specified in the policy, include identifying and distributing food and information that would help safeguard the health of both the mothers and their children. We could measure success in accomplishing this goal by comparing the percentages of low-birth-weight babies born before and after the policy was implemented in a specified area.

In contrast, if the specified goals and activities had been simply to distribute surplus food to pregnant women and children, program administrators could just distribute any surplus food rather than food and information that would improve the health of the target population. Under these circumstances, evaluation of the program would focus on how much food was distributed rather than the health of the mothers and their children. From a strengths perspective, it is important for us to examine what outcomes will result for clients if the goal is attained.

Incorporating Clients' Perspectives   Typically, the goal of the policy as well as the type of intervention the policy prescribes are determined by policy makers who may not possess expertise in the underlying issue. In such cases, the policy makers turn to "experts" who often don't provide the perspective of the target population. As we discussed earlier in the chapter, these experts frequently are members of privileged or higher-status groups who may have little knowledge of the clients' reality. Failure to incorporate the clients' perspective often leads to the adoption of inappropriate and ineffective goals (Rapp, Pettus, & Goscha, in press).

For example, people with developmental disabilities who want a decent job may instead have received a lifetime of "vocational training" at a developmental achievement center because the prescribed policy goal was to provide them with such training. Not coincidentally, this goal reflected the input of experts who ran the centers. In contrast, a policy developed using the strengths perspective would reflect the clients' goals of securing and maintaining a paying job. Although vocational training can certainly help people build on their strengths, when it becomes an end in itself rather than a means to attaining a paying job, many clients would not endorse vocational training as an appropriate end goal.

Benefits or Services Provided

Another component of social policies and programs that should be examined is the benefits or services provided by the policy or program. Benefits and services can include food stamps, counseling services, job coaching, a Social Security check, and the opportunity to vote. In certain cases, the benefits may be stigmatizing. For example, school systems sometimes provide vouchers that can be presented at specific local department stores to purchase back-to-school clothing. If the clothing voucher clearly marks the shopper as indigent, the child may feel ashamed and become stigmatized.

Analyzing benefits and services from a strengths perspective leads to a number of questions: Is the benefit or service designed to remove societal barriers that prevent people from meeting their needs? Alternatively, does the benefit or service focus primarily on correcting the behavior of the target population? How much consumer choice is allowed? Cash provides the most choice; however, if a service is unavailable, cash does not help. For example, if children with disabilities need therapeutic preschools and none are available, then the service must be developed to address the need.

The strengths perspective also raises the question of whether the benefits or services take into account the strengths and resources of the community. For example, policies may prescribe that nutrition programs for seniors serve a uniform menu across the city. Alternatively, they may permit local groups to develop different menus that comply with nutrition guidelines. Cooks who make the ethnic dishes long favored by elders in the community could be hired and consulted in developing a healthful menu built on their talents. A policy could also set nutrition guidelines, and permit different communities to figure out how best to meet them without requiring uniform menus. In the case of the Homeless Assistance Act, funds are provided to a wide variety of programs that assist homeless people. Such an approach makes it possible to build on existing community resources and tailor programs to the community. On the negative side, however, the quality of the programs funded by the act will also vary widely.

Finally, it is crucial to evaluate whether the benefit or service will alleviate the identified need and result in positive outcomes for your clients. For example, when the goal is to reduce drug use among teenagers and the service provided is a rack of pamphlets in each high school warning against drug use, the policy will probably be ineffective.

Eligibility Rules

Eligibility rules stipulate who receives the benefit or service. Some rules require that people may receive benefits only if they have made prior contributions. For example, Social Security retirement benefits are available only to workers who have been employed in a covered job and have paid into the system for the required amount of time; spouses of qualified workers are also eligible for certain benefits. Other benefits are available based on attachment to the workforce and do not require employee contribution. For example, workers' compensation is funded by employers. As a social worker, you should always consider social justice and equity issues when you examine eligibility rules. For example, women historically have been disadvantaged when eligibility for public benefits was based on attachment to the workforce because they were less likely than men to have held paid jobs. Similarly, people of color were less likely to have worked in jobs that provide Social Security benefits.

The eligibility rules for many of the services and benefits received by your clients require a means test. For example, many policies provide for financial aid only to people who have income and assets below a certain level. In addition, some policies require functional need as well as financial need. For example, older adults can receive Medicaid funding for nursing facility care only if they have exhausted their financial resources and are also severely functionally impaired. Means tests can be stigmatizing and can discourage people in need from applying for services. At the same time, however, benefits provided with less stringent eligibility rules may lead to overwhelming cost. In the case of the Homeless Assistance Act, programs that serve the homeless population and meet other specified requirements are eligible for funding, and the definition of homelessness is specified in the law.

Eligibility rules may also be based on judicial decisions. For example, a judge can rule that a family should receive services designed to prevent further child abuse. Similarly, a teen may be assigned to probation during which he will receive the services of a probation officer. In addition, many health and mental health benefits require that licensed professionals certify the need for services. Although there typically are rules or guidelines, professionals, such as physicians, nurses, and social workers, have some discretion in deciding who will receive services.

When considering eligibility rules from a strengths perspective, you should examine the structure of these rules to determine if they create incentives for people to develop their capacity to meet their own needs. At the same time, you should ask whether such positive steps could result in loss of benefits. For example, do low-income parents automatically become ineligible for a day care subsidy if they manage to land higher-paying jobs?

Service Delivery Systems

The system for delivering services or benefits also influences policy effectiveness. Therefore, any comprehensive policy analysis includes an examination of the delivery system. Remember that services can be delivered by public or private agencies. In addition, publicly funded services can be provided by private institutions supervised by public agencies. For example, the publicly funded Medicaid program pays for long-term care health services that are often provided by private church-affiliated nursing facilities. Similarly, Medicaid-funded acute health care is often provided by private hospitals that are regulated by public agencies.

Services can be delivered in a variety of ways, for example, by social workers in a hospital, nursing facility, or family service center or by case managers working in a senior center. Taking advantage of modern technology, social workers are now experimenting with delivering services such as support groups online. In addition, certain benefits, such as Social Security payments, can be delivered through direct bank deposit or the U.S. mail.

As is true of the other topics we have examined, the delivery system can be examined from a strengths perspective. To do this, you need to consider whether the service delivery system is designed to build on assets that already exist in the community, such as schools, churches, medical services, and community centers. Alternatively, does the delivery system create separate structures for serving the target population? For example, separate schools and recreation facilities can be set up for people with disabilities, or, instead, existing schools and recreation facilities can be modified so that people with disabilities can use them. History has illustrated again and again that separate structures are inherently unequal.

Further consider whether a service delivery system offers clients choice. For example, food stamps allow people to shop in a variety of grocery stores. Alternatively, clients could be required to receive the service in only one place. Historically, people had to go to a surplus-food distribution site to receive publicly subsidized food benefits.

Service delivery systems should be staffed by workers who reflect the ethnic diversity found within the target population, and services should be accessible to people of all ethnic backgrounds. For example, locating a program in an all-white neighborhood that does not have public transportation will limit access to that service by low-income people of color who don't have other transportation. Of course, policies can be designed to require service delivery systems that are not accessible to certain groups, to change the way they provide services. However, most policies focus change efforts on the individual clients rather than on problems in the service delivery system.

The most important question to ask when evaluating the effectiveness of a service delivery system is "Can this system deliver services or benefits in a cost-effective manner that achieves the desired outcomes for clients?" It is crucial that we always return to the question of outcomes for clients. However, attention to outcomes must be coupled with attention to cost-effectiveness. Cost-effectiveness is critical to policy makers who will determine whether to continue the policy or program, and it is important in evaluating overall effectiveness.

Financing

Another important element of any policy or program is the method by which it is financed. Chapter 4 provides a detailed discussion of funding for social welfare programs, including the difference between private and public funding and funding of programs by different levels of government. You need to consider the sources of funding when you analyze a social policy or program so that you may determine its stability and adequacy. When funding is not ensured from year to year, the result can be chaos for staff and clients. Entitlements have the most year-to-year stability. However, as seen with the abolition of Aid to Families with Dependent Children (AFDC) in 1996, even publicly funded entitlements can be eliminated. Public funding generally provides more stable and adequate funding than do other sources. In contrast, because private funding is dependent on voluntary giving, stability and adequacy will fluctuate depending on the givers.

Recall that certain publicly funded programs, such as the Social Security retirement program, are based on the insurance principle and require prior contributions. Other public programs, such as Temporary Aid for Needy Families (TANF), are funded through general revenue appropriations that specify how tax dollars are to be spent. Some public programs are funded totally through taxes collected at the federal level, others are funded solely with state revenues, and still others are funded with a combination of federal and state monies. In the case of the programs funded through the Homeless Assistance Act, federal funds are made available to augment state, local, and private funds.

Programs can also be funded by out-of-pocket payments made by the people who receive the service. For example, a religious denomination might institute a day care program that requires parents to pay for the service out of pocket. Clients also may pay privately for counseling.

When analyzing financing strategies, it is also important to consider how providers of services are reimbursed or paid, whether by public or private sources. If service providers are paid the same amount regardless of the outcome for clients, then they have less incentive to attain the policy goals. For this reason, the reimbursement system should support the policy goals. Again, social workers should focus on the outcome for their clients. We will discuss the impact of reimbursement systems on policy and program effectiveness in more detail in coming chapters.

CONCLUSION

Each element of the policy and program analysis framework explained above must be examined in order to determine how it contributes to overall effectiveness. Cost-effectiveness and outcomes for clients should be evaluated for each element. Such evaluation is very useful in determining the merit of a policy or program and in convincing policy makers that the program should continue to receive funding or should be modified.

You can utilize the insights gained from the framework for analysis and the discussion of needs determination and claimsmaking presented in this chapter to evaluate any social policy or program. Your analysis may identify areas in which policies and programs can be improved, and it may also demonstrate that certain policies result in negative outcomes for clients. For example, eligibility rules that limit TANF payments to five years will most certainly create hardships for children whose parents have not been able to find stable, long-term employment. As a professional social worker, you will be expected to be capable of judging the merits of existing policies and programs and advocating for more effective policies.

MAIN POINTS

- There are multiple ways of viewing social problems or needs. The way in which the problem or need is framed will greatly influence the policy solutions developed.

- Understanding how a problem is defined and documented, focusing on how values, ideologies, and self-interest influence policy, and examining what causal theories have been developed based on the definition of social problems provide the foundation for effective policy analysis.

- Strengths-based policy analysis asks questions that seek to identify the needs of people as well as their strengths, goals, and resources in order to guide future policy and program development.

- The goals, strengths, and resources of the people who are experiencing the problem or need (the target population) should be clearly reflected in the definition of need.

- Claimsmaking is the process of promoting recognition of a social condition as deserving of action by policy makers. In addition to recognized need, there must be a successful claim made for societal responsibility and action to meet that need before social policy will be enacted.

- Claims can be based on rights, comparative disadvantage, and appeals for social justice.

- A strengths-based policy and program analysis framework focusing on the following areas can help determine effectiveness: policy or program goals, benefits or services provided, eligibility rules, service delivery system, and financing.

EXERCISES: PRACTICING SOCIAL WORK

Working with the Sanchez Family

Immigration policy influences the Sanchez family in multiple ways. Examine how people interested in immigration reform are engaging in claimsmaking to get policies changed. On what basis are they asserting that policies need to change—human rights, comparative disadvantage, or social justice? Are member of the target group actively involved in this process? Give examples.

Working with the Black Feather Community

Analyze the No Child Left Behind legislation included in the Resources section of the Black Feather case.

1. What are the goals of the legislation?

2. How is it financed?

Read the article by the National Indian Education Association, *No Child Left Behind in Indian Country* available at: www.mhhe.com/chapin1.

1. Do you think this legislation reflects a strengths approach to working with indigenous communities?

2. What changes to the No Child Left Behind legislation do you think are needed to make it more effective for Native American students?

EXERCISES: THE SOCIAL WORK LIBRARY

Values and Self-interest

Read "Value differences between social workers and members of the working and middle classes" (Hodge, 2003), and respond to the following:

1. As you read through Hodge's article on value differences, think about the issues that were addressed in this study. What are your values regarding the particular social issues discussed?

2. How do you think the government should prioritize current spending areas discussed in this article?

3. What factors do you think influence the value differences discussed in the article?

4. How do you think these value differences may be reflected in policy?

Claimsmaking

Read "Claimsmakers in the child sexual abuse 'wars': Who are they and what do they want?" (Mildred, 2003), and respond to the following:

1. Claimsmakers are instrumental in defining social problems and gaining support for policy change. Mildred's article suggests claimsmakers can be viewed on a continuum. Explain what she means.

2. Given the differences in viewpoints and ideas for change expressed by various claimsmakers, how is it possible to decide what policy to implement?

OTHER EXERCISES

1. Go to www.mhhe.com/chapin1 for a link to a site that contains detailed information about how to access legislation. This Web link will be a valuable resource as you analyze each stage of the policy and program analysis framework.

2. The Special Supplemental Nutrition Program for Women, Infants, and Children (WIC) Web site has a section that illustrates how research has been done to determine cost-effectiveness and outcomes for clients. Go to www.mhhe.com/chapin1 for a link, and then examine this material to get a firsthand look at policy and program evaluations.

CHAPTER 6

Social Policy Development and Policy Practice

> *While there is no guarantee that democracies will act rationally in formulating their social policies, it is also abundantly clear that they cannot even be expected to do so unless they are made aware of the full implications of the choices available to them.*
>
> —EVELINE M. BURNS, 1956

POLICY DEVELOPMENT MAY SEEM LIKE A MYSTERIOUS PROCESS; however, it is a process you can come to understand and even influence. Policy development is the process by which policies are created and implemented in order to meet identified need. The purpose of policy practice is to influence this process. As we discussed in the previous chapter, policies can be designed to build on strengths and reflect the goals of the target group.

In this chapter, we first explore the process of policy development in detail, examining the different steps in that process. We then focus explicitly on the ways in which social workers can intervene in that process. Many of the ideas on policy practice we will discuss in this chapter were briefly introduced in Chapter 1. In addition, we will explore various ways that social workers engaged in policy practice can use the strengths principles discussed in the previous chapter to shape social policy. If you think a policy is serving your clients poorly, then you can help change it.

STEPS IN POLICY DEVELOPMENT

We have already examined some of the steps in policy development in the context of policy analysis. The policy development process differs from the policy analysis process in that emphasis shifts from analyzing each element of an existing policy to examining the steps in the process of developing new policy or revising existing policy. However, an analysis of policy alternatives is part of the policy development process. Therefore, you can apply the ability to analyze need and existing policies, which you developed in Chapter 5, to understand policy development.

The list presented below provides an overview of the components of the policy development process and also incorporates material covered in earlier chapters. Each component includes information on how the strengths perspective can be integrated into that component. We will examine these components in greater detail in the next part of the chapter.

- **Define needs or social problem and strengths.** Definitions are viewed as negotiated. The perspectives of the target group should be included in defining goals and strengths as well as in identifying needs and structural barriers to meeting needs.

- **Document need, strengths, and goals.** Measure the amount of needs, the dimensions of structural barriers, and the clients' strengths and goals.

- **Identify initial policy goals.** Clients' goals are privileged, that is, information on client goals should explicitly be sought out and given careful consideration.

- **Engage in claimsmaking.** Claimsmaking is based on the right to self-determination and social justice necessary for people to meet their goals.

- **Negotiate definition of policy goals.** Work with policy makers to ensure that they include the clients' goals when developing policy goals.

- **Legitimize policy goals with the public.** Building public consensus is key. Publicize information on the opportunities and resources necessary for people to meet their goals.

- **Formulate policy alternatives that meet established goals.** Identify ways in which barriers to reaching goals are currently overcome by clients (strengths) and through programs (best practice). Formulate policy informed by consumer collaboration. In addition, assess workability at this stage. Evaluate the various elements of the proposed policy alternatives using the policy analysis framework presented in Chapter 5.

- **Develop, enact, and implement the policy or program.** Policy and program design and implementation should be informed by consumer involvement.

- **Evaluate outcomes.** Evaluation and assessment should emphasize client outcomes and client feedback to improve policy.

Determining Need and Making Claims

Determining needs and making claims based on those needs form the foundation for the policy development process. Chapter 5 detailed ways in which needs were defined and claims made for existing policies. This chapter highlights what can be added when developing new social policy or reforming existing policy using the strengths perspective. Adopting a strengths-based approach enables policy makers to shift their focus from what has typically been done in the past to alternative strategies. One example of how to shift focus is by identifying assets in the community to aid in policy development. Most impoverished communities have been the subject of numerous needs assessments that emphasize deficits such as unemployment rates, low rates of homeownership, school dropout rates, and crime rates. However, their many assets, such as community associations, businesses, agencies, and community leaders, have not been assessed as carefully as their needs. Neither have the myriad barriers that prevent members of the target group from meeting their goals and needs. For example, in low-income communities, access to banking services such as home loans is often limited. Assessing needs, strengths, and barriers provides information that supports a claim for assistance in overcoming barriers that other people might not face.

Further, the people engaging in needs assessment typically identify initial policy goals early in the needs assessment and claimsmaking processes because these individuals generally have some idea of the types of policies that they expect to champion. For example, if civic leaders have noted a lack of after-school activities and increasing gang membership, they may propose a policy to provide funding for after-school programs through the park and recreation departments. It is important to scrutinize policy goals from the beginning to ensure that they include the goals of the client group. In the case of the after-school program, asking the young people in the community directly about their needs—about preferred location and activities and involving them in the policy development process—will make it much more likely that any program that is developed will be well attended. We will consider methods for making these assessments in the policy practice segment of this chapter.

Groups Involved in Needs Determination and Claimsmaking   Major policies are rarely crafted quickly. Rather, they generally emerge from a process of development. Typically, there are a variety of provider groups, client groups, and advocacy groups who have identified needs, are engaging in claimsmaking, and are trying to provide direction for policy development. These groups may be operating independently and even in opposition to one another. Particular groups may have identified specific policy makers to champion their cause. For example, in the legislative arena, an advocacy group for people with developmental disabilities may be working closely with a senator who has a son who is developmentally disabled. Similarly, a service provider group that owns independent living facilities may have the ear of a legislator who formerly owned such facilities.

On the executive or agency side, a retired inspector of independent living facilities may now be lobbying on behalf of a client group with his former agency colleagues, who likely will be involved in drafting any legislation that involves such facilities. There also may be researchers associated with national organizations such as the Child Welfare League of America or with universities that have conducted research on best practices for people with developmental disabilities and are publicizing information on client needs and making recommendations for policy initiatives.

Legislators bring varying amounts of expertise on different subjects to policy making. For example, they may be very familiar with transportation needs because of their careers in the trucking business but might know little about social services. In such cases, they turn to people they know who possess expertise on the subject. However, they receive input on a huge variety of policy initiatives. Legislators are being pressed to enact agricultural policy, water standards, educational reform, and many other initiatives of importance to their constituents. Pleas for increases in social services will have to vie with many competing claims for the legislator's attention.

The Legislative Agenda Fundamentally, claimsmakers who want legislation enacted must compete to get on the legislative agenda. The term *agenda,* as used here, means "the list of subjects or problems to which government officials, and people outside of government closely associated with those officials, are paying some serious attention at any given time" (Kingdon, 2003, p. 3). Claims for attention from policy makers must compete with many other claims that may be more compelling. The policy practice section of this chapter contains a detailed discussion of methods for garnering policy makers' attention to your clients' needs and goals.

In many cases, the groups involved in claimsmaking described earlier might already be considering areas in which policy making is needed. They might even be in the process of drafting legislation. In a sense, these issues already are on the legislator's agenda. However, in order for the issue to progress to the point that a bill is introduced and acted upon, it somehow will need to move to what is termed the "decision agenda" (Kingdon, 2003). We will explore a real-life example of getting on the agenda later in the chapter.

A problem or need must press on the policy maker in some way in order to attract sufficient attention to move to the decision agenda. For example, if the media are covering a problem or need and advocating for change, then there may be pressure for change. Public opinion also influences the policy agenda. A crisis may help focus attention. For example, when the state's news media report that an older nursing home resident wandered away and died of exposure due to inadequate staff oversight, a public clamor for more stringent regulation of nursing facility staffing levels might arise. At this point, perceptions can be influenced by providing policy makers with information on the need for more adequate staffing. In fact, if specialists have accumulated knowledge about the need and best practice, this may be the time that the information will be used.

Elections have an influence on which issues move to the decision-making agenda. For example, a politician who promises to work to restrict access to abortion will press to get attention for reforming abortion regulations if elected. Similarly, constituents who contribute financially to a legislator's campaign or otherwise help the legislator get elected will generally receive greater attention to legislative issues they want on the agenda than other people or groups will.

The process by which a policy issue moves to the decision agenda influences the resulting policy. For example, public outrage may prompt rapid action. However, if the public is convinced that an emergency exists, then policy changes to deal with the specific emergency may be enacted quickly without sufficient attention to underlying problems.

It should be clear by now that policy development is not a technical, step-by-step process. Rather, it tends to be messy and inexact. Many individuals and groups participate in the process. When input from these different groups converges at a time when policy makers are open to considering initiatives in that particular area, then policy can be developed or changed.

Initial Steps in Policy Development: A Summary   To review and help you understand the policy development process, the components we have discussed thus far are listed below:

- Need must be determined. Information on strengths, needs, goals, and assets of the target group can also inform policy development. Initial policy goals are typically formulated during this stage.

- A claim for attention must be developed.

- Claimsmakers must get access to key policy makers.

- Pressure and direction for policy change from a sufficient number of key actors must converge to place the issue on the agenda.

- There must be a window of opportunity when other, more pressing policy issues aren't higher on the decision agenda. At this point, if there is sufficient consensus, new policy will be made or current policy reformed.

Finally, remember that the policy development process is not linear. For example, a person who will become a claimsmaker may have access to a key policy maker before the claim is developed. In fact, that access might be the reason why that individual will be asked to help out. As an example, family members of legislators and other elected officials frequently are asked to help promote education or conservation initiatives.

Crafting Policy Goals

Crafting policy goals includes negotiating the definition of policy goals with policy makers and legitimizing policy goals with the public. Once goals are determined, various policy alternatives that meet the established goals can be formulated and evaluated. The ideas of key actors about potential ways to meet needs and reach goals typically emerge as the need-identification and claims-making process develops. Remember, key actors are those individuals and groups who hold significant power to influence policy making by virtue of their position, political influence, or expertise. They include elected officials, agency staff, advocacy groups, and researchers. Of course, the target group for the policy also should be recognized as having expertise by virtue of their lived experience. However, this expertise is often not acknowledged. The goals and ideas of clients are less likely to be heard unless advocates work to get attention for their perspectives.

Additionally, policy makers at the local, state, and national levels might be working on the same policy issues largely unaware of initiatives under way at other levels. All of these groups may be defining policy goals very differently. These diverse ideas and definitions of policy goals may surface during the policy development process.

Achieving Consensus   Consensus among groups sufficient to get new policies enacted must somehow be developed. Different key actors often hold quite diverse goals. For example, groups pressing for more services for people with developmental disabilities may all agree on the general policy goal of more public support for these people. However, some groups may advocate more funds for independent living facilities, whereas other groups favor family-directed care available in the home.

Often, interviewing key actors and policy makers about their views of the problem and the particular policy options they are considering makes it possible to identify policy goals and options on which consensus may be reached. For example, when research companies are hired by states to help craft policies, they typically conduct extensive interviews with key actors early in the process. They particularly target **stakeholders,** those people who likely will experience either substantial gain or loss as a result of the policy change. So people working to craft policy goals typically perform a thorough literature review and are knowledgeable about potential goals and solutions, and they also can contact key stakeholders influential with legislators who may suggest solutions and then become vested in seeing a policy initiative implemented. This strategy may make passage of the policy much more likely. Although the major purpose of such interviews is to listen to stakeholders, these interviews can also be used to provide information about how members of the client group understand their needs and define their goals. My experience and the experience of many seasoned policy makers I interviewed is that policy proposals that actually get implemented usually incorporate a variety of ideas that one person or even a small group of people would not have developed. It is easier to craft policy goals and options around which consensus may develop when you are familiar with stakeholders' opinions and goals.

In addition, achieving consensus on policy goals is easier if the goals are general. For example, most policy makers would agree that it is important to have healthy babies. However, details such as the type and amount of assistance their mothers should receive will be more contentious. As we have discussed, self-interest, wealth and political power, values, and social movements can all influence policy goals. In addition, public opinion influences the passage of social policy. Although social policies sometimes are passed with little public attention, widespread public opposition to policy goals can help defeat a social policy. Advocacy groups and the media involved in the claimsmaking process can help legitimize policy goals with the public.

Utilizing the Strengths Perspective   The strengths perspective mandates that efforts to develop public consensus and legitimize policy goals include assertive outreach to client groups. Public hearings are often held to get feedback on proposed policies and to lend legitimacy to the policies that ultimately are passed. Clients could provide feedback, but without support such as transportation and help in preparation, they might be unable to attend these hearings. The media may be open to presenting the clients' perspectives on their needs and the most effective ways to help them meet those needs but often lack insight into these perspectives. Social workers can help clients make their voices heard by assisting with transportation and preparation and by encouraging members of the media to expand their perspectives and expose themselves to the whole story.

Examining the Workability of Policy Alternatives

A great many potential solutions to problems may be vying for expression as policy goals and implementation strategies. It is much like a group making stew against a backdrop of social, economic, and political factors that are influencing the participants. Feasibility or workability of proposed solutions must be considered. People attempting to develop policies try to craft a workable solution and then convince policy makers to support it.

The following elements should be considered in determining whether a solution is workable:

- *Expected outcomes.* First and foremost, can the proposed solution realistically be expected to help the target population reach their goals and fill their needs? (Some proposals actually make things worse.)

- *Value base.* Are the values supported by this proposal consistent with social work values and the strengths perspective?

- *Level of risk.* Is the proposed solution low-risk? Is it likely to succeed? What is the probability of risking resources and leaving the target population worse off?

- *Ease of implementation.* How difficult would it be to develop an adequate and accessible benefit or service delivery system?

- *Cost.* Can the policy be funded with existing resources or with grants that are likely to be secured? If a tax increase would be needed to fund the proposal, what is the likelihood it would be passed?

- *Flexibility.* Is the policy flexible enough to withstand environmental stressors like economic downturns, to provide some choice to members of the target group who will not all have exactly the same needs, and to address additional societal goals important to the citizenry?

- *Communicability.* Can the policy be easily communicated to policy makers, the public, and the target population?

- *Likelihood of passage.* What is the likelihood that the policy will be passed? Are there sufficient numbers of policy makers and constituent groups that would support or could be persuaded to support its passage? How strong is the opposition?

Here is an example of how to use these criteria to consider a policy designed to improve the performance of low-income children in school and ultimately to increase their graduation rate. Parents and the larger community are united in supporting this goal. In addition, many members of the target group want this outcome. Social justice and equal opportunity are values that motivate interest in increasing high school graduation rates. Community activists therefore propose a policy to provide full-day preschool programs at existing schools. Research indicates that if these programs are correctly implemented and made accessible, they will lead to higher graduation rates. It further reveals that such programs are cost-effective and that state and federal funding as well as foundation money may be available. The proposal is low-risk in that many communities have already successfully implemented such programs. In addition, the preschool classes will be conducted at existing schools. Allowing each school the flexibility to decide how best to reach parents in its area, to respond to unique ethnic and cultural issues, and to help support the program will increase the likelihood of sustained success. Such an approach will address criteria concerned with *expected outcomes, value base, level of risk, costs,* and *ease of implementation.*

The concept of all-day preschool is easily communicated to parents and the media. Widespread parental support for the proposal makes its passage more likely. However, some taxpayers oppose any new school program that will increase property taxes. Therefore, securing federal, state, or foundation support for the program will be crucial to obtaining the approval of the school board. This proposal meets the criteria of *communicability* and *likelihood of passage,* provided the always difficult issue of funding can be successfully negotiated. In coming to judgment, this proposal appears to be workable and one that social workers could support.

In contrast, a policy that does not fit the *values and strengths perspective* criteria is one that would require parents to attend parenting classes conducted by a trained social worker as a condition of allowing their children into the preschool program. The assumption behind such a policy is that low-income people are deficient parents. Clearly, this is not a strengths-based approach. In fact, voluntary rather than required participation for clients is typically a hallmark of strengths-based policy approaches. Therefore, offering voluntary parenting classes and maximizing the opportunities for parents to become involved in their children's education is very important and would be in keeping with the strengths perspective. These parents would be provided resources and opportunities to help their children to succeed that may have previously been unavailable to them. For example, they can be taught how to prepare for and participate effectively in parent-teacher conferences and school and community meetings. A voluntary policy that strongly supports parental involvement would be considered workable based on the criteria discussed above.

If a policy proposal does not fit these criteria, then it may be eliminated from consideration. In some cases, however, a policy proposal that is generally distasteful is presented to motivate decision makers to compromise and pass the preferred policy before the alternative policy gains momentum. For example, citizen groups might put forward a proposal to abolish free after-school programs for all junior high school students in a district in order to save tax dollars. However, the policy they actually favor is to require middle- and upper-income families to pay a fee for their children to use the service. Nevertheless, they propose abolishing the program in the hope that people who oppose any change in the program will believe the very existence of the program is threatened and consequently will be willing to compromise.

Enacting and Implementing Policy

The next phase of the policy development process focuses on how policies get enacted and are subsequently implemented. Steps in this process will vary depending on who has been given authority to enact policy. Legislators at the state and federal level are typically the policy makers we consider. In Chapter 4, we examined the steps necessary to pass legislation. However, the legislative branch is not the only branch that makes policy. As discussed in earlier chapters, the executive and judicial branches also make policy. The religious organization, corporation, or agency where you may be employed also makes many policies that govern your work.

The specific processes of determining need, making claims, and enacting policy will vary somewhat depending on the setting, but the concepts are essentially the same. Need must be recognized and defined, claimsmaking must take place, and the issue must gain sufficient attention from policy makers to warrant action.

Generally, once a policy is approved, money must be appropriated to implement it. Many times, legislation has limited impact because the separate process of appropriating funds was not understood and successfully negotiated so that adequate funding was made available. The segment of this chapter that focuses on policy practice provides specific strategies to employ when pressing for policy enactment.

After a policy is enacted, agency staff will be charged with implementing the policy and/or establishing a program. It is at this stage that the details of who will be eligible, how the benefit or service will be delivered, and how service providers will be paid are worked out. If a state agency is involved in implementing the policy, often a manual of rules and regulations—or procedures—is developed. Some local and private agencies also will codify their implementation plans in this way. If you are involved with a service agency, you can best understand the specifics of policy implementation by examining the written manuals as well as discussing the program with staff members. You also can research how the rules and regulations were written.

Policies are seldom so specific that administrators know exactly what is to be done. For example, legislation may be passed giving a state agency the authority to license and regulate day care providers. However, the legislation might not specify the number of infants who can be cared for or the type of space that is appropriate. In such a case, a series of meetings with legislators, providers, and parents might be held to develop written rules and regulations. Many times, federal, state, and even local agencies may be required to engage in a rule-making process in which public input is gathered and must be considered. In other instances, a few staff people or perhaps only one staff person develops guidelines for implementation that may or may not be written. Some agencies have few, if any, written guidelines for implementing policies and programs.

Client groups can and should be part of the implementation process. Their input should be sought when rules are developed. Such participation promotes service delivery that is sensitive to the ethnic backgrounds of client groups. Often, clients can become service providers. Additionally, community agencies with which clients are already comfortable can be used to provide services.

Evaluating Policy Outcomes

Once enacted, programs developed to implement the policies should be evaluated so that future policy development can focus on reforms if necessary. Evaluation involves determining whether the goals of the policy were accomplished and the identified problems or needs were met or at least reduced. From a strengths perspective, clients should be part of the evaluation process, the evaluation should examine outcomes for clients, and, if possible, clients' views on the effectiveness of the program should be brought to the attention of the program administrators and policy makers.

Evaluating policies and programs is a very important type of research for social workers. Even if you are not involved in actually conducting formal program evaluation research, examining the effectiveness of the policies and programs you will help implement is part of your professional practice. You can read the social work professional literature that contains evaluations of the type of policies and programs you will implement. In addition, you can find out how the agencies where you will work evaluate policies and programs and become familiar with the results.

Providing evaluative information to policy makers is a crucial component of policy development. When there is pressure for changing a policy, change is often made without knowledge of the results of evaluations of current programs. In fact, in some cases, evaluations might not have been completed because program staff did not think it was important. However, credible evaluations can help save effective programs and identify strategies for improving less-effective programs. Unless policy and program evaluations are carefully conducted and the outcomes are used by professionals and publicized to policy makers, the development of more-effective policies and programs will be hampered.

Although policy makers may try to anticipate outcomes, policies frequently generate **unanticipated consequences,** defined as unexpected events that result from the implementation of a policy. A policy can make things better for the general population but worse for the target group, or better or worse for some other groups (Ellis, 2003). For example, building a housing project for older adults with low incomes may involve tearing down existing housing that serves low-income families. In this case, the unanticipated consequence will be an increase in the number of homeless families. Of course, these consequences could have been foreseen if policy makers had developed outcome scenarios to try to determine displacement effects prior to implementing the policy. Other unanticipated consequences may be higher or lower costs than expected. Clearly, no matter how carefully policy results are anticipated, there will likely be unexpected consequences. It is important to have contingency plans and to monitor implementation so that unanticipated outcomes can be discovered as early as possible and a plan for dealing with the unanticipated outcome can be formulated.

SOCIAL WORK POLICY PRACTICE AND THE ECOLOGICAL PERSPECTIVE

Having examined the various steps in the policy development process, we now address the question: What is the role of the social worker in this process? More to the point, what can your role be? Remember, the NASW *Code of Ethics* directs us to engage in policy practice in order to put our values into action. Analysis is necessary but not sufficient. Social workers are expected to take action to bring about policy changes that benefit their clients. Engaging in policy practice means making "efforts to change policies in legislative, agency and community settings whether by establishing new policies, improving existing ones, or defeating the policy initiatives of other people" (Jansson, 2003, p. 15). People across the political spectrum can engage in policy practice: liberals, conservatives, death penalty advocates, health care advocates, advocates of mercy killing, and so on. Social workers can learn a great deal about the successful strategies and tactics used to shape policy from people across the political and professional spectrum.

However, this book focuses specifically on social work policy practice, that is, work to change social policy that influences your clients and your profession and that is informed by the *Code of Ethics* (Jansson, 2003). In the interest of brevity, however, I will simply use the term *policy practice* to refer to social work policy practice. This section will consider how social workers can help develop social policy, and it will examine how the ecological perspective can inform policy practice.

Although every social worker is directed by the *Code* to engage in policy practice at some level, certain social workers have full-time policy practice jobs such as lobbying, working for legislators, or rule making in public social service agencies. Others in public and private social service agencies may be designated to monitor legislation that affects their agencies and to testify at legislative committee hearings. Many social service agencies realize too late that they need to keep track of changes in relevant legislation if they are to stay in business. Some social workers believe that if they work to do good, then that is enough, and the rest will take care of itself. Unfortunately, many times there are people interested in cutting funding for social services who are willing to invest their time, money, and labor, and their efforts win the day.

Social workers whose primary duties involve direct service also have a responsibility to engage in policy practice. Like most social workers, you will likely be providing direct service. You will have a very busy work life in addition to home and community responsibilities. As one person, what can you do? The next part of this chapter focuses on the choices you have for becoming involved in policy practice. We have examined the elements of policy development. We will now use this information to identify places where you can help shape the policy development process. You will be equipped with beginning tools that you can choose to use to influence social policy in areas where you have passion. When you see foster children shunted through multiple foster homes, or when you see old people die alone with inadequate care, then hopefully you won't feel powerless but rather passionate about carving out some time for policy practice. You will also have some concrete ideas about how to proceed.

The ecological perspective used in your practice classes provides insight into the policy practice process. The **ecological perspective** in social work focuses on the ways in which people and their environments influence, change, and shape each other (Germain, 1991). Social policies and programs are part of our ecology. **Ecology** is the set of relationships between people and their environment. Further, the ecological perspective directs attention to the risks and protective factors in the environment that either help or impede people's efforts to reach their goals. Social policies and program can help your clients by providing needed benefits and services, or they can create barriers for your clients when, for example, they foster discrimination. The ecological perspective views the interaction between individuals and their different environments as a two-way exchange in which interactions are connected by complex feedback loops. Social workers can therefore use an ecological perspective to examine context and to understand the interactions and feedback mechanisms that connect clients and policies in order to shape effective policy.

The ecological perspective can help us discern why certain groups are disadvantaged in meeting their needs and how we may engage in policy practice to remove these barriers. Jim Taylor, a social work theorist, built on the ecological perspective in examining community factors and exploring the concept of "social niches." **Social niches** are "the environmental habitat of people including the resources they utilize and the people with which they associate" (Taylor, 1997). A housing development, school, or community center and the people and resources associated with each of them can all be components of social niches.

Taylor further distinguished between entrapping niches and enabling niches. People in **entrapping niches** face barriers that prevent them from filling their needs. For example, they frequently have restricted access to

The Social Work Library

Visit www.mhhe.com/ chapin1 for articles that will help you learn more about the ecological perspective.

people or resources outside their niche. Within entrapping niches, there are few economic resources and few chances to learn the skills and adopt the expectations that would facilitate escape. Entrapping niches are stigmatizing. For example, people in high-rise housing projects and homeless people living on the streets are caught in entrapping niches. Clearly, people in these niches have strengths, and their communities contain some resources. However, significant barriers to access to community resources are hallmarks of entrapping niches.

In contrast, people in **enabling niches** have resources readily available to help them meet their needs. Enabling niches provide resources, rewards, and incentives instead of barriers. For example, Kretzmann and McKnight (1993) have identified community assets such as excellent educational resources, interested adults, and vocational training programs that offer access to well-paying jobs after high school. Communities that offer such assets are providing enabling niches for their young people.

Taylor proposed that many of the social worker's clients are isolated in niches in society where very few empowering resources are available to them. These clients often have little money, they work long hours, and they spend any additional time they have taking care of their homes and families. Thus, they have little or no time or money for education or participation in religious or community groups. As a result, they do not come into contact with people, ideas, information, and opportunities that might help make them more effective at achieving the goals of an adequate income, education for themselves and their children, and perhaps even homeownership. Language and literacy barriers may be among the information barriers they face.

Transporting niches are places where people can get the help they need to move out of entrapping niches. Social work has sought to create transporting niches via settlement houses and community centers. Social policies can provide funds and promote programs to create transporting niches.

By adopting a broader perspective on their clients' goals and the resources they need to meet them, social workers can help develop policy options that help to overcome barriers to accessing these resources. For example, they can promote policies to provide free language programs to low-income immigrants as well as low-interest loans and training for people who want to start small businesses. Community centers often house these programs and reach out to people in their community. Needs and goals may be understood in new ways and redefined as policy options are explored.

The strengths perspective builds on the ecological approach. Reality is co-constructed, that is, people influence one another's views of reality. Positive expectations are created when you ask people, "What are your strengths and community resources, and how can they be developed?" Both these questions and questions about need and problems are important in formulating effective policy strategies.

The Social Work Library

If you are unfamiliar with the work of Kretzmann and McKnight, visit the Institute for Policy Research at Northwestern University at www.mhhe.com/chapin1 and go to the work of John Kretzmann, Faculty Associate, to learn more about these initiatives.

POLICY PRACTICE: BASIC SKILLS AND TASKS

To help create a reality for ourselves and our clients that provides opportunities for self-determination and increased access to necessary resources, social workers need to develop a well-honed set of policy practice skills. These skills include the ability to conduct policy analysis, as presented in Chapter 5. You also will need to know how to conduct literature reviews, research demographic information on various target groups, and identify best practices. The e-content attached to this text can give you guidance if you feel that you need additional preparation to perform these tasks. Beyond analytic and research skills, social workers need political skills, value-clarifying skills, and organizing skills in order to be effective policy practitioners (Jansson, 2003). Political skills enable social workers to understand and use power effectively. Value-clarifying skills help them to determine if the policy options under consideration are consistent with social work values. Finally, organizational skills assist social workers in negotiating consensus on policy and program directions. Your practice classes will help you build skills in these areas that you can use as you find opportunities to engage in policy practice. These skills are used in performing the following policy practice tasks:

The Social Work Library

View e-content on how to do policy research at the Chapin Web site.

- Identifying the target population

- Examining your perspective

- Getting on the agenda

- Identifying policy options that include the clients' perspectives

- Negotiating consensus on policy goals

- Helping to get policy enacted

- Evaluating policy based on client outcomes

This list of tasks builds on Jansson's formulation of basic policy practice tasks (2003). We discuss each task and the ways in which strengths perspective policy principles can be used to accomplish that task below. The discussion particularly highlights policy principle 7, which states that the role of the social worker is not that of the expert who helps shape policy for hapless victims. Rather, it is that of collaborator and resource to help attract attention to the perspectives of the target group.

Web Link

You can review the strengths policy principles by visiting the link at www.mhhe.com/chapin1.

For the purpose of helping you understand the basics of how to engage in policy practice, the tasks are presented in linear order. In reality, however, you may be working on several tasks simultaneously and may therefore revisit each step while working on another element. For example, while conducting a literature review focusing on the needs of your target population, you may come upon interesting policy proposals as well as information useful for claimsmaking. Begin to keep notes at each stage.

Identifying and Defining the Target Population

As you become experienced social workers, you will likely become very familiar with individual members of the target population for policies that you want to see changed. In order to consider policy change, it is important to clearly identify, define, and describe the characteristics of the target group in aggregate. For example, if you are interested in foster children, you need to be aware of the legal definitions specifying who is considered a foster child. You need to identify and define the group (Ellis, 2003, p. 24). How many members of the target population live in your town, state, and nation? What is their age, gender, ethnicity? What is their socioeconomic status? How many have a physical or mental disability? For example, if you were interested in reducing the number of placements foster children experience, it would be important to examine how gender, age, race, and disability level upon entering the foster care system influence the number of placements experienced. The state agency in charge of foster care may be able to provide this information. You need to know the size and variation of the target population and receive direct input from its members.

The Social Work Library

View Kids Count *information at www.mhhe.com/chapin1.*

Social workers should also attempt to document individual and community strengths and assets as well as the barriers confronting the target population. Identifying strengths can help in constructing solutions to seemingly unsolvable problems. Publications such as *Kids Count* and *Kansas Elder Count* provide some useful information on this subject at both the state and county levels (Annie E. Casey Foundation, 2004; Center on Aging, 2002). Additionally, you can use sources reviewed in Chapter 5 to access these data.

Often, members of the target group are already involved in political action. As discussed previously, your community and state have many such organizations, which you can access by asking your professors, attending legislative hearings, consulting resource guides, and performing online research. However, sometimes there is no official state or local organization that is already active on behalf of a target group, or there may be a variety of fragmented organizations that have difficulty accessing policy makers and lack a unified message.

Certainly, in any group you will find diverse opinions. You can use your social work skills to help develop a shared vision of preferred reality. Basically, developing a **preferred reality** means helping your clients articulate what they want changed. Social work has a long-standing commitment to improving conditions for clients, that is, to helping create a preferred reality. Beyond listening, you can help create a preferred reality by identifying common ground between the views of clients and policy makers and by considering which policy change initiatives have the best chance of passing. Grand or sweeping changes may not be the place to start. Indeed, as a social worker who is not a member of the target group, you must carefully consider both the necessary efforts and the possible consequences for the target population before championing a high-risk policy change initiative.

Sometimes, members of the target group have faced so much oppression that they need help to expand their vision. Here, again, your social work skills will be useful. You can encourage them to think about their goals and demonstrate respect for their views. You can also share information about what kinds of programs and services have helped people in similar circumstances in other areas.

To summarize, the following is a list of concrete, initial tasks that can help you identify the needs, strengths, and goals of the target population with whom you are involved:

- Contact advocacy groups with client membership to get their perspectives.

- Conduct a literature review that includes newspaper articles.

- Note how various groups have portrayed the target group and characterized their problems.

- Ask social workers practicing with the target population to identify their clients' strengths, needs, and goals.

- Analyze demographics, identify location, and estimate the size of the target group.

- Help formulate an analysis of the target group's strengths, needs, and goals that incorporates the target group's vision of preferred reality.

Once you and your clients have developed a preferred reality, you can provide support for that reality and help to craft a claim for policy makers' attention. The time you spend in becoming familiar with and documenting the needs, strengths, and goals of the target population will be invaluable in helping to craft a compelling message that gets their needs on the agenda. This information is also critical to developing effective policy options.

Examining Your Perspective

From the time you begin working with client groups and continuing through your performance of other policy practice tasks, take time to examine your views on the policies being considered. As discussed in earlier chapters, the way in which a situation is viewed is significantly influenced by the viewer. This observation applies to you as a social worker. Therefore, it is important for you to examine your views and their effect on your policy practice. Ask yourself, "How did your family background shape your views? What education and experiences influenced your perspective?" After all, it is your perspective and passion that will motivate your policy practice.

Understanding your perspective will also help you identify potential allies. For example, if your perspectives have been influenced by membership in a church, faith-based groups are potential allies. The views of the target population should also have informed your perspective. If not, getting involved with advocacy groups that include members of the target group becomes even more important.

Getting on the Agenda

We explored the process of setting an agenda in some depth earlier in the chapter. Here, we focus more specifically on how social workers can help clients get their issues onto the policy makers' decision agendas. Remember that policies and needs of all sorts are vying for policy makers' attention. Typically, interest in policy change develops gradually as need is recognized and claims are successfully made. Policy makers, whether in the agency or the legislature, become aware of the issue. At this point, we can say that the issue is on their agenda. Recall, however, that there is a separate decision agenda of issues where action will be taken and policy perhaps will change (Kingdon, 2003).

The example below illustrates the incremental process typical of efforts to get onto the agenda and then on to the decision agenda. You will note that not only the need but also a possible policy strategy was presented as part of the effort. Following the example, specific strategies you can use to get on the agenda are discussed.

Getting on the Agenda: A Real-Life Scenario   In one of my first jobs in a state department of human services, I was asked to write up an idea I had read about whereby parents of children with severe developmental disabilities would be eligible for special state-backed loans to buy homes on behalf of their children. This approach is strengths-based in that (1) it reflects the wishes of many people with severe developmental disabilities to remain in their communities; (2) it meets their needs in nonsegregated, normative ways; and (3) it builds on the strengths of families. Because I was familiar with the work of local advocacy groups for people with developmental disabilities, I was aware that these groups supported these general policy goals. I managed to bring the idea to the attention of the head of my department by talking with her in the cafeteria before work. I wrote up the idea in June, hoping it would be the subject of legislative decision making during the coming term, which began in January.

In September, I was congratulated because my concept paper would likely be incorporated into the "C" Budget of the agency's legislative proposals. However, I subsequently discovered that the "C" Budget was the agency's wish list and that it would probably be years before this particular initiative would be the subject of legislative decision making. A proposal moves from the "C" to the "B" Budget and finally to the "A" Budget only if there is sufficient money, political pressure, and time to move it to the top. Policies to develop home-ownership loans finally were enacted primarily because of the work of clients' families, but I felt I had a small part in making it happen.

This example illustrates how social workers can carve out a little time for policy practice and use relationships, research, and writing skills to place an issue on the agenda. It also illustrates the importance of exercising patience, being in for the long haul, and becoming savvy by means of often painful experience.

Strategies for Utilizing the Strengths Approach The strengths perspective asserts that the clients' perspectives should be emphasized even at the point of getting on the agenda. How can you help ensure that policy makers under-stand clients' needs, strengths, and goals? Consider the concrete suggestions discussed below.

You can begin by collecting stories that illustrate capacity rather than inca-pacity. Create "story banks" of clients' struggles and successes that you can draw upon when you have a chance to talk to policy makers or influence public opinion. You may want to keep written notes so that your stories will be richer and can help policy makers understand the realities of people's lives. Of course, to protect client privacy, you must never make specific names and identifying information public.

You can also find out if researchers are doing participatory action research in your area. In participatory action research, practitioners, researchers, and people in groups under study join together to conduct research with the purpose of contributing to social action. After obtaining written consent, researchers may engage people in the groups under study to tell their own stories. Your social work professors might already be doing this type of research. If you can become involved with participatory action research, it could be an exciting opportunity.

When you are involved in research as well as in other interactions with clients, look carefully at the interpretation of the clients' situation that is reflected back to them. If the questions asked clearly indicate that the client is perceived as sick, isolated, and incapacitated, the power of such language influ-ences how clients see themselves. If you become involved early in the research process, perhaps you can reframe the questions to focus on client strengths and capacities. Reformulating the questions might also change clients' responses. If you aren't actually involved with the research, you can certainly find out what the researchers discovered. Community meetings, surveys, interviews, and focus groups involving members of the target population can also help you gather information on needs, strengths, and goals.

Think of yourself as a resource who can support the vision of the target group and bring new ideas and information to the policy development process. Ideally, as discussed in the previous section, you will have identified client organizations with which to collaborate. Such organizations often have local and state offices that would welcome your efforts. You can also conduct a literature search on the most effective practices for building on strengths and community resources with the client population you serve. Conferring with professional contacts, calling social workers and state agency staff, brainstorming with a group of colleagues, and conducting Internet searches also provides information that is not easily accessible to target group members. Additionally, you should consider approaches that have worked in other policy arenas. For example, if longitudinally monitoring and widely publicizing client outcomes for children, such as rising numbers institutionalized, have helped reduce institutionalization, then policies to monitor and publicize institutionalization rates of older adults may also result in decreased institutionalization.

You can also help develop and provide information to agency policy makers, the news media, and legislators. Watch for the window of opportunity that is created when media coverage increases around a crisis. Other, more predictable openings occur when policies or programs are up for renewal, routine evaluation reports are made, or budgets are being negotiated. You will need to use your assessment skills to evaluate your work environment and determine what is allowable if you want to remain employed. However, many agencies now understand the need for policy practice and would welcome your efforts if they are well thought out. You will likely not do all of the things discussed thus far to help get your clients' issues on the policy agenda, but you can choose to do something.

Working with Other Individuals and Groups   It is also critical to locate and work with other people or advocacy groups as well as clients when you are engaged in claimsmaking for the purpose of getting on policy makers' agendas. Social work professors typically can help guide you to such groups, as can Internet searches and attending legislative committee hearings on the topic of interest. If you go to an advocacy group meeting and have some time and energy to give, you will most likely be very welcome. Below is a list of concrete, beginning tasks that can help with claimsmaking for the target population in whom you are interested.

- Identify members of the target population and other groups that would be willing to help with claimsmaking.

- If the target group has historically been oppressed, consider how a social justice claim may be made based on rights to equal treatment. Examine how claims have been made in the past for this and other groups and what approaches have been effective. Adapt them, if appropriate, to emphasize the strengths and contributions as well as the needs of the target population.

- Identify key actors who must be convinced of the merit of the claim and consider how the claim might need to be framed in order to garner their support.

- In collaboration with members of the target group as well as other key actors, develop a clear and easy-to-communicate statement that explains why policy makers should provide benefits or services to your target population.

- Begin to contact media and key actors so you can publicize the claim.

Identifying Policy Options that Include Client Perspectives

Your skills at gathering information as described above will be very useful when you are examining policy alternatives. You can employ the following strategies to identify policy alternatives that build on clients' strengths and help access resources to meet the needs of the target population.

- List proposed policy options identified by target groups members and other experts during the claimsmaking process. Consider which options are strengths-based. Determine whether any of these options are widely supported. If possible, brainstorm with people who may be your allies about how ideas might be combined and options crafted.

- Conduct a literature review and contact concerned national organizations to determine whether similar initiatives have been tried in other places.

- Consider history. Much like the analysis you did in Chapter 2, you should determine whether conditions are the same or different in the current time and location when considering policy options similar to those tried in the past. Whole new policy ideas typically do not suddenly appear; rather, familiar elements may be recombined into a new structure. This is one of the reasons why a historical policy perspective is important.

Negotiating Consensus on Policy Goals

Recall that in the section on policy development, we discussed the role of key actors and the importance of clients' perspectives in negotiating policy consensus. You can be part of the process that is necessary to negotiate such a consensus. You can help gain attention to clients' perspectives and goals through the media and by facilitating client-legislator interaction. For example, social workers involved with older adults routinely invite legislators to speak at senior centers, and they provide transportation so that large groups of older adults can visit their legislators. Preparation for such meetings could emphasize how to focus the interaction on specific policy goals that clients support.

As a citizen and a constituent, you should have access to your legislators. As a social worker, and most certainly as a student, you can request time from elected leaders or their staffs to hear their ideas concerning policy strategies that will meet your clients' needs and to share your clients' perspectives. Of course, you must always protect your clients' confidentiality. Armed with firsthand knowledge acquired from talking with clients and reviewing the professional literature on the subject, you will be ready to engage in a discussion from which both parties can learn a great deal. Such interactions will help you identify which strengths-based policy goals would likely receive legislative support. If you make certain to follow up with a thank you and any written information you have that may be helpful, you will establish a contact that allows you to provide and receive feedback. Every semester, I have students who successfully use this strategy to establish ongoing relationships with their legislators.

These strategies combine analytical and relationship-building skills. Finding ways to increase access to key actors is basic to effective policy practice. Of course, having access is not the same as having power. Contributions from key players and coalitions of voters can exert considerable power over legislative decisions. However, information can also help change people's minds. When attempting to influence policy, time spent in practicing the strategies discussed here will be much more useful than time spent trying to first write a proposal on your own and then get support from key actors, including client advocacy groups.

Helping to Get Policy Enacted

We have discussed how to identify policy options and achieve consensus on policy goals. We will now focus on how to determine which of the identified policy options you should support and try to get enacted. When you are considering new policies, it is crucial to think carefully about which options offer workable or feasible solutions. Look back at the criteria used to evaluate workability in the "Examining the Workability of Policy Alternatives" segment at the beginning of this chapter. These criteria can help you identify workable solutions. Further, you need to consider whether the policy can actually be implemented given the available time, talent, and funding. Social workers often champion policy options before giving much thought to these factors. Although it is important to dream on a grand scale, you should carefully consider the feasibility of your ideas before suggesting them to policy makers.

Considering Whether a New Law Is Needed   Many times, when social workers see a problem, there already is an applicable law, policy, or program in place that is ineffective because it is underfunded or incompetently implemented or monitored. In such cases, the appropriate policy change is not new legislation but, rather, increased funding or more-enforceable regulations. Keep in mind that when new laws are enacted, the effective portions of the previous law are often repealed. Try to determine which parts of the system work well and why. Are there minor policy or program enhancements that could bolster those parts? Policy practice focused solely on increasing funding for effective but underfunded programs is very important work. Although it is more glamorous to advocate an entirely new approach, when infrastructure and experience in administering a policy or program already exist, working for adequate funding can be the most effective approach.

In addition, funding regulations may be rewritten to create sanctions for ineffective implementation of a policy or program. When a program is sanctioned for ineffectiveness, funds can be withheld or fines can be levied. Conversely, incentives in the form of greater funding or other rewards can be offered for meeting or exceeding the specified outcomes.

Agency rules and regulations that specify how a program is to be administered can often be changed without passing new legislation. Modifying administrative and organizational behavior may help eliminate barriers to clients' reaching their goals and thus enhance the effectiveness of social work practice. Policy advocacy might also be needed to ensure that staff charged with implementing the program are properly trained. If agency rules or regulations do not require training and funds are not available to provide it, then little, if any, training may be provided. When program staff are not adequately trained, programs frequently do not work because they are inadequately implemented. Before you attempt to modify a law or major policy, you should investigate whether program staff are properly trained and the program has been implemented correctly.

Using the Policy Analysis Framework   In analyzing a proposed new policy that will result in new social programs, you should analyze each of the policy and program elements of the policy analysis framework detailed in Chapter 5. The elements are goals, benefits or services, eligibility rules, service delivery system, and financing. If you have not already committed this list to memory, please take time to do so because you will use it often in the future. Each element should be examined for congruence with the strengths perspective. For example, policy options in terms of eligibility rules and type of service offered should be analyzed for capacity to increase access to resources that will allow clients to meet their goals in ways similar to those of other community members.

Consider the case in which eligibility rules for a service stipulate it will be provided only to people with disabilities who live in institutions or attend segregated special schools or adult achievement centers. The eligibility rule and the type of service or benefit provided entrap clients in a niche separated from the rest of the community and from other rich community resources. Such a policy is not strengths based if it disregards the client's goal to remain a part of the larger community. Additionally, remember that the eligibility rules involve rationing. Policy advocacy can be aimed at ensuring that eligibility rules direct the majority of resources to people with the greatest need.

Going further, the service delivery system for policy or program implementation should build on existing resources rather than create separate, often redundant delivery systems. The development of service delivery systems is yet another area where social workers can engage in policy practice. Social workers in public and private agencies frequently are involved in implementing the service delivery system for a new policy. For example, when foster care is privatized in a state, social workers in private agencies such as Catholic Charities or Lutheran Social Services could help develop agency policies that emphasize working closely with local churches and other community organizations in order to recruit more foster parents. Alternatively, they can develop agency policy to fund group homes. They can adopt a policy of referring children to the local mental health system, or they can develop specialized separate mental health services for foster children.

Social workers should analyze proposed financing of new legislation for adequacy and stability. Additionally, they should analyze the incentives created for providers by the way the service is reimbursed to ensure that there are no financial incentives to underserve clients or, conversely, to continue treating clients indefinitely.

Analyzing Costs   An analysis of costs and benefits is a critical component of the process whereby the feasibility of proposed legislation is examined. Preliminary budgets are often part of policy proposals. The budget analyst at the state legislative research office or a budget analyst in the agency that will administer proposed policies may be willing to provide information to help craft or evaluate a draft budget.

A cost-benefit analysis can be very complex. It is important to draw attention to the costs to clients and to society of not implementing policies. Although policy makers certainly base decisions on more than cost, cost-effectiveness is an important element. There are many intangibles to which it is difficult to assign a value. Working with an expert to help perform the cost-benefit analysis or using already completed analyses usually is the preferred way to add such analysis to your arguments in support of new policy. If a bill dealing with the policy in which you have an interest has already been introduced, the state agency involved has likely been asked to generate a financial impact statement. If you contact the legislators who sponsored the bill, they may be able to tell you which agency official is responsible for examining the costs and benefits of a bill. The legislator or state agency staff may be able to give you a copy of the financial impact statement. Agency staff may also be willing to talk with you about the assumptions they used to determine financial impact. You may be able to use this information either to bolster or to refute cost-benefit claims made by other groups.

One simple but effective way of analyzing costs and benefits based on outcome is to examine costs to taxpayers if effective intervention does not take place and, for example, a child goes to foster care or a correctional facility or an older adult is admitted to a nursing home, runs out of money, and goes on Medicaid. The cost of institutionalization for a year has usually already been calculated and may be obtained from the state agency in charge of reimbursing institutions. Most agencies also have calculated an average cost per year for serving a client in the community. You then can compare the cost of social work intervention and service to maintain the client in the community to the cost of institutionalization. The cost of providing service to a large number of people in the community is often much less and can be offset if the cost of just one person entering an institution is avoided.

Evaluating Policy Based on Client Outcomes

Finally, it is important, even at the early stages of policy consideration, to think about how the effectiveness of the policy will be evaluated. If policy makers agree on outcomes they would like to see for clients after the policy is implemented, evaluation can then focus on these outcomes. If policy makers can be convinced to specify in the enabling legislation that evaluation will be based on outcomes for clients, then client-focused information will be made available to evaluate policy effectiveness and improve the policy.

For example, a student in one of my classes who had been a foster child worked with a child advocacy group to develop a policy proposal with the goal of increasing educational attainment for children who have been in foster care. They proposed legislation to guarantee funding for postsecondary education at a state college, community college, or county technical institute for former foster children. Because policy makers were concerned with the large numbers of former foster children who were entering homeless shelters as adults, they were interested in initiatives that might increase the ability of these individuals to become self-supporting.

Significantly, the specified goal—increased educational attainment for people who had been in foster care—could be tracked, and my student advocated that tracking be mandated in the initial legislation. Because the educational attainment of people who had grown up in foster care in previous years had been documented as part of the needs determination process, changes after the policy is implemented could be measured. Also, if this outcome is routinely tracked and monitored for people who have been in foster care, the impact of other changes in the foster care system and the magnitude of the change in educational outcomes can be monitored over time. It is important to think about outcome measures that include clients' goals as well as policy makers' goals early in the policy enactment process so that both sets of goals can be evaluated. In the case described above, policy makers were interested in improving educational achievement for former foster children, thereby decreasing their numbers in homeless shelters. These outcomes could all be monitored.

The failure to evaluate policies can contribute to ineffectiveness and even loss of service, because the outcomes of the prescribed intervention are not recorded and analyzed. For example, a policy may specify that juvenile offenders receive services in a group home. However, if the people who work with juvenile offenders placed in group homes fail to track recidivism rates (rates of repeat offenses), then policy makers cannot determine whether the program is effective or needs major revamping. Further, the social workers who staff the group home will not be able to defend the efficacy and cost-effectiveness of their work in the face of budget cuts that could ultimately result in closing the group home. In fact, I have witnessed just this scenario. Of course, savvy social workers will monitor client outcomes regardless of whether such monitoring is required in order to avoid such a situation.

In order to analyze outcomes once a policy is enacted, we must know the condition of the target group prior to the intervention. This information is called **base line data.** Ideally, information gathered in the need determination stage of policy development will provide base line data; otherwise, these data will need to be gathered. Of course, if outcomes improve after the policy is implemented, it does not necessarily follow that the intervention or policy made the difference. There is a correlation rather than a causal link. You do know that the outcome improved after implementation of a policy change, but it will take more research to establish that the policy change actually caused the improved outcome. Nonetheless, if more members of the target groups had a positive outcome after receiving services or benefits compared to members of the same groups in the base line year, then policy makers will be interested in knowing that the policy change didn't cause the situation to deteriorate and might have improved conditions.

A PLACE TO START

You may already be passionate about an area of social policy in which you want to get involved in policy practice. Involvement with social work agencies often helps students focus on needed policy changes. Think critically about the social work agencies where you volunteer or do fieldwork. What policies govern their programs? How does funding drive the program? How is the program evaluated? Are outcomes for clients a component of the evaluation? Are

evaluation results used to improve policy and program? If clients have griev-
ances, does the agency give them a chance for a fair hearing? Examining the
issues raised in these hearings may provide indicators of where policy is not
working effectively. If clients do not have the opportunity for this kind of due
process, there may be a need for policy advocacy so that they do have some
recourse.

Seeking Support

If you are in field placement, ask your field instructor for guidance and ideas
about where to start engaging in policy practice. Remember, policy practice is
important at the agency level as well as at the legislative level. At the legislative
level, the agency may already have staff designated to follow legislation and
talk to policy makers about needed changes. If so, see if you can work with
them. If you have been a volunteer, agency staff may be willing to talk with you
about the legislative policy changes they would like to see. Becoming a skilled
policy practitioner means learning how to work effectively with agencies and
other concerned groups to shape policies and programs.

During your social work career, your policy practice work may include
forming coalitions with clients and key constituent groups, finding or helping
to elect supportive legislators, analyzing proposals, developing proposals, communicating ideas effectively, and advocating for policy enactment. You may become involved in efforts to take an issue to court. Some schools of social work
offer joint degrees with their affiliated law schools. Seeking out people who
were involved in these programs and enlisting the help of your local or national
NASW chapter are starting places in evaluating the feasibility of a lawsuit.
NASW also initiates or participates in development of legal briefs on selected
social and practice issues. These briefs are called *amicus curiae* (friend of the
court) briefs and may be available through your library under the topic of
NASW Amicus Briefs.

Many NASW chapters also sponsor training programs to increase the political effectiveness of social workers. Be sure to find out what the local NASW
chapters are doing in your state. Nationally, NASW seeks to educate and mobilize social workers and other groups to press for a more just society. NASW
publishes an excellent resource titled *Social Work Speaks*; it provides policy statements on a variety of social work issues, which can be used to guide social work
political activism and policy advocacy (National Association of Social Workers,
2003). NASW also has a political action arm called Political Action for Candidate Election (PACE). PACE endorses and contributes financially to candidates
from any party who support the policy agenda of NASW.

We know that people are most familiar with policy issues that have a
direct impact on them, their friends, and their families. If legislative bodies

reflected the makeup of the voting public more closely, they would contain many more women, people of color, and people who grew up in low-income families. Such legislators might be more likely to vote for many of the policies social workers champion. However, large numbers of eligible voters who could help elect such candidates are not registered to vote. Two-thirds of the millions of registered voters who do not vote are below the median income line (National Association of Social Workers, 2003). Given this lack of voter involvement, particularly among low-income citizens, there is a great need for political activism. **Political activism** is defined as actions taken for the purpose of influencing the outcome of elections or government decision making.

Taking Action

When you are ready to take action, the task descriptions presented earlier in the chapter, from determining needs to developing and evaluating proposed policy, can guide your efforts. The tasks listed in each of those sections can help you develop steps for an action plan when you become involved in policy practice. You will need help and support from other groups, including the target population, to do what needs to be done. However, in most change efforts I have seen succeed, there have been a handful of determined people who endure until the change occurs. Don't be discouraged if at first you attract only small numbers of people who are willing to help out. Even a few people who are actually willing to work on an issue can make a huge difference.

The Social Work Library

Take time to explore the Sample Action Plan available at www.mhhe.com/chapin1 and consider how it could be modified to develop an action plan for an issue where you have passion.

An **action plan** is very important. It details steps to take in planning and implementing your action strategy. A thoughtful plan can help make you aware of the potential influence of your actions and those of your group members. An example of an action plan is included with this text. Two principles guide my development of action plans:

- First, keep it simple (KIS) so that everyone understands what is to be done. Remember, the goal is to involve people from a variety of backgrounds. If the plan is too long and detailed, MEGO (my eyes glaze over) will overtake group members, and they will lose interest.

- Second, if your group expends most of its energy in planning, there won't be any gas left in the tank to put the plan into action. As with detailed analysis of social problems, I have seen time and again that well-meaning groups admire the problem and plan and then lose momentum before much else is accomplished. Think realistically about how much time and effort group members have to give, and then contain the planning so that it doesn't use up most of their energy.

Integrating Other People into Action Plans   A written action plan is very useful because it helps clarify strategy and assignment of responsibility. Also, if the action plan is developed as a group endeavor, that process can help create consensus about what needs to be done. Additionally, when other people are involved in drafting the action plan, they will also be more likely to work to implement it. However, instead of creating a comprehensive written action plan containing all the tasks we have covered thus far, a concise action plan can be developed, as illustrated in the Sample Action Plan.

It is important to have a solid, carefully thought-out action plan and to make certain that everyone who is responsible for a task has agreed to do it, knows how to do it, is aware of the due date, has a copy of the plan, and expects to be held accountable. Your action plan can also include strategies for dealing with important stakeholders and gaining public support (Ellis, 2003).

After developing the action plan, review it with people who have experience with change efforts in your chosen area. They often can identify misinformation and omissions, and they can offer constructive feedback. They may also join your effort or know other people who will. You also will have to monitor the action plan as it is implemented and modify it as needed. At the very least, you will need a list of tasks. You will also need to determine who will do what and in what order.

Focusing Your Efforts   Working from a strengths perspective, you could, for example, focus your policy practice efforts on simply increasing public awareness of a policy alternative that builds on the strengths and goals of your target group. One approach would be to help your local newspaper or public radio station develop a series of stories. Stories about innovative strengths-based policy alternatives that address the desperate need for affordable high-quality day care for single working mothers or for affordable home and community services for low-income elders are good examples of possible subjects. There likely are advocacy groups in your state that are already working on these issues where you could find people interested in collaborating with you. Initially, it is best to seek guidance from a seasoned policy practitioner to help prevent any breach of ethics concerning confidentiality and privacy. If you have begun to keep a story bank of clients' successes and struggles, as explained earlier, you will already have rich material to share. Media pieces may also contain contact phone numbers or e-mail addresses of advocacy groups working on these issues, for people who want to get involved. Your action plan could include identifying interested reporters, convincing them of the merit of the stories, supplying information and perhaps speakers from the target group, and then evaluating the results of the effort.

When the work involved in making an impact seems overwhelming, break it down into small, manageable tasks. Take action where you can. Your skills will improve with practice, and other people will take notice because the ability to work effectively and persistently to bring about change is very valuable in a great variety of settings.

Interacting with Your Opposition   Expect to encounter opposition. Remember, there are groups in the policy stew who are committed to many different policy options. There may be groups whose goal is simply to block any and all initiatives. They are made up of people who feel they are best benefited by maintaining the status quo. You will need to learn how to work with people who share your concerns and to deal with people who don't.

You need to become savvy about vested interests and people who espouse ideologies that are very different from your own. Consider how much power they have and what methods they used to acquire power. Strategies to counter these forces may include forming coalitions with clients and key constituent groups and finding or helping to elect supportive legislators. Realistically assessing the barriers to changing policy is important. You also will find key actors in government agencies and in the legislature who will be your allies.

Working with the Target Group   Members of the target group may already possess well-developed political skills. If they don't, however, you can help connect them with advocacy training opportunities. Their involvement is key, but always temper efforts to encourage their involvement with a careful assessment of the level of risk that such involvement represents for them. This assessment is particularly important when you are considering confrontational strategies. Confrontation is often necessary, but it also involves higher levels of risk. Therefore, you should exhaust low-risk strategies first.

Interacting with Policy Makers   When communicating with key actors such as legislators, it helps to prepare by doing a little research on their backgrounds and philosophies. Today, many legislators have their own Web sites. Perhaps they put out newsletters. With just a little effort, you can learn their underlying philosophies and the areas in which they are active. As you examine the history of attempts to address needs in a particular area, pay attention to who has been involved in past initiatives. You know the importance of "starting where the client is" in practice. Similarly, "starting where policy makers are" and framing proposals to fit in with their ideas and approaches without compromising essential elements will likely generate more support. At the very least, a little research will help you avoid alienating a policy maker needlessly by, for example, beginning your interaction decrying "a bootstrap mentality" when the person you're talking to fancies himself a "self-made man." People who believe citizens should rely on themselves and pull themselves out of difficulty by their own bootstraps are very cautious about increasing spending on public welfare programs.

Don't rely on technical information and logic alone to make your case. Consider normative affective strategies also. This means you should try to identify legislators who may be interested in an issue because of past involvement on a personal or professional level. For example, if a legislator has a disability or a family member with disabilities, she or he might take greater interest in policies and programs for people with disabilities.

Package your ideas so that they are attractive to policy makers. A one-page brief is recommended because policy makers must deal with such a huge volume of issues that you need to get their attention and make major points as briefly as possible. Sometimes, an "incremental approach"—that is, an approach that presses for a small change to an existing program rather than radical change—is more appealing to policy makers. However, there are times when radical change is needed.

Policy change efforts undoubtedly are going on in your state, and you could help out with them. Start with one contact or one action. You may be surprised at the opportunities for policy practice that are readily available to you.

Facing Limits on Political Activism   Sometimes, social workers do not get involved in political activism because they believe it would violate the terms of their employment. In fact, limits on political activism in social service agencies are frequently misunderstood. For example, agencies may indicate that all sorts of political activism are prohibited under the Hatch Act, a federal law that restricts the political activity of federal employees, District of Columbia government employees, and some state and local employees who are involved with federally funded programs. However, there are a great many ways in which a social worker employed by public or private agencies can be politically active without violating the Hatch Act. There may be additional state or agency prohibitions against political activism in places where you will work. However, if you examine the written policy closely, you may find that it is not nearly as restrictive as agency personnel who haven't actually taken time to examine the policy closely may believe.

The Social Work Library

An example of a one-page brief is available at www.mhhe.com/chapin1.

Web Link

Limitations under the Hatch Act are explained in detail on the federal government Web site of the U.S. Office of the Special Counsel found at www.mhhe.com/chapin1.

CONCLUSION

This chapter provided an overview of the policy development process and of policy practice, examined your responsibility and opportunities to become involved, and suggested some beginning strategies. Your social work practice classes will help you further develop skills that can be applied to influencing policy.

Additionally, there are many books that detail strategies and tactics to use in policy practice (Haynes & Mickelson, 2003; MacEarchern, 1994; Schneider &

Lester, 2001). Some of these books are very specialized. For example, the focus may be entirely on how to use the Internet to build coalitions and get information to the people who need it. As you become engaged in social work practice with a specific client group, such as children in foster care or older adults with long-term care needs, chances to be involved in policy practice will abound if you are attuned to the opportunities and your obligation to be involved in influencing policy and program.

MAIN POINTS

- Policy development is the process by which policies are created and implemented to meet identified need. Policies can also be developed that build on strengths and reflect the goals of the target group.

- Tasks in the policy development process include defining needs, social problems, and strengths; documenting needs, strengths, and goals; identifying initial policy goals; engaging in claimsmaking; crafting broadly supported policy goals; formulating policy alternatives that meet established goals; developing, enacting, and implementing the policy or program; and evaluating outcomes.

- Social, cultural, and community factors influence social policies.

- Policy practice involves working "to change policies in legislative, agency and community settings whether by establishing new policies, improving existing ones, or defeating the policy initiatives of other people" (Jansson, 2003, p. 15).

- All social workers have a responsibility to be involved in some level of social work policy practice, as outlined in the NASW *Code of Ethics*. Involvement requires many skills, including policy analysis, political, value-clarifying, and organizational skills.

- Policy practice tasks include understanding the target population, examining your perspective on the issue, getting on the agenda, identifying policy options that include the clients' perspectives, negotiating consensus on policy goals, getting the policy enacted, and evaluating the policy in terms of client outcomes.

- A written action plan can help guide policy practice. However, think realistically about how much time and effort your group has to give and avoid using all the group's energy on planning.

- You can use the ideas presented in this chapter to become involved in policy practice in an area for which you have passion.

You are a social work student with a practicum placement in the public school system. You are working with one of the children in the Sanchez family and during a conversation with Mrs. Sanchez, she tells you she is very worried about health insurance for her children. Mr. Sanchez currently has health insurance through his employer. However, his job as a laborer is precarious and he changes employers often. Some jobs offer no health insurance, but his income though low, is too high to qualify for the State Children's Health Initiative Program (SCHIP), which is available to children in families with income below 150% of the federal poverty level (FPL) in their state. With the Sanchez family of 5 people, this is an income of approximately $33,045 (150% FPL). In a school setting, you have heard from many families without health insurance and have seen the negative impact of inadequate health care on their children. You decide that you would like to impact policy so that more children will be covered by health insurance. The following action plan delineates steps that you and others you enlist might take to increase SCHIP benefits in states where families with incomes above 150% of the FPL are ineligible for the program.

CASE VIGNETTE

Sample Action Plan

ACTION PLAN

ACTION PLAN TASKS	WHO WILL DO IT?	DATE DONE

Month 1–2: Identifying the Target Population and Examining Your Perspective
 	
1. **Identify target population**
  • Contact state advocacy groups and use the Internet to determine:
    – How many children in your state are uninsured with a family income level above 150% of the federal poverty level? How many children would qualify for benefits if the law changed to 200% or 300% of the FPL? What are the characteristics such as age and race of uninsured children?
  • Consider what you know from your own practice experience about the strengths of the target group. Are members of the group politically active currently on issues related to their well-being?
    – Many cities have active Hispanic Political Action Groups as well as parent groups who lobby on behalf of their children. Is this true in your community? Members of the client group and other social workers who practice with them can provide additional information.		

continued

CASE
VIGNETTE

*Sample
Action Plan*
continued

ACTION PLAN TASKS	WHO WILL DO IT?	DATE DONE

2. Do a literature search to research possible solutions
 • Access your State Department of Health on the Internet to view a description of the SCHIP program in your state.
 • Investigate other state programs to determine differences and similarities. The Henry J. Kaiser Foundation provides state-by-state comparisons of SCHIP income eligibility at www.statehealthfacts.kff.org.
  – Many states have higher family income eligibility, up to 350% of the FPL.
 • Identify advocacy groups at the local, state, and national level with similar interests.
  – Families USA is a national organization that provides valuable information about SCHIP on their Web site, www.familiesusa.org, in addition to being active advocates for change.
 3. Examine your perspectives
 • Why are you interested in this issue? What is your motivation in advocating for change? Do you belong to civic or church groups that might share your interest in the topic? If you are a student member of the NASW or school social work groups in your area, you may find likely allies in those groups.
  – By identifying your interest in the issue, it might be possible to identify others with similar interests that will work with you to change policy.
 	
 Month 2–3: Getting on the Agenda
 	
 1. Talk to key actors about the issue
 • Speak to advocacy groups about whether they are already working on the issue or interested in focusing on the issue. If not interested, ask if they are aware of other people or groups interested or knowledgeable about the issue.
 • Contact your state legislator. You can identify your legislator by visiting your state legislature's Web site, accessible from www.stateline.org.
  – Meeting with your legislator allows you to introduce yourself, the issue, and assess their interest in the topic. Remember to protect confidentiality of your clients when explaining the need for change. Be sure to thank your legislator for the visit.		

ACTION PLAN TASKS	WHO WILL DO IT?	DATE DONE

2. Locate and engage with people who want to be involved with the issue
• Examples could include other students, members of the target population, an advocacy group, local NASW members, and a state legislator willing to sponsor a bill. They may join you in contacting legislators and trying to get this issue on the agenda.
3. Try to get media coverage
• Write a letter to the editor of your local newspaper.
• Call the local radio station and see if they will air a story on your issue.
If you have time to take only the actions listed above, you have made a great start and have created a foundation for future involvement.
 	
Month 3–4: Identifying Policy Options and Negotiating Consensus on Policy Goals
 	
1. Clarify the issue and discuss policy goals and solutions
• Work with like-minded advocates to ensure you have a clear statement of the issue, uninsured children that articulate reasons policymakers should provide health care coverage to additional low-income working families.
• Identify alternative solutions to addressing the issue.
  – Think about the solutions in terms of goals, benefits or services provided, eligibility rules, service delivery system, and financing.
2. Negotiate consensus
• Meet with client advocacy groups to determine a mutually acceptable goal and solution to addressing the issue in your state.
  – The goal may be to increase the family income level to 200% of the FPL. Although an increase to 300% would be ideal, an incremental change will be more easily passed through the legislature.
• Develop a one-page information sheet about the issue and actions desired so that a consistent and concise message can be delivered to legislators.		

CASE VIGNETTE

Sample Action Plan
continued

continued

CASE
VIGNETTE

*Sample
Action Plan*
continued

ACTION PLAN TASKS	WHO WILL DO IT?	DATE DONE
Month 5–6: During Legislative Session		
1. Tracking the legislative process		
• Continue to speak with legislators and look for a legislator who will introduce and/or support the bill. Help families without health insurance voice their concerns to legislators. Don't be surprised if a bill is not introduced during the first year.		
• Maintain contact with key actors. Attend meetings held by the advocacy group.		
• Continue to increase public awareness of the issue.		
Month 7–8: Evaluating Campaign		
1. Evaluate campaign		
• The legislation you supported may not have been introduced. Although the legislation was not introduced, public awareness and support of the issue was gained. In addition, a few legislators expressed interest in pursuing the bill in the next legislative session.		
• Awareness of SCHIP increased across the state and more families already eligible applied for the program and currently have health care coverage.		
2. Use evaluation to think about strategies for next year. Strategies may include:		
• Periodically meeting with interested legislators to encourage them to sponsor a bill. See if some of the families without health insurance would be willing to go along and tell their stories in person.		
• Organizing a letter writing campaign encouraging the families without health insurance to write to their legislator in order to increase awareness of the need for health care coverage.		
• Staying in close contact with advocacy groups to strategize about how best to accomplish your goals.		

EXERCISES: PRACTICING SOCIAL WORK

Working with the Black Feather Community

1. In the Engage segment, read about the principle agencies and people who live in the Black Feather region. What do you see as some of the strengths of the area? Identify some resources that would be important to bring into the community.

2. Based on your review of the components of the Black Feather case study, who are the key actors that you can identify to interview about their ideas for policy reforms in the Black Feather community?

3. Answer the questions below. These questions are similar to the Critical Thinking questions in the Engage segment. However, they have been modified to focus on policy practice.

   a. What are the perceived needs and issues facing the elder community? What are some potential sources for addressing these issues?

   b. For the youth focus group, identify the main concerns of the young people and the possible underlying factors that are contributing to these concerns.

   c. What are the biggest differences between the Medicine Wheel approach and the "risk and protective factors" approach to engaging the community in identifying their needs?

   d. Based upon your analysis of the focus group data, how do the views of the youth and elders converge or diverge in terms of their respective views of the community?

4. Write a critique of the approaches used with elders and children as described in the Assessment component of this interactive case. What components of these approaches were effective in identifying the strengths, needs, and goals of this community? Do you have suggestions about how their methods could have been improved with more emphasis on the strengths approach?

5. Identify four strategies you might use to get the needs of the Black Feather community on the agenda of the state legislature.

6. What have you learned from this case about policy practice that you might go out and apply in a real community?

EXERCISES: THE SOCIAL WORK LIBRARY

Ecological Perspective

Read "The ecological perspective" (Germain & Gitterman, 1995), and respond to the following:

1. How does the ecological perspective define the relationship between person and environment?

2. According to the ecological perspective, how can the relationship between person and environment have a negative impact on oppressed populations?

3. Applying the concepts of the ecological perspective, identify specific ways in which social workers can advocate for clients in the political arena.

Policy Advocacy and Collaboration

Read "Innovations in social policy: Collaborative policy advocacy" (Sherraden, Slosar & Sherraden, 2002), and respond to the following:

1. What are the strengths that students, researchers, practitioners, and educational and advocacy organizations can bring to the policy-making process?

2. How did the various actors influence the coalition and the policy process?

CHAPTER 7

Civil Rights

Never doubt that a small group of thoughtful committed citizens can change the world; indeed it's the only thing that ever has.

— MARGARET MEAD

CIVIL RIGHTS ARE LEGALLY ENFORCEABLE PROTECTIONS afforded to citizens to prevent arbitrary abuse by the state or other individuals. The rights taken for granted by the majority population, such as the right to vote, the right to an adequate education, the right to live where desired, and the right to marry, often are denied to oppressed populations. This reality has driven oppressed groups and their allies to advocate for civil rights policies and their enforcement in order to eliminate discrimination and promote equality. In this chapter, we will examine major civil rights policies as well as some of the challenges faced in securing civil rights for specific oppressed groups. The first section of the chapter offers a brief overview of the recent and current status of various oppressed groups, building on the historical base provided in Chapters 2 and 3. The second section focuses more narrowly on key laws and court rulings directed toward securing and expanding the basic rights of marginalized groups in the United States.

One of the many benefits of being a social worker is getting to know people from diverse cultures and backgrounds. Social workers who embrace diversity believe that a range of human characteristics—age, race, gender, ability level, sexual orientation—is normal and acceptable. These characteristics are not a valid basis for withholding basic societal benefits such as the right to an adequate education, housing, health care, employment, and social services. Yet, African Americans, American Indians, Hispanics or Latinos, Asian Americans, women, people with disabilities, gay men and lesbians, and older adults all face threats to their civil rights, which contributes to the problems that bring them into contact with social workers. The capacity to help these clients reach their goals is either impeded or bolstered by the quality of the civil rights policies that protect them.

When you have completed this chapter, you will understand why it was necessary to enact legislation that has protected and increased people's civil rights. Moreover, you will be more aware of additional areas in which people are still being denied their basic rights and will be able to use what you learn to help improve conditions for members of oppressed groups throughout your social work career.

BACKGROUND AND HISTORY

Knowledge about diverse cultures and backgrounds is important in order to understand how policies and programs influence outcomes for members of these groups and how policies that work more effectively for these groups might be crafted. Taking an ecological approach helps us focus on the environmental barriers all of these groups face in meeting their needs and achieving their goals. The most obvious barrier they encounter is being underrepresented or not represented at all in the halls of the U.S. Congress, in most state legislatures, in executive positions in corporate America, and even in leadership positions in many social service agencies.

As explained in the policy practice section of Chapter 6, when people are making policy for target groups whom they perceive as unlike themselves—that is, the "other"—those policies likely will not adequately reflect the goals and needs of the target group. In fact, many policies have actually erected barriers and promoted discrimination that increased the power and wealth of dominant groups. Members of oppressed groups may be subjected to racism, sexism, homophobia, ageism, and discrimination in employment and housing. **Racism** is "stereotyping and generalizing about people, usually negatively, because of their race; commonly a basis of discrimination against members of racial groups" (Barker, 2003, p. 357). The validity of race as a concept is currently under dispute. Nonetheless, racism clearly continues to influence interactions in our society. A key component of racial ideologies is that they connect physical characteristics with intellectual or behavioral traits such as intelligence and criminal behavior. Consequently, they tend to divide humanity into "superior" and "inferior" groups. **Sexism** is discrimination based solely on gender. **Homophobia** is the fear of, and discrimination against, people who are gay, lesbian, transgender, or bisexual, on the basis of their sexual orientation. **Ageism** is discrimination based on age, usually directed toward older adults, but often toward children as well.

Members of oppressed groups receive inequitable treatment in many areas. For example, they frequently are provided poorer medical care and police protection. Portrayals of their strengths and capacities are often hard to find in the media, and discrimination against them is often ignored or glossed over. If you examine social and economic outcome indicators for various groups of Americans, you will see large differences for oppressed groups. For example, take a look at the national outcome indicators documented in *Kids Count Data Book*, a book published yearly by the Annie E. Casey Foundation that draws attention to the disparate outcomes for children across the United States.

 Web Link

Visit the Kids Count Web site found at www.mhhe.com/chapin1.

You will see that people of color have very high poverty rates. Other statistics, such as rates of suicide, incarceration, infant mortality, school dropout, and unemployment, may also be much higher for a given group. As we have seen, throughout history people often have attributed poorer outcomes to individual deficits of group members. If you still think individual failings and group characteristics rather than societal barriers are primarily to blame for these poor group outcomes, please challenge yourself to reexamine the realities of the lives of many members of these groups.

As policy analysts, you need to ask how social policies and programs contribute to these poorer outcomes. Further, as policy practitioners, you need to work with oppressed groups to craft policies that more effectively help them fill needs and reach goals. Policies designed to ensure civil rights, as well as policies that institutionalize discrimination, need careful attention. Box 7.1 lists a few of the most pressing negative outcomes for oppressed groups that can be addressed using policy practice skills. Perhaps one of these outcomes represents an issue for which you have passion enough to spark involvement.

When examining civil rights, it is critical to consider not only equal rights but also policies that can help oppressed groups who have suffered structural discrimination for years to surmount the effects of that prolonged discrimination. **Structural discrimination** refers to entrenched and long-lasting societal practices that favor one group over another based on group characteristics such as skin color. The concept of structural discrimination can be more easily understood by considering its effects for a group such as inner-city Mexican American girls. Take a moment to think back about the concepts related to empowering niches presented in Chapter 6. What are the barriers that keep assets such as adequate educational opportunities, access to well-paying jobs, health care, and adequate family income out of the inner-city area? Discrimination in hiring, lack of Mexican American physicians, and state school funding policies that negatively impact poor communities are just a few of the reasons you and your classmates may list.

In examining policy options and strategies for decreasing discrimination, it is important to also consider the strengths and resources of oppressed groups. For example, voting rights for African Americans were secured in large part because church leaders in African American communities, where churches have traditionally been major community resources, mobilized and provided leadership. Similarly, as discussed in Chapter 3, Cesar Chavez and other Latino activists organized farm laborers to press for an end to discriminatory employment

BOX 7.1

*Focus on
Outcomes*

- **High rates of violence against women.** In 2002, 216,090 women over the age of 12 reported being victims of rape, attempted rape, or sexual assault. This is equivalent to 1.8 victims per 1,000 women over the age of 12. This number only represents the number of violent crimes reported, estimated at only 54 percent of victims (Rennison & Rand, 2003).

- **Large differences in educational attainment between whites and people of color.** The percentage of Americans age 25 and older with a bachelor's degrees varies greatly, with 37 percent of Asian Americans and 22 percent of whites having a bachelor's degree compared to 11 percent of blacks and 9 percent of Hispanics and Native Americans (Kao & Thompson, 2003).

- **Income disparities between men and women.** The median earnings for full-time, year-round workers age 15 and older is $39,429 for men and $30,203 for women (DeNavas-Walt, Cleveland, & Webster, 2003).

- **Very high poverty rates for black women age 75 and older.** Black women age 75 and older have a poverty rate of 31 percent, which is more than double the overall poverty rate of 12.7 percent (U.S. Census Bureau, 2005).

- **High rates of concentrated poverty in inner cities and other isolated areas for people of color.** African Americans are the largest racial/ethnic group living in areas of high poverty where 40 percent or more of the population is poor. Blacks represent 39 percent of the population in high poverty areas, followed by Hispanics or Latinos at 29 percent and whites with 24 percent (Jargowsky, 2003).

- **Elevated school dropout rates for Hispanics.** Of Hispanics or Latinos age 16–24, 27 percent are not enrolled in high school and have not completed high school (U.S. Department of Education, National Center for Education Statistics, 2003).

- **Large numbers of people of color without health insurance.** Overall, 32 percent of Hispanics or Latinos are without health insurance, compared to 20 percent of African Americans and 11 percent of non-Hispanic whites in the United States (Mills & Bhandari, 2003).

- **Low employment rates for people with physical and mental disabilities who want to work.** Recent data reveal that 23 percent of people with non-severe disabilities and 74 percent of people with severe disabilities are not employed. Researchers reported 79 percent of nonemployed people with disabilities indicated that they wanted a job (Stoddard, Jans, Ripple, & Kraus, 1998).

practices. If differences can be embraced and strengths recognized, then the need for people to relinquish their cultural roots and diverse backgrounds to be accepted in U.S. society may diminish. Instead, we can draw on these strengths to help create more equitable social policies.

Social work students, like their clients, come from varied backgrounds. You may have grown up on stories of Cesar Chavez and his work to organize migrant workers. You also may be familiar with the historical images of "Whites

Only" water fountains and lunch counters, and you even might have memorized some of Martin Luther King's speeches. Conversely, you may have limited familiarity with the history of civil rights. If you need or want to learn more than what is covered in this chapter and the history chapters, you can see the faces and hear the voices of famous civil rights leaders via the book's Web site.

The Social Work Library

Browse the "I Have a Dream" speech and the Leadership Conference on Civil Rights.

CIVIL RIGHTS POLICIES IN THE UNITED STATES

The historical milestones in securing civil rights are integral parts of the history of U.S. social policy and as such have been discussed in the history chapters. This section examines how these milestones have affected the current status of marginalized groups in this country. It focuses both on the progress that has been achieved and on the challenges that continue to confront us.

The foundation of civil rights protection in the United States is the U.S. Constitution, particularly the Bill of Rights. The Bill of Rights refers to the first 10 amendments to the Constitution, which were ratified in 1791. These amendments identify the basic civil rights of U.S. citizens, which include:

- Freedom of religion; freedom of speech; freedom of the press; the right to assemble (First Amendment)

- Freedom from "unreasonable searches and seizures" (Fourth Amendment)

- Protection against self-incrimination (Fifth Amendment)

- The right to "a speedy and public trial, by an impartial jury" (Sixth Amendment)

- Protection against excessive bail and "cruel and unusual punishments" (Eighth Amendment)

In addition, the civil rights of individuals and groups have been expanded on numerous occasions through subsequent amendments to the Constitution. For example, as shown in Chapter 2, the amendments approved during Reconstruction officially abolished slavery and extended voting rights and due process to the former slaves. Because we discussed the role of the Constitution with regard to civil rights in the history chapters, this chapter only briefly highlights particular amendments as they pertain to specific oppressed groups.

Disenfranchised Groups and Civil Rights

Many groups of citizens have faced discrimination in the United States. We discussed the history of these groups in Chapters 2 and 3. In this section, we will focus on the successes and shortcomings of efforts to enhance the civil rights of these groups. To do this, we must also examine the effects of social policies directed toward these groups.

Web Link

For more information on the history of African Americans visit the National Association for the Advancement of Colored People's site at www.mhhe.com/chapin1.

African Americans   Chapters 2 and 3 trace the historical struggle for African American civil rights, from slavery, to Jim Crow, through the civil rights movement and the implementation of affirmative action. The landmark laws in this movement are the Civil Rights Act of 1964, which outlaws racial discrimination in employment and mandates equal access to public accommodations, and the Voting Rights Act of 1965. We will examine these laws in detail later in the chapter. Another key ruling is *Brown vs. Board of Education,* which declared school segregation to be unconstitutional. Today, however, 80 percent of young black children go to schools that are more than 50 percent black, and 60 percent of white children attend schools that are more than 50 percent white. In addition, the unemployment rate for African Americans is still double that for white Americans, and almost twice as many African Americans as white Americans do not have health insurance (Jargowsky, 2003). The struggle is not over.

We have also discussed the leadership roles of African Americans who were instrumental in shaping the civil rights movement. They blazed a trail that provided inspiration for other social movements focused on women's rights, disability rights, and rights for other minority groups. The events leading up to the passage of civil rights legislation as well as the difficulties encountered in enforcing civil rights make clear that it takes the long-term commitment of people who are passionate about civil rights to enact needed policies. Moreover, once policies are enacted, their proponents must continue to be vigilant to ensure that they are enforced. Leadership for civil rights efforts most often comes from members of the group experiencing discrimination. However, other groups are often motivated to join the struggle when they witness the harm done by discrimination. As discussed in previous chapters, economic, social, and historical factors contribute to support for discriminatory practices, and change does not happen without conflict. During these conflicts, the strengths of oppressed groups become clear. In fact, it is often through engaging in conflict that individuals and communities build their strengths. The African American community continues to provide leadership in the struggle for civil rights.

American Indians   Like African Americans, American Indians were denied basic civil rights throughout most of the nation's history. Of central concern for many American Indians is **tribal sovereignty,** which refers to the right of Indian peoples to govern themselves, determine tribal membership, regulate tribal business and domestic relations, and manage tribal property. Sovereignty implies a government-to-government relationship between the federal government and the tribes. However, as seen in Chapter 2, as far back as 1831, the Supreme Court ruled in *Cherokee Nation vs. Georgia* that Indian tribes are "domestic dependent nations" and in effect declared them to be wards of the federal government (Commager, 1958, p. 256). Subsequent government actions such as the Dawes Act of 1887 further undermined tribal sovereignty. In 1934, the Indian Reorganization Act gave tribes more autonomy in handling their own affairs. However, the termination policies instituted in the 1950s further eroded both tribal sovereignty and traditional cultural practices. To challenge these policies, groups such as the American Indian Movement (AIM) resorted to direct action, such as the occupation of Alcatraz and Wounded Knee. Other groups used the courts to press for the restoration of traditional land, water, and fishing rights. The Indian Self-Determination and Education Assistance Act of 1975 affirmed American Indians' rights to be self-governing and to have greater autonomy and authority over federal programs for Indians.

Native Americans continue to fight for their civil rights, often on the basis of treaties and sovereignty rather than the Constitution. It is important to recognize that tribal sovereignty occurs within the economic and cultural contexts of the dominant culture in the United States. Cultural issues that influence the ability to practice and pass on traditional religious beliefs, languages, and social practices without fear of discrimination are particularly important to many Native Americans. For example, their religious freedom has been compromised by denial of access to religious sites by the government, and their ability to worship through traditional means has been restricted. As one example, in 1988, the U.S. Supreme Court refused to prevent the government from building roads through forest lands that certain tribes considered sacred, even though one justice acknowledged that this construction "could have devastating effects on traditional Indian religious practices" (Postrel, 1988).

Visit the Native Americans Rights Fund site through the link at www.mhhe.com/chapin1.

American Indians are also pressing for adequate funding to fully implement the Indian Child Welfare Act (ICWA) of 1978. This legislation is discussed in detail in Chapter 9. The ICWA mandates that tribes and tribal courts oversee decision making regarding Native American children who are facing out-of-home placement, thus making it more likely that their cultures will be preserved. However, lack of adequate federal funding makes such oversight very difficult for small tribes with limited resources.

To learn more about current initiatives to protect American Indian children, go to the National Indian Child Welfare Association (NICWA) Web site, found at www.mhhe.com/chapin1.

Native Americans have suffered long-term bias and discrimination. Consequently, outcomes for Indian peoples include disproportionately high rates of poverty, infant mortality, unemployment, and alcohol abuse in addition to low high school completion rates. Securing equal employment and educational opportunity is necessary if these outcomes are to change. Many tribes have opted to open casinos on their lands in order to use gambling as a source of income. However, prior to opening a casino, the tribe must obtain permission from the state government. This requirement has resulted in many legal disputes between tribes and states concerning tribal sovereignty.

Native American groups as well as other minority groups are also concerned about the "digital divide," the disparity in access to computers and the Internet between majority and minority groups. Some Alaskan Natives and American Indians have yet to be connected even to basic telephone networks. Lack of access to communication and information technology puts these groups at even greater risk of being unable to take advantage of educational and employment opportunities.

Web Link

For more information on Hispanic Americans, access the National Council of La Raza site at www.mhhe.com/chapin1.

Hispanics or Latinos Chapters 2 and 3 traced the history of Mexican Americans—also referred to as Latinos and Chicanos—in the Southwest. This group, as well as legal and undocumented migrant workers, has served as a source of inexpensive labor, particularly in the agricultural sector. As such, they lived and worked under difficult and often unhealthy conditions. In addition to Mexican Americans, immigrants from Spanish-speaking countries in Central and South America as well as Puerto Ricans have experienced widespread discrimination and abuse even as they provided the labor that helped build this country. Today, many Americans are demanding that the government limit legal immigration and strengthen border patrols to prevent undocumented immigrants from entering the country. In addition, the question of whether to provide educational and social services for undocumented immigrants continues to be a topic of heated debate.

In recent decades, the Hispanic population in the United States has grown significantly. During the period 1980–2000, almost half of all immigrants to the United States came from Latin America or the Caribbean. Consequently, according to the 2000 census, Hispanics now outnumber African Americans, and they constitute the largest ethnic group in the nation (Kaplan, Wheeler, & Holloway, 2004). Unfortunately, Hispanic families continue to be overrepresented within the low-income ranges. However, because this population has grown so rapidly, Hispanic voters are now receiving attention from politicians with diverse agendas who are intent on winning their votes. The numbers of Hispanic legislators and government officials are increasing. Thus, there is reason to hope that the power of an expanding number of Hispanic voters and elected officials will lead to the passage of policies to reduce discrimination.

Asian Americans Asian Americans are people living in the United States who personally identify themselves as having Asian or Pacific Islander ancestry. Because Asia comprises myriad countries and regions, the Asian American population is very diverse. Although small in comparison to other ethnic groups in the United States, its numbers are growing. However, discrimination is an experience that many Asian Americans share with other ethnic and racial minorities. For example, Chinese immigrants have experienced continuing exploitation in the workplace, from the early periods when they performed very dangerous work in building the nation's railways to the present time when newly arrived immigrants toil in urban sweatshops.

Japanese Americans experienced discrimination during World War II. In particular, Japanese Americans living on the West Coast, whom the government determined to be security risks, were incarcerated and sent to internment camps while their lands were confiscated. This policy was carried out even as family members were volunteering for and serving in the military. The internment of Japanese Americans demonstrates how concerns about safety and national security can lead to disregard for the civil rights of particular groups.

Because certain Asian Americans have worked hard to receive higher educations and have secured good jobs, people sometimes assume that all Asian Americans are doing well. In fact, this stereotype often leads to the portrayal of Asian Americans as the "model minority." However, this image obscures the fact that Asian Americans experience discrimination and some groups have high rates of poverty. Asian American advocacy groups are working to dispel stereotypes and develop the necessary political influence to remove remaining barriers to their full participation in society. The accompanying Web sites will provide you with more information about the history of Asian Americans and these advocacy groups.

 Web Links

Links to both the Japanese American Citizens League Web site and the Southeast Asia Resource Action Center Web site can be found at www.mhhe.com/chapin1.

Civil Rights and Sexual Orientation The struggle for equal rights for people who are gay, lesbian, bisexual, and transgender marks another milestone in the 20th-century struggle for human rights. Historically, millions of Americans regularly suffered discrimination based on **sexual orientation,** defined as "the tendency to experience erotic or romantic responses to men, women, or both, and the resulting sense of oneself" (NASW, 2003d). The 1950s saw the development of gay and lesbian activist organizations such as the Mattachine Society and the Daughters of Bilitis.

Although the 1950s were a period of social isolation for gays and lesbians, the groundwork was being laid for the gay rights movement. A major turning point in this struggle was the Stonewall Riot of 1969. When New York police raided a gay bar in Greenwich Village and the patrons resisted, gay and lesbian groups around the country began to coalesce. Their activities and the new perspectives they advocated convinced several professional organizations to modify existing policies regarding sexual orientation. For example, in 1974, the American Psychiatric Association (APA) reversed its previous policy and removed homosexuality from its official list of mental disorders (Oltmanns & Emery, 1995). Homosexuality was defined instead as an alternative form of biopsychosocial development. Three years later, the delegate assembly of the National Association of Social Workers passed a public policy statement that called on social workers to help eradicate homophobia. It further proposed that the NASW establish a National Task Force on Gay Rights to begin implementing this policy (Tice & Perkins, 2002).

In recent years, advocates for gay and lesbian rights have experienced a combination of successes and reversals. They achieved a major victory in 1996

 **The Social Work Library**

For ideas about what social workers can do to help reduce homophobia, visit The Social Work Library and read National Association of Social Workers, lesbian, gay, and bisexual issues, in Social work speaks: National Association of Social Workers policy statements, 2003–2006.

when the Supreme Court, in *Romer vs. Evans*, struck down an amendment to Colorado's constitution that barred cities and localities from enacting laws protecting homosexuals against discrimination. Among the court's arguments was that the amendment violated the "equal protection of the laws" provision of the 14th Amendment (Dripps, 1996). Despite this ruling, however, discrimination in housing and employment remains widespread, and hate crimes are regularly reported.

People in same-sex relationships do not have the right to make medical decisions for each other in medical emergencies, they do not have rights of inheritance, and they can be legally denied custody of their children and the opportunity to provide adoptive and foster care. Lesbian, gay, bisexual, and transgender people encounter barriers that often cause their needs for services, from housing to family counseling, to go largely unmet. Some states have passed **domestic partnership** legislation, which provides legal recognition or registration of committed lesbian and gay relationships. These laws do not provide the same entitlements and protections that marriage does in the state and federal systems. In 1996, Congress passed the Defense of Marriage Act (DOMA), which prohibited the recognition of same-sex marriages at the federal level and allowed states to ignore marriages of same-sex couples that are performed in other states. In addition to the federal government, 38 states had adopted DOMA laws by 2004.

 Web Link

The PFLAG Transgender Network can be accessed at www.mhhe.com/chapin1.

Gay and lesbian couples are working hard across the nation to secure the right to marry. In November 2003, the Massachusetts Supreme Court ruled that denying gay marriage violated the state constitution. Consequently, same-sex couples could legally marry beginning on May 17, 2004, in Massachusetts. This decision incited opponents in Massachusetts and more than 30 other states to introduce laws as well as amendments to state constitutions that would ban same-sex marriages. A state constitutional amendment banning same-sex marriage has gained preliminary approval in Massachusetts. If it is approved in the 2005 legislative session, a statewide vote to change the constitution will take place in 2006 (Peterson, 2004). Opponents also have called for a federal constitutional ban on same-sex marriages in order to uphold the "traditional definition of marriage as a union between a man and a woman" (Peterson, 2003). In 2004, President George W. Bush publicly stated his support for a constitutional amendment prohibiting same-sex marriages, thus interjecting the issue into the presidential campaign. In contrast, the NASW is committed to full legal and social acceptance and recognition of lesbian, gay, bisexual, and transgender people (NASW, 2003d).

People with Disabilities   The advocacy efforts of people with disabilities and their families have changed the face of social policy in the education and employment sectors. The Education for All Handicapped Children Act of 1975 mandates free public education for all children with disabilities. Amendments passed in 1986 extend services to children with disabilities from birth through age five (Pollard, 1995). Other legislation such as the Mental Health Bill of Rights Act and the Developmentally Disabled and Assistance Bill of Rights expand protection and care for people with mental illness and developmental disabilities. However, these laws offer protection only in activities and programs involving the government (NASW, 2003e).

As discussed in Chapter 3, the Americans with Disabilities Act (ADA) of 1990 helped remove deterrents to full citizenship for people with disabilities (Pollard, 1995). The ADA requires businesses and employers to make "reasonable accommodations" in order to allow people with disabilities the opportunity to perform job functions. This law has significantly increased the access of people with disabilities to needed resources. We will explore the ADA in depth in the section on major policies and programs.

In 1999, the Supreme Court held in the landmark decision *Olmstead vs. L.C.* that Title II of the ADA requires states, whenever possible, to place qualified individuals with disabilities in community settings rather than in institutions. The Supreme Court called on the states to develop "comprehensive, effectively working plans" to provide services to people with disabilities in the most integrated settings possible. Executive Order No. 13217, Community-Based Alternatives for Individuals with Disabilities, was signed on June 18, 2001. This initiative went beyond the decision to direct and mandate the federal government be involved in quickly accomplishing the task set out for the states. Instead, it called on federal agencies to assist the states and to examine their own policies and procedures to determine whether these policies presented barriers to community-based services. The attorney general and the secretary of the Department of Health and Human Services (DHHS) were empowered to enforce the *Olmstead* decision (U.S. Department of Health and Human Services, 2001). The *Olmstead* decision may lead to greater community integration for people with mental as well as physical disabilities.

People with mental illness have experienced both gains and setbacks in their pursuit of civil rights. Although people with mental illness have the right to refuse treatment, they may be committed involuntarily for treatment in a psychiatric hospital if they exhibit dangerous behavior or are incapable of self-care. However, once committed, they have the right to treatment. The legislative tenets of a client's right to treatment in the least restrictive community environment and to freedom from harm have been less well established (Marty & Chapin, 2000). One reason for this ambiguity is that the courts have been unwilling to protect the right to treatment outside of the institution when states cut back community-based options because of funding shortfalls. Deinstitutionalization of people with mental disabilities and the recognition of their right to refuse treatment help protect their civil rights. However, unless their right to treatment after they have reentered the community is established and

The Social Work Library

To find out more about clients' right to treatment in the community, read Marty, D., & Chapin, R. (2000), The legislative tenets of client's right to treatment in the least restrictive environment and freedom from harm: Implications for community providers.

Web Link

The Bazelon Center for Mental Health and the Law provides in-depth coverage of current civil rights issues for people with mental disabilities. You will find its Web site at www.mhhe.com/chapin1.

protected, they are in danger of struggling with mental illness without the needed supports or treatment.

The number of people with disabilities will grow much larger as (1) the baby boom generation ages and (2) new medical advances make it possible to save people with injuries so serious that they would have died even a few years ago. Disability rights groups can be expected to continue to press their case legislatively as well as through the courts. The combination of growth in the disability population and the loudly voiced goal of the majority of people with disabilities to remain in the community will create fiscal challenges for states and will require creative strategic planning to best use limited public resources.

Older Adults   The 1964 Civil Rights Act didn't prohibit discrimination on the basis of age. Three years later, however, the Age Discrimination in Employment Act (ADEA) prohibited employment discrimination against people between the ages of 40 and 70. Although this law protected workers within this age range, the cap on age allowed employers to enforce mandatory retirement and pursue other age-based discriminatory practices with employees and job applicants over the age of 70. In 1986, the ADEA was amended to eliminate the age cap. This revision abolished mandatory retirement for most employment and made age discrimination illegal for all age groups (Equal Employment Opportunity Commission, 1999). In 1990, the Older Workers Benefit Protection Act (OWBPA) further amended the ADEA to specifically prohibit employers from denying benefits to older employees. Despite the numerous laws enacted to protect older workers, alleged age-based discrimination is the fastest-growing source of litigation for unfair dismissal (Hooyman & Kiyak, 2002). Further, *compassionate ageism*—the stereotypical belief that all older adults are frail and incapacitated—has led to the development of public and corporate policies that hinder older adults who are fit and capable from fully participating in society. Contrary to widespread stereotypes, the older-adult population is quite diverse, and social policies must be adjusted to reflect this diversity.

Older adults also suffer discrimination when their right to self-determination in end-of-life decisions is abrogated. The Patient's Self-Determination Act of 1990 requires all hospitals participating in Medicare and Medicaid to inquire whether adult inpatients have advanced health care directives and to provide information on pertinent state laws and hospital policies. An **advanced directive** is a document or statement produced by the patient specifying her or his choices for medical treatment or designating a person to make those choices should the patient be unable to do so. Although the 1990 law was intended to protect patients at the end of life, the lack of trained hospital staff who could effectively implement the policy has limited its effectiveness. Further, as a society, we have yet to effectively address the unacceptably high levels of untreated pain that many older adults experience at the end of life. Conflict surrounding assisted suicide continues to compromise the rights of patients, including older adults, to self-determination at end of life. We will examine policy initiatives to secure and protect the rights of older adults in these areas in Chapter 11.

Women and Civil Rights   As we observed in reviewing the struggle for gender equality in Chapter 3, the struggle for voting rights and for the rights to equity in education and athletics was long and difficult. Although women have made great gains in education and training and can enter many professions that were previously closed to them, the struggle against gender-based discrimination is not over. For example, women working full-time still earn only 77 percent of the salaries of full-time male workers (DeNavas-Walt, Cleveland, & Webster, 2003). Because women are more often the primary caregivers for children and elders, the lack of policies to adequately support people who work and care for dependents continues to place female workers at a disadvantage. This combination of factors contributes to the **"feminization of poverty,"** that is, the disproportionately high number of women and their children who are living in poverty. Moreover, women who have been poor all their lives face old age with inadequate retirement savings and pensions. The poverty rate for people age 65 and older decreases for men but increases slightly for women (U.S. Census Bureau, 2003). Finally, the current trend of dual-income families in the United States means that all family members, including men, suffer from lower wages paid to women (NASW, 2003b). Low wages for women are a major cause of childhood poverty.

Women also continue to fight for the right to control their own bodies, and they are much more likely than men to be the victims of domestic violence. The economic disadvantages women still face make it more difficult to leave abusive relationships. Affirmative action has helped women achieve gains in the workplace. However, as we shall see in the next segment of this chapter, changes in affirmative action as well as other polices and programs have differential effects on women and men.

Affirmative Action

As discussed in Chapter 3, affirmative action evolved in the 1970s as advocates of equal opportunity became convinced that simply banning discrimination was insufficient to help marginalized groups overcome the effects of past discrimination. Affirmative action is often misunderstood and misrepresented. It is best understood as a tool for reducing discrimination in employment and education (NASW, 2003a). The basic affirmative action strategies—proportional representation, numerical quotas, and set-asides for women and minorities— have been relatively successful in securing access to opportunities previously restricted largely to white males. Nevertheless, affirmative action has always been—and continues to be—highly controversial. Critics question the fairness

---

www.ncwge.org

To view information on progress made in achieving gender equity, read National Coalition for Women and Girls in Education (2002), Title IX at 30: Report card on gender equity.

---

www.now.org/issues/ abortion/roe30/timeline.html

For more information on the struggle for reproductive rights, read National Organization for Women (2004), Reproductive rights historical highlights.

---

www.usdoj.gov/ovw/

For more information on violence against women and enforcement of the Violence Against Women Act, go to the Office on Violence Against Women, U.S. Department of justice.

Source: Copyright © 2003 Mike Keefe. All rights reserved. Used with permission of Cagle Cartoons. www.caglecartoons.com

and effectiveness of affirmative action, especially concerning its effects on white men. They frequently refer to affirmative action as reverse discrimination, defined as discrimination against the majority group arising from policies designed to overcome discrimination against minority groups. They have consistently challenged such policies and programs in the courts. In 1978, *The Regents of the University of California vs. Bakke* came before the Supreme Court. Allan Bakke, a white male, had been denied admission to the medical school, even though he had a higher grade point average than some minority candidates who were admitted. The court ruling in the *Bakke* case can be interpreted as a partial victory for both opponents and advocates of affirmative action. On the one hand, the court struck down the use of strict racial quotas in determining school admissions. Consequently, Bakke was admitted to the medical school. On the other hand, the ruling upheld the use of race as one determinant of admission to higher education. The *Bakke* decision fueled the reverse discrimination controversy.

In 2003, two major Supreme Court decisions essentially upheld the *Bakke* ruling. Both cases involved the University of Michigan. The university's College of Literature, Science, and the Arts had instituted an admissions system in which all candidates who received a rating of 100 points on a scale of 150 were accepted. In 1998, the college instituted an affirmative action program that automatically awarded 20 points to all Native American, African American, and Hispanic applicants. Two white students challenged this system as an exercise in reverse discrimination. In *Gratz vs. Bollinger*, the court upheld this challenge and declared the program unconstitutional. However, in *Grutter vs. Bollinger*, it ruled in favor of the law school's program, which considers race a factor in admissions but does not employ a strict numerical system. Significantly, the court confirmed the argument of affirmative action proponents that promoting racial and ethnic diversity on college campuses is a legitimate strategy for achieving social justice (Greenhouse, 2003).

At the same time, the Supreme Court has placed greater restrictions on affirmative action policies concerning employment. In the 1995 case *Adarand Constructors vs. Peña*, the court invalidated a set-aside program established by the federal government that awarded special consideration to minority-owned construction firms. The ruling specified that such an arrangement is legitimate only when the minority recipient could demonstrate that she or he had been the victim of clearly identified acts of discrimination in the past. It further mandated that all federal affirmative action programs be subjected to "strict scrutiny" (Weiss, 1997).

The federal government is able to influence state and local policies as well as businesses and corporations by requiring adherence to specific regulations and stipulations as a condition for receiving federal funds. The federal government used this power to require affirmative action to advance civil rights across the United States. However, as discussed in previous chapters, we are now witnessing a return to more state control. Widespread discrimination under state rule in the 1960s spurred federal involvement in civil rights protection. The return to more state control could therefore lead to diminished support for civil rights.

Affirmative action will undoubtedly remain an inflammatory issue for the foreseeable future. As the representation of minorities in different fields has increased, many people have come to believe that our society has reached a point at which we no longer need affirmative action. Conversely, others believe that we still have a long way to go before we achieve equality and that affirmative action remains essential to this process.

MAJOR POLICIES AND PROGRAMS

Our examination of the history of civil rights provided ample illustrations of social policies that served to deny rather than protect the civil rights of African Americans, Native Americans, Hispanics, Asian Americans, women, people with disabilities, gay men and lesbians, and older adults. Major policies and programs discussed below were implemented more recently to protect civil rights, to eliminate discrimination, and to help repair the damage done by previous discriminatory policies. As such, they represent efforts to secure social justice for people of diverse backgrounds. Examining them in detail provides us with insight into what additional policies and programs are needed to achieve further progress in civil rights.

BOX 7.2

Civil Rights Act, 1964

Policy Goals	To remove barriers to voter registration, end discrimination in public accommodations and programs receiving federal assistance, encourage school desegregation, and establish the Equal Employment Opportunity Commission to oversee antidiscrimination efforts in the workplace.
Benefits or Services Provided	Enforcement of the right to register to vote; the right to use public accommodations such as hotels, restaurants, and theaters; desegregation of schools; and the right to obtain employment.
Eligibility Rules	All people regardless of race, color, religion, or national origin. Employment protection also covers discrimination based on sex.
Service Delivery System	Mandated places of public accommodation to remove barriers to use by desegregating facilities. Attorney general authorized to file suits to enforce rights.
Financing	Federal general revenue used to fund enforcement agencies.

Source: Adapted from "Major features of the Civil Rights Act of 1964," by CongressLink, n.d. www.congresslink.org/civil/essay.html. Copyright 2004 Dirksen Congressional Center. Used with permission.

The Civil Rights Act of 1964

The Civil Rights Act of 1964 was an omnibus bill directed against the various forms of segregation and discrimination that characterized U.S. society—particularly the southern states—in the 1960s. This landmark law attempted to decrease discrimination by (1) barring unequal application of voter registration requirements; (2) outlawing segregation in hotels, restaurants, theaters, and other public accommodations; (3) encouraging school desegregation and authorizing the U.S. attorney general to file lawsuits against schools that resisted integration; (4) empowering federal agencies to withhold funds from programs that practiced segregation; and (5) creating the Equal Employment Opportunity Commission (EEOC) to oversee antidiscrimination efforts in employment. Box 7.2 summarizes the central features of the act.

 Web Link

The Leadership Conference on Civil Rights (LCCR) has developed a timeline, which you may view at its Web site, that allows you to learn more about civil rights legislation. You'll find the Web site at www.mhhe.com/chapin1.

The Civil Rights Restoration Act of 1987, which became law in spite of President Reagan's veto, amended the Civil Rights Act of 1964 by strengthening enforcement of nondiscrimination laws in private institutions that receive federal funds. The Civil Rights Act of 1991 further amended the 1964 law. This legislation was designed to address a series of Supreme Court decisions that rolled back support for employees who sued their employers for discrimination. It strengthened and improved federal civil rights enforcement by mandating

Policy Goals	To enforce the 15th Amendment to the Constitution granting all citizens an equal opportunity to vote.
Benefits or Services Provided	Provided protection against the use of literacy tests or other election laws that denied or reduced voting rights.
Eligibility Rules	All citizens eligible to vote regardless of race or color.
Service Delivery System	Federal examiners register voters and approve election law practices prior to their use. Attorney general directed to enforce the law and challenge discriminatory practices.
Financing	Federal general revenue used to fund enforcement agencies.

BOX 7.3

Voting Rights Act, 1965

Source: From "Introduction to federal voting rights laws," by U.S. Department of Justice, 2000. www.usdoj.gov.

monetary damages in cases of intentional employment discrimination and by extending protection against employment discrimination to employees of Congress and some high-level political appointees. In addition, it extended civil rights legislation to include U.S. and U.S.-controlled employers operating abroad. Although the legislation broadened many aspects of civil rights law, it also included provisions prohibiting the use of quotas, and it placed a cap on the damages paid in cases of intentional employment discrimination and unlawful harassment.

The Voting Rights Act of 1965

By 1965, escalating violence, televised accounts of the protest march from Selma to Montgomery, Alabama, where the marchers faced resistance from state troopers, and the murder of voting rights activists made it clear that stronger federal intervention was necessary to overcome state and local practices that disenfranchised African Americans. President Lyndon Johnson and many civil rights activists issued a call for strong voting rights legislation that resulted in the passage of the Voting Rights Act. This legislation temporarily suspended literacy tests, and it provided for the appointment of federal examiners with the power to approve election practices prior to their use and register qualified citizens to vote (U.S. Department of Justice, 2000). See Box 7.3 for an overview of the specifics of the Voting Rights Act. Amendments to the act in 1975 added protections from voting discrimination for groups whose native language is not English. In addition, the 24th Amendment to the U.S. Constitution had outlawed the use of poll taxes.

The effectiveness of the Voting Rights Act was evident within the first five years of its passage. From 1964 to 1968, the percentage of eligible black voters

BOX 7.4		
Education for All Handicapped Children Act, 1975	**Policy Goals**	To provide free and appropriate public education to all children.
	Benefits or Services Provided	Special education and related services. Use of an Individualized Education Plan (IEP) for each eligible child. Education provided in the least restrictive environment.
	Eligibility Rules	Children ages 3–21 with disabilities.
	Service Delivery System	Public schools provide appropriate education. IEPs are prepared by multidisciplinary teams within the public schools and include input from the families and students.
	Financing	Federal funding provided to states to encourage public education of children with disabilities.

Source: From "Education for All Handicapped Children Act of 1975." Pub. L. 94–142, s. 6.

who were registered rose from 23 percent to 59 percent in the Deep South states of Alabama, Georgia, Louisiana, Mississippi, and South Carolina. As the number of registered black voters increased, so did the number of black elected officials. Prior to 1965, there were less than 100 black elected officials in the previously mentioned five states plus Virginia and North Carolina. By 1975, that number had risen to more than 1,000, primarily in county and municipal offices. One black man was serving in Congress, and 68 African Americans were state legislators (Hudson, 1998).

The Education for All Handicapped Children Act of 1975

www.ed.gov/policy/speced/
leg/idea/history.html

For more information, read the U.S. Department of Education report Twenty-five Years of Progress in Educating Children with Disabilities through IDEA.

The Education for All Handicapped Children Act of 1975 mandated that all children with disabilities have available to them a free and appropriate public education. The law specified that education and related services should be designed to meet the unique needs of these children and would ensure that the rights of children with disabilities and their parents or guardians are protected. The act also required that students with disabilities be "mainstreamed," that is, educated with peers without disabilities to the maximum extent appropriate. The federal government was to assist states and localities so they could provide for the education of all children with disabilities. Federal oversight to assess and assure the effectiveness of efforts to educate children with disabilities was also mandated. You can examine the details of this law in Box 7.4.

In 1990, this statute was amended, and the title was changed to Individuals with Disabilities Education Act (IDEA). Additional amendments made in 1997 are commonly referred to as IDEA 97. IDEA secures the right of children to a "free and appropriate public education" by making federal funding for special education contingent upon compliance with IDEA. School districts are required to formulate an *individualized education plan* (IEP) for each student with disabilities and to provide education in the *least restrictive environment* (LRE). Inclusion—that is, the education of children with disabilities in the classroom with their peers—is required to the maximum extent possible. Although school districts continue to struggle to meet the mandates of this legislation, children with disabilities now have a much greater chance of receiving an adequate public education than they did before the legislation was enacted.

The Americans with Disabilities Act of 1990

The Americans with Disabilities Act (ADA), which is summarized in Box 7.5, illustrates how legislation can be formulated based on the goals of the target group. The ADA was designed to press for full access to services and benefits for people with disabilities. The purposes of this act are as follows:

- To provide a clear and comprehensive national mandate for the elimination of discrimination against individuals with disabilities

- To provide clear, strong, consistent, enforceable standards addressing discrimination against individuals with disabilities

- To ensure that the federal government plays a central role in enforcing the standards established in this act on behalf of individuals with disabilities

---

BOX 7.5

Americans with Disabilities Act, 1990

Policy Goals	To eradicate discrimination directed toward people with disabilities, increase employment opportunities, and ensure equality of opportunity and access.
Benefits or Services Provided	Protection of right to equal opportunity in public accommodations, employment, transportation, state and local government services, and telecommunications.
Eligibility Rules	People with a physical or mental impairment that limits one or more major life activities.
Service Delivery System	Businesses and employers make and pay for reasonable accomodations. Department of Justice negotiates, mediates, and files suit in cases of discrimination unless employment related, in which case the Equal Employment Opportunity Commission handles the complaint.
Financing	Federal general revenue used to fund enforcement agencies.

Source: From "ADA Homepage," by U.S. Department of Justice, 2004. www.ada.gov.

- To invoke the sweep of congressional authority, including the power to enforce the 14th Amendment and to regulate commerce, in order to address the major areas of day-to-day discrimination faced by people with disabilities (Americans with Disabilities Act of 1990, 2, 204)

Web Link

To learn more about the ADA Watch project, visit their link at www.mhhe.com/chapin1.

The principles of strengths-based policy development, as detailed in previous chapters, are clearly reflected in this policy. Over the last 30 years, society's view of people with disabilities has evolved from one in which they were segregated and devalued to one in which they are active participants in our communities, with the decision-making capacity to control their own lives (NASW, 2003e). There is a guiding principle in the disability community: "Nothing about us without us." In keeping with that principle, groups made up of people with disabilities and their families, including the *independent living* (IL) movement, worked to craft this legislation and were tireless in their efforts to secure passage of the ADA. The people who crafted this legislation clearly understood that disability is a social construct and, as such, is open to interpretation and modification (NASW, 2003e). Disability is no longer viewed as occurring solely in the individual but rather in the interface between personal capacity and environmental demands. Disability can thus be ameliorated by transforming the environment rather than by focusing primarily on what an individual is unable to do.

People with disabilities and their families worked hard to change the definition of the "problem of disability" from a focus on individual deficiencies to one that insisted that strengths, needs, and goals of people with disabilities be given center stage. The IL movement helped to create sociopolitical forces that reshaped policy makers' understanding of the nature of disability and resulting needs. It did so by shifting the approach to understanding need from considering disability as a problem to examining the environmental barriers that prevented people who were "differently able" from accessing needed resources. Professionals collaborated with the target group in crafting the legislation. Claimsmaking was based on appeals to social justice, equity, and the right to self-determination, all core social work values that reflect the strengths perspective. The focus was on civil rights for people with disabilities.

Since the bill became law, employment and educational outcomes for people with disabilities continue to be carefully monitored to ensure that the goals of the target group are being achieved. Although the ADA has not ended discrimination against people with disabilities and enforcement has been problematic, this legislative initiative provides a powerful example of how the strengths perspective can be reflected in crafting policy.

Web Link

For more information on the Americans with Disabilities Act and enforcement issues, go to the ADA Homepage.

Some businesses and employers have challenged the need to comply with the ADA. Their reasons for resistance to making reasonable accommodations include fear of financial hardship and concern that people with disabilities create heightened liability risks both as employees and as customers (NASW, 2003e). Courts have often sided with the defendant rather than the person with a disability. However, efforts to promote voluntary compliance, coupled with a willingness to pursue mandatory compliance through the courts, have resulted in increased access to many businesses and faculties that were previously inaccessible for many people with disabilities.

EVALUATING CIVIL RIGHTS POLICIES AND PROGRAMS

The following discussion acknowledges advances in securing civil rights and also examines work yet to be done. There is no question that the United States made significant progress during the 20th century toward protecting and enhancing the civil rights of many oppressed groups. Perhaps one of the most important changes has been an increased recognition of discrimination and a willingness to speak up and use a variety of strategies to end discriminatory practices. Groups that have experienced discrimination, including people of color, women, people with disabilities, and people discriminated against based on sexual orientation, have demanded changes in social policies and programs and an end to unfair treatment. However, people of color are still experiencing discrimination, which results in the disproportionately negative educational, health, and employment outcomes discussed in this chapter. Because of **de facto segregation**—segregation caused by social practices, political acts, or economic circumstances but not by actual laws—disproportionate numbers of people of color continue to live in inner-city and other isolated low-income neighborhoods with segregated schools and severely limited job opportunities.

Discrimination Based on Race and Gender

We have examined disparities in poverty rates, retirement programs, and employment for women and people of color. A major reason why wages earned by women and people of color are lower than those of white males is that they are still disproportionately represented in the lowest-paying jobs, sometimes termed the **secondary labor market.** This tendency is referred to as **occupational segregation** (NASW, 2003b). Employment in the secondary labor market also negatively influences the health of these groups because these jobs generally do not provide health insurance. For example, many childcare, housekeeping, and public school paraprofessional positions provide low pay and few benefits. Although it is important to open up more job categories to women and people of color, it is also important to adequately compensate people who perform traditionally female work. To accomplish this goal, we need to develop methods of determining the comparable worth of jobs and strategies for implementing comparable pay scales.

Harassment on the job is also a civil rights issue. Sexual harassment and harassment based on race and ethnicity create a hostile working environment and can limit employment longevity and promotion. Many people who encounter harassment on the job either put up with it or leave. Preventing harassment is key to equal access to employment and promotion.

Web Link

For more information on initiatives to protect civil liberties, access the American Civil Liberties Union Web site at www.mhhe.com/chapin1.

Affirmative action, although successful in increasing access for groups previously excluded from many employment and educational opportunities, has certainly not leveled the playing field. For example, in 2004, the National Urban League reported that the mean income of black men is 70 percent of that of white men (a $16,876 gap). Similarly, the mean income of black women is 83 percent of their white counterparts (a $6,370 difference) (National Urban League, 2004). The differences are even starker when the asset accumulations of blacks and whites are compared. Further, affirmative action is under attack in many quarters. Discrimination on the basis of sexual orientation is still accepted social policy, and women's rights must constantly be defended. The need to make sure all children receive adequate basic education generates a great deal of discussion; however, the funding strategies to make adequate education a reality for all children have yet to materialize in many states.

Immigrants and undocumented workers are often blamed for many of our nation's woes, and efforts to restrict immigration have been a recurring theme in our history. Many states and localities continue to introduce initiatives requiring all residents to speak English only. Human rights violations in other parts of the world contribute to the flow of refugees into our country. Therefore, we must reform our immigration and refugee policies in a way that (1) reaffirms the contributions immigrants have made to this country, (2) permits the United States to respond humanely to political refugees, and (3) provides fiscal relief to states and communities that provide services to large numbers of immigrants and refugees (NASW, 2003c).

Civil Rights Amid a Climate of Fear

Given the current war on terror and the accompanying climate of fear, people in this country who are Muslims or have family roots in the Middle East are at risk for increased discrimination. Following the 9/11 terrorist attacks, Arab Americans increasingly have been targets of hate crimes and physical violence and have encountered discrimination on airlines, in employment, and at schools. There is growing concern that the USA Patriot Act is eroding their civil liberties, particularly the right of due process (American-Arab Anti Discrimination Committee, 2002).

Indeed, in previous periods when the United States has been gripped by fear, repression of citizens from a variety of backgrounds has escalated. For example, during the 1950s, when the U.S. public was very fearful of commu-nism, Senator Joseph McCarthy (a Wisconsin Republican) spearheaded an in-famous effort to stifle political dissent. McCarthy claimed that the State Department was composed of a large number of communists. He garnered widespread attention to his claims about the prevalence of communism in the government and raised suspicions about the alleged communist affiliations of prominent citizens. A new term developed from this model of accusation and attack: *McCarthyism.* Other such attacks, which often included inaccurate evi-dence and sensationalist tactics, are still referred to by this term. Given the cur-rent climate of fear in the United States, social workers need to be alert to the possibility of the emergence of another era of McCarthyism that seeks to stifle dissent. During such periods, the kind of speaking up and speaking out that is vital to securing and protecting civil rights for all citizens may become more difficult.

NEXT STEPS

How, then, are civil rights to be secured and protected for people of diverse backgrounds in our country? Clearly, social workers are called upon to advocate for equal rights for all citizens in the NASW *Code of Ethics.* Some people incor-rectly believe that the strengths perspective is incompatible with conflict strategies to help oppressed groups. In fact, there is a close relationship between the strengths perspective and empowerment theory, which is rooted in conflict theory. Conflict theory focuses on how individuals and groups struggle to in-crease their power and maximize benefits, which in turn leads to political and social change. Strengths-based and empowerment-oriented interventions both focus on client and environmental strengths and strategies, including educa-tion (transfer of knowledge and skills, often among individuals in similar cir-cumstances), self-help, social networks, advocacy, and social action, to help clients increase their power over their own lives. Both approaches strongly sup-port client participation in all aspects of decision making that affect their lives. Moreover, both strategies seek egalitarian working relationships between social workers and their clients (Chapin & Cox, 2001).

Finally, commitment to social justice is an overarching value guiding both approaches. Work that identifies and bolsters the strengths of oppressed groups and helps them remove barriers to reaching their goals is at the heart of the strengths perspective; it also supports empowerment strategies. Conflict as well as consensus building may be necessary in collaborating with oppressed groups to achieve their goals. The strengths perspective provides tools for supporting the strengths of oppressed populations and for helping them acquire the nec-essary resources for successful civil rights initiatives.

The Social Work Library

If you would like to learn more about the connections between empowerment and strengths-based approaches, see Chapin & Cox, Changing the paradigm: Strengths-based and empowerment-oriented social work with frail elders, found at www.mhhe.com/chapin1.

Reconsidering "Neutral" Policies

Social workers must analyze policies that in theory apply equally to all citizens so as to determine whether in practice they adversely affect people from diverse backgrounds. Policies apply to large categories of people, and individualizing policies to fit diverse needs is a complicated process. For example, low-income elders with disabilities are eligible to have their nursing home care paid for through Medicaid. Theoretically, Native Americans should have equal access to that benefit because providers of Medicaid benefits are prohibited from discriminating on the basis of race or ethnicity. However, nursing home policies often require certain types of beds and bed heights and certain dietary regimens. An elder raised in a traditional Native American culture may be more at ease in a bed at a lower level surrounded by sacred objects from home. In addition, the kinds of food and food preparation provided in the nursing facility may be foreign to them and put them at risk of severe weight loss. When perceived from this perspective, nursing home policies that are not sensitive to racial and ethnic differences create barriers that limit access even though they appear neutral on the surface.

Exploring this issue from a strengths perspective suggests alternative approaches. For example, nursing home regulations could incorporate traditional values of tribal caring, and Native American tribes could be provided resources to design community-based, long-term care alternatives that reflect their lifestyle. The negative impact of nursing home policies is just one example of the many ways in which supposedly neutral policies actually create barriers to benefits and services for already disadvantaged groups. If you begin to look carefully at the differential effects of policies, you undoubtedly will find many more examples. It is important to try to educate policy makers about cultural differences and to help craft more culturally sensitive policies. However, until people of color and other disadvantaged groups are much better represented among the ranks of policy makers, it will be difficult for policy makers to foresee the barriers much less craft effective alternatives.

The Role of Social Workers

The NASW is committed to affirmative action and is working to increase diversity in the profession (NASW, 2003b). Attracting social workers from diverse backgrounds will prove helpful in identifying policies that don't work well for specific populations. Schools of social work have also instituted new curriculum policies to help sensitize their students to groups who have experienced historical discrimination. Each new piece of proposed legislation needs to be scrutinized for differential negative effects on people of different backgrounds.

Because legislation typically is quite broad, rules and regulations are written to determine how legislation will be implemented. Discriminatory rules and regulations can often be changed without creating new legislation. Social workers on the front lines who are aware that certain policies perpetuate discrimination can help policy makers and administrators craft more-effective rules and regulations. Typically, the more flexible the rules and regulations, the greater the opportunity for professionals to tailor services in ways better suited to people of diverse backgrounds. Although greater flexibility may also lead to abuse, it is impossible to legislate for all eventualities. Rather, allowing providers latitude, creating incentives for compliance, and then closely monitoring for outcomes that indicate equal access to services can be expected to reap more satisfactory results.

Social workers can also publicize information concerning progress toward equal opportunity in a form that most citizens can understand. For example, the National Urban League has developed the Equality Index, a statistical measurement of disparities that exist between blacks and whites in economics, education, health, housing, civic engagement, and social justice. A weighted index value of 1 is assigned to whites. An Equality Index value of less than 1 indicates that the group being compared is doing worse than whites in a category, whereas a value of 1 or more means the comparison group is doing as well as or better than whites. The league's analysis indicates that the mean income of black workers is significantly less than that of their white counterparts. However, the index focused on service to country indicates higher rates of military service among black as opposed to white Americans (National Urban League, 2004). Social workers need to help make their fellow citizens aware that inequality continues to be a problem in our society.

Web Links

You can find out more about this analysis and the Equity Index by visiting the National Urban League Web site www.mhhe.com/chapin1.

Because public as well as private monitoring of outcomes is necessary for laws to be effective, social workers can also advocate for more effective, comprehensive monitoring by federal and state agencies charged with enforcing civil rights legislation. These efforts should include demands for adequate funding for these agencies. Further, a huge impediment to progress in civil rights as well as in the social service arena is that legislation is passed and mandates are given, but funds to make the required changes are in very short supply.

If professionals in service settings do not see their clear responsibility to be involved in policy practice and to call attention to policies that lead to unequal access, such policies and practices will continue to put disadvantaged groups at even greater risk. Box 7.6 lists some questions that can help alert you to possible discrimination in social work settings where you practice. Consider these questions in relation to an agency with which you are familiar. If you conclude that access to service is unequal, then you can utilize the information contained in Chapter 6 to generate some ideas about how you might resolve this problem.

Social workers and the social service systems in which they work often reflect the dominant culture in which they are immersed. Service delivery from diagnosis and assessment to financing, reimbursement, and general organization is shaped by this culture. At the same time, clients who come from different cultures have also been influenced by their backgrounds. Unfortunately, social workers frequently are ill equipped to recognize and negotiate the

BOX 7.6

*Agency
Analysis*

- Does the agency serve a larger proportion of people from one race or gender than is found in the service area? If so, why?
- Does the agency typically contact the mother when working with a family?
- Where is the agency located? Location of service in itself can create access problems for certain groups.
- Is the agency accessible by people with physical disabilities?
- Who works in the agency? Does the gender and racial composition resemble that of the population served?
- Does the gender and racial composition of administrators and managers resemble that of the population served?
- Are staff who speak their language available to applicants and clients who do not speak English?
- Does the agency attempt to build on the racial and cultural identities of clients, or does it typically impose the identity of the staff?
- Does the agency acknowledge and serve same-sex couples and families?
- How do agency policies help support or undermine positive outcomes for clients in the areas discussed above?
- What agency policies or practices contribute to or reduce experiences of discrimination on a personal level?

cultural differences that can influence the effectiveness of services. If equal access to services tailored to diverse needs is to become a reality, then service providers must be trained to recognize and respond effectively to their clients' cultural backgrounds. Policies that promote diversity in service provider backgrounds are needed. The goal is to find ways to celebrate differences and to draw strength from diversity.

CONCLUSION

The United States is home to an array of cultures, races, and ethnicities. People of diverse backgrounds bring energy, optimism, global perspectives, and productive contributions to all areas of contemporary life. Social workers can help celebrate these differences and not allow them to be the basis for denying access to education, employment, health, or social services. We need to join together with other concerned groups to develop more cogent and effective policies and programs in order to ensure that these goals are realized in our society and communities (NASW, 2003a).

MAIN POINTS

- Civil rights are legally enforceable protections afforded to citizens for the purpose of preventing arbitrary abuse by the state or other individuals. Societal barriers to accessing equal rights for oppressed groups affect outcomes such as poverty, unemployment rates, and school dropout rates.

- The Constitution, including the Bill of Rights, is the foundation of civil rights protection. Subsequent constitutional amendments, the Civil War, and the civil rights movement of the 1950s and 1960s have helped secure additional rights for oppressed groups and ensure recognition of those rights by the majority population.

- The struggle of people of color to attain equal rights is central to the civil rights movement. Besides having to struggle to secure citizenship and individual civil rights, Native Americans have fought for tribal sovereignty in the United States.

- Religious leaders, particularly in the African American community, have often been instrumental in the fight for civil rights.

- Efforts to reduce discrimination based on sexual orientation have focused on employment, housing, education, and legal rights in marriage as well as reduction of hate crimes.

- People with disabilities have fought for access to services, benefits, and non-institutionalized care. Civil rights for older adults have also been pressed in employment and end-of-life decisions.

- Women's rights' initiatives have focused on suffrage, education, employment, reproductive freedom, and the unsuccessful push for the passage of the Equal Rights Amendment.

- Affirmative action is based on the idea that past and present discrimination warrants compensation. It has been used as an effective tool for reducing discrimination, but it remains controversial.

- Major legislation influencing the rights of people regardless of race, color, religion, and national origin includes the Civil Rights Act of 1964 as amended in 1987 and 1991 and the Voting Rights Act of 1965.

- The Education for All Handicapped Children Act of 1975 provides for free and appropriate public education for all children with disabilities. The Americans with Disabilities Act of 1990 mandates equal opportunity in applying for and securing access to jobs.

- Social workers have a commitment to social justice. By identifying the strengths of oppressed groups and removing barriers to goal attainment through conflict and consensus building, they can increase social justice.

- Significant strides have been made in the civil rights arena, but additional advocacy is needed to reduce the discrimination still present in U.S. society.

EXERCISES: PRACTICING SOCIAL WORK

Working with the Sanchez Family

1. The Sanchez family discussed in the case vignettes is Mexican American. What historical policies and programs have had a negative impact on their ability to reach their goals? Identify a policy change that would improve the quality of life for the Sanchez family. How could you help bring about that policy change?

2. Go the National Council of La Raza Web site which can be accessed through the Resources Folder under Relevant Web sites, in the Sanchez Family case and examine the topics under Civil Rights and Justice. Pick one of the policies covered under this heading and explain likely implications for the Sanchez family.

Working with the Black Feather Community

1. In reviewing information about the Black Feather community, it is clear that the legacy of oppression of Native Americans has produced environmental conditions that have led to public health outcomes that are poorer for Native Americans than for the general population. In your opinion, what additional pieces of legislation, at the federal, state, or local level, are needed to equalize conditions between poorer Native American communities and their more affluent non-native counterparts?

2. As you learned in your text, American Indian tribes have pressed for a sovereign relationship with the federal government. Explain what is meant by a sovereign relationship and identify at least two implications for social policy based on your understanding of this relationship. You can inform your understanding of these issues by reading about legislation in the Resources section of the Black Feather case study and by reviewing information on the agencies in the Bios file in the Engage segment.

EXERCISES: THE SOCIAL WORK LIBRARY

Read "Race, politics, and social policy" (Parham & Quadagno, 2000), and respond to the following:

1. How did the cultural milieu affect social policies regarding race from the New Deal until current times? (Refer to Chapters 2 and 3 for additional history.)

2. What is affirmative action? How has affirmative action changed since the 1960s?

Read "Lesbian, gay, and bisexual issues" (National Association of Social Workers, 2003), and respond to the following:

1. Were any of the issues specific to the lesbian, gay, and bisexual population discussed in this policy statement unfamiliar to you?

2. How can the NASW *Code of Ethics* be used to guide social work practice with lesbian, gay, and bisexual people?

3. The issue of gay marriage has been heavily debated in many states recently. What is the current status of this debate in your state of residence? (Hint: Start your search at www.stateline.org.)

CHAPTER 8

Income- and Asset-Based
Social Policies and Programs

I have . . .	I need . . .
hopes,	*food,*
dreams,	*shelter,*
goals,	*a check,*
children.	*a chance.*

Anonymous: A Mother

SOCIAL WORKERS PRACTICE WITH PEOPLE OF ALL INCOME LEVELS. However, many of their clients live in poverty. As discussed in the section on needs determination in Chapter 5, there may be many reasons a person has a low income, including physical and mental disabilities, lack of education, alcohol and drug abuse, discriminatory hiring practices, and lack of well-paying jobs in the community. Basically, people are poor because they lack the power to acquire resources to meet their needs. Although there are many strategies for overcoming the barriers faced by people in poverty, the most immediate requirement is access to incomes that are adequate to acquire necessities such as food and shelter.

This chapter examines the major government policies and programs designed to reduce poverty. Its primary emphasis is on those policies and programs that provide cash to clients. However, because food stamps and housing subsidies also directly help ameliorate the effects of poverty, we will analyze these policies and programs as well. In addition, because Temporary Assistance to Needy Families (TANF), the major program that supports women and children who are living in poverty, also contains a large jobs program, this chapter also covers employment policy in the context of TANF. Additionally, to help you understand the structure and functions of government antipoverty policies and programs, we will analyze official definitions of poverty, contrast universal with selective programs, and examine in greater detail the major asset-based policies currently advocated by social workers. As in previous chapters, we will use strengths perspective principles to analyze various income-support policies.

DEFINITIONS OF POVERTY

Poverty may be defined in a variety of ways. Experts who define poverty frequently distinguish between absolute and relative poverty. **Absolute poverty** refers to a system whereby the government determines an objective income level threshold or *poverty line,* which is used as a measure of who is poor. More specifically, the government calculates food, housing, and other basic needs in terms of the minimum level of income needed to survive. If an individual's or a family's income falls below the poverty line, then that individual or family is defined as poor. Absolute measures of poverty typically are used when setting social policy.

Poverty can also be defined in terms of a relative poverty threshold. **Relative poverty** is influenced heavily by societal standards in determining a threshold of income that allows people to afford what is generally considered by the citizenry to be an adequate standard of living at a given time in a society. For example, housing considered to be adequate by U.S. standards is different from housing considered adequate in developing countries. Likewise, what is considered a necessary material possession varies from country to country and even among people within the United States. For example, many Americans might not consider a television to be a necessity, but perhaps all Americans would define a refrigerator as a basic necessity. One common measure for relative poverty is an income that is less than 50 percent of the median family income in a country. Median income is the income point at which half of the citizens have a higher income and half have a lower income.

The Poverty Line

The government uses an absolute income level threshold, or **poverty line,** to determine who is poor. The poverty line has also been described as the *poverty index, poverty threshold,* or *poverty level,* depending on the context. Mollie Orshansky, a social science research analyst on the staff of the Social Security Administration, initially developed the official poverty threshold used by the U.S. government. Orshansky constructed this measure based on a survey of American households conducted in 1955. The results of this survey indicated that families of three or more members spent approximately one-third of their post-tax monthly income on food. Orshansky established the measurement of poverty by selecting the cheapest of four economy food plans developed by the Department of Agriculture and then multiplying the cost of that plan by three. Significantly, this food plan—referred to as the "Thrifty Food Plan"—outlined a nutritionally adequate diet for families under economic constraints or facing an emergency situation that might not be adequate on a long-term basis (Fischer, 1992).

Currently, the U.S. Census Bureau is responsible for measuring poverty. In 2004, the poverty threshold for a family of four with two children under the

The Social Work Library

You can find more in-depth information about the development of poverty measures and Mollie Orshansky's work at www.mhhe.com/chapin1.

age of 18 was $19,157, meaning that if a family's income was lower than this amount, the family was considered poor (U.S. Census Bureau, 2004). This income level, which is adjusted yearly for inflation, is supposed to satisfy a family's minimal needs. In 2004, 37 million people in the United States—approximately 12.7 percent of the overall population—were living below the poverty line (U.S. Census Bureau, 2005b). This was an increase over 2003. However, many public means-tested programs such as Medicaid and TANF require clients to fall far below the poverty line in order to qualify for assistance.

Calculations to determine who is poor are based on actual pretax income including financial assistance from the government such as Social Security and Supplemental Security Income (SSI). However, it does not consider noncash benefits such as housing subsidies and food stamps, nor does it include a family's assets or liabilities. Unlike earlier federal calculations of poverty levels that considered such factors as farm and nonfarm residence and the sex of the family head, the current poverty line is adjusted only for family size and ages of family members. The poverty line also does not take into consideration the geographical location of families, except for those living in either Hawaii or Alaska (U.S. Census Bureau, 2003). Consequently, it does not differentiate families in large urban areas from families living in small, rural communities where the cost of living may be lower.

Poverty Guidelines

Web Link

To find out more about poverty thresholds and which programs use the DHHS guidelines, go to www.mhhe.com/chapin1 and explore the link at the Institute for Research on Poverty.

The poverty line is one means the federal government uses to measure poverty, though primarily for statistical purposes. In contrast, poverty guidelines represent different measures that are used to determine financial eligibility for various federal programs. One way that these guidelines differ from the poverty line is that they do not differentiate for age. The U.S. Department of Health and Human Services (DHHS) publishes poverty guidelines in the *Federal Register*. In 2005, the poverty guideline for a family of four was $19,350 (U.S. Department of Health and Human Services, 2005). Some of the programs that use the DHHS poverty guidelines are the Food Stamp Program, Head Start, and Children's Health Insurance Programs (CHIP).

MAJOR INCOME-SUPPORT POLICIES AND PROGRAMS

Unlike many other developed countries, the United States does not have policies that guarantee a minimum income for each child or paid family leave. Instead, we have enacted policies to provide a patchwork of income-support programs. Some of these programs require prior attachment to the workforce (i.e., worker, spouse of worker, or child of worker) as a condition of eligibility.

Other programs are available only to low-income citizens who meet some additional category of eligibility such as disability or having children in the family. Because income-support programs are so central to social work with people in poverty, Chapter 3 discussed the development of these policies and programs in detail.

Income-support programs are categorized as either universal or selective. Although all of these programs have eligibility requirements, *universal programs* are provided to eligible citizens regardless of income, whereas *selective programs* are means-tested and are designed solely for people in poverty (Blau, 2004). Some of the programs are entitlement programs, meaning that the government has a legal obligation to provide payments or benefits to all individuals who meet the eligibility requirements. Recall that we discussed entitlements in Chapter 4 in the context of mandatory versus discretionary spending and the federal budget. Mandatory spending at the federal level—which includes entitlement programs—is authorized by permanent laws rather than by annual appropriation bills. Thus, it is more difficult for the federal government to eliminate or drastically reduce entitlements.

Some entitlement programs, such as unemployment insurance and Old Age, Survivors, Disability and Health Insurance—which includes Medicare—are universal and require attachment to the workforce in order to qualify for benefits and services. Other entitlement programs, including food stamps, SSI, and the Earned Income Tax Credit, are selective and means-tested. Veterans' benefits are an entitlement based on prior military service.

Many of the programs that serve people in poverty are not entitlement programs. These programs include TANF, General Assistance, the Special Supplemental Nutrition Program for Women, Infants, and Children (WIC), the Elder Nutrition Program under the Older Americans Act, public housing, and Section 8 housing. People who apply and are eligible may not receive the benefits and services they need, depending on federal and state budgetary constraints.

In the following sections, we turn our attention to policies governing major programs that provide income support as well as housing and food assistance programs. We also examine housing, food, and jobs policies as they relate to TANF legislation.

UNIVERSAL PROGRAMS

In this section, we consider universal programs designed to provide income in the face of predictable age and unpredictable work-related events that cause people to be unable to continue to work. These programs also help stabilize the economy, because beneficiaries typically spend the income right away on necessities such as food, clothing, shelter, and health care.

Old Age, Survivors, and Disability Insurance

As presented in Chapter 3, the Social Security Act established several major income-support programs, including unemployment compensation and financial assistance for aged and blind individuals and dependent children. Nevertheless, as popularly used, the term *Social Security* generally refers to the program titled **Old Age, Survivors, and Disability Insurance (OASDI).** OASDI was established to provide pensions to workers and their families when income is lost due to retirement, old age, or disability. It was expanded to include health insurance when Medicare was enacted in 1965. We will examine Medicare in greater detail in Chapter 10.

At the end of 2003, almost 40 million people were receiving OASDI benefits, and an additional 7.6 million were getting disability insurance benefits. Currently 98 percent of U.S. workers are covered by the Social Security system. The future of the Social Security system and proposals to reform it have emerged as a highly controversial political issue. We will consider these proposals later in this chapter.

Eligibility for OASDI benefits is dependent on age and work credits earned. For example, to be eligible for old-age retirement pensions, a person has to complete 40 credits of work. A person earns 4 credits each year by working for a certain amount of wages, $890 in 2003 (Social Security Administration, 2003c). Eligibility for survivors' and disability benefits require fewer credits when death or disability occurs at a younger age. Once people earn the appropriate numbers of credits, they become eligible for early retirement benefits at age 62. Early retirees receive a lower monthly pension. People born before 1938 are eligible for full Social Security benefits at the age of 65. However, beginning in 2003, the age at which full benefits are payable increases in gradual steps from 65 to 67 (Social Security Administration, 2003c). People born after 1959 are not eligible to receive benefits until the age of 67. Some experts advocate moving the age of eligibility for full retirement yet higher as life expectancy increases. Currently, if a person voluntarily elects to delay retirement until age 70, then her or his benefits increase for each month that OASDI payments are postponed.

Benefit payments take the form of either a monthly check mailed to the recipient or funds transferred directly to the recipient's bank account. In 2003, the average monthly benefit for a retired worker was $895; for a retired couple, it was $1,483. Beneficiaries with disabilities received average monthly payments of $833; those with a spouse and one child received $1,395. A young surviving spouse with two children averaged $1,838 per month (Social Security Administration, 2003c). Local Social Security Administration (SSA) offices determine eligibility for benefits, and the checks are processed through the U.S. Treasury Department.

The administrative costs associated with providing OASDI are low. While people are in the labor force, their earnings are taxed to pay for Social Security

The Social Work Library

For more detailed information on Social Security, go to www.mhhe.com/chapin1 and browse "Understanding the Benefits (Social Security)."

Policy Goals	To protect workers and their families from loss of income due to retirement, disability, or death.
Benefits or Services Provided	Monthly checks.
Eligibility Rules	Determined by age, payment of payroll taxes, and disability.
Service Delivery System	Social Security Administration offices determine eligibility, and funds are sent by check via U.S. mail or by electronic bank transfer.
Financing	Payroll taxes paid by employees and their employers.

BOX 8.1

Old Age, Survivors, and Disability Insurance (OASDI), 1935

benefits. Social Security payroll taxes are collected under authority of the Federal Insurance Contributions Act (FICA). Payroll taxes are listed on pay stubs as FICA. Funds collected from people in the workforce are used to pay benefits to people who have already retired. Currently, the government collects a good deal more taxes than are needed to pay benefits for retirees. The surplus is being invested in U.S. Treasury bonds. In 2003, some 154 million people paid payroll taxes on earnings (Board of Trustees, 2004). Both employers and employees pay the FICA tax up to a certain income. In 2003, employers and employees each paid 6.2 percent of an employee's gross income, for a total of 12.4 percent. Significantly, FICA taxes currently are not deducted from income in excess of $87,000 in one year (Social Security Administration, 2003c).

Box 8.1 summarizes information on OASDI using the policy and program analysis framework introduced in Chapter 5. The date shown in Box 8.1 is the year in which the original policy legislation was passed. Although this and subsequent boxes do not encompass all the details provided in the text and at Web links, they provide the basics in a format you can easily remember. If you practice using the framework with each new policy or program you encounter, the process will become automatic, and you will more easily understand major elements of the policy or program.

 Web Link

To find more information about OASDI, visit the Web site at www.mhhe.com/chapin1.

Unemployment Insurance

Unemployment insurance serves two primary functions: (1) it ensures that unemployed workers receive minimal cash assistance, allowing them to meet basic needs such as housing, food, and clothing; and (2) it provides cash assistance during periods of high unemployment, which helps stabilize the economy. In 2004, an estimated 128.5 million workers were covered by unemployment insurance, and 10.2 million unemployed workers received benefits.

Eligibility for benefits is based on attachment to the labor force, which is determined by examining wages and weeks worked at the time of unemployment.

BOX 8.2 *Unemployment Insurance, 1935*	**Policy Goals**	To provide income to meet basic needs for workers who have lost jobs and to stabilize the economy by encouraging spending.
	Benefits or Services Provided	Cash assistance for up to 26 weeks in most states. Extended benefits are available during high unemployment.
	Eligibility Rules	Workers must be unemployed due to no fault of their own and must meet requirements of wages earned and weeks worked in the past year. They also must be actively seeking work.
	Service Delivery System	State agencies determine eligibility for claims. Claims are filed weekly or biweekly until employment is secured.
	Financing	Funded primarily by taxes on employers.

Benefits are intended for people who are unemployed due to external circumstances and will continue to actively seek work. Beneficiaries also must be able to work if an appropriate job becomes available.

Web Link

For additional information on unemployment insurance, visit www.mhhe.com/chapin1.

Unemployment insurance is unique in that it is the only universal program created by the states with federal oversight by the U.S. Department of Labor. Individual states have the opportunity to design the program's benefit structure and state tax structure. This arrangement causes some variations across states in terms of eligibility and actual benefits. In all but three states, unemployment insurance is funded entirely by taxes on employers. The remaining three states tax employees as well. These taxes are collected by both the states and the federal government, and companies that comply with state requirements are eligible for substantial tax credits (U.S. Department of Labor, 2004). During periods of economic growth, taxes are collected and saved for times when larger numbers of workers become unemployed. Most states pay benefits for up to 26 weeks, with "extended benefits" funded jointly by states and federal sources during periods of high unemployment. Box 8.2 summarizes the features of the unemployment insurance program.

Workers' Compensation

Enacted by Congress in 1908, workers' compensation was the first social insurance program in the United States. This program—which, like unemployment insurance, is funded by employers—provides some protection for workers who are injured or killed at work and also offers benefits to their families. In addition to paying for medical care to treat the injury or disability, workers'

BOX 8.3

*Workers' Compen-
sation, 1908*

Policy Goals	To protect workers against the effects of occupational injuries or illnesses.
Benefits or Services Provided	Cash and medical assistance.
Eligibility Rules	Workers must be injured or killed on the job in accidents unrelated to intoxication, gross negligence, or willful misconduct.
Service Delivery System	Programs are organized by states under federal legislation. Insurance companies receive claims and award benefits.
Financing	Employers purchase policies from insurance companies.

compensation provides cash assistance to ensure that people are not without income due to work-related injuries. Benefit levels vary from state to state. Most states pay recipients two-thirds of the worker's weekly earning at the time of injury or death. The duration of payments depends on whether the disability is temporary or permanent. Survivors of deceased workers receive burial expenses and payments until they remarry, and children receive benefits until a certain age that is set by the state.

In 2001, some 127 million workers—the vast majority of the nation's wage and salary workers—were covered by workers' compensation. In general, people are eligible for benefits regardless of fault or blame for the accident. The major exceptions to this rule are gross negligence, willful misconduct, and intoxication while working. In 2001, benefit payments totaled $49.4 billion. Of this total, $27.4 billion was paid as compensation, and the remaining $22.0 billion covered medical and hospitalization costs (Social Security Administration, 2004a).

Private employers purchase policies through insurance companies that distribute benefits following an injury or accident. These insurance companies are governed by state and federal statutes. In most cases, the program delivery system is organized by the state. Businesses pay premiums that are based on company size and level of risk to employees. Box 8.3 summarizes the workers' compensation program.

 Web Link

To find out more about workers' compensation in your state, explore the site at www.mhhe.com/chapin1.

Veterans' Benefits

Veterans' benefits include pensions to veterans with disabilities. Benefits are intended to restore veterans' capabilities to the greatest extent possible and to improve the quality of their lives and the lives of their families. Currently, there are more than 26 million living veterans. Of this group, 2.7 million receive disability compensation and pensions. In addition, approximately 600,000 family members of deceased veterans receive death compensation and pensions (Department of Veterans Affairs, 2003).

The Social Work Library

Read more about veterans' benefits at www.mhhe.com/chapin1.

To be eligible for veterans' benefits, an individual must have been discharged from active military service. A veteran who received an honorable or general discharge from active military services is eligible for most benefits, but dishonorable discharge likely makes a person ineligible. Disability compensation is paid for injury, disability, or death that occurs while the veteran was serving in the armed forces. The level of compensation payments depends on the degree of disability, ranging from monthly payments of $106 to $2,239. In contrast, disability pensions are selective, means-tested benefits paid either to low-income veterans with a permanent and total disability that is not service-connected or to low-income veterans age 65 or older regardless of physical condition (Compensation & Pension Service, 2003). Veterans' benefits are financed primarily through federal general revenues, with some co-payments made by military personnel, and are administered through the Compensation and Pension Service, a division of the Department of Veterans' Affairs (VA). The benefits and eligibility qualifications are too varied to be presented in a summary table.

SELECTIVE PROGRAMS

Selective policies and programs that require a person to be impoverished as a condition of eligibility can be more clearly understood if you first think about who is considered poor in our society and why. Of the 37 million people who fell below the poverty line in 2004, 27.3 million (or 74 percent) were women and children (U.S. Census Bureau, 2005a). In addition, 46 percent were white, non-Hispanic. Women of color age 75 and over were at particularly high risk of poverty. Specifically, 31 percent of black women, 20 percent of Hispanic or Latino women, and 14 percent of Asian women in this age category were living in poverty, compared to 10.4 percent of non-Hispanic white women (U.S. Census Bureau, 2005a).

Many younger single women and older women are poor for some of the same reasons. They have spent most of their lives as unpaid caretakers; in addition, many poor women and people of color held temporary or part-time jobs that were not covered by OASDI.

Women faced discrimination in hiring in the past and continue to do so. Although 59 percent of working-age women are in the labor force, they still are disproportionately represented among those holding low-paying jobs with few benefits. Moreover, with so many women of all income and age levels now joining the workforce, there has been erosion in the beliefs that (1) caring for children is a full-time job for women and (2) all low-income mothers therefore are worthy of government support in that role. There is no longer strong societal pressure for women to be at home full-time to take care of their children.

However, the decision to stay at home to care for children is generally supported by the public when the family provides the income necessary to support the mother and children or when the primary breadwinner had sufficient work history to qualify for OASDI prior to death or disability.

Now public priorities have shifted. Consequently, work requirements are a central component of TANF, even for single mothers with young children. However, analysis indicates these mothers work predominantly in low-paying jobs that do not provide benefits and therefore do not allow them to move out of poverty. In sum, then, the majority of the people who are poor are women and children for whom the usual sources of support, such as family and the labor market, have been and continue to be insufficient.

Temporary Assistance to Needy Families

Recall from Chapter 3 that the 1996 Personal Responsibility and Work Opportunity Reconciliation Act (PRWORA) replaced Aid to Families with Dependent Children (AFDC) with TANF. AFDC (originally ADC) was the federal cash public assistance program established as an entitlement under the Social Security Act. The 1996 TANF legislation eliminated the individual entitlement to cash assistance. Formerly, under the AFDC program, states were required to aid all families that met the state income requirements for eligibility. The federal government contributed at least half of the AFDC benefit costs, so federal welfare spending increased on an open-ended basis as AFDC caseloads rose. In contrast, TANF is a state-level block grant that empowers each state to determine when and under what circumstances it will provide cash assistance to families in poverty. States are no longer required to provide assistance to any individual or family (Committee on Ways and Means, 2000).

 Web Link

To find out about TANF in your state, visit the Coalition on Human Needs Web site and go to "State Fact Sheets on TANF," found at www.mhhe.com/chapin1.

In 2004, federal TANF funding totaled $17 billion (Office of Family Assistance, 2004). States get a lump-sum payment that represents roughly what they received for AFDC and related services in 1994, and they have a "maintenance of effort" requirement to continue to spend 75 percent to 80 percent of the amount they spent on AFDC and related services in 1994 (Committee on Ways and Means, 2000). They also must meet some federal stipulations including work requirements and the cumulative five-year limit on cash assistance using federal funds.

In June 2002, the average monthly state payment for a family receiving TANF was $411.69 (Social Security Administration, 2004). The payments ranged from $164 per month for a family of three in Alabama to $923 per month for a family of three in Alaska (Administration for Children and Families, 2004). On average, a family of three on TANF received $4,940.28 per year. That same year, the federal poverty line for a family of three was $14,494. Clearly, then, TANF payments by themselves are not nearly adequate to lift a family out of poverty.

History and Development of TANF   The importance of historical, economic, social, and political contexts in shaping social policy is clearly illustrated by the debates leading up to the passage of the legislation that created TANF. Many of the themes that emerged during the welfare reform debate of the 1990s were not new. Ideological issues and concerns revolving around the morality of single motherhood, "deserving" versus "undeserving" poor people, and race have long historical roots, and we have examined them in previous chapters. Furthermore, under the previous AFDC program, low benefit levels meant that, historically, many recipients already engaged in paid labor (Abramovitz, 1996).

As the number of families receiving AFDC continued to rise in the 1970s, the focus increasingly shifted to moving recipients into paid work. However, with the increasing participation of middle- and upper-income women in the workforce, strict work requirements, even for mothers with preschool children, gained much more political support in the 1990s. Although many women with young children of all income levels are working outside the home, proponents of work requirements overlook the crucial fact that—unlike TANF recipients, who are disproportionately single mothers—most mothers are not the sole breadwinners, homemakers, and caregivers in their families. Working outside the home and also being the only parent to handle childcare and household tasks is a monumental undertaking. Children of working mothers can thrive if they have high-quality day care and plenty of parental involvement in their lives. However, TANF did not change the reality of the social context that shapes these families. Affordable high-quality day care for mothers on TANF continues to be in short supply, and when one person is working full-time and also doing all of the home chores, time for parental involvement is greatly reduced.

We know that poverty is a powerful predictor of all sorts of negative outcomes for children, from dropping out of school to teen pregnancy to juvenile crime. Children in families receiving TANF are still living in poverty, and the protective factors of high-quality day care—whether provided in a facility or by the mother—and time for parental involvement are not adequately supported by current TANF policy. As you will see when we examine TANF goals in the next section, the need for improved day care if mothers are required to work outside the home is not explicitly addressed in the purpose statement.

TANF Goals   Section 401(a) of the Social Security Act states that the purpose of TANF is to give states more flexibility in operating a program that is intended to accomplish the following purposes:

- Provide assistance to needy families so that children may be cared for in their own homes or in the homes of relatives

- End dependence on government benefits by promoting job preparation, work, and marriage for needy parents

- Prevent and reduce the incidence of out-of-wedlock pregnancies and establish annual numerical goals for preventing and reducing the incidence of these pregnancies.

- Encourage the formation and maintenance of two-parent families (Committee on Ways and Means, 2000).

Note that decreasing poverty is not one of these goals. Remember, effectiveness of a policy should be evaluated based on stated goals. According to the strengths perspective, the goal of the target group not to live in poverty should be reflected in the policy goals statement. Were that the case, then reduction of poverty would be the central outcome on which the program's effectiveness would be judged. Instead, claims of success for TANF are centered on reduction of caseloads and increases in employment.

At the time the TANF legislation was passed, 4.4 million families were receiving cash public assistance (Committee on Ways and Means, 2000). For FY 2001, the average monthly number of TANF families was 2.1 million (Office of Family Assistance, 2003). Thus, the number of caseloads had been cut in half within five years. Many supporters of TANF interpreted this development as positive. Viewed from a different perspective, however, caseload declines in both TANF and food stamps have greatly exceeded declines in poverty, which means that a substantially smaller percentage of poor families now receive public income support (Committee on Ways and Means, 2000).

At the same time, educational and workplace discrimination have prevented some people of color from getting jobs covered by OASDI and unemployment insurance, and therefore they are not eligible for those benefits. Because TANF may be the only income-support program for which these citizens qualify, insufficiencies in TANF create disproportionate hardships for these groups. In 2002, 32 percent of TANF recipients were white non-Hispanic, 38 percent were African American, and 25 percent were Hispanic or Latino with an increasing shift from white non-Hispanic families to Hispanic families. Other groups, including Native American and Asian families, made up less than 6 percent of recipients (Administration for Children and Families, 2004).

Family Formation Goals   As we have seen, one stated goal of TANF is to reduce the number of out-of-wedlock pregnancies and births by promoting marriage (Office of Family Assistance, 2003). The TANF legislation gives states more flexibility to provide assistance to two-parent families. It also provides bonuses to states with the highest rates of reduction in births to unmarried mothers as well as reduced abortion rates. Further, it empowers states to deny assistance to minor parents who are unmarried, not in school, and not living with relatives or other adults. It also provides federal funding for "abstinence only" sex education. States have the option of instituting family caps that deny assistance to additional children born while a family is receiving TANF. To date, 20 states have established caps that provide either no assistance or reduced benefits for additional children. Despite these stringent measures, however, the majority of the TANF evaluations that examined issues of family formation, such as marriage and birth rates for single parents, reported that the TANF guidelines have had no discernible impact on these trends (Committee on Ways and Means, 2000).

TANF Work Requirements and Sanctions   We have already seen that a major impetus for the creation of TANF came from pressure to place more aid recipients in the paid workforce. Not surprisingly, then, the PRWORA mandated that a specific percentage of families receiving TANF be involved in work activities and that this percentage rise over time. In 1997, the requirement was 25 percent; it increased to 50 percent in 2002. All states require recipients to be involved in work activities within two years after they begin to receive assistance; many states impose immediate work requirements. States may choose to exempt parents with a child under the age of 12 months (Administration for Children and Families, 2004).

The PRWORA further requires states to reduce TANF cash benefits of adults who do not meet the work requirement. Additionally, some states have chosen to eliminate food stamps and/or Medicaid benefits if the family head does not meet work requirements. The federal government will also reduce the amount of the block grant to any state in which the specified percentage of TANF recipients are not participating in work activities. As a partial balance to these requirements, states have the option of exempting up to 20 percent of families receiving TANF from the five-year time limit. Additionally, states may use their funds (but not federal monies) to continue assistance to families who have exceeded the limit. Box 8.4 summarizes the major features of TANF.

 Web Link

For more information on employment policy and needed reforms, go the Workforce Investment Act Web site, found at www.mhhe.com/chapin1.

The 1996 PRWORA legislation also combined welfare and employment policy so that a large portion of employment policy is now focused on welfare recipients. The 1997 Balanced Budget Act established welfare-to-work (WTW) grants as a component of the TANF Funding Work Incentive Program (Committee on Ways and Means, 2000). The following year, the Workforce Investment Act required that a wide range of state programs, including WTW, employment services, unemployment insurance, vocational rehabilitation, adult education, and postsecondary vocational education, be brought together into a one-stop system.

Noncash Programs That Assist Low-Income Families

A number of other programs help low-income families meet basic survival needs without providing direct cash assistance. These programs include the Food Stamp Program, the Special Supplemental Nutrition Program for Women,

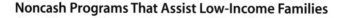

Policy Goals	To promote families by helping them care for children in their own home, supporting two-parent families, and discouraging out-of-wedlock pregnancies. To reduce dependency of needy families by focusing on job preparation, work, and marriage.	**BOX 8.4** *Temporary Assistance to Needy Families (TANF), 1996*
Benefits or Services Provided	Monthly cash assistance. Services to promote work and reduce dependency.	
Eligibility Rules	Means-tested. Families with children must meet work requirements and not exceed time limit.	
Service Delivery System	State welfare agencies determine eligibility and administer payments to eligible families.	
Financing	Federal block grant given to each state, with states required to contribute additional funding.	

Infants, and Children (WIC), public housing, and the Tenant-Based Housing Assistance Program (Section 8). We discuss these selective programs only briefly here. However, the margin notes provide links to Web sites where you may learn about these programs in more depth.

The Food Stamp Program   The **Food Stamp Program** was established to address hunger in the United States by helping low-income people to purchase nutritionally adequate food. In FY 2004, the Food Stamp Program assisted 10.2 million households, or 23.9 million individuals (Food and Nutrition Service, 2005). To be eligible for benefits, individuals or families must have incomes that are less than 130 percent of the federal poverty guidelines and countable assets under $2,000. For people who are eligible, food stamps are an entitlement. All public assistance recipients are eligible for food stamps, as are other people who meet the federal and state requirements (Food and Nutrition Service, 2003a).

Monthly allotments in the form of Electronic Benefit Transfer (EBT) cards are provided to eligible beneficiaries based on the Thrifty Food Plan discussed at the beginning of the chapter. Recipients then use these cards to purchase specified food items in retail stores. In FY 2004, the average monthly benefit was $86 per individual and $194 per family (Food and Nutrition Service, 2005).

The Food Stamp Program is funded through general tax revenues. At the federal level, the Department of Agriculture administers the program through the Food and Nutrition Service, which has established certain eligibility, allotment, and benefit distribution guidelines. State- and local-level programs determine eligibility, allotments, and distribution of benefits within the parameters of the federal regulations.

 Web Link

You can find more information about the Food Stamp Program at www.mhhe.com/chapin1.

The WIC Nutrition Program   The **Special Supplemental Nutrition Program for Women, Infants, and Children (WIC)** was established to help improve the health of low-income women, infants, and children up to age five who are nutritionally at risk for medically based or diet-based reasons (Food and Nutrition Service, 2003b). More specifically, WIC recipients must meet the following criteria:

- All recipients must have incomes at or below 185 percent of the poverty line and must be determined to be nutritionally at risk by a health professional.

- Women are eligible if they are pregnant. After the baby is born, the mother receives benefits for one year if she breastfeeds and for six months if she does not. A woman need not be a single mother to be eligible.

- Infants are eligible for specifically designed benefits and services until their first birthdays.

- Children are eligible for other WIC benefits until their fifth birthdays.

WIC benefits include nutritious food, nutrition counseling and education, and referrals to health care and other social services when needed. Vouchers are usually issued for recipients to purchase food at local retail stores.

 Web Link

Find more information about WIC at its Web site, listed at www.mhhe.com/chapin1.

WIC is funded by a federal grant appropriated by Congress, which may not be sufficient to cover all eligible women, infants, and children. WIC is not an entitlement program; nevertheless, current estimates suggest that it serves 90 percent of eligible individuals in these categories. At the federal level, WIC, like the Food Stamp Program, is administered by the Food and Nutrition Service. On the state and local levels, various agencies administer programs through locations such as state and county health departments, hospitals, community centers, schools, and Indian health facilities.

Public Housing   Subsidized rental housing may be available to families, older adults, and people with disabilities who cannot afford to pay full rental costs in the private market. The goal of such programs is to provide safe, decent, affordable housing. Approximately 1.3 million households currently live in public housing. In addition, there is a long list of eligible people waiting for housing to become available (U.S. Department of Housing and Urban Development, 2000).

Income level is used to determine eligibility for public housing. Specifically, families and individuals are eligible if they earn less than 80 percent of the median income in the geographic area. Families, elders, and people with disabilities whose incomes are below 50 percent of the median income in the area receive preference (U.S. Department of Housing and Urban Development, 2000). Housing policies are therefore unique in that they define need in terms of relative poverty as measured in the person's geographical location. TANF and SSI recipients also meet the income limits for public housing, and they often need to live in public housing in order to survive on the small cash benefits they receive. Public housing is denied to people who have not exhibited good habits at other rental properties and have the potential to be detrimental to other tenants or the environment of the housing complexes. A person or a family can continue to live in public housing until their income is assessed as high enough to afford housing in the private market.

The public housing program is financed at the federal level through general revenues. The U.S. Department of Housing and Urban Development (HUD) provides federal funds to local housing offices, which actually manage the housing. These offices are in charge of collecting rent from tenants, enforcing leases, and maintaining the housing so that it continues to be safe and decent (U.S. Department of Housing and Urban Development, 2000).

The Social Work Library

More information about public housing is available at www.mhhe.com/chapin1.

The Tenant-Based Housing Assistance Program   This program has the same purpose as the public housing program: to provide low-income people with decent, safe, and affordable places to live. It is commonly referred to as "Section 8" housing because the regulations governing the program are codified in Section 8 of the Code of Federal Regulations, Title 24. However, the Section 8 approach is different from that of public housing. Instead of providing an actual apartment or home, Section 8 uses a voucher system that permits eligible families to choose privately owned houses or apartments that meet program requirements and have reasonable rent that will be subsidized (U.S. Department of Housing and Urban Development, 2001).

People who apply for Section 8 housing and public housing recipients must meet the same income eligibility standards. Vouchers are limited, and families are placed on a waiting list when they apply. Section 8 housing is financed through general revenues at the federal level. HUD provides the funds to local housing offices, which issue vouchers to families when their names come to the top of the waiting list.

Web Link

You can get more information from the Tenant-Based Housing Assistance Program Web site, found at www.mhhe.com/chapin1.

Supplemental Security Income

Before Congress passed legislation creating the **Supplemental Security Income (SSI)** program in 1974, states had a patchwork of programs that provided assistance to people with limited or no income who are elderly or blind or have disabilities. The federal legislation replaced this arrangement with a means-tested entitlement program that is uniform across the nation. By January 2003, 6.5 million Americans were receiving monthly SSI benefits,

BOX 8.5 *Supplemental Security Income (SSI), 1974*	**Policy Goals**	To provide income assistance to the aged, blind individuals, and people with disabilities who have limited income and resources.
	Benefits or Services Provided	Monthly check.
	Eligibility Rules	Means-tested. Must be 65 or older, blind, or disabled.
	Service Delivery System	Social Security Administration offices administer the program, and funds are sent by check via U.S. mail or by electronic bank transfer.
	Financing	General tax revenue at the federal level.

which amounted to approximately 2 percent of the overall population (Social Security Administration, 2003a). To receive SSI benefits, individuals must have very low incomes, including both cash and noncash assistance. In addition, the person's assets must be below $2,000, excluding certain items such as a home, a car, and life insurance policies under $1,500 (Social Security Administration, 2003b). Other eligibility requirements are age (65 or older for age-based benefits), physical or mental disability that prevents work for at least one year, or blindness.

 **The Social Work Library**

Find out more about SSI at www.mhhe.com/chapin1.

SSI provides monthly cash benefits to eligible people. Benefits are not dependent on work history or marital status. The maximum monthly benefit in January 2003 was $552 for individuals and $829 for couples when two individuals residing together were receiving SSI benefits (Social Security Administration, 2003b). The average monthly benefit was $381 (Social Security Administration, 2003a). These benefits are funded by general tax revenues. The Social Security Administration (SSA) runs the SSI program through regional and district offices. SSA can contract with state or local agencies to administer the program. Box 8.5 summarizes the features of the SSI program.

As discussed in earlier chapters, prior to the passage of the PRWORA in 1996, legal immigrants were eligible to receive SSI assistance from the federal government. Currently, most immigrants in the United States are ineligible for most means-tested programs including SSI, food stamps, TANF, and Medicaid until they obtain citizenship or reside in the United States legally for five years (U.S. Department of Health and Human Services, 2003).

General Assistance

General Assistance (GA) is provided to assist poor individuals and families who do not qualify for or are waiting for approval for federal programs such as SSI and TANF. GA programs provide minimal assistance and are generally a

Policy Goals	To help low-income people who are ineligible for federal assistance programs or waiting for approval meet their basic survival needs.	**BOX 8.6**
Benefits or Services Provided	Temporary or long-term cash or in-kind assistance and medical care.	*General Assistance (GA), 1935*
Eligibility Rules	Means-tested. Eligibility varies but usually is reserved for people with very little or no income.	
Service Delivery System	States, counties, and localities determine eligibility and provide either cash or in-kind assistance.	
Financing	Funded entirely by the states, counties, and localities that administer the programs.	

last resort for people in need. According to one estimate, more than 1 million people are receiving benefits from GA programs nationwide (Blau, 2004). However, due to differences in reporting and in the types of GA programs offered by localities, the number of recipients is probably higher than has been reported. Nevertheless, the availability of GA is very limited, and the total number of GA beneficiaries in most states is reported to be less than 15 percent the number of TANF recipients.

General Assistance is administered by states, counties, and localities and is not funded or regulated by the federal government. Some states provide no GA. The states, counties, or localities administer the programs, determining both the benefits and the service delivery system. Many of the programs are called General Assistance, but some are referred to by a variety of names such as General Relief, Poor Relief, City Welfare, and General Public Assistance. Programs vary drastically in terms of the amounts and duration of benefits as well as eligibility rules. However, payments are generally low and may be as little as $100 a month. Payments take the form of cash or in-kind benefits such as food or clothing. In addition, some GA programs offer minimal medical assistance. Box 8.6 provides a policy analysis of General Assistance.

 Web Link

You can get more information about General Assistance at the book's Web site www.mhhe.com/chapin1.

The Earned Income Tax Credit

As discussed in Chapter 3, Congress enacted the Earned Income Tax Credit (EITC) in 1975 in order to decrease the impact of Medicare and Social Security taxes that are deducted from the wages earned by low-income families with children (Internal Revenue Service, 2003). The goal of EITC is to encourage people to work and assist them in paying for expenses incurred because of work. It is estimated that in 2002, EITC benefits raised 4.8 million adults and children

BOX 8.7

Earned Income Tax Credit (EITC), 1975

Policy Goals	To decrease the impact of payroll taxes on low-income families with children. To encourage nonworkers to enter the workforce.
Benefits or Services Provided	Tax credit of up to $4,300 in 2004. Credit can be used to reduce federal taxes owed or provide a cash refund.
Eligibility Rules	In 2004, recipients had to earn a work income below $34,458 ($35,458 for married, filing jointly) if they have two or more children, $30,338 ($31,338 for married, filing jointly) if they have only one child, or $11,490 ($12,490 for married, filing jointly) if they have no children.
Service Delivery System	Recipients must file tax returns with the Internal Revenue Service, which refunds a check.
Financing	Funded through general tax revenue and decreases the tax revenue collected by the federal government.

above the poverty line. EITC has been described as the "largest anti-poverty program in the United States" (Beverly, 2002, p. 259).

Only U.S. citizens or resident aliens are eligible for the EITC. In 2004, recipients had to earn an income from work that was less than $34,458 ($35,458 for married, filing jointly) if they had two or more children, $30,338 ($31,338 for married, filing jointly) if they had only one child, or $11,490 ($12,490 for married, filing jointly) if they had no children (Internal Revenue Service, 2004). Benefits vary depending on the family's income level and number of children. The EITC reduces taxes owed to the federal government and provides a refund if fewer or no taxes are owed. In 2004, the maximum credit was $4,300 (Internal Revenue Service, 2004). The benefit can be received in one lump-sum check at the end of the year, or it can be added to paychecks in smaller allotments throughout the year. Receiving a refund doesn't affect eligibility for Medicaid, SSI, food stamps, or low-income housing if the recipient spends the refund within a certain time frame. TANF eligibility and benefits might be affected by the EITC, depending on the state (Beverly, 2002).

To apply for the EITC, people must file a federal tax return with the Internal Revenue Service (IRS). The IRS administers the program and sends a check to each recipient who is eligible for a refund. The program is financed by general revenue at the federal level. As a result of the benefit, fewer taxes are collected from individual tax returns. This reduces the general revenue funds available to the federal government. See Box 8.7 for a policy analysis of the EITC.

The Social Work Library

You can find more information about the Earned Income Tax Credit at www.mhhe.com/chapin1.

EVALUATION OF INCOME-SUPPORT POLICIES AND PROGRAMS

We have examined a number of income-support policies and programs. The next section provides a more in-depth evaluation of two of the major programs, TANF and OASDI, based on the strengths perspective and guided by the strengths policy principles articulated in earlier chapters. Recall that removing structural barriers to necessary resources is a key tenet of the strengths perspective. Therefore, policy and program goals and design should focus on access, choice, and opportunities that lead to empowerment. In addition, the effectiveness of these programs should be judged not only on whether they achieve societal goals but also on whether they help clients achieve their goals.

Attention to the voices of client groups is essential to meaningful evaluation of TANF. The strengths perspective asserts that clients are experts on their own needs and goals and therefore should be consulted when policy is developed and evaluated. Welfare rights groups provide a variety of opinions.

Some people feel that rearing children should again be considered a full-time job worthy of public support. Caring for children is a socially and economically valuable activity, and there are costs when mothers no longer provide such care. As discussed earlier, low-income single parents face great challenges when they are required to be the sole breadwinners, homemakers, and caregivers. In contrast, middle-class women whose children already have many resources unavailable to children in low-income homes are often urged to stay at home "for the sake of their children."

However, given the realities of women in the workforce, welfare rights groups have also pointed to the desperate need for high-quality, low-cost day care for the 11 million families categorized as the working poor (TANF recipient and welfare rights organizer, personal interview, 2003). Day care is also an important investment in all of our futures, because these children will be the people who will support and care for us in our old age. Without adequate care and education during their childhood, they will experience more negative outcomes including higher dropout rates, reduced ability to find well-paying jobs, and higher incarceration rates.

Adequate transportation is also crucial. A number of large corporations have made a commitment to locating new facilities only in cities that have adequate mass transportation so that more workers have access to these facilities.

TANF and Poverty   A central, broadly shared goal of TANF clients is to move their families out of poverty. It is clear that the meager income provided through TANF will not end poverty. Indeed, the program is not designed to do so; rather, it is designed to lessen dependence on the public coffers. Research conducted to evaluate the success of TANF indicates that welfare caseloads have gone down and employment has gone up. Keep in mind, of course, that states

The Social Work Library

If you would like to review the strengths principles, please go to "TANF from the strengths perspective," at www.mhhe.com/chapin1.

Web Links

Visit the Web sites of welfare rights groups made up of consumers and other advocates. The National Welfare Rights Union provides links, which are listed at www.mhhe.com/chapin1. Some welfare rights groups are also part of the global struggle for human rights. The National Welfare Rights Union Web site also provides links to information on the United Nations' Universal Declaration of Human Rights, the international standard for human rights.

Web Link

To view work that ensures the voices of welfare recipients and other low-income citizens are heard, access the Community Voices Heard site at www.mhhe.com/chapin1.

can decrease their caseloads simply by changing their eligibility requirements. The decline in caseloads and increases in employment were due in part to the strong economy in the latter half of the 1990s and to changes in the EITC. However, in the first years of the new century, employment rates declined because of the sluggish economy.

The findings on income, earnings, and the ability of former TANF families to escape poverty are much more mixed. Between 2000 and 2004, the overall child poverty rate, as measured by the U.S. Census Bureau, increased from 16.2 percent to 17.8 percent. This increase followed a seven-year decline in which rates dropped from 22.7 percent in 1993. The poverty rate for children under age 18 is higher than those for adults age 18 to 64 and older adults age 65 and older. The African American child poverty rate reached a low of 30.2 percent in 2001 and then rose to 33.6 percent in 2004. Similarly, the poverty rate for Hispanic or Latino children rose from 28 percent in 2001 to 29 percent in 2004 (U.S. Census Bureau, 2005a). About 1 child in 12 in married two-parent families was poor, compared to more than 1 in 3 children living in a female-headed, single-parent family (U.S. Census Bureau, 2005a). These data indicate that although child poverty rates for some groups dropped precipitously during the latter half of the 1990s, they are again rising. The large percentages of African American children and Hispanic or Latino children still living in poverty are particularly troubling.

The link between growing up in poverty and a myriad of negative outcomes for children is well documented. The impact of TANF on child well-being will have serious consequences for years to come and thus should be carefully monitored in evaluating TANF.

The outcomes of welfare leavers should be monitored by race and ethnicity to determine if discrimination either by welfare agencies or by employers is disproportionately disadvantaging people of color in meeting TANF requirements. Rigorous enforcement of antidiscrimination laws should accompany TANF work requirements if recipients are to move out of poverty.

Average incomes among the poorest quintile of single mothers have actually fallen (Committee on Ways and Means, 2000). People leaving TANF for employment typically are finding jobs with wages that are below the poverty level. To compound this problem, they often don't receive employer benefits such as health care, and many of them fail to receive other public income supports for which they would be eligible, such as childcare assistance, Medicaid coverage, and food stamps (Committee on Ways and Means, 2000; Peterson, 2002).

Many welfare rights groups endorse the living wage movement as a strategy for alleviating the problems associated with poverty-level wages. "Living wage campaigns seek to pass local ordinances requiring private businesses that benefit from public money to pay their workers a living wage" (ACORN Living Wage Resource Center, 2003). A **living wage** is the income level necessary to live adequately within a given community, according to the calculations of advocates.

 Web Link

To learn more about living wage campaigns, go to the Web site found at www.mhhe.com/chapin1.

Generally speaking, each campaign defines this wage for its community. Many campaigns base the living wage calculation on the poverty line for a family of four. Using this formula, the standard living wage is $8.20 for employees who work a 40-hour week for 52 weeks each year. Overall, living wages have ranged from $6.25 to $12.00 per hour in ordinances passed. Some living wage movements also advocate for benefits such as health coverage, paid vacation, and community hiring goals. Living wage ordinances generally cover city and county service contractors and other employers who receive grants, loans, tax abatements, or other government support.

Reforming TANF from a Strengths Perspective What changes in TANF policies and programs should be considered so as to effectively meet the needs and support the goals of low-income families? As discussed previously, welfare rights advocates argue that single parents receiving TANF should be given the option to care for their children on a full-time basis. Further, parents in the paid workforce should have access to high-quality day care, transportation, and training and education for jobs that pay a living wage. The strengths perspective also encourages us to carefully analyze the barriers that impede or prevent families from reaching the goal of self-support, including inadequate education, substance abuse, domestic violence, physical or mental illness, and the need to care for a chronically ill child. Significantly, families who are experiencing difficulties in meeting TANF work requirements often face many of these barriers simultaneously. Focusing on overcoming these barriers rather than primarily on enforcing work requirements would better serve these families.

Web Link

To explore more ideas for how states can help low-income families move up the economic ladder, check out the Web site at www.mhhe.com/chapin1.

The current emphasis on "work first" limits education and training options for TANF families. The "work first" emphasis can push women into traditionally low-paying, female-dominated occupations that frequently do not pay a living wage. In fact, TANF requirements can ensure low-wage employers a large workforce made up of women who don't have the qualifications that would enable them to leave for higher-paying jobs. Amending TANF requirements to enable women to enter educational and training programs can help them attain higher-paying jobs and move their families out of poverty. Analysis of TANF based on the strengths perspective clearly points to the need to restructure TANF policies to help women secure such jobs.

The Social Work Library

To learn more about needed reform to help low-income workers get higher-paying jobs, go to www.mhhe.com/chapin1.

Other needed reforms grounded in the strengths perspective and social work values include policies to protect a woman's choice of whether to marry or remain married, particularly for survivors of domestic violence. Additionally, policies to encourage parental involvement in the lives of their children, such as the option of working part-time outside the home or receiving work credits for involvement in school activities, may help mitigate the heightened risks of school failure, teen pregnancy, and delinquency that poor children face. Factors that discourage mothers and fathers from being more involved with their children, particularly in families headed by unmarried couples, need to be examined, and additional strategies to increase parental involvement should be crafted based on that analysis.

Restoring the federal entitlement status of AFDC is one policy change that could help ensure that at least the basic survival needs of children in poor families are met. Receiving TANF is a survival strategy for women. They turn to TANF when other sources of support such as the family and the labor markets fail. Our nation's children should be provided with a safety net when other systems fail them.

Although some people argue that TANF block grant funding to states is now too high given the reductions in caseloads, it is also possible to redirect any excess funds to help low-income working families more generally (Lazere, Fremstad, & Goldberg, 2002). For example, subsidies to help more low-income working families afford high-quality day care can also help improve school success and ultimately enhance the chances of breaking the cycle of poverty. Moreover, in times of recession, caseloads will undoubtedly rise again, and the additional block grant funds will be needed to provide assistance to eligible families.

Another strategy to reform TANF so that it reflects strengths principles is to reconsider the five-year time limit on receipt of federal funds. Families who do work may not earn enough money to survive without public income support even after five years. The five-year time limit fails to take into account the realities of caring for a family member with disabilities, domestic violence, economic recession, and low wages. If the five-year limit is not abolished, it needs to be modified to address these realities by stipulating that the clock may be stopped in such instances. For example, policies could be enacted specifying that periods when a parent must care full-time for a severely disabled family member will not be counted in calculating the five-year limit. Benefits also need to be restored for legal immigrants.

Policies should be developed that meet the survival needs of poor families and support their efforts to move out of poverty. Investment of public monies in such strategies will mean that parents will be able to reach the goal of adequately caring for their children even in the face of hardship. This outcome is much more important than reductions in caseloads for our nation's future.

When TANF was established in 1996, funding was authorized through September 2002. Eight short-term extensions have maintained the program's operation and funding, but full long-term reauthorization has not been achieved. The eighth extension expires in 2005. Welfare reform clearly continues to be a hotly contested topic and is a challenging but crucial arena for policy practice.

OASDI from the Strengths Perspective

OASDI has been a great success story in lessening poverty for the people who are eligible for this program. From a strengths perspective, any evaluation of OASDI should start by examining the opinions of the target group. Consumer

Web Links

To learn more about TANF reform, get the latest information on TANF reauthorization, and find out how you can get involved in pressing for reform, go to the National Association of Social Workers site and the Center on Budget and Policy Priorities site, found at www.mhhe.com/chapin1.

groups such as the Older Women's League and the Gray Panthers provide insights about how OASDI has benefited generations of Americans as well as point out needed changes. They speak to the importance of OASDI in protecting workers and their families from loss of income due to retirement, disability, or death. The monthly check provides consumers with choice in how best to meet their needs. Eligibility is determined by age, payment of payroll taxes, and disability, and beneficiaries do not have to submit to humiliating means tests.

 Web Link

You can view insights on OASDI reform from two consumer groups, the Older Women's League and the Gray Panthers, at www.mhhe.com/chapin1.

Women and OASDI   Because OASDI is employment based and has its roots in the male-breadwinner family model, women historically have been disadvantaged by this system. Most women's retirement income is, in large part, determined by wages earned during their own or their spouses' current or past employment. Because older women have experienced gender inequality in educational and employment opportunities over a lifetime, they often enter old age with shorter, inconsistent, and lower-paid employment histories. Although the policy of providing coverage for a spouse in the amount of half of the worker's earnings does partially recognize the role of the spouse in supporting the worker, this amount varies not by the contribution of the spouse but by the earnings of the worker. In addition, couples who divorce before their tenth anniversaries are not eligible for survivors' insurance. Additionally, when both spouses work outside the home, the couple may pay more taxes and receive lower yearly Social Security benefits at retirement than a one-earner couple with the same income (Quadagno, 1999, p. 355).

Social Security credits are not earned for the unpaid labor necessary to care for children and older adults. Therefore, women, who have traditionally been expected to assume these duties, are disadvantaged initially by lack of payment for their work and at the time of retirement by lack of recognition of their contributions (Older Women's League, 1998). It is obvious that, given the role of caretaker and the insecurities of a postmodern working life, many women will be unable to secure adequate retirement income based on their work record unless a method for providing Social Security credits for caregiving is devised.

 Web Link

To learn more about Social Security reform proposals from the Older Women's League, visit the site at www.mhhe.com/chapin1.

People of Color and OASDI   People who have experienced racial discrimination during their work lives also are less adequately served by a system that bases eligibility on amount of salary earned and time spent in covered jobs. Because benefits are earnings related, white, male, educated professionals who earn higher wages receive higher benefits. Additionally, because African Americans and Native Americans have shorter life expectancies than white Americans do, raising the retirement age for full eligibility for old-age pensions to 67 reduces the likelihood that these groups will ever receive retirement benefits for which they have contributed. However, this argument overlooks the fact that minority-group workers receive disability and survivors' benefits. Because people of color are more likely to be employed in hazardous jobs, these benefits are especially important for them.

Is OASDI Regressive or Progressive?   The Social Security tax is regressive because both high- and low-income employees pay at the same rate and in 2005 the tax was not paid on income in excess of $90,000. However, distribution of benefits is progressive in that low-wage earners receive a proportionally higher rate of return. In this way, OASDI has a redistributive function that benefits citizens with low incomes or disabilities. Low government administrative costs, equaling less than 1 percent of each Social Security tax dollar collected, also benefit participants in the Social Security system.

Web Link

To learn more about the OASDI Trust Funds Board of Trustees' report on the solvency of the program, and suggestions for reform, browse the site at www.mhhe.com/chapin1.

How Solvent Is OASDI?   The solvency of OASDI is perhaps the biggest issue in most citizens' minds. Some critics have warned that the system is in a state of "crisis" that requires immediate and drastic changes. In reality, the program is solvent through 2042 (Board of Trustees, 2004). Moreover, even after that point, it could continue to pay a substantial proportion of benefits. Nevertheless, some modest adjustments should be made soon to the Social Security system so that more drastic changes will not be required later. Proposals for reforming the system include the following:

- Raising the retirement age, although workers in physically demanding or stressful jobs may find it difficult to continue working longer

- Increasing the tax that workers and employers pay into the system

- Requiring that people with incomes above $90,000 continue to pay into the system

- Dedicating taxes on estates worth more than $3.5 million to Social Security

- Mandating that all federal and state workers take part in the national retirement program

The existing link between retirement benefits and increases in the country's overall living standard could also be removed. Instead of being based on wage increases, benefits could be tied to price inflation. Prices tend to rise more slowly than wages, so future payments also would rise more slowly. However, such a change would result in large reductions in retirement income to beneficiaries.

Young people have questioned whether Social Security benefits will be there for them. However, the fact is that the benefit is already there for them in the form of disability and survivors' benefits that many young people currently receive. This insurance element of OASDI is often overlooked.

One highly controversial proposal for reforming Social Security is to privatize the system. However, with the decline in the stock market in the first years of this century, enthusiasm for privatization plans seems to have cooled. President George W. Bush's proposal to use Social Security funds to create private or personal accounts has been opposed by many individuals and groups, including the American Association of Retired Persons (AARP). Under his plan, younger workers who pay into OASDI could redirect a portion of their FICA taxes into private accounts where the money would be invested in various options. However, setting up and administering such a system would involve substantial costs. In addition, private accounts would divert funds from the current program.

Although promoting strategies to help people with low incomes save and accumulate assets is in keeping with the strengths perspective, doing so by reducing benefits guaranteed through our current, very modest income-support programs could intensify the economic problems of future older adults. Social Security is a contract among generations, and as long as that contract is intact, relatively minor adjustments to payroll taxes, benefits, and eligibility rules can ensure solvency far into the future.

From the strengths perspective, OASDI provides consumer choice. It is non-stigmatizing and is a universal benefit. The program still enjoys public support despite well-funded efforts to undermine and dismantle it. A similar universal approach to protect all our nation's children could dramatically lessen the number of young people growing up in poverty.

 Web Link

To learn more about President Bush's proposed reforms and the AARP position on Social Security reform, go to the White House Web link at www.mhhe.com/chapin1.

Proposals for Fundamental Reform

In addition to proposing adjustments to existing programs, critics of U.S. policies designed to help people in need have proposed some fundamental reforms to the ways in which support is provided. Two notable proposals are the basic income grant and asset-based, as opposed to income-based, programs.

Basic Income Grant We have examined a number of income-support programs. Sometimes programs overlap, but more often there are huge gaps, and many people still live in dire poverty. Policy analysts have suggested replacing this patchwork system with a basic income grant (BIG) for all citizens (Blau, 2004). According to this plan, every family, regardless of income, would receive a uniform benefit, perhaps $14,000. For high-income families, the benefit would be taxed at 50 percent. BIG payments to low-income families would go largely untaxed.

Such a program would make great strides in lifting families out of poverty. However, like earlier proposals to create a minimum family income in this country, concerns about cost and work disincentives mitigate against its passage. Such a program would clearly be costly. However, the benefits as well as cost avoidance due to reduction or elimination of other income-support programs are complex to evaluate, and therefore the true cost-benefit is difficult to predict. Further, the program might provide a work disincentive in that it could encourage people who currently earn less than the BIG grant to work fewer hours. The extent to which people, especially women with young children, would reduce their work time if such a program were instituted is unclear.

Asset-Based Policies   The last section of this chapter focuses on asset-based policies and programs. These programs have been discussed briefly in other chapters, and the role social workers have played in formulating and implementing these policies has been highlighted. The term *assets* includes equity in a home, savings accounts, stocks and mutual funds, rental property, vehicles, and certificates of deposit (CDs). Inequality in asset distribution in the United States is vastly greater than income inequality. Overall, the wealthiest 20 percent of people in the United States own 83 percent of the nation's assets, whereas the poorest 40 percent own only 1 percent (Edwards & Mason, 2003). This considerable inequality has prompted people to research differences in assets and to propose policies to increase the assets of low-income people.

Historically, few policies have focused on assets. Two noteworthy exceptions, discussed in Chapters 2 and 3, are the Homestead Act of 1862, which increased the number of landowners in the United States, and the 1944 GI Bill of Rights, which helped returning veterans purchase homes, start businesses, and attend college. Other asset-building policies focus primarily on the middle and upper classes in the form of provisions made through the tax system to encourage home ownership and contributions to retirement accounts (Edwards & Mason, 2003).

Michael Sherraden, a social worker, has been one of the primary advocates for a different approach to welfare policy that stresses the importance of asset accumulation as well as income support. In his 1991 book *Assets and the poor: A new American welfare policy*, he proposed that the United States needs a shift in paradigms from welfare benefits that focus exclusively on income maintenance to policies that would encourage and help low-income citizens obtain assets. His emphasis on assets was meant to "complement" income assistance, not replace it.

Sherraden suggested establishing Individual Development Accounts (IDAs) that in many ways mirror Individual Retirement Accounts (IRAs), which are not utilized frequently by lower-income citizens. IDAs are savings accounts for poor people that are matched through public or private sources. Sherraden proposed that these IDAs be made available to all people in the future, with increased matched amounts and greater incentives available for people in poverty who choose to participate in the plan. Low-income people could invest monies from public benefits they receive as well as from income from work or other sources. These savings could be matched or augmented by contributions from the government, corporations, foundations, community groups, and individual donors (Sherraden, 2000). The goal of the IDA program is to help people in poverty accumulate wealth gradually as a long-term investment. People can use

IDAs for education, job training, homeownership, operating a small business, or other development purposes.

IDAs benefit individuals by helping them to obtain needed resources to compete effectively in the economy. At the same time, they benefit society by encouraging people to save money for purposes that are in the public interest (Sherraden, 1991). Sherraden (2000) asserted that our nation has begun the paradigm shift to focusing on asset accumulation through the continued establishment and growth of asset-based programs such as College Savings Plans, IRAs, Roth IRAs, 401(k)s, and Medical Savings Accounts. Moreover, IDAs are gaining support, bolstered by initial research statistics that attest to their ability to assist people living in poverty (Schreiner, Clancy, & Sherraden, 2002; Zhan, 2003). By 2003, some 34 states, Washington, DC, and Puerto Rico had passed IDA legislation. An additional two pieces of legislation have been passed at the federal level, with ongoing proposals in both the House and the Senate to increase the programs. Significantly, with the passage of the PRWORA, the federal government determined that IDAs cannot be considered as assets when eligibility for means-tested programs is being established (Edwards & Mason, 2003).

IDAs could complement but not replace income-support programs. However, they also shift our focus to the need for individual savings and away from the structural barriers, such as discrimination in employment and inadequate salaries and income supports, that keep people in poverty. This shift in attention may decrease the likelihood that such barriers will be effectively addressed.

Sherraden and others have also suggested a lump-sum payment from the federal government to children at birth. Significantly, most other developed countries provide some sort of children's allowance. This payment could go into an IDA-type account that could later be used for education, health care, or other designated purposes. Although passage of such a policy may be unlikely at this time, asset-based policies have the potential to help some families escape poverty if they are sufficiently funded. However, current federal and state funds to help low-income families meet survival needs are not adequate, and funneling those funds into asset-based programs, which may be more politically popular, could further erode an already badly frayed safety net for low-income families and their children.

CONCLUSION

Helping people to meet their basic needs for food, shelter, and income is the first step in effective social work practice. In psychology and human behavior courses, you have learned about the importance of tending to basic needs before expecting other therapeutic efforts to meet with success. As a social worker, you will likely come into contact with families who struggle constantly on very low incomes. It is incumbent on social workers to make certain their clients know about the benefits discussed in this chapter. Clients may also need help in filling out the often very complicated application forms. Unfortunately, benefits frequently are inadequate and in short supply. Policy practice that is focused on expanding benefits and increasing access to eligible citizens is sorely needed.

MAIN POINTS

- The government typically defines poverty in terms of a poverty line, which was $19,157 for a family of four in 2004. People with incomes below the poverty line are considered poor. Poverty can also be defined in terms of relative poverty, whereby people are judged to be poor if they do not have sufficient resources to maintain a standard of living considered adequate in a given society at a particular time

- Income-support programs may be categorized as universal or selective. Some universal and selective programs are entitlement programs, which require benefits to be distributed to all people who meet the program criteria.

- Universal income-support programs that are provided to eligible citizens regardless of income include Old Age, Survivors, and Disability Insurance (OASDI); Unemployment Insurance; workers' compensation; and veterans' benefits.

- Selective programs are means-tested and include Temporary Assistance to Needy Families (TANF), the Food Stamp Program, the Special Supplemental Nutrition Program for Women, Infants, and Children (WIC), public housing, Section 8 housing, Supplemental Security Income (SSI), General Assistance, and the Earned Income Tax Credit (EITC).

- When evaluating the effectiveness of these policies and programs, strengths perspective principles emphasize examination of client goals and outcomes. Policy and program goals and design should focus on removing structural barriers and increasing access, choice, and opportunities that can lead to client empowerment. The effectiveness of the programs should be judged not only on whether they achieve societal goals but also on whether outcomes for clients are consistent with clients' goals.

- Asset-based policies and programs are gaining support in the United States. Individual Development Accounts (IDAs) have been instituted to assist families and individuals in saving for homes, education, and businesses in order to combat the inequality in asset distribution in the United States.

- Asset-based programs may complement but should not replace income-support programs.

EXERCISES: PRACTICING SOCIAL WORK

Working with the Sanchez Family

1. Based on your knowledge of family members, what benefits discussed in this chapter do you think Joey and Vicki might be eligible to receive? What further information would you need on each person in order to more clearly determine eligibility? In crafting your answer, list the family member's name, programs for which she or he might be eligible and additional information needed.

Working with the Black Feather Community

1. It is clear that poverty is a major issue in the Black Feather community. Taking into account the American Indian culture as described in the Black Feather case study, what kind of asset-based approaches do you think might be effective in this community?

EXERCISES: THE SOCIAL WORK LIBRARY

Poverty Is Widespread in the Adult Population

Read "The likelihood of poverty across the American adult life span," (Rank & Hirschl, 1999), and respond to the following:

1. What was your reaction to the results of the study discussed in this article? Were you aware that the majority of people in the United States experience poverty at some point in their lives? Did this article cause you to reexamine your views of people in poverty in United States?

2. The authors suggest that people would be motivated to change social policies related to poverty if a self-interest argument were made. What did they mean by this statement? Do you think that this approach would be an effective way to advocate for social policies related to alleviating poverty?

Asset-based Policy:

Read "From research to policy: Lessons from Individual Development Accounts" (Sherraden, 2000), and respond to the following:

1. The introduction of Individual Development Accounts has spawned increased focus on asset-based policies. Since 1990 when IDAs were first mentioned, what process did Michael Sherraden pursue to increase awareness and support for asset-based policies?

2. What are the results of this process in terms of support for asset-based policies?

OTHER EXERCISES

Taking Action

1. If you don't already know people receiving TANF with whom you can talk, consider volunteering time at a community center in a low-income area, or perhaps in a day care center in that area. This experience will give you a chance to learn about the barriers to meeting basic needs faced by low-income families.

Think about how you might most effectively approach the Sanchez family to help them get benefits. Identify the steps you would take.

2. How could you become part of the effort in your area to promote a living wage? List the steps you would take.

3. Ask a member of your family who is age 65 or over what Social Security means for her or him.

4. Issues such as high-quality, low-cost day care, mass transit, and a living wage are likely issues that people in your community are already actively trying to push in the local and state policy arena. You can find out how to join with other social workers and consumer groups to advocate for needed welfare reform by going to www.mhhe.com/chapin1 and clicking on the NASW Web link.

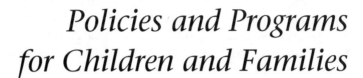

CHAPTER 9

Policies and Programs for Children and Families

WHEN WE SEARCH FOR STRENGTHS AND RESOURCES IN THE family and community, our attention turns naturally to children. We know that children can thrive if they have adequate food, shelter, education, health care, and sufficient adult guidance. Many adults devote their lives to helping children build on their strengths, thus enhancing both the present and the future of our families and communities. Nevertheless, in the United States, one in six children under age 18 is growing up in poverty (U.S. Census Bureau, 2005). For children age 5 and under, the number is one in five. Poor children eat less-nutritious meals, often live in unsafe homes, and are more likely to be victims of abuse and neglect. They are less healthy and less successful in school, and they are three times more likely to die in childhood. In addition, more than 500,000 children currently are in foster care (U.S. Department of Health and Human Services, 2004). On a regular basis, nearly 7 million children between ages 5 to 14 care for themselves without any adult supervision (Children's Defense Fund, 2001). Suicide is the second leading cause of death among teenagers.

The statistics are even bleaker for children of color (Petr, 2004). To begin with, the infant mortality rate for black children is more than twice that of white children (Annie E. Casey Foundation, 2004). Further, 33.6 percent of African American children and 29.7 percent of Hispanic or Latino children are living in poverty. Hispanic or Latino and African American youth are twice as likely as white youth to be neither in school nor working (Annie E. Casey Foundation, 2004). The percentage of children of color who are removed from their homes and placed in foster care is disproportionately higher than would be expected given the percentage of children of color in the United States. For example, 37 percent of children in foster care are African American, despite the fact that African Americans represent only 15 percent of all children in the United States under age 18 (U.S. Department of Health and Human Services, 2004). Although our children are our future, current policies and programs are failing to meet the needs of many of our youngest and most vulnerable citizens. Child welfare policies have developed primarily when the family and other systems that serve our children have failed (Briar Lawson & Drews, 2000). These programs have been largely residual, and they have often focused on child saving rather than on strengthening families (Lindsey, 1994). That is, they have emphasized the child in danger, but supports such as adequate day care and family allowances that many other developed countries provide for all families are still not in place in the United States. Thus, intervention is targeted to crisis situations rather than to providing vulnerable children and their families with the resources to avoid crisis situations. The result has been programs that are less effective in terms of both fiscal and human outcomes.

In Chapter 8, we discussed and critiqued the major programs designed to provide income support to children: EITC, TANF, and OASDI. We do not have children's allowances to help support all of our nation's children, and the policies and programs we do have leave many children to grow up in dire poverty. Our lack of effective income-support programs is a grave risk factor for our children. Chapter 8 explained in detail the need for additional, more-adequate income-support programs. In this chapter, we focus on policies and programs dealing with child protection, family preservation, permanency planning, adoption and foster care, and juvenile justice. Children in need of care are found in all of these systems. Additionally, children and families who are involved in the juvenile system because a child has been charged with a crime are also often involved with other child welfare service providers. For example, the child may be in foster care, or the family may be receiving family preservation services. Finally, we will examine programs for children with special needs as well as child-support enforcement policies.

This chapter provides information that will help develop your understanding of child welfare and family policy and how they can be improved. Many social workers are employed in the child welfare system. Further, social workers in all settings will undoubtedly deal with issues of child welfare and thus need to be familiar with basic child welfare policies and programs. Therefore, this chapter also explores the steps necessary for crafting effective child welfare and family policy using the strengths perspective. By taking a strengths approach, we can develop policies and programs that enhance the ability of families to care for their children and reduce cases of family dysfunction that put children at risk.

HISTORY AND BACKGROUND OF PROGRAMS PROTECTING CHILDREN AND FAMILIES

Social workers have long been leaders in the field of child welfare. In contrast to fields such as health care and education where other professions dominate, the child welfare system has been primarily a social work domain since the beginning of the 20th century (Hartman, 1990). As discussed in previous chapters, historical strategies for dealing with children in need of care included indenture, orphan trains, and large orphan asylums. In colonial times, children were subject to the same rules of criminal responsibility as adults, but reformers early on began to press for different treatment for children and youth (NASW, 2003g). For example, Jane Addams and her colleagues from Hull House lobbied the Illinois state legislature for a separate juvenile court. As a result of their efforts, the first juvenile court opened in Cook County, Illinois, in 1899 (Allard & Young, 2002). This approach spread across the country, so that by 1925, all but two states had juvenile courts.

Most states did not pass laws to protect children from physical abuse by parents until the mid-1800s to late 1800s. Even then, it took determined efforts by women's groups and other concerned citizens to convince legislators to pass such laws. Widely publicized cases of severe abuse helped build public support for these laws, which allowed the courts to remove children in need of protection from their parents and place them in orphanages, asylums, and other families. However, the laws did not specify who was responsible for investigating child abuse and enforcing child protection statutes. Consequently, private societies were established to provide these services (Petr, 2004).

In 1875, the first Society for the Prevention of Cruelty to Children was founded in New York. Similar private societies subsequently were established across the United States. These societies investigated cases of alleged child abuse and neglect, presented the cases in court, and advocated for legislation to safeguard children's welfare (Downs, Costin, & McFadden, 1996). Because private societies dedicated to the protection of animals were much more organized than groups aiming to protect children during this period, private child protection societies modeled their programs and strategies on those of the animal protection societies.

The Social Work Library

You may review the legislative initiatives and the role of pioneer social workers in building our child welfare system at the Social Work History Station, found at www.mhhe.com/chapin1.

As far back as 1935, Title IV-B, the Child Welfare Services Program of the Social Security Act, established the protection of children as a focus of public social service. Nevertheless, it was not until the powerful medical profession "rediscovered" child abuse in the 1960s that child maltreatment appeared on the policy agenda across the nation (Brissett-Chapman, 1995). The 1963 publication of a medical survey on "battered child syndrome" ignited public action. By presenting child abuse as a medical syndrome recognized by the medical profession, the 1963 report enhanced the validity of claims for the need for legislative intervention. By the mid-1960s, every state had passed legislation for the reporting of child abuse and the protection of children (Petr, 2004).

Currently, federal funds are provided to states and counties to help support child welfare services (Briar Lawson & Drews, 2000). Specifically, Title XX of the Social Security Act provides block grants for social services to states. In addition, Title IV-E provides reimbursement for a portion of the state's costs for foster care and adoption. Finally, Title IV-B provides grants to states for case

Web Link

To learn more about the work of the Children's Bureau, go to the link found at www.mhhe.com/chapin1.

management and prevention. The U.S. Children's Bureau, established in 1912, now oversees policies and funding affecting child welfare systems.

CHILDREN AND FAMILIES TODAY

By examining the environment in which children are growing up, we can gain insight into why child welfare policies succeed or fail. Today, children are growing up in much smaller families than was the case during the baby boom of 1945–1964. In addition, children represent a smaller proportion of our population today than in 1960. In 2000, only 26 percent of the population was under the age of 18, compared with 36 percent in 1960. Moreover, this percentage is projected to decrease to 24 percent by 2010 and then remain stable until 2030 (U.S. Department of Health and Human Services, 2002c). Consequently, there will be proportionally more adults to help support dependent children in the near future. However, it is unclear whether these adults will be willing to dedicate sufficient time and money to adequately nurturing these children.

Families have also become much more mobile. Many times, family members live far apart and therefore are less able to provide support and guidance. Further, the number of single-parent families increased from 7.9 million in 1990 to 9.7 million in 2001 (Annie E. Casey Foundation, 2003). In 2002, 19.8 million (27.3 percent) of U.S. children were living in single-parent homes, and 34 percent of all births were to unmarried women (U.S. Census Bureau, 2003; Annie E. Casey Foundation, 2004). Having two parents and many siblings doesn't ensure that children will receive the support they need, as those adults who grew up with abuse in two-parent homes and who often were hungry because there were so many mouths to feed can attest. However, the absence of fathers, siblings, and grandparents from the lives of children does mean that children have access to fewer of the resources that have traditionally supported and guided them.

The percentage of U.S. children who are African American and Hispanic is also increasing. In 1980, 74 percent of children under age 18 were Caucasian, 15 percent were African American, 9 percent were Hispanic, and 2 percent were Asian/Pacific Islander (U.S. Department of Health and Human Services, 2002d). By 2004, the percentage of Caucasian children had dropped to 59 percent, the African American population had increased to 17 percent, the Hispanic population had more than doubled to 19 percent, and the Asian/Pacific Islander population had doubled to 5 percent (U.S. Census Bureau, 2005). Experts project that Hispanic children will increase to 26 percent, of the child population by 2030, and Asian/Pacific Islander children will represent 6 percent of the child population by the same year. During this same period, the percentage of Caucasian children will decrease to 53 percent, while the percentage of African American children will decline slightly to 14 percent (U.S. Department of

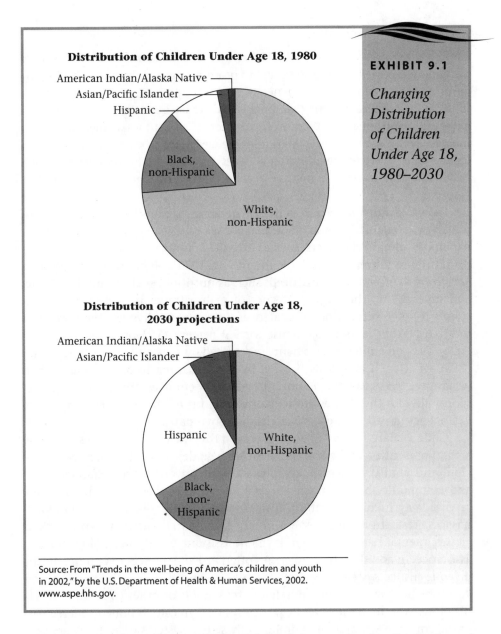

Distribution of Children Under Age 18, 1980

American Indian/Alaska Native
Asian/Pacific Islander
Hispanic
Black, non-Hispanic
White, non-Hispanic

Distribution of Children Under Age 18, 2030 projections

American Indian/Alaska Native
Asian/Pacific Islander
Hispanic
White, non-Hispanic
Black, non-Hispanic

EXHIBIT 9.1

Changing Distribution of Children Under Age 18, 1980–2030

Source: From "Trends in the well-being of America's children and youth in 2002," by the U.S. Department of Health & Human Services, 2002. www.aspe.hhs.gov.

Health and Human Services, 2002c). Exhibit 9.1 contrasts the distribution of children under age 18 in 1980 with the projected distribution for 2030.

These numbers indicate that our nation's children are now more ethnically diverse, more likely to be growing up in single-parent homes, and more likely to have a smaller kinship network. Therefore, they may rely on new kinds of family support that are not based on the traditional biological definitions of families. Policies and practices that do not take into account these new realities are less likely to be effective.

The Child Welfare System

Child welfare policy has created a **child welfare system.** "The child welfare system is a group of services designed to promote the well-being of children by ensuring safety, achieving permanency, and strengthening families to successfully care for their children" (National Clearinghouse on Child Abuse and Neglect, 2003). Although the child welfare system is sometimes defined broadly to include services, such as Head Start, that are designed to be preventive, the core child welfare services are adoption services and services for families in which child abuse or neglect, sometimes called *child maltreatment,* is reported or suspected.

Federal law defines **child maltreatment** as "serious harm (neglect, physical abuse, sexual abuse, and emotional abuse or neglect) caused to children by parents or primary caregivers, such as extended family members or babysitters" (Child Abuse Prevention and Treatment Act, 1974). **Neglect** is the failure of caregivers to provide for basic needs such as nutrition, shelter, emotional care, and supervision. The largest category of maltreatment is neglect, which accounts for 60.5 percent of all incidences. In contrast, physical abuse accounts for 18.6 percent, and sexual abuse for 9.9 percent (McDonald & Associates, 2004). Data on child maltreatment are reported by state child protective service (CPS) agencies. If a child is harmed by an acquaintance or a stranger, child welfare agencies generally do not intervene; law enforcement agencies have responsibility for those cases. If the maltreatment is not investigated by the state CPS agency, it will not be included in the above statistics.

Child welfare systems are complex, and they vary from state to state. They are not one entity. Rather, public agencies (e.g., departments of social services, child and family services) may contract with private child welfare agencies and community-based organizations to provide services to families. These services may include adoption, foster care, in-home ("family preservation") services, residential treatment, substance abuse treatment, parenting skills classes, mental health care, employment assistance, and financial or housing assistance. In addition, these agencies often provide services to children in the juvenile justice system as well as to children and families who seek out services on their own or who are referred by schools or other community organizations. Although the juvenile justice system typically is not considered part of the child welfare system, families in these two systems often face very similar problems. You will need to understand the policies and programs that structure each of these systems if you are to work effectively with children and families.

The Juvenile Justice System

Children and youth who are charged with crimes receive services through the **juvenile justice system.** The emphasis on rehabilitation within the juvenile justice system reflects the concept that young people are developmentally different from adults and therefore are more amenable to treatment. Children and youths who come into the juvenile justice system may be experiencing mental illness, substance abuse, or learning disabilities. They may have a history of abuse and of multiple placements in foster homes. Their backgrounds may be very similar to those of children in need of care who are receiving treatment through the child protection and foster care system. However, the juvenile justice system has been under criticism for years from people who feel that it often fails to rehabilitate youths.

Although the general public perception is that young people have become more crime prone and dangerous, recent studies indicate that this is not the case (Sentencing Project, 2003). In the late 1980s, juvenile violent crime arrests grew until they reached their peak level in 1994. From 1994 to 2002, however, the number of arrests actually declined. By 2002, juvenile arrest rates for violent crimes had reached their lowest level since at least 1980, and they were 47 percent below 1994 arrest rates (Snyder, 2004).

Despite these trends, during the 1980s and 1990s, states slowly began to reduce the age of criminal responsibility for some crimes and to respond more punitively to juvenile crime. In 1991, some 176,000 juveniles were tried as adults in criminal court (Sickmund, 1994). Today, that number exceeds 200,000. Further, in 2000, more than 7,600 prison inmates younger than 18 were being held as adults, an increase of 14 percent since 1994 (Sickmund, 2004). Significantly, many of the cases transferred to adult court are for nonviolent drug or property offenses rather than for violent crimes (Sentencing Project, 2003).

Holding youthful offenders as adults has many serious consequences. For example, juveniles in adult prisons are more than seven times more likely to commit suicide, five times more likely to be sexually abused, and twice as likely to be assaulted with a weapon as their adult counterparts (Sentencing Project, 2003). Moreover, after these youths are released, they are rearrested sooner, more often, and for more serious offenses than are their counterparts who received treatment through the juvenile court system.

Particularly troubling is the inequitable processing of African American youth through the system such that they are overrepresented in both the justice system and adult prisons. More than 69 percent of the juveniles in adult court and 75 percent of the youth sent to adult prisons are African American. Children and youth with special needs are also increasingly being incarcerated. The negative outcomes for children in our correctional system and the racial disparities in incarceration rates indicate that this is an area where effective reform measures are badly needed. We will discuss some promising reform initiatives later in the chapter.

One sign that perhaps our society is ready to reconsider some of the most onerous policies that affect children is the March 2005 U.S. Supreme Court

Web Link

For more information on the experiences of juveniles in adult criminal courts, visit the Sentencing Project Web site, found at www.mhhe.com/chapin1.

ruling *Roper vs. Simmons,* which abolished the death penalty for juvenile criminals. Before this change was made, the only countries that permitted the exe-
cution of offenders under the age of 18 were Iran, Nigeria, Saudi Arabia, and
the United States. Of these nations, the United States was responsible for 70
percent of all juvenile executions worldwide between the years 1998–2002
(Amnesty International, 2002).

MAJOR POLICIES AND PROGRAMS AFFECTING CHILD WELFARE AND JUVENILE JUSTICE

 Web Link

*For state-by-state informa-
tion on child abuse and
neglect, visit the National
Clearinghouse on Child
Abuse and Neglect
Web site, found at
www.mhhe.com/chapin1.
This Web site is maintained
by the Children's Bureau of
the Department of Health
and Human Services and is
an excellent source of the
most up-to-date information
on child abuse.*

The following section examines major federal child welfare policies and
programs as well as juvenile justice policies and legislation for children with
special needs. As we explore these policies, you will observe that policy emphasis shifts back and forth between protecting children and preserving families. Similarly, ideological and societal shifts strongly influence the extent to
which juvenile justice policy emphasizes rehabilitation at a given time. You
will also find that states have the primary responsibility for administering
child welfare and juvenile justice programs. Therefore, the quality and types
of public services available for children and families vary greatly from state to
state.

The Child Abuse Prevention and Treatment Act

In 1974, the federal government became involved in child abuse prevention
with the passage of the **Child Abuse Prevention and Treatment Act
(CAPTA)** (P.L. 93-247). The CAPTA provided states with federal funds to
develop reporting systems for investigation of abuse and neglect. The law also
established the National Center on Child Abuse and Neglect, whose mission
was to "assess the extent of the problem, to examine models for prevention and
treatment and to act as a catalyst for change" (NASW, 2003f, p. 32). This center
was a valuable source of funds for research into both the causes of child abuse
and neglect and models for effective treatment and prevention.

Congress has amended the CAPTA six times to reauthorize the program and
to strengthen and expand programs centered on prevention and reporting. In
1978, it was amended to include provisions for comprehensive state adoption
programs. The CAPTA was most recently amended by the Keeping Children and
Families Safe Act of 2003 (P.L. 108-36, 6/25/03), which provided community-
based grants for the prevention of child abuse and neglect. Box 9.1 applies the
policy analysis framework introduced in Chapter 5 to the CAPTA. These short
summary exhibits are not intended to be comprehensive, but they can help you
remember major elements of the policy.

Policy Goals	To strengthen the identification, reporting, and investigation of child maltreatment. Monitor research and publish information about child abuse and neglect.
Benefits or Services Provided	Programs for reporting, investigating, treating, and preventing child abuse and neglect. National Center on Child Abuse and Neglect established as an information clearinghouse.
Eligibility Rules	Children under age 18 at risk for or a victim of abuse or neglect.
Service Delivery System	At the federal level, the Office on Child Abuse and Neglect in the Children's Bureau of DHHS administers the act. State and local welfare agencies responsible for investigating and treating abuse and neglect implement the programs.
Financing	Federal grant to the state based on population under age 18.

BOX 9.1

Child Abuse Prevention and Treatment Act (CAPTA), 1974

The Juvenile Justice and Delinquency Prevention Act

In 1974, Congress also passed the **Juvenile Justice and Delinquency Prevention Act (JJDP Act)** (P.L. 93-415), which was last reauthorized in 2002. The goals of the original act were to aid state and local governments in preventing and controlling juvenile delinquency and to improve the juvenile justice system. An additional important element was to protect juveniles from being inappropriately placed in the juvenile justice system and from being harmed by exposure to adult inmates. This act also emphasized the importance of community-based treatment for juvenile offenders.

The 2002 reauthorization of the JJDP Act requires states to develop and implement strategies to comply with four core protections for juveniles as a condition of receiving grants under the act. The core protections are:

- Reduction of the disproportionate number of juvenile minority-group members who come into contact with the juvenile justice system

- Separation of juveniles from adult offenders

- Removal of juveniles from adult jails

- Deinstitutionalization of juveniles who are status offenders, that is, who have committed crimes that would not be criminal if committed by an adult (Office of Juvenile Justice and Delinquency Prevention, 2002)

BOX 9.2 *Juvenile Justice and Delinquency Prevention (JJDP) Act, 1974*		
	Policy Goals	To prevent and control juvenile delinquency and improve the juvenile justice system.
	Benefits or Services Provided	Community-based treatment provided when appropriate to protect juveniles from unnecessary placement in the juvenile justice system and from harm incurred from exposure to adult inmates.
	Eligibility Rules	Juveniles adjudicated delinquent and at-risk children.
	Service Delivery System	Office of Juvenile Justice and Delinquency Prevention in the U.S. Department of Justice has oversight over state and local government actions taken to reach goals.
	Financing	Federal funds provided to state and local governments.

 Web Link

For more information on juvenile justice legislation, visit the Office of Juvenile Justice and Delinquency Prevention (OJJDP) Web site by going to www.mhhe.com/chapin1.

The Office of Juvenile Justice and Delinquency Prevention (OJJDP) in the U.S. Department of Justice works to achieve these goals. Although this act focused on rehabilitating youthful offenders, it did not provide sufficient resources to build an effective system. State and local government will need much more funding if they are to develop juvenile justice systems that can achieve the goals of the act. Box 9.2 summarizes the features of the JJDP Act.

The Indian Child Welfare Act

Because the Indian Child Welfare Act is an excellent example of policy change guided by the client group, we have already examined the historical context for this legislation and discussed how it reflects strengths perspective principles. Here, we briefly review the background of the act in order to restate the conditions that propelled the passage of this unique piece of child welfare legislation. Recall that federal policy for Native Americans historically has emphasized forced acculturation. Religious conversion was forced, and children were placed in boarding schools and other institutions and were systematically stripped of their native cultures. Between 1969 and 1974, approximately 35 percent of Native American children were in foster homes and institutions (Matheson, 1996). Moreover, 85 percent of these placements were in non-Indian homes (U.S. Department of Health and Human Services, 2003a).

Native American leaders were determined to halt this cultural genocide. A number of tribes worked together to convince Congress to pass the **Indian Child Welfare Act (ICWA)** (P.L. 95-608) of 1978. The ICWA mandates that active efforts be made to ensure that Native American children remain with their families, and it empowers tribes and tribal courts to oversee decision making regarding Native American children. Box 9.3 applies the policy analysis framework to the ICWA.

Policy Goals	To protect the best interests of Native American children and families. To set minimum standards for removal and placement of Indian children and termination of parental rights. To recognize and strengthen the role of tribal government.	**BOX 9.3** *Indian Child Welfare Act (ICWA), 1978*
Benefits or Services Provided	Endorse maintenance of Native American children with their families or placement in homes that reflect their culture. Tribes are actively involved in decision making.	
Eligibility Rules	All children who are members of federally recognized tribes, with membership determined by individual tribes.	
Service Delivery System	Tribal and urban Native American agencies have authority over state and federal courts to protect the best interests of their communities' children.	
Financing	Federal funds provided to tribal and urban Native American agencies.	

Tribes vary greatly in their capacity to implement the ICWA. Unfortunately, federal funding has been insufficient. In order to implement the ICWA more fully, the government must provide adequate funding to establish Indian child and family services and additional funding for training and monitoring. In addition, greater cooperation between states and tribes and increased employment and retention of Native American staff are essential if the ICWA is to achieve its goals (Petr, 2004).

 Web Link

You may view the specific procedural safeguards for the custody and placement of Native American children created by the ICWA at the National Indian Child Welfare Association (NICWA) Web site, found at www.mhhe.com/chapin1.

The Adoption Assistance and Child Welfare Act

Widely considered to be the most important piece of federal legislation to impact child welfare practice, the **Adoption Assistance and Child Welfare Act (AACWA) of 1980** (P.L. 96-272) established family preservation as a major goal of the child welfare system. Before this law was enacted, extensive research had documented the impermanence of foster placement. In the 1960s and 1970s, the philosophies, financial incentives, and professional attitudes in state foster care systems emphasized "child saving" rather than "family saving" (Petr, 2004). Thousands of children grew up in foster care, with no permanent ties to any family. Because the system did not emphasize permanent relationships in biological and adoptive families, these children often grew up without the supports and family bonds that are considered important to healthy development.

BOX 9.4 *Adoption Assistance and Child Welfare Act, 1980*	**Policy Goals**	To reduce the number of children in foster care for extended lengths of time through written permanency plans that emphasize family preservation, reunification, or adoption.
	Benefits or Services Provided	"Reasonable efforts" made to preserve the family. Establishment of a permanency plan for all children in the foster care system.
	Eligibility Rules	Children and families involved in investigation of and treatment for abuse and neglect.
	Service Delivery System	DHHS is responsible for federal oversight. State and local agencies responsible for investigating and treating abuse and neglect implement program changes. Periodic court reviews are conducted for each foster child case.
	Financing	Federal funds attached to incentives to reach goals.

The AACWA established financial incentives for states to emphasize permanency planning. In order to receive certain federal funding to help pay for their child welfare services, states are required to make a judicial determination that "reasonable efforts" were made to prevent unnecessary out-of-home placement (Petr, 2004). If such placements are found necessary, then states subsequently must make "reasonable efforts" to reunite the families. Unfortunately, the legislation did not define what constituted "reasonable efforts." State child welfare agencies thus varied widely in their efforts to increase permanency, and children continued to languish in foster care. Box 9.4 summarizes the features of the AACWA.

Family Preservation and Support Services

Over the years, many states and counties have experimented with family preservation initiatives to prevent placement and support reunification. This work was reinforced by **Family Preservation and Support Services** (P.L. 103-66), enacted as part of the Omnibus Budget Reconciliation Act of 1993.

The Family Preservation and Support Services provisions encourage the development of cohesive, community-based family preservation and support strategies that involve collaboration between child protection and child welfare workers and other service providers to implement family-centered interventions (Briar Lawson & Drews, 2000). The goals are to support the well-being of all family members and to enable parents to create safe, nurturing home environments. Federal funding is provided to the states, which establish the programs and services. Family support services may include activities such as support groups, home visits, and childcare with the purpose of increasing family strength and stability. Family preservation encompasses counseling or respite care as well as other interventions that help families at risk or in crisis keep their children in their homes (Ahsan, 1996). Children and families at risk of abuse or neglect or in crisis are eligible for these services.

These provisions were reauthorized as the Promoting Safe and Stable Families (PSSF) program in 1997. The most recent reauthorization was in 2002. This is one of the very few programs for which federal funds are made available to state child welfare services that focus on prevention and support of vulnerable families.

Web Link

You can find more information on the PSSF at the Web site found at www.mhhe.com/chapin1.

The Multi-Ethnic Placement Act

The intent of the **Multi-Ethnic Placement Act (MEPA) of 1994** (P.L. 103-82) and the 1996 amendment, the Interethnic Adoption Provisions (MEPA-IEP), is to remove barriers to permanency for children in the child protective system. Specific goals are (1) to eliminate discrimination based on race, color, or national origin of the child or the prospective parent; (2) to shorten the time that children wait to be adopted; and (3) to facilitate the recruitment and retention of adoptive and foster care parents who can meet the distinctive needs of children awaiting placement (Hollinger, 1998).

The MEPA-IEP prohibits states and other entities involved in foster care or adoption placements that receive federal financial assistance under Title IV-E, Title IV-B, or any other federal program from delaying or denying a child's foster care or adoptive placement because of the child's or the prospective parent's race, color, or national origin, or denying the opportunity to become a foster or adoptive parent for the same reasons. This act also requires states to diligently recruit foster and adoptive parents who reflect the racial and ethnic diversity of the children in the state in need of foster and adoptive homes in order to remain eligible for federal assistance for their child welfare programs (Hollinger, 1998). Box 9.5 summarizes the provisions of the MEPA-IEP.

The MEPA-IEP does not apply to children covered under the ICWA because of the unique political relationship between the Indian tribes and the federal government. In contrast to the ICWA, the MEPA-IEP is designed to break down barriers to interracial adoption. However, the law does require increased efforts to recruit and retain a multi-ethnic pool of prospective parents who reflect the racial and ethnic diversity of children in foster care.

Children of color, particularly African American children, were lingering disproportionately long in the system. Now, child welfare workers are to consider race as well as other factors in placement. Although the MEPA is designed

BOX 9.5 *Multi-Ethnic Placement Act, 1994*	**Policy Goals**	To remove barriers to permanency by eliminating discrimination based on race, color, or national origin of the child or the prospective parent and reducing the waiting time before adoption.
	Benefits or Services Provided	Guidelines established for placement of children with prospective parents and recruitment and retention of adoptive and foster care parents.
	Eligibility Rules	All children in foster care awaiting adoption except for children covered under the Indian Child Welfare Act.
	Service Delivery System	State and local child protection agencies follow the federal guidelines in order to ensure funding for programs.
	Financing	Federal funds given to states.

to increase the number of homes available for same-race adoption while simultaneously removing barriers to cross-racial adoption, children of color are still spending comparatively longer amounts of time in foster care before they are permanently placed. Even though agencies are increasing their efforts to recruit black families, some critics question whether this goal is realistic, given that black parents currently adopt foster children at a rate that is double their proportion in the population (Geen, 2003).

Transracial adoptions increased from 8 percent of adoptions in 1987 to 21 percent in 2001 (Geen, 2003). As the number of transracial adoptions increases, the impact on children of color of being raised in white homes is still hotly debated. Most research completed on transracial adoption indicates that the practice does not negatively affect the child's psychosocial and overall well-being. However, this research has been questioned on both theoretical and methodological grounds. For example, some studies indicate that minority children adopted into Caucasian families are prone to identify with the culture of their adopted families instead of their own races and cultures. This process can be problematic because identifying with one's own race and culture is correlated with fewer adjustment difficulties (Frasch & Brooks, 2003).

 Web Link

For more detailed information on this legislation, see the guide to the Multiethnic Placement Act of 1994 and the 1996 amendment, the Interethnic Adoption Provisions, available at the Children's Bureau Web site, found at www.mhhe.com/chapin1.

The Adoption and Safe Families Act

The **Adoption and Safe Families Act (ASFA) of 1997** (P.L. 105-89) amended the Adoption Assistance and Child Welfare Act (AACWA) of 1980. The AACWA made reunification the primary goal for children who were removed from their homes. The law mandated that reasonable efforts be made to reunite the child and family, and it placed an 18-month time limit on foster care before termination of parental rights was initiated. Despite these stipulations, however, the number of children in foster care had increased to about 468,000 by 1994 (Baum, Crase, & Crase, 2001).

In 1997, Congress enacted the Adoption and Safe Families Act, which placed more emphasis on child safety and was intended to increase adoptions. The ASFA provides that states are not required to make reasonable efforts to preserve or reunify families once a court has determined that (1) the parent subjected the child to "aggravated circumstances"; (2) the parent committed a felony assault that resulted in serious bodily injury to the child or another of the parent's children; (3) the parent is guilty of murder or voluntary manslaughter of another of her or his children, or abetted, aided, solicited, or conspired to commit such a crime; or (4) parental rights with another child had been terminated. ASFA further required that termination of parental rights be initiated for any child who had been out of the home for 15 of the prior 22 months (Wan, 1999). This change was intended to enable a quicker adoption process and thus to reduce the amount of time a child spends in limbo between foster care and either reunification or adoption.

Since the inception of this policy, the number of children served each year by the foster care system has decreased only slightly, from 817,000 in 1998 to 810,000 in 2002. The number of children in foster care has also declined. At the end of 1998, there were 559,000 children in foster care; by the end of 2003, that number had declined to 523,000 (U.S. Department of Health and Human Services, 2003c, 2004).

When children are removed from the home, they become eligible for the benefits provided by ASFA. The intent of ASFA is to provide safe, stable, and permanent homes to these children in a timely manner. ASFA asserts that health and safety should be paramount in every decision made about children. The reasonable effort requirement for permanency planning was altered to provide for the best interest of the child. The act further requires that permanency hearings be held within 12 months of the time when the child enters foster care. If reasonable efforts are not required, then the time frame is reduced to 30 days. Additionally, for children who have been in foster care for 15 of the prior 22 months, termination of parental rights must be initiated unless (1) a child is being cared for by a relative, (2) a compelling reason why termination would not be in the best interests of the child can be shown, or (3) the state has not provided the child's family with the necessary or timely services that would enable the child to return safely to the home.

In order to expedite the process of permanency, ASFA authorizes the use of concurrent planning, when appropriate. **Concurrent planning** provides states with the option of working on an alternative plan for the child even while it is attempting reunification (Adler, 2001). Despite all these changes, however, children continue to remain in the foster care system longer than the policy intends, and they continue to enter the system faster than they find permanency.

ASFA is a federal program and is funded through federal dollars and some state matching grants. ASFA provides states with incentive payments of $4,000 per child for any increase in the number of adoptions over the number in a base year. It also provides an additional $2,000 if children with special needs are adopted, and it makes health insurance available for children with special needs who cannot be adopted without such insurance. ASFA also removes geographic barriers to adoption by allowing children to be adopted outside the jurisdiction that is responsible for them (Adler, 2001).

ASFA services are delivered by a diverse group of professionals. The court system is involved in deciding the best interests of the child. The court makes this decision within 12 months of placement in the system or within 30 days if it decides that reasonable efforts are not required to keep a child in her or his family of origin. Social workers and other professionals who provide case management and therapeutic services are responsible for planning treatment and for working with the courts to make recommendations for placing the child. Providing competent services for children in foster care clearly is critical. Nevertheless, many staff who work with children are not properly trained.

ASFA was also designed to enhance state capacity and accountability. It provides additional funds to states to develop innovative new approaches. ASFA also provides funding for the Department of Health and Human Services (DHHS) to make technical assistance available to states, communities, and courts. Furthermore, it requires states to submit an annual performance report to DHHS. In turn, DHHS is responsible for reporting each state's annual performance and for developing performance-based financial incentives for states (Adler, 2001). Finally, ASFA requires states to implement standards that ensure that children in foster care are provided with quality services that protect their health and safety (Adler, 2001). Box 9.6 summarizes the major provisions of ASFA.

Some states have experimented with privatizing foster care and adoption. As discussed in earlier chapters, *privatization* refers to the process whereby services formerly provided by the public sector are transferred to the private sector. The results of privatizing foster care and adoption have been mixed in terms of outcomes for children. In addition, privatized programs have not proved to be less expensive. The cost for foster care is high, and it continues to grow as the number of children in the foster care system increases. We examine privatization and other strategies for improving the child welfare system in more detail later in the chapter.

The Child Support Enforcement Program

Many children living with only one of their biological parents do not receive adequate financial support from the noncustodial parent. The Child Support

Policy Goals	To place emphasis on child safety and the best interests of children. To promote permanency for children in foster care and accelerate permanent placement. To increase accountability of the child welfare system.	**BOX 9.6** *Adoption and Safe Families Act (ASFA), 1997*
Benefits or Services Provided	Accelerates permanent placement by promoting adoption and shortening time limits for termination of parental rights.	
Eligibility Rules	Children are eligible when they are removed from their homes.	
Service Delivery System	Federal oversight of state and local child welfare agencies that implement mandated changes. Court system decides the best interests of the child with recommendations from social workers and other professionals that provide case management and therapeutic services.	
Financing	Federal funding with some state matching funds. Federal incentives given to states that have an increase in adoptions.	

Enforcement (CSE) Program is designed to help remedy this situation. The CSE Program was established in 1975 as part of Title IV-D of the Social Security Act. At the federal level, the Office of Child Support Enforcement in the Administration for Children and Families (ACF) within DHHS oversees child support enforcement. This federal, state, and local program provides the following services:

- Establishes paternity

- Locates noncustodial parents

- Establishes child support obligations

- Collects child support for families

Currently, each state administers a child support program. In addition, Indian tribes may administer these programs. Different states place child support enforcement under the auspices of various agencies. In some states, the human services department is responsible for enforcement; in other states, the department of revenue performs this role. A parent with custody of a child who has a parent living outside the home may receive services through the CSE Program by applying to the agencies that administer the programs. For families receiving assistance through TANF, services are automatic. Part of the child support collected for these families is used to reimburse the federal and state governments for the TANF payments the family has received. Child support payments for families not receiving TANF are sent directly to the families (U.S. Department of Health and Human Services, 2002c).

Although it was not technically a component of the CSE Program, the 1996 TANF legislation improved the states' capacity to collect child support. The law established a national new-hire and wage-reporting system and instituted uniform interstate child support forms. It also provided funds to computerize statewide collection systems, and it authorized tough new penalties such as revoking driver's licenses for nonpayment of child support. Following these reforms, child support collection increased nationally to a record $18 billion in 2000 (U.S. Department of Health and Human Services, 2002b).

States and other service providers are also experimenting with programs designed to help noncustodial parents improve their ability to provide both financial and emotional support for their children. These programs help young unmarried fathers find employment and improve their parenting skills. Because the service delivery system varies significantly from state to state, I have not provided a summary chart on CSE.

Legislation for Children with Special Educational Needs

Children who require special educational provisions because of a physical or mental disability are considered to have special educational needs. Legislation for children with special needs, such as the Education for All Handicapped Children Act of 1975 and its reauthorization, the Individuals with Disabilities Education Act (IDEA) of 1990, require states to provide education and services to meet these children's needs in the "least restrictive environment" (Briar Lawson & Drews, 2000). The Individuals with Disabilities Education Act was reauthorized in 2004 (P.L. 108-446). Measures designed to hold the educational system more accountable for learning outcomes for children with disabilities are a major component of the reauthorization legislation. However, federal funding to help schools meet the new requirements has been inadequate.

Movements on behalf of children with special needs have helped draw attention to the importance of "least restrictive" placements and "least intrusive" interventions. Advocates have also promoted normalization for children with special needs. **Normalization** is a policy whereby schools endeavor to create an environment similar to that experienced by children without special needs. Parents and other advocates, including many educators and social workers, have lobbied tirelessly to implement policies that would allow children with special needs to receive inclusionary services in the public schools. Their work has reinforced the importance of these principles in child welfare services for all children.

Web Links

You can find out more about the Child Support Enforcement Program and programs for noncustodial parents by visiting the Web sites at www.mhhe.com/chapin1.

The Social Work Library

Access the User's Guide to the 2004 IDEA Reauthorization (P.L. 108-446) *at www.mhhe.com/chapin1. You may examine the changes made by the acts and the implications for parents and schools at this link.*

Web Links

Learn more about the advocacy group ARC and a variety of groups working to improve conditions for children with special needs, by visiting the Office of Special Education Programs in the U.S. Department of Education to find out about federal initiatives and best practices in special education. Browse the Federal Resource Center for Special Education for more about programs for children with special needs through www.mhhe.com/chapin1.

Social workers in schools and other agencies regularly serve children with special educational needs. It is important that you become familiar with policies and programs targeted to these children. For information specific to your state's programs, contact your state department of education.

EVALUATING POLICIES AND PROGRAMS FOR CHILDREN AND FAMILIES

The family is the foundation for the support of children. The application of strengths perspective policy principles when evaluating child welfare policies focuses attention on enhancing the family's capacity to support its children. Policies and programs need to be attuned to the racial, political, cultural, and economic contexts of families' lives. In addition, they must provide additional resources so that work with families may help to overcome barriers such as inadequate wages, lack of jobs, lack of training, and discrimination in the workforce. Families need assistance in obtaining access to knowledge and resources to address problems such as substance abuse and mental illness. The extent to which the child safety and permanency goals of child welfare policies and programs are met will be determined in large part by success in family capacity building. Family capacity building could include developing occupational ladders for economically stressed families whereby former clients who have been trained as adoption and foster support aides, parent aides, and reunification aides could deliver services (Briar Lawson & Drews, 2000).

As discussed in previous chapters, evaluating policies and programs using the strengths perspective involves seeking clients' input. Regarding child welfare, there are Web sites that provide parents' perspectives on child welfare policy, especially for children with special needs. For example, Family Voices, a national grassroots network of families and advocates for children with special needs, promotes the inclusion of all families as decision makers and supports partnerships between families and professionals. Family Voices makes available publications, funded in part by DHHS, that describe mandates and strategies for involving families in developing and evaluating programs.

 Web Link

You can find out more about the work of Family Voices at www.mhhe.com/chapin1.

Strengths-based policy principles also stress involving the target group in designing and delivering services. Families are defining themselves in new ways, and initiatives to identify and work with support networks that are not based on biological relationship can help bolster parents' capacities to care effectively for their children. Strengths-based approaches to reforming child welfare services include instituting policies that promote self-help and mutual assistance at the community level and investing in economic and occupational approaches that help families overcome the barriers that keep them in poverty.

Examining client outcomes is central to evaluation from a strengths perspective. However, because states vary widely in the statistics they keep, it is

 Web Link

For more information on outcomes for children at the state and national levels, access the Kids Count Data Book Web site at www.mhhe.com/chapin1.

very difficult to develop a clear picture of outcomes for children on a national basis. Improving and standardizing state data systems are critical to enhancing our understanding of the success and failure of child welfare policy.

In the next section, we will evaluate selected components of child protection and juvenile justice policy, and we will consider next steps and necessary changes in the role of social workers in the child welfare system. We will also examine policy strategies to increase the effectiveness of social work within this system.

Child Protection Policy from the Strengths Perspective

There are two different policy paradigms for child protection. One focuses on children's legal rights and views abusive parental behaviors as crimes requiring police-style investigation (Pelton, 1989). The second emphasizes social work–style investigation that focuses on assessing not only risk and safety but also the need for a range of interventions and services. Ineffective investigative practices and lawsuits have contributed to the development of litigation oriented rather than social work–operated child protection systems. However, research studies have indicated that providing biological parents with needed support can generate improved child welfare outcomes (Briar Lawson & Drews, 2000). In line with this research, the National Association of Public Child Welfare Administrators (NAPCWA) published revised guidelines for a model system of child protective services. It has also sponsored the development of cross-disciplinary work, including the report *Bringing Systems Together* (American Public Human Services Association, 2002).

The NAPCWA report calls for much greater integration and tracking of outcomes across the mental health, domestic abuse, substance abuse, child welfare, and child protection systems in a way that focuses on families. The same children and families are often shuffled among these systems rather than receiving integrated, effective service. For example, it is estimated that more than half of all child welfare families have substance abuse as a presenting problem. Yet, few states have enacted policies that allow even drug-using pregnant mothers priority access to treatment beds for substance abuse (Briar Lawson & Drews, 2000).

The report further recommends that child protective services function as an interrelated and integrated set of services that are part of a community-wide early prevention, intervention, and treatment system. It notes that since the mid-1990s, there has been an increased focus on assessing family and community strengths as well as safety and risk. It further asserts that work with families needs to be strengths based and empowerment based. The authors recommend adopting policies that provide greater flexibility in conducting investigations rather than adhering to a standardized, "one-size-fits-all" approach regardless of the specifics of the case.

The report also expresses concern regarding the continued use of a law-enforcement approach to investigating black families, given the discrimination

The Social Work Library

You can view a more detailed evaluation of child protection policy and practice in the full NAPCWA report, available at www.mhhe.com/chapin1.

that African American families have experienced within that system. African American families are disproportionately represented in the child protection system. Consequently, sensitivity to diversity is particularly important to successful child protection intervention. In some states, nonminority, nonpoor children may be served more often in the mental health and disabilities system rather than in the child welfare system.

Family Rights and Child Safety As discussed earlier, the Adoption and Safe Families Act of 1997 (ASFA), which amended the Adoption Assistance and Child Welfare Act (AACWA) of 1980, was enacted to place more emphasis on child safety and to increase the number of adoptions, thereby reducing the amount of time that children spend in the foster care system. Despite the passage of the ASFA, however, the length of stay and the number of children in the foster care system have decreased only slightly. Children are still lingering in the system, bouncing from one foster home to another. These children are not able to reap the benefits of living in a stable, healthy home environment.

Moving children out of the foster care system has proved to be difficult. Meanwhile, reports of abuse and neglect continue to rise. One reason for this increase is improved reporting systems and increased detection, such as screening newborn infants for drug exposure and mothers for substance abuse. However, poverty, inequality, and underemployment are also major contributors to family stressors that increase child abuse (Briar Lawson & Drews, 2000). At the same time, traditional support systems provided by extended families, schools, and churches are no longer as available. Further research that examines risk factors for abuse and attempts to unravel the relationships among these contributing factors clearly is needed.

Policy changes in the ASFA allow for the rights of parents to be terminated more easily than was true under the AACWA. Advocates of these changes believed that this approach would enhance the potential for timely permanent placement. Critics contend, however, that the revised policies work against family reunification. Although cases move into permanency planning more quickly because of the ASFA, the 12-month time line may not allow sufficient time for families to successfully work on their problems and get their children back. Consider, for example, that many children are removed from their homes owing to substance abuse issues. In fact, about 80 percent of substantiated abuse and neglect cases are associated with drug abuse (Cox, 1998). A 12-month limit does not allow the parents enough time to rectify their situations to the point at which they can regain custody of their children.

In general, then, severing the rights of parents has not accomplished the goal of getting children into a permanent home setting. Rather, it has intensified the problem by creating "legal orphans" of children in the foster care system. To change this outcome, we need to develop policies and programs that (1) put more emphasis on kinship care, which means placing children with relatives,

The Social Work Library

The National Association of Public Child Welfare Administrators (NAPCWA) published revised guidelines for a model system of child protective services. You can view these guidelines at www.mhhe.com/chapin1.

Web Link

To learn more about cross-disciplinary work in child welfare, go to the APHSA Web site at www.mhhe.com/chapin1.

and (2) allow parents more time to regain some control over issues that are impeding them from being effective parents without severing ties to the biological family. To encourage more kinship care placements, it may be necessary to modify foster care guidelines so that more families can become eligible.

Family Reunification   High caseloads and financial disincentives work against family reunification. Most federal child welfare funding supports out-of-home rather than in-home services (Briar Lawson & Drews, 2000). In addition, the policies of many residential facilities do not support family reintegration. When facilities are located far from families, when family visits and phone calls are considered privileges rather than rights, and when there are no residential staff responsible for working with families to facilitate discharge and reintegration into the community, family reintegration is less likely.

Web Link

Find out more about GLASS at its Web site, found at www.mhhe.com/chapin1.

Gay and lesbian youth may have a particularly hard time in foster care. Some communities have experimented with group homes created specifically for these youth. For example, Gay and Lesbian Adolescent Social Services (GLASS) has established such group homes in Los Angeles (Petr, 2004).

Policy principles such as "reasonable efforts" in preventing placement, the child's right to the least intrusive intervention and the least restrictive environment in placement, and emphasis on normalization, although laudable, are difficult to define and operationalize. Nevertheless, they promote a philosophy of child welfare intervention that is consistent with the strengths perspective in that they focus on child development and well-being as well as safety. As is the case in most policy arenas, there are many gray areas. However, these policy principles make it clear that extremes such as large, isolated children's institutions and foster care drift, which means that children spend years moving from one temporary placement to another, are no longer acceptable. When these principles are incorporated into law, they help fortify the efforts of child welfare advocates who are petitioning hard-pressed state legislatures for additional funds and for reform of the child welfare system.

Many children in state custody have traditionally received services from private providers, such as church-affiliated nonprofit group homes. Modifying the ways in which the state reimburses these private entities could promote more positive outcomes for children. Traditional reimbursement strategies that pay providers a set fee for each day children remain in out-of-home care create a financial disincentive for family reunification and effective permanency planning. Recognizing this problem, some states have begun paying for permanency and have instituted financial disincentives for allowing children to linger too long in foster care.

Privatization   As discussed earlier, the provision of child welfare services is becoming increasingly privatized. A privatized system relies much more heavily on market forces and competition to improve the system. Some private sector providers—particularly foster parents and church-affiliated group homes—traditionally have been part of the public child welfare system. However, for-profit providers are becoming more involved with the system. Even the jobs of adoption and foster care case managers and administrators, formerly located in the public sector, are being privatized.

A principal privatization strategy is for public entities to buy services for clients through **purchase-of-service (POS) contracting** rather than to provide services directly (Petr, 2004). The state then monitors and oversees the provision of services. In one form of privatization, POS vouchers are provided directly to recipients or their families. Modified managed care models, whereby private entities are paid a set amount per person to provide all needed services, have also been developed. We will discuss managed care in more detail in Chapter 10 on health care.

Rigorous research is needed to evaluate the efficacy of these various privatization initiatives. Consistent with the strengths perspective, such research must carefully examine outcomes for clients as well as cost-effectiveness. At present, it is not clear how the profit motive will result in higher-quality services in the adoption and foster care arena. Additionally, child welfare advocates continually have emphasized the need for more cooperation and integration among service providers. Again, it is unclear how a greater emphasis on competition will increase cooperation. Finally, evaluative research must examine the impact of privatization on child welfare workers. It is very difficult to recruit and retain skilled workers if the workplace does not provide adequate pay, benefits, and job stability. Because private agencies compete for contracts to provide services and may lose these contracts, job stability is reduced. Further, when cost is a driving factor, an agency that provides lower pay and fewer benefits for its workforce, and therefore offers services more cheaply, is more likely to win the contract.

 Web Link

Learn more about evaluations of privatization initiatives at the Kansas Action for Children Web site, found at www.mhhe.com/chapin1.

Strategies for Supporting Families More Effectively   Children who are victims of child abuse sometimes have co-occurring symptoms of disability and mental illness. They may also be involved with the juvenile justice system. Thus, under traditional categorical approaches to policy and services, a family could be involved with as many as 15 workers from different agencies at one time. Regardless of which system children and their families enter, policies must ensure that they receive home- and community-based options whenever possible and that the services are tailored to their individual needs. Foster parents should be trained, and services should be delivered by professionals with expertise and appropriate professional training (Briar Lawson & Drews, 2000).

It is crucial that policies and adequate funding be in place to provide services at the point that the child has been reported as endangered and the family is in crisis. Initiatives such as the Homebuilders Model of family preservation hold promise that intensive services can effectively build family

Web Link

You can find out about re-search on the Homebuilders Model and school-based programs that wrap services around families at the National Coalition for Child Protection Reform (NCCPR) Web site. Go to the issue paper Does Family Preservation Work? *found at www.mhhe.com/chapin1.*

capacity. Under the Homebuilders Model, workers with small caseloads focus on helping families find strategies to stay together, including ways of accessing formal and informal resources and support. School-based policies and programs that help families remain intact and keep children safe through wraparound services have also been developed. Research on the effectiveness of such models continues. Rigorous study of various models will be necessary to determine which interventions are most effective in achieving specific outcomes with different types of families (Petr, 2004).

Long-term models of counseling and support may be necessary for families in "perpetual crisis." Families coping with serious ongoing problems such as substance abuse, extreme poverty, and chronic unemployment will likely need more than short-term services if their children are to remain safely at home and not reenter the foster care system. High rates of system reentry after children are returned to their families indicate that these families continue to be vulnerable (Briar Lawson & Drews, 2000). Some advocates have endorsed long-term, low-cost support strategies such as self-help and mutual aid groups. As with other policy approaches, these programs must be evaluated to assess their effectiveness.

Finally, the promotion of child welfare requires government, community, and workplace policies that support workers in their roles as parents and build on the strengths of families and kinship networks. Examples of such policies are paid family leave at childbirth, flexible working hours, resources for caregivers, and on-site daycare at the workplace. Although they are promoted as a strategy to prevent problems, "preventive" programs that improve outcomes for children, such as Head Start and home nursing visits for high-risk infants, actually provide needed resources that help families build on their strengths and, ultimately, flourish. Advocates have further recommended that when new children enter either the child welfare or the juvenile justice system, their cases should be reviewed in order to determine which preventive services failed to reach them (Briar Lawson & Drews, 2000). That information can then be used to develop new outreach approaches.

Juvenile Justice from the Strengths Perspective

Although studies of change in juvenile crime rates indicate otherwise, public perceptions of increasing juvenile crime have triggered a policy response in some states that emphasizes punishment rather than builds on the concept that young people are developmentally different from adults and therefore more amenable to treatment and rehabilitation (NASW, 2003g). Not surprisingly, then, programs aimed at prevention and early intervention receive insufficient funding and attention.

The social work profession has adopted a clear position in support of early intervention and prevention programs. The NASW "Policy Statement on

Juvenile Justice and Delinquency Prevention," issued in 2003, recommends policy changes that would establish a continuum of care for troubled youth, pre-delinquents, and delinquents. It also recommends oversight of the juvenile justice system in order to identify and correct the biases that result in the disproportionate incarceration of indigent and minority youth. Finally, NASW opposes the incarceration of youth under 18 in adult facilities (NASW, 2003g). Recall that the 2002 reauthorization of the federal Juvenile Justice and Delinquency Prevention Act requires states to decrease disproportionate minority contact with their juvenile justice systems and to separate children from adults.

Assessment and treatment tailored to the individual youth in the home community are much more likely to be effective than are generalized treatment programs in large facilities far from home. Effective post-release plans and after-care programs are also important. Policies and funding that make such treatment approaches viable are needed.

Social workers can advocate for establishing and fully funding juvenile delinquency prevention programs, diversion programs, and early intervention programs across the nation. Many examples of such programs that have been evaluated and shown to be effective are available in publications on juveniles in adult criminal courts.

Some of these programs could be implemented through policy changes at the agency level. Others would require state or federal legislative action to increase funding or establish new policy. However, the first step in establishing these programs is to make practitioners and policy makers aware of cost-effective approaches that have been successful in reducing juvenile crime. As a social worker, you can be part of that effort.

 Web Links

For more information on juvenile justice and on specific promising programs, visit the Web sites of the Office of Juvenile Justice and Delinquency Prevention and the Center for the Study and Prevention of Violence, Blueprints for Violence Prevention, both found at www.mhhe.com/chapin1.

The Role of Social Workers in the Child Welfare System

Although social work has traditionally been the lead profession in public child welfare, the recruitment and retention of professionally trained social workers in this area has been declining over the past decade (NASW, 2003h). High caseloads, low pay, and increasing interest on the part of social work students in more clinically oriented careers have contributed to decreased involvement of social workers in the public child welfare system. In addition, some states have attempted to save money by reclassifying public child welfare positions so that people without social work degrees may deliver these services. Other states have privatized their foster care and adoption systems. As we saw in Chapter 4, these kinds of funding decisions have a substantial impact on the services that clients receive and ultimately on the lives of our most vulnerable families and children.

The NASW has issued a policy statement asserting that (1) these families have a right to the same level and quality of services as people served by professional social workers in other fields of practice and (2) an undergraduate or graduate degree in social work should be required for the delivery and administration of public child welfare services (NASW, 2003h). Social workers need to help educate the public and policy makers about the importance of public child welfare services so that these services are adequately provided and supported.

CONCLUSION

Despite the high correlation of poverty with child abuse, neglect, and involvement with the juvenile justice system, symptom-focused problem remediation, rather than efforts to secure an adequate income base and increase access to jobs that pay a living wage, remains the major focus of work with the families of these children (Briar Lawson & Drews, 2000). Because families are the primary providers for children, policies that support and strengthen families in that role are basic to promoting child welfare. Social workers need to partner with families to advocate for policies that build on family strengths. Respect for diversity in families, including immigrant and gay and lesbian families, should be reinforced in policy. Policies that create or promote adequate families income supports, a living wage, educational and training opportunities for parents, affordable high-quality health care, day care, and housing also help protect our nation's children and enable families to care effectively for their children. Such policies enhance family functioning and lessen the need for intensive intervention to alleviate problems.

The media can help develop a public perception of the strengths and needs of the family that promotes support for such policies. Social workers can provide media representatives with ideas for stories that reinforce these views and urge media groups to present them. Topics include grassroots community development efforts to create jobs and initiatives to provide innovative programs for families through the schools. As always, social workers must be careful not to jeopardize their clients' confidentiality.

Many public and private organizations are working to improve outcomes for children. Several major foundations have supported innovation in child welfare services. This type of public-private partnership could help craft more-effective child welfare policies.

 Web Links

You can visit the Web sites of foundations promoting the welfare of children. Learn about the work of the Annie E. Casey Foundation, the Edna McConnell Clark Foundation, and the W. K. Kellogg Foundation at their Web sites, found at www.mhhe.com/chapin1.

MAIN POINTS

- Historically, child welfare policies emphasized child saving rather than family strengthening. Currently, there is ongoing tension between the family's right to preservation and the public's desire to protect children and keep them safe.

- The demographics of children in the United States has changed in the past 40 years. Children under age 18 represent a smaller proportion of the U.S. population, the racial composition is shifting with an increase in Hispanic children and a decrease in white non-Hispanic children, and more children are living in single-parent households. These trends will continue.

- The child welfare system promotes child well-being by focusing on safety, permanency, and family support when providing adoption services and services for families with reports of suspected abuse and neglect. Child maltreatment is considered to be harm caused by parents or primary care-givers and includes neglect, physical abuse, sexual abuse, and emotional abuse or neglect.

- The first major federal social policy specifically intended to prevent child maltreatment was the Child Abuse Prevention and Treatment Act of 1974. This act emphasized the need for increased state efforts in reporting and investigating child abuse and neglect.

- The juvenile justice system was established to promote rehabilitation of young offenders. The Juvenile Justice and Delinquency Prevention Act of 1974 was passed to prevent and control juvenile delinquency and improve the juvenile justice system.

- Legislative policies that have influenced the child welfare system include efforts to ensure that Native American children remain with their families, prohibition of race consideration in placement decisions of non–Native American children, and emphasis on family preservation and reunification, which was later tempered by emphasis on safety and permanency.

- Legislation for children with special needs emphasizes the importance of meeting education needs in the least restrictive environment and normalization.

- The social work profession has been the lead profession in child welfare, but professionals working in public child welfare are decreasing. The NASW asserts that families have the right to the delivery and administration of public child welfare services by trained social workers.

- Despite the high correlation of poverty with child abuse, neglect, and involvement with the juvenile justice system, symptom-focused problem remediation remains the major focus of work with the families of these children. The strengths perspective urges greater focus on wraparound services and family capacity building, including attention to increasing income and job opportunities.

EXERCISES: PRACTICING SOCIAL WORK

Working with the Sanchez Family

1. What child welfare policies and programs could influence the ability of the Sanchez grandparents to continue to provide kinship care for their grandchild?

2. What types of supports do you believe the Sanchez grandparents need in order to keep their grandson in kinship care? What polices and programs are needed to make that support possible?

3. Go the Child Welfare Home Page which can be accessed through the Resources Folder under Relevant Web sites, in the Sanchez Family case. Click on your state. Explore the many resources listed. Pick one program described on the site and explain how it might be of help to the Sanchez Family.

Working with the Black Feather Community

1. Familiarize yourself with the legislation reviewed in the Resources segment of the Black Feather case material. Both the Indian Child Welfare Act (ICWA) and the Multi-Ethnic Placement Act (MEPA) were passed to address civil rights issues that influence out-of-home placement of children. Yet they prescribe very different criteria to consider when deciding on appropriate out-of-home placements for children. How do you account for those differences?

2. Risk and protective factors for Black Feather youth are identified in the Resources segment of the case materials. Note that risk factors are clearly spelled out, but protective factors are not. What do you think might be some of the protective factors that could be enhanced to reduce substance abuse in the Black Feather community? What types of policies and programs might decrease risk factors? Increase protective factors?

3. When Melinda Sage, the social worker at the mental health center, has reason to suspect child abuse and/or neglect, she notifies the Department of Human Services. DHS workers proceed under the rules established by ASFA and ICWA. Discuss how social work practice operates differently when these two laws must be integrated. Is the work of the child welfare worker made more difficult? How?

EXERCISES: THE SOCIAL WORK LIBRARY

Juvenile Justice Policy

Read "Youth crime, public policy, and practice in the juvenile justice system: Recent trends and needed reforms" (Jenson & Howard, 1998), and respond to the following:

1. Explain the cycle of juvenile justice reform discussed in this article. Currently, where are juvenile justice policy and practice located along this cycle?

2. What connection can be made between juvenile crime rates and juvenile justice practice and policy?

3. What is the strength of the juvenile justice system according to the authors' claims? Based on the article and this chapter, what evidence is there to support this claim? Do you agree or disagree with their claim?

Transracial Adoption

Read "Adoption and race: Implementing the Multiethnic Placement Act and the Interethnic Adoption Provisions" (Brooks, Barth, Bussiere & Patterson, 1999), and respond to the following:

1. What were the primary factors that led to the passage of the Multiethnic Placement Act and the Interethnic Adoption Provisions legislation?

2. How do the practice principles for child welfare professionals proposed by the Work Group discussed in this article fit within the mandates of this legislation? Do any of the principles seem inconsistent with the legislation, the values of the social work profession, or your own personal values?

OTHER EXERCISES

Improving State Policies for Children and Families

Identify specific steps you and your classmates could take to improve child welfare policy in your state or community. What stops you from taking action? Brainstorm strategies for overcoming those barriers.

Health and Mental Health Policies and Programs

HEALTH AND MENTAL HEALTH POLICY AND PROGRAMS INFLUENCE social workers in all areas of practice. Because many of the factors that shape health care also shape mental health practice, this chapter begins with an overview and evaluation of health care policies and programs. We will also examine mental health policy in detail and discuss possible directions for improvement of health and mental health policies and programs.

HEALTH CARE IN THE UNITED STATES

In the United States, health care is rationed based on a person's ability to pay. In other words, it is treated as a commodity. Like other commodities in the marketplace such as cars and houses, health care has a price. Not surprisingly, then, people with more money get a better quality of goods or service (Blau, 2004).

We all need health care. Significantly, most other developed countries have chosen to treat health care, not as a commodity, but as a social utility. That is, basic health care is paid for publicly and is available to everyone as a right of citizenship. The recognition that people need to be healthy if they are to be productive citizens, and that untreated health problems can be dangerous to fellow citizens, underpins this approach to health care. Although these countries also ration care, this rationing is done by methods such as creating waiting lists for elective surgery and restricting referrals to specialists.

In contrast, in our country, publicly supported health care is guaranteed without regard to income only for people age 65 and over who are eligible for Medicare. This means that some people who are 65 and over and most people younger than 65 do not qualify for publicly supported health care. Although many citizens receive health insurance as a benefit through their places of employment, almost 16 percent of the population had no health insurance in 2003.

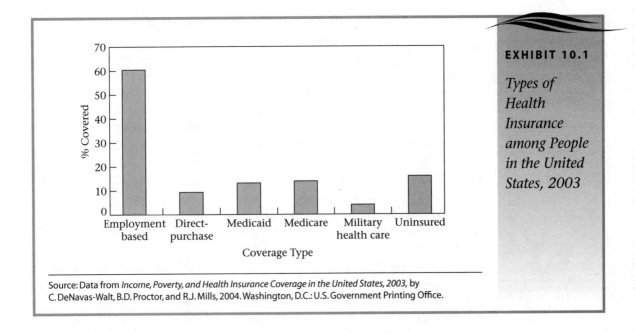

EXHIBIT 10.1

Types of Health Insurance among People in the United States, 2003

Source: Data from *Income, Poverty, and Health Insurance Coverage in the United States, 2003,* by C. DeNavas-Walt, B.D. Proctor, and R.J. Mills, 2004. Washington, D.C.: U.S. Government Printing Office.

People who are insured receive their health insurance through either the private or the public (government) sector. Private health insurance includes employment-based insurance and direct-purchase insurance. Government health insurance includes Medicaid, Medicare, the State Children's Health Insurance Program, and military health coverage. Some people have multiple forms of insurance. For instance, they receive Medicare in conjunction with employment-based insurance, or they receive Medicaid and Medicare benefits simultaneously. People who do not have either private or government health insurance fit into the category of uninsured.

Exhibit 10.1 identifies the percentage of people in the United States with health insurance by coverage type. In 2003, approximately 174 million people (60.4 percent of the population) had health insurance through their employment or a family member's employment. This number includes about 83 percent of working adults, age 18 to 64, and 61 percent of children. As these numbers indicate, many people in the United States do not have private health insurance. Some of these people either are not employed or hold jobs that don't provide insurance. Others cannot afford to pay high premiums on a limited income. Government health insurance accounted for approximately 26 percent of all health insurance coverage, providing insurance for almost 77 million people. Meanwhile, 45 million people (15.6 percent) had neither public nor private health insurance (U.S. Census Bureau, 2005).

Going further, in 2003, almost 31 percent of people in the United States with incomes below the poverty line had no health insurance at all (U.S. Census

Bureau, 2004). This rate is more than double that for people who were not poor. Health insurance coverage also varies substantially by race and ethnicity (Center on Budget and Policy Priorities, 2003). For example, approximately 11 percent of white, non-Hispanic Americans were uninsured in 2003, compared to 19 percent of African Americans, 33 percent of Hispanics or Latinos, and 19 percent of Asians. Of immigrants who are non-citizens, 45 percent were uninsured. The percentage of people without health insurance in all racial and ethnic groups reached a 10-year high in 1998, followed by 2 years of decline. Since 2000, the percentage has increased for all racial and ethnic groups (U.S. Census Bureau, 2005). Social risk factors such as low income, English as a second language, and minority group membership are associated with decreased access to adequate health care and ultimately with poorer health outcomes and early death for many of the people whom social workers serve.

For people who can afford health care, the advanced medical technology available in the United States is excellent. Many people in the United States receive adequate health care. However, even for those people who now have insurance, the rationing of services by health maintenance organizations (HMOs), decreasing benefits, and spiraling costs compromise the quality of health care they can afford.

The High Cost of Health Care

The United States spent approximately $5,670 per person on health care in 2003, up from $5,264 per person the previous year (Smith, Cowan, Sensenig, Catlin, & The Health Accounts Team, 2005). Per capita health care costs in the United States are much higher than those of all other industrialized countries, including Canada, Japan, and Switzerland. By way of contrast, in 2002, Canada spent $2,931 per person, Japan spent $2,077, and Switzerland spent $3,446 (Organisation for Economic Co-operation and Development, 2004). However, even though the United States spends the most money on health care, some of our basic health outcomes are not as favorable as those of countries that spend much less. For example, in 2001, life expectancy at birth in the United States was 79.8 years for females and 74.4 years for males. In comparison, Japan had one of the highest life expectancies in the world: 84.9 years for females and 78.1 years for males. For Canada, the numbers were 82.2 years for females and 77.1 years for males. As another example, the 2001 infant mortality rate in the United States, 6.8 deaths per 1,000 infants, is among the highest for the industrialized countries. Canada also has a relatively high rate of infant mortality, with 5.2 deaths per 1,000, whereas Japan has a relatively low rate of 3.0 deaths per 1,000 (Organisation for Economic Co-operation and Development, 2004).

The federal Centers for Medicare and Medicaid Services (CMS) reported that in 2003, people in the United States spent $1.7 trillion on health care (Smith et al., 2005). This total represented an increase of 7.7 percent over the previous year. The increase was fueled by rising hospital spending and prescription drug costs, and it outstripped growth in the economy for the fourth consecutive year.

Although spending on publicly funded health care in the United States accounts for only a portion of total health care spending, publicly funded health care costs are very hard to control. Unlike income-maintenance programs, for which the government can calculate the annual cost per person for Social Security retirement benefits or Supplemental Security Income benefits, federal and state policy makers do not know how much health care an individual eligible for Medicaid, Medicare, or SCHIP will actually need. They also cannot know what costly but effective new medical technologies or medications may be developed in the coming year. Thus, predicting and controlling the costs of health care is very difficult for public policy makers, particularly when there are multiple private as well as public insurers.

Health care constitutes approximately 14 percent of the U.S. economy (NASW, 2003n). About 10 percent of the workforce is employed in health care–related jobs. When we examine current public social policies and programs that support health care in the United States, the interaction of ideology and values, social movements, economics, and history becomes evident (Blau, 2004). We have discussed these factors in detail in earlier chapters. In this section, we will examine them briefly as they specifically pertain to health care.

History and Background of Health Care Programs

Prior to the 20th century, the involvement of the federal government in health care was limited to care for military personnel and veterans. At the state level, all states had established some type of department of public health by 1909. In 1943, the Internal Revenue Service ruled that employees did not have to pay taxes on their employers' contributions to group health benefits. This ruling made offering health benefits to recruit employees an attractive option. However, as discussed in Chapter 4, this tax break also represents a tax expenditure. The result is that the United States puts tax dollars that would have been collected by the government into employer-based health insurance. This approach reflects economic preference for private initiatives, the lack of a sufficiently strong social movement to bring about public health insurance, and the continued reliance on attachment to the workforce as the basis for provision of non-stigmatized benefits.

Federal Involvement in Health Care   In 1946, Congress passed the **Hill Burton Act,** which provides public funds for hospital construction. In return, hospitals are to provide some free or reduced-charge care for indigent citizens (Division of Facilities Compliance and Recovery, 2003). In fact, concerns about reimbursement for the care that some hospitals were providing for people who could not pay created an impetus for legislation to provide federal funds to help impoverished families pay for health care.

In addition, the need for a productive labor force and healthy recruits for the military, along with humanitarian concerns and fear of epidemics, contributed to growing support for limited public entitlement to health care. Moreover, as longevity increased in the 20th century, a respected political constituency developed that consisted of older adults with sufficient numbers to press successfully for policy change. This group helped get Social Security legislation passed in 1935. Older adults later helped press for the addition of Medicare (a categorical program primarily for older adults) and Medicaid (a categorical program for people with very low incomes) in 1965. Recall that we discussed the genesis of these programs in Chapter 2. Additionally, advocates pressing for the end to racial discrimination in health care gained ground when the Social Security Administration (SSA) required hospitals applying for Medicare certification to prove they were not engaging in discrimination. Some experts credit Medicare with integrating southern hospitals (Quadagno, 2000).

Retrospective versus Prospective Approaches   Both Medicaid and Medicare were structured to be retrospective **fee-for-service systems.** That is, the government acts as insurer and reimburses private health care providers for services rendered. This approach is termed a **retrospective payment system** because the private provider submits a bill after services have been rendered and the insurer then reimburses the provider. This approach creates incentives to provide additional services while offering no incentives to control costs. In fact, it may lead to overservice, that is, performing tests or procedures that might not be necessary. Consequently, health care costs accelerated, prompting the government as well as private insurers to experiment with a variety of cost-control strategies. Many of these strategies involved **prospective payment,** in which insurers determine ahead of time the average cost for a procedure, such as an appendectomy or uncomplicated childbirth, in a previous year and then prospectively (before treatment) set an amount they will reimburse the providers. Hospitals are reimbursed based on fixed rates for specific diagnosis or diagnosis-related groups (DRGs) regardless of the length of the hospital stay or the particular services provided.

This same prospective approach may be used to determine the average annual costs, or perhaps the amount that would cover the costs, for 75 percent of healthy people in a certain age range. Public and private insurers can use such an approach to decide how much to pay a **health maintenance organization (HMO)** to care for each such person enrolled in its system for the year. HMOs offer comprehensive health care to enrolled members. Members, their employers, or the government prepays a fixed amount to enroll for a specified time, typically one year. Health care services are offered through designated providers who contract with the HMO. HMOs provide managed care.

HMOs assume responsibility for the health care services and the costs of care for their members. Under such a **capitated approach,** the HMO or managed care provider is expected to provide all elements of health care covered in the enrollee's contract in return for a fixed monthly or annual payment per person enrolled. The same basic techniques can be used to determine prospective payment amounts and institute prospective payment systems for various high-risk groups served through Medicare and Medicaid, such as older adults with disabilities or people with mental retardation.

Managed Care: A Critique   In contrast to the incentive for overservice inherent in the fee-for-service retrospective approach, the incentive in prospective payment systems is for underservice. Under **managed care,** the insurer controls the person's health care. If services can be provided more cheaply than the prospective payment rate or avoided completely, then the provider makes a profit. The role of physicians in these systems is to act as gatekeepers, manage care more cost-effectively, and control access to costly specialists and services. Managed care also typically involves administrative oversight to determine whether treatments recommended by physicians are necessary and should be approved. Further, managed care generally does not cover services provided outside the network of doctors under contract to the HMO.

Problems in access to service and quality of service can be expected to increase given these new incentives. To address these problems, statements of patient rights need to be developed and enforced. Some progress has been made in this area. For example, some states have passed laws that prohibit gag clauses in HMO contracts with health care providers. Gag clauses prohibit physicians from telling patients about expensive or alternative options not covered by their HMOs.

Patients also need effective appeals processes. Additional public and private oversight and appeals procedures that are clear and easy to use can help protect patients. Further, the effectiveness of managed care approaches in holding down costs when examined in light of quality concerns and increased bureaucracy is certainly not clear-cut. Most important, none of the financial strategies discussed thus far addresses the basic problem in our health care system of millions of families who lack public or private insurance.

Additional Health Care Reform Initiatives   A major initiative by the Clinton administration to institute national health care insurance failed in 1994. Nevertheless, the government has enacted some limited health care reforms. For example, the **Health Insurance Portability and Accountability Act (HIPAA) of 1996** (P.L. 104-191) provides that workers must be able to continue purchasing their health insurance if they lose their jobs or change jobs (NASW, 2003n). It also prohibits insurance companies from denying coverage to people with preexisting conditions, and it introduces medical savings accounts.

Medical savings accounts allow people who are self-employed or working for small businesses to place their own pretax money in an account that can then be used to pay for routine or long-term care (NASW, 2003n).

Such an approach could lead to a privatized insurance model for healthy and/or wealthy citizens, leaving lower-income and less-healthy people in the traditional insurance pool to pay higher premiums (NASW, 2003n). Because insurance premiums are based on the expected cost of taking care of the people in the insured pool or group, when healthy people leave the pool, average costs per person, and thus premiums, inevitably rise.

In addition to this law, Congress passed the Mental Health Parity Act in 1996. One year later, the State Children's Health Insurance Program was created as part of the Balanced Budget Act of 1997. We discuss both of these acts in detail later in this chapter.

Web Link

For the latest information on federal drug abuse policy, go to the Office of National Drug Control Policy (ONDCP) Web site, found at www.mhhe.com/chapin1.

Substance Abuse, Pandemics, and the Health Care System U.S. health care policies are particularly deficient in two areas: treatment of substance abuse and response to pandemics. Regarding substance abuse, the federal government has not given sufficient support to policies to provide treatment through medical and mental health interventions. Instead, most federal legislation reflects the belief that use and abuse of drugs should be controlled primarily through law enforcement and punishment. For example, the Anti–Drug Abuse Act of 1988 focuses on control strategies rather than treatment. Policies dealing with substance abuse have created particular challenges for social workers who provide services to clients who abuse alcohol and drugs.

Pandemics are epidemics that occur across large geographic regions. Two well-known examples are acquired immune deficiency syndrome (AIDS) and human immunodeficiency virus (HIV). Since the 1980s, these pandemics have presented major challenges to our health care system, and the federal government often has been slow to respond. In fact, the Ryan White Comprehensive AIDS Resources Emergency (CARE) Act of 1990 is the only major federal policy implemented as a direct response to AIDS/HIV in our country (Segal & Brzuzy, 1998). Passed only after years of work by advocacy groups, this legislation authorized federal funds for health care services for people who have AIDS or are HIV-positive.

Web Link

More information on the Ryan White Comprehensive AIDS Resources Emergency (CARE) Act of 1990 can be found at the Health Resources and Services Administration (HRSA), Department of Health and Human Service HIV/AIDS Bureau (HAB), Web site, found at www.mhhe.com/chapin1.

Because AIDS/HIV patients were initially perceived to be members of marginalized groups, particularly gay men and intravenous drug users, social values that held these people responsible for their illness interfered with mounting a timely and effective public health response. The devastating effects of pandemics such as AIDS/HIV make it increasingly clear that U.S. health-policy makers must pay more attention to the influence of global health conditions.

Social Workers and Health Care Policy Social workers in hospitals, nursing homes, and other health care settings are directly involved in determining eligibility for public health insurance programs as well as in helping to sort out private insurance problems. Social workers in all settings need to know which public programs are available and how to help their clients determine if they are eligible for these programs. Social workers have been active in efforts to increase access to health care. They must continue to work for health care reform if a more equitable system is to develop.

MAJOR HEALTH CARE POLICIES AND PROGRAMS

Major public health insurance programs in the United States include Medicaid, Medicare, and the State Children's Health Insurance Program (SCHIP). In this section, we discuss these programs as well as the policies that govern them. Among the specific topics we examine are differences in eligibility rules, service delivery systems, and financing. Of particular significance are the effects of these policies on the people who receive the benefits. Although the Americans with Disabilities Act (ADA) of 1990 has increased access to both mental health and health care for people with disabilities, that legislation is fundamentally about increasing access in areas much broader than health and mental health. We examined the ADA in detail in Chapter 7, so we do not consider it here.

Medicaid

Title XIX of the Social Security Act established a program with the goal of providing health insurance and medical assistance to families with low incomes and few assets and to certain individuals with disabilities. The program, known as **Medicaid,** is jointly funded by the federal and state governments. Medicaid is the largest program that provides medical and health-related services to America's poorest families and children. It is also the largest single provider of direct medical care for people with AIDS. Finally, it is the largest single funding source in the United States for nursing homes and for facilities for people with developmental disabilities (Provost & Hughes, 2000). Millions of people in the United States need access to medical care and Medicaid provides health insurance for certain segments of this population.

Medicaid payments for nursing home care account for 49 percent of the total nursing home payments made nationwide, with overall governmental funding accounting for 64 percent of nursing home costs (Levit, Smith, Cowan, Sensenig, Catlin, & The Health Accounts Team, 2004). About 35 percent of all Medicaid spending nationwide is for nursing facility care (Blau, 2004). Many nursing home residents become "medically needy" because of the costs of nursing home care and thus become eligible for Medicaid in old age. Medicaid also helps shore up the gaps in Medicare for low-income older adults.

Many younger people with disabilities also qualify for Medicaid. Older adults as well as younger people who would be eligible for Medicaid if they were in institutions can be served in the community via a Medicaid waiver. Waivers allow states to disregard certain requirements—for example, service must be provided in a Medicaid-certified facility—for people with severe disabilities. Waivers have made home- and community-based services available for some older adults and younger people with severe disabilities. Nevertheless, unlike nursing home care, these services are not an entitlement, and a number of states have long waiting lists.

In 2003, approximately 35.6 million people, or 12.4 percent of the population, were receiving Medicaid (U.S. Census Bureau, 2005). Although Medicaid is supposed to make health care available to poor people, only about 42 percent of people in poverty actually receive Medicaid (U.S. Census Bureau, 2004). Not all people who fall below the poverty level are eligible for Medicaid. Rather, recipients must meet specific eligibility criteria. For example, childless, non-elderly adults who do not have permanent disabilities typically are not eligible. Moreover, many potentially eligible people either are unaware that they might be eligible or feel it would be too stigmatizing to admit they are impoverished in order to get help. Despite these limitations, however, were it not for Medicaid, the number of uninsured people could balloon to as many as 80 million (Mills & Bhandari, 2003).

Mandatory and Optional Coverage   States have some discretion in determining the groups that are eligible for Medicaid as well as the financial criteria for eligibility. To be eligible for federal funds, states are required to provide Medicaid coverage for most individuals who receive federally assisted income-maintenance payments and for related groups that are not receiving cash payments. The following are examples of such groups:

- Low-income families with children who meet eligibility criteria for State AFDC benefits that were in effect in 1996

- Supplemental Security Income (SSI) recipients

- Infants born to Medicaid-eligible pregnant women

- Recipients of adoption assistance and foster care under Title IV-E of the Social Security Act

- Children under age six and pregnant women with a family income below 133 percent of the federal poverty level

States also have the option to provide Medicaid coverage for other "categorically needy" groups such as:

- Infants up to age one and pregnant women not covered under the mandatory rules but whose family incomes are below 185 percent of the federal poverty level (actual percentage to be set by each state)

- Certain aged or blind adults or adults with disabilities who have incomes above those that require mandatory coverage but below the federal poverty level

- Children under age 21 who meet income and resources requirements for TANF but who otherwise are not eligible for TANF

- Institutionalized individuals whose income and resources fall below specified limits

- Persons receiving care under home- and community-based services waivers

- Recipients of state supplementary payments

In addition, states have the option to implement a "medically needy" program. This option empowers states to extend Medicaid eligibility to additional qualified persons whose incomes are too high for them to be included under the mandatory or categorically needy groups. It allows these people to "spend down" to Medicaid eligibility by incurring medical and/or remedial care expenses, thereby reducing their incomes to a level below the maximum allowed by their states' Medicaid plans. Older adults and people with disabilities who need long-term care benefit from this option in many states. In addition, approximately 30 states use this option to provide prescription drugs for people designated as medically needy.

 Web Link

You will find detailed information on eligibility, covered services, and how to help clients access benefits at the Medicaid site, found at www.mhhe.com/chapin1.

Variations among States   The standard Medicaid benefits are health insurance and medical assistance. Recipients thus achieve access to medical care, including long-term care in nursing facilities and institutions. Within broad federal guidelines, each of the states (1) establishes its own eligibility standards; (2) determines the type, amount, duration, and scope of services; (3) sets the rate of payment for services; and (4) administers its own program. Thus, the Medicaid program varies considerably from state to state as well as within each state over time (Health Care Financing Administration, 2000). Each state designates an agency to administer its Medicaid program. Local branches of that agency typically determine eligibility. Social workers in hospitals and nursing facilities often assist medically needy people in applying for Medicaid. Public and private providers are then paid for costs incurred for covered services.

BOX 10.1 *Medicaid, 1965*	**Policy Goals**	To provide health insurance to certain categories of low-income people (includes people who are aged, disabled, blind, or members of families with dependent children) to improve access to medical and health care.
	Benefits or Services Provided	Health insurance for medical and health-related services. Pays for nursing facility care for low-income residents.
	Eligibility Rules	Low-income people with minimal assets that fall within the state's "categorically needy" groups.
	Service Delivery System	State development and administration under federal regulations. Federal oversight by the Centers for Medicaid and Medicare Services. Applications typically are filled out at local welfare offices, and eligible recipients choose doctors or providers in the private or public sector who accept Medicaid to deliver the health services.
	Financing	Joint funding by the federal and state governments based on the state's average per capita income level.

Web Link

You can find out about how your state's health care spending for Medicaid and other public programs compares to that of other states by visiting www.mhhe.com/ chapin1 and browsing Kaiser Family Foundation State Facts Online.

The federal and state governments share the cost of Medicaid services via a matching formula that is adjusted annually. The federal matching rate, which is inversely related to a state's average per capita income level, can range from 50 percent to 83 percent. States are allowed to establish their own service reimbursement policies within federal guidelines. In 2002, the program cost $244 billion, with $139 billion coming from the federal government and $105 billion from the states (U.S. Department of Health and Human Services, 2003). See Box 10.1 for a summary of Medicaid based on the basic policy analysis framework outlined earlier in this text.

Medicaid and the PRWORA   In 1996, the Personal Responsibility and Work Opportunity Reconciliation Act (PRWORA) decoupled Medicaid from public assistance and allowed states more latitude to expand Medicaid assistance to people in poverty who were not formerly covered. A new Medicaid coverage category for low-income families with children was established under Section 1931, which maintained the AFDC eligibility criteria that were in place in 1996. However, with the passage of the PRWORA, eligibility for Medicaid was separated from eligibility for income-support programs. As a result, Medicaid eligibility and termination were no longer automatically determined based on eligibility for cash assistance. Nevertheless, many families who were still eligible for Medicaid lost their benefits because they were ruled ineligible for cash assistance (Provost & Hughes, 2000). Families who receive TANF benefits are not guaranteed Medicaid, and states have the option of using one application for the two programs or using separate applications (Peller & Shaner, 1998).

The PRWORA also changed Medicaid and SSI eligibility for legal immigrants. Immigrants who arrived after August 22, 1996, are ineligible for Medicaid and SSI benefits until they have resided in the country for five years, except in the case of emergency care (Centers for Medicare and Medicaid Services, 2003a). In addition, if legal immigrants lose SSI eligibility, they will also lose Medicaid benefits unless they are eligible for benefits under another category of need.

As a result of the PRWORA and a stronger economy, including lower rates of unemployment and fewer people living in poverty, Medicaid enrollment dropped from 31.5 million in 1996 to 27.9 million in 1999 (Provost & Hughes, 2000). Enrollment then increased drastically each year, reaching 35.6 million in 2003 (U.S. Census Bureau, 2005). It continued to increase in 2004 (U.S. Census Bureau, 2005). This increase was fueled by the weak economy and by increased efforts in some states to enroll eligible people in Medicaid programs (Levit et al., 2004).

Limitations   After Congress passed the 1997 Balanced Budget Act, states were no longer required to obtain waivers to enroll Medicaid recipients in managed care organizations. Consequently, by 2002, well over half (57.6 percent) of all Medicaid recipients were enrolled in managed care (Centers for Medicare and Medicaid Services, 2003c). Unfortunately, managed care plans often have not had much experience with high-risk clients. Also, clients may have difficulty accessing and using the information they need for choosing plans. Managed care plans may not be a good match for Medicaid recipients (Blau, 2004).

Medicaid provides health insurance for people who otherwise would likely have none. This policy is compatible with values such as social justice and adequacy to the extent that it provides some opportunity for oppressed groups to access health care. However, information about Medicaid eligibility needs to be made more accessible to a culturally diverse U.S. population. Values of adequacy and social justice would be much more effectively addressed via a universal health care policy that includes preventive care and access to home care.

Another problem associated with Medicaid is low reimbursement rates. Because of these low rates, many physicians are unwilling to serve Medicaid patients. A final limitation involves the eligibility requirements. Because people are required to "spend down" on health care until they are impoverished before they qualify for Medicaid, the eligibility requirements undermine people's strengths. If assets are accumulated, then benefits are lost. Thus, Medicaid clearly is ineffective in many ways, and it obviously does not provide health insurance to a large percentage of uninsured people. However, because certain categories of needy people are currently "entitled" to health insurance guaranteed by both the federal and state governments, it would be unwise to declare the Medicaid policy so flawed that it should be repealed unless it is replaced by a more universal health care plan.

Medicare

Medicare was created by Title XVIII of the Social Security Act. It is a national health insurance program designed primarily for people age 65 or older. To be eligible, an individual must be a citizen or a permanent resident of the United States. In addition, the person or his or her spouse must have worked for at least 10 years in Medicare-covered employment. Younger people with disabilities who receive cash benefits for 24 months under the Social Security program and persons with end-stage renal disease (permanent kidney failure requiring dialysis or a kidney transplant) are also eligible for Medicare benefits. About 40 million older adults and people with disabilities receive Medicare. People may sign up for Medicare through their local Social Security office. Box 10.2 summarizes the program's features.

Medicare focuses primarily on *acute* care, that is, short-term medical care, especially for serious disease or trauma. However, it also provides for rehabilitation of up to 100 days in a nursing facility. Contrary to what many older adults believe, Medicare does not pay for the long-term care needed for *chronic* conditions in a nursing facility, although it does pay for hospice benefits. These benefits have made end-of-life care more widely available for older adults who wish to forgo curative treatment and receive palliative care instead. The intent of hospice is to improve the quality of care for dying patients and to reduce health care costs by decreasing the use of high-cost treatment options.

Medicare Plans   **Medicare Part A** is paid for through payroll taxes. It helps cover the cost of inpatient hospital care, rehabilitation in skilled nursing facilities, some home health care, and hospice care. Each time patients are hospitalized during a new benefit period, they must pay a deductible equal to the cost of a single day in the hospital, which now exceeds $875. They also must pay additional charges if the hospitalization lasts beyond 60 days (U.S. Department of Health and Human Services, 2004).

Medicare Part B is an optional program that enables people age 65 and over to purchase medical care. Part B helps pay for outpatient hospital care, doctors' services, laboratory services, and certain other medical procedures not covered by Part A, such as occupational and physical therapy and some home health care. Beneficiaries pay a monthly premium, currently more than $50 per month. They also must pay substantial deductibles. Medicare then pays 80 percent of its established fee schedule for the service. If people do not sign up for Part B insurance when they become eligible upon turning 65, they will pay a substantial penalty if they decide to purchase it in later years.

Policy Goals	To improve access to medical care by providing health insurance for eligible older adults and people with disabilities.	**BOX 10.2** *Medicare, 1965*
Benefits or Services Provided	Health insurance. Part A covers hospital inpatient care. Part B covers doctor visits and outpatient hospital care. Limited prescription drug benefits.	
Eligibility Rules	People age 65, people with certain disabilities, or people with end-stage renal disease. Part A eligibility is linked to work history or additional payment of premiums.	
Service Delivery System	Federal administration by the Centers for Medicare and Medicaid Services. Recipients choose physicians or hospitals for care, and Medicare reimburses providers for the service.	
Financing	Part A is funded by payroll taxes. Part B is funded through premium payments from older adults and federal general revenue.	

Older adults with Medicare Parts A and B coverage still may have to pay for nearly half of their acute care costs. These adults may purchase Medigap policies, which are designed to provide more comprehensive coverage, from private insurers. However, Medigap policies could cost as much as $4,000 dollars a year (Moon, 2001).

Managed care options such as HMOs are increasingly being relied upon to stem spiraling health care costs. As we have seen, however, mixed outcomes in terms of enhanced care and cost have fueled debate about the efficacy of this approach. Indeed, some HMOs are canceling coverage for older adults when Medicare reimbursement rates do not provide the profit margin they had anticipated.

Because of the costs of Medicare Part B, gaps in Medicare coverage, and high deductibles, many elders cannot afford the health care they need. In fact, there are so many gaps that the typical beneficiary spends 22 percent of her or his income on health care (Blau, 2004). Nevertheless, Medicare has helped many older Americans access health care, and it has contributed to increasing longevity.

The Balanced Budget Act of 1997 created Medicare Part C, recently renamed *Medicare Advantage* to replace the name *Medicare + Choice*. Medicare Advantage allows private companies to contract with Medicare to provide health coverage through managed care plans or private fee-for-service plans. People who receive both Medicare Part A and Part B are eligible to enroll in Medicare Advantage if there is a plan in their area. The private companies reduce out-of-pocket

Web Link

You will find detailed information on eligibility, covered services, and how to help clients access benefits at the Medicare site, found at www.mhhe.com/chapin1.

expenses and coordinate care. In addition, some plans pay for prescription medications (U.S. Department of Health and Human Services, 2004).

The **Centers for Medicare and Medicaid Services (CMS)** is the federal agency that administers both Medicare and Medicaid. Medicare is federally funded, primarily through payroll taxes. Part A is financed through the Medicare payroll tax paid by both employers and employees. The premiums for Part B are supposed to cover 25 percent of its costs, with general tax revenues covering the rest (Blau, 2004). Significantly, Medicare is administered for a fraction of the cost of many private health insurance programs.

In 2002, Medicare cost approximately $265.7 billion. When we subtract the Part B premiums collected, the net federal outlay totaled $239 billion (Board of Trustees, 2003). The Medicare Trust Fund is projected to remain solvent until 2020 (Centers for Medicare and Medicaid Services, 2005).

The Medicare Prescription Drug, Improvement, and Modernization Act   In 2003, Congress passed the **Medicare Prescription Drug, Improvement, and Modernization Act,** which provides prescription drug coverage to more than 40 million Medicare beneficiaries. The Medicare prescription drug benefit is referred to as Part D. Previously, Medicare did not pay for prescription drugs administered outside the hospital, and due to ever-increasing costs, many older adults could not afford to buy the medications their doctors prescribed. The 2003 law provided that discount cards for prescription drugs would be made available for Medicare beneficiaries after June 1, 2004. Savings are estimated to be 10–25 percent off the retail price on many drugs. Medicare beneficiaries with low incomes may qualify for an additional $600 credit to help pay for prescription drugs.

In 2006, the prescription drug benefit will be fully added to Medicare. The features of the basic benefit are:

- Monthly premium of $35

- $250 annual deductible

- Medicare pays 75 percent of drug costs between the deductible and $2,250

- Beneficiaries pay 100 percent of costs between $2,250 and $5,100

- Catastrophic protection after $3,600 total out-of-pocket expenses

- Medicare pays 95 percent of costs above $5,100

This legislation also improves payments to Medicare providers to ensure continued access to basic health care services for older adults and individuals with disabilities, especially those living in rural communities. Further, Medicare rather than Medicaid will now be responsible for providing prescription drug coverage to dual-eligible beneficiaries, the term for people who are eligible for both programs.

These changes will have a major impact on state Medicaid programs, both fiscally and administratively. State Medicaid agencies and Social Security offices will now accept and evaluate applications from Medicare beneficiaries who want financial assistance through Medicare's Part D program. Financial assistance with the Part D premium, deductible, and cost-sharing obligations will be provided to Medicare beneficiaries with incomes below 150 percent of the poverty line who can also meet an asset test (Guyer, 2003).

The 2003 law is complex and has been widely debated. For example, Robert Greenstein (2003), the executive director for the Center on Budget and Policy Priorities, a nonpartisan research organization and policy institute, contends that the act has major flaws, including the following:

- It lacks any provisions to moderate spiraling increases in the cost of drugs.

- It provides subsidies to HMOs.

- It contains provisions that could cause low-income Medicaid recipients to actually pay more for their prescriptions.

- There are large gaps in coverage.

The cost of this coverage is projected to be $37.4 billion in 2006 and $724 billion for the period 2006–2015 (Kaiser Family Foundation, 2005).

The State Children's Health Insurance Program

Although Medicaid had made strides in enrolling low-income children, significant numbers of children remained uninsured. In fact, from 1988 to 1998, the percentage of the nation's children who had no health insurance grew from 13.1 percent to 15.4 percent. In order to help remedy this problem, the Balanced Budget Act of 1997 created a new children's health insurance program called the **State Children's Health Insurance Program (SCHIP).** The act established SCHIP under Title XXI of the Social Security Act and made health insurance for children more widely available.

This law authorized states to offer health insurance for children up to age 19 who are not already insured. SCHIP is state administered, and each state sets its own guidelines regarding eligibility and services. Eligibility rules for SCHIP are much more generous than are those for Medicaid, and working families without insurance may qualify. States have different eligibility rules, but in most states, uninsured children under the age of 19 whose families earn up to $36,200 a year (for a family of four) are eligible. SCHIP pays for doctor visits, hospitalization, emergency room visits, and immunizations (Centers for Medicare and Medicaid Services, 2003b). Services provided to children under SCHIP are the same as services received by Medicaid recipients in each state.

 Web Link

The full text of the Medicare Prescription Drug, Improvement, and Modernization Act of 2003 is available at the Centers for Medicare and Medicaid Services (CMS) Web site, found at www.mhhe.com/chapin1.

 Web Link

The Families USA Information on the Medicare Prescription Drug, Improvement, and Modernization Act of 2003 is easy to understand and may be accessed at www.mhhe.com/chapin1.

 **The Social Work Library**

Kaiser Family Foundation Medicare Information is also presented in an easy-to-understand format at www.mhhe.com/chapin1.

BOX 10.3 *State Children's Health Insurance Program, 1997*	**Policy Goals**	To increase the number of children with health insurance.
	Benefits or Services Provided	Doctor visits, hospitalizations, emergency room visits, and immunizations. Benefits mirror Medicaid benefits in each state.
	Eligibility Rules	Uninsured children under the age of 19 whose families earn up to $36,200 a year (for a family of four).
	Service Delivery System	State administration. Federal oversight by the Centers for Medicaid and Medicare Services. Applications filled out at local welfare offices. Recipients choose a doctor or provider for health services.
	Financing	Jointly funded by the federal and state governments. Federal funds are capped.

 Web Link

You can get information about SCHIP in your state at the Centers for Medicare and Medicaid Services Web site, found at www.mhhe.com/chapin1.

Both federal and state taxes are used to fund SCHIP. The federal-state matching formula varies from state to state. The states contribute 70 percent of the share of Medicaid they pay, and the federal government contributes the rest. Federal funds allocated for SCHIP are capped. SCHIP is not an entitlement. The federal allocation for SCHIP is $4 billion per year for FY 2005 through FY 2006 (Centers for Medicare and Medicaid Services, 2003b). Box 10.3 summarizes the features of SCHIP.

MENTAL HEALTH POLICIES AND PROGRAMS

Mental health has never received the same attention in public policy as health care. Many people in the United States have not understood that good mental health is essential to good physical health. Public funding is available primarily for people with severe psychiatric problems, and even then it is not adequate. For that reason, mental health advocates are divided about whether efforts to increase public support for mental health care should be pressed as part of the fight for adequate health insurance or whether they should be a separate initiative. Alternatively, they can be both. Holistic approaches to health care, which attempt to treat both the body and the mind, are receiving increased support. Improving both mental health and physical health is integral to improving health care in the United States.

By examining the barriers to adequate care for people with mental illness, reviewing the history of our current mental health system, and analyzing the major legislation that shapes the system, we will be able to identify the next steps that should be taken to improve mental health policy and programs. Major barriers to caring for people with mental health problems include the stigma that surrounds mental illness, unfair treatment limitations and financial requirements placed on mental health benefits in private insurance, and a fragmented mental health delivery system. Mental health experts contend that the current system is focused on managing the disabilities associated with mental illness rather than on promoting recovery (President's New Freedom Commission on Mental Health, 2003). As with other forms of health care, when public funding is available, it is only for people who are categorically eligible. That is, they are eligible based on age or disability and impoverishment. Both Medicaid and Medicare provide funding for treatment for people with mental disorders.

Major mental disorders such as schizophrenia, autism, depression and bipolar disorder, and panic disorder are found worldwide, across racial and ethnic groups (U.S. Public Health Service Office of the Surgeon General, 2001). Tragic and devastating disorders such as schizophrenia, depression and bipolar disorder, Alzheimer's disease, and the mental and behavioral disorders suffered by children affect nearly one in five Americans in any year. Adults over age 18 who have been diagnosed with a major mental illness that results in functional impairment and substantially limits their ability to perform activities of daily living are designated as having **serious and persistent mental illness (SPMI).** This designation is used to determine eligibility for certain public programs.

Although African Americans, Hispanics or Latinos, American Indians, and Asian Americans are no less likely than whites to suffer from mental illness, they often do not get the help they need. If they do get access to treatment, the treatment may be substandard or too late. Barriers to adequate care that create these disparities include the large percentage of families in these groups who lack health insurance, treatment that is not tailored to people from different cultures who speak different languages, lack of research specific to minorities, and lack of mental health services in isolated areas (U.S. Public Health Service Office of the Surgeon General, 2001). Additionally, concerns about stigma and lack of physicians, particularly specialists, from these ethnic groups negatively influence treatment. Disparities in access to mental health services need to be eliminated.

History and Background of Mental Health Programs

As discussed in Chapter 2, policies on mental health care have undergone major shifts. Prior to the 1800s, mentally ill people were cared for either at home or in almshouses. During the early 1800s, some small, privately funded hospitals were established that emphasized therapeutic rather than custodial care. However, they could serve only a tiny portion of the population with mental illness. During the mid-1800s, Dorothea Dix led a social movement to garner

The Social Work Library

If you would like to read the full text of the President's New Freedom Commission on Mental Health report, Achieving the promise: Transforming mental health care in America, go to the article at www.mhhe.com/chapin1.

Web Link

Learn about research currently being funded by linking to the National Institute of Mental Health Web site, found at www.mhhe.com/chapin1.

national attention for the plight of people with mental illness. She wanted the federal government to provide for institutions for these people. Although she was not successful in securing federal support, more than 30 state hospitals were established by the mid-1800s. The period witnessed a growing belief in the efficacy of treatment for people with mental illness. However, inadequate funding soon led to overcrowding and largely custodial care in some state institutions.

The mental hygiene movement, which emphasized community care, gained momentum after World War I, fueled by the recognition of the impact of mental health problems on soldiers. The federal government became involved in the delivery of mental health services to the general citizenry with the passage of the 1946 Mental Health Act, which established the National Institute of Mental Health. The **National Institute of Mental Health** (**NIMH**) is part of the National Institutes of Health in the Department of Health and Human Services (DHHS). NIMH is the federal agency that is primarily responsible for research on mental and behavioral disorders. Research conducted through this agency helps shape the nation's mental health policies and programs.

Community Mental Health and Deinstitutionalization   Although interest in community mental health care grew in the 1950s, much of the treatment for people with serious mental illness continued to be provided in state mental institutions. However, the development of medications that helped people with mental illness function outside of the institution, combined with growing awareness of deplorable conditions in some state institutions, led to the passage of the Mental Retardation and Community Mental Health Centers Construction Act of 1963. This landmark legislation, which we discuss in the following section on mental health policies and programs, provided communities with federal funds to construct community mental health centers, thereby providing outpatient services to people with serious mental illness. However, the community mental health movement continued to suffer from underfunding.

The deinstitutionalization movement swept through the states, propelled by hopes that community mental health treatment would be more cost-effective and humane. **Deinstitutionalization** refers to the policy of providing community-based services for people with disabilities who were formerly served in institutions. Thousands of people with mental illness left state institutions, new admissions to state institutions were strictly limited, and many state hospitals closed. Many of the people who were released were successfully reintegrated into communities. However, due to inadequate funding and services, large numbers of people received little or no mental health care. As a result, some people with mental illness have been reinstitutionalized in prisons or nursing homes, while others are living in homeless shelters or on the streets. Initiatives are under way to screen people in these settings for mental illness and, when necessary, refer them for treatment. However, detection and treatment of mental illness is certainly not a primary aim of these facilities.

Therefore, they are unlikely to meet the treatment needs of people with mental illness who are reinstitutionalized in these settings.

Although inadequate funding continues to plague the community mental health movement, the two major federal health insurance programs, Medicaid and Medicare, do provide funding for some mental health services for eligible citizens. Medicaid pays for mental health care for people with mental illness who meet income and disability criteria. Medicare pays for mental health care for people who are elderly, regardless of income, and for former workers who have been disabled for two years (NASW, 2003o). Additionally, the Social Security Disability Insurance (SSDI) program provides cash assistance for former workers who have developed mental illness. Finally, SSI provides cash assistance for people who have little or no income and meet stringent disability criteria.

In the late 1960s, many states revised their mental health codes to protect consumers' civil rights and to standardize criteria for involuntary hospitalization (NASW 2003o). In most cases, in order to be involuntarily hospitalized, a person must be found to be a current danger to self or others or gravely disabled and incapable of self-care by reason of mental illness. The Mental Health Systems Act of 1980 contained a model bill of rights that states were expected to enact and enforce so as to protect the civil rights of people with mental illness.

As part of the Reagan New Federalism initiative of the 1980s, several NIMH categorical programs for substance abuse and mental health were collapsed into a single Alcohol, Drug Abuse, and Mental Health block grant to states, and funding was cut by 20 percent (Monitz & Gorin, 2003). Although mental health care is still primarily the responsibility of the states, the State Comprehensive Mental Health Services Plan Act of 1986 encouraged a federal-state partnership in this area. This legislation allowed each state to use its block grant to expand community mental health services. We discuss this law in greater detail later in the chapter.

The Substance Abuse and Mental Health Services Administration An agency within DHHS, the Substance Abuse and Mental Health Services Administration (SAMHSA) was established in 1992. Its purpose is to improve the lives of people with or at risk for mental and substance abuse disorders. SAMHSA supports the development of policy, programs, and knowledge regarding mental health services and the prevention and treatment of substance abuse (Substance Abuse and Mental Health Services Administration, 2003). A priority area for SAMHSA is the estimated 10 million people in the United States who annually meet the criteria for both mental disorders and substance abuse, a condition known as co-occurring conditions (Center for Mental Health Services, 1997). Effective policies and programs that address the treatment, social service, and housing needs of people with these disorders are desperately needed.

BOX 10.4

Mental Retardation and Community Mental Health Centers Construction Act, 1963

Policy Goals	To reduce the number of patients in state mental hospitals. To develop a system of community mental health centers to provide services in the least restrictive environment.
Benefits or Services Provided	Community mental health services.
Eligibility Rules	Formerly institutionalized people living in the community and community-dwelling people with mental illness and developmental disabilities.
Service Delivery System	Community mental health centers provide local services.
Financing	Federal block grant to the state.

Major Mental Health Policies and Programs

Two major pieces of federal legislation have shaped mental health services. They are the Mental Retardation and Community Mental Health Centers Construction Act and the State Comprehensive Mental Health Services Plan Act.

The Mental Retardation and Community Mental Health Centers Construction Act
As previously discussed, development of medication to control symptoms of people with chronic mental illness, the exposure of inhumane treatment of patients in some state mental hospitals, and the high expense of custodial care in these facilities led to the passage of **The Mental Retardation and Community Mental Health Centers Construction Act of 1963 (P.L. 88-164).** The goals of this legislation were to reduce the number of patients in state mental hospitals and to develop a system of community mental health centers that would provide services to the deinstitutionalized people. Federal funds were provided to the states through block grants. Funding, although inadequate, was to provide for the construction of community mental health centers where mental health services could be delivered locally by center staff.

Although the intent was to provide care for formerly institutionalized people in the least restrictive environment, in the community and with family, inadequate funding and staffing of formal services often pressured families to provide care beyond their means. Many people with chronic and severe mental illness were not adequately monitored, resulting in increased homelessness among people with mental illness. On the positive side, however, local access to mental health services did increase as a result of this legislation. See Box 10.4 for a summary of the act's provisions.

The 1975 amendments to the Community Mental Health Act, in combination with the Medicare provisions of the Social Security Amendments of 1965,

Policy Goals	To provide support for community mental health services.	**BOX 10.5**
Benefits or Services Provided	Increased and expanded mental health services.	*State*
Eligibility Rules	People eligible for mental health services as defined by state.	*Comprehensive Mental Health*
Service Delivery System	State agency oversees network of mental health services.	*Services Plan*
Financing	Federal block grant to the state.	*Act, 1986*

also changed the availability of mental health services to older adults (Tice & Perkins, 1996). Medicare provided the financial vehicle for at least limited access to mental health services for older adults.

The State Comprehensive Mental Health Services Plan Act   Although the federal government has never taken a major role in providing mental health services, Congress encouraged the federal-state partnership approach when it passed the State Comprehensive Mental Health Services Plan Act of 1986 (P.L. 99-660). As discussed, this legislation authorized states to use federal block grants to expand community mental health services. At the federal level, the Substance Abuse and Mental Health Services Administration of DHHS administers the block grants. At the same time, each state designates an agency to operate or oversee the statewide network of mental health services. Box 10.5 summarizes the act's provisions.

Although the law permitted states greater flexibility in spending the federal block grants, the amount of money made available was not adequate to build an effective community mental health system. To compound this problem, states did not dedicate sufficient state funds to make comprehensive community-based mental health services a reality.

EVALUATING HEALTH AND MENTAL HEALTH POLICIES AND PROGRAMS

As we have seen throughout this chapter, U.S. health care policies have produced mixed results. One group that seems to have benefited from these policies is children. It is true that between 2000 and 2003, the percentage of children covered by private health insurance dropped from 69.8 percent to 65.9 percent (U.S. Census Bureau, 2005). However, this decline was offset by an increase in the percentage of children covered by public health insurance. The percentage of children in the United States covered by publicly funded health insurance rose from 24.4 percent in 2000 to 29.1 percent in 2003 (U.S. Census Bureau, 2005). Coverage was provided principally through Medicaid and SCHIP (Ku, 2003). In some states, improved enrollment procedures for Medicaid and SCHIP made it simpler for families of newly unemployed workers to receive coverage.

Expansion in public health insurance for children has lessened the health care access problem for children to some extent. However, many adults still have no health insurance. In fact, U.S. Census Bureau data indicate that more people in the United States lacked health insurance in 2004 than in 2000. This growing problem has serious implications for public health as well as for personal health. Despite this reality, however, we have yet to develop a consensus in this country about effective and acceptable solutions to this health care crisis. As a result, millions of Americans continue to go without basic health care. Given the current state of health care in the United States, it is crucial that Medicaid continue as an entitlement. We turn now to consider in more detail the reasons why Medicaid should not be capped.

Benefits of Maintaining Medicaid as an Entitlement

Although there have been concerted efforts to reduce services and benefits that are entitlements in general, Medicaid's entitlement status allows it to play a countercyclical role in times of economic downturn like that experienced in 2002. Medicaid expenditures rose to cover some of the adults and children who lost their insurance coverage during the economic slowdown. Because of Medicaid's entitlement funding structure, federal funding levels automatically increased in 2002 to match states' Medicaid expenditures and were not limited by predetermined federal funding caps or grant levels. If Medicaid funding were capped and provided to the states as block grants, as various individuals and groups have proposed, federal funding would not have been as responsive as needs increased with the economic downturn (Center on Budget and Policy Priorities, 2003).

During times of economic downturn, states often face budget deficits and cannot afford to pay for millions of new low-income enrollees entirely with state funds. Instead, states would have had to take harsh actions to cut Medicaid expenditures, such as (1) disqualifying whole categories of low-income elders, people with disabilities, parents, and children; (2) putting eligible Medicaid applicants on waiting lists and leaving them uninsured until "coverage slots" open; and (3) eliminating coverage for certain medical services. Although the number of people without health insurance is increasing, the problem could become much worse if Medicaid were capped. If states were forced to limit Medicaid enrollment in the face of rising unemployment, increasing poverty, and eroding private health care coverage, then the numbers of uninsured Americans would increase even more dramatically (Center on Budget and Policy Priorities, 2003).

When state revenues decrease, states often do cut back on discretionary Medicaid spending, particularly for people with disabilities who are served in the community instead of in nursing facilities under Medicaid waiver programs.

However, the entitlement status of core Medicaid programs helps lessen hardship during these times.

Challenges to the Medicare System

In this section, we address major challenges to the existing Medicare system. One pressing issue is the failure to control medical costs. Both the federal and state governments insure large numbers of people and therefore have leverage in negotiating with the health care industry for better prices. However, even this kind of government effort to control escalating health care costs has been limited. For example, the Medicare prescription drug legislation passed in 2003 prohibits Medicare from negotiating with drug companies for lower prices, even though the Veterans' Administration performs this service for veterans and private health insurance companies do so for employer-based health plans. Consequently, each of the 40 million Medicare beneficiaries is in an individual buying group, and individual seniors lack the leverage to negotiate for lower prescription drug prices. This situation could be rectified by authorizing DHHS to negotiate lower prices on behalf of Medicare beneficiaries.

As medical costs continue to increase, the expenses involved in maintaining the Medicare system will also rise substantially. Remember, the Medicare Trust Fund is projected to run out of money in 2020 (Centers for Medicare and Medicaid Services, 2005). Options for containing the costs of Medicare generally fall into one of three categories: limiting services, raising the age of eligibility, and shifting costs to older adults by increasing out-of-pocket costs (Quadagno, 1999). All of these options will disproportionately affect low-income older adults, particularly women age 75 and older, because of their relatively lower incomes in old age. Remember that, unlike Social Security, in which costs per beneficiary are determined by law and can be known, Medicare costs are determined in large part by the type and amount of health care received by beneficiaries and the costs of providing it (Binstock, 1999).

These issues will become more serious when costs increase as the baby boom generation retires. Between 2010, when the first of the baby boomers will turn 65, and 2030, when all baby boomers will be 65 or older, Medicare costs as a percentage of gross domestic product (GDP) are projected to rise by 73 percent (Binstock, 1999). Before that time, methods of controlling health care costs will need serious national debate. We discuss the future of Medicare in greater detail in the next chapter, which focuses on older adults.

Next Steps for Promoting More Effective Health and Mental Health Policies

Universal access to both health and mental health services is vital to well-being. The best way to achieve this outcome is hotly debated. Given the preference in the United States for public-private partnerships and the already established system of private health insurance provided through the workplace, an approach that incorporates both the public and private sectors may be most likely to succeed. For example, the United States could implement strategies that continue to rely on employment-based health insurance for most citizens but make insurance available and affordable for uninsured people through public financing. The SCHIP program contains elements of such a strategy.

However, because SCHIP is not an entitlement and varies from state to state, it falls far short of guaranteeing health insurance even for children. Further, because the costs of health care are rising so quickly, it is doubtful that we can continue to afford such piecemeal approaches to extending coverage to people without insurance. Because no single entity is acting as the universal insurer, it is difficult to control increases in health care costs by negotiating with health care providers and pharmaceutical companies based on buying power. Effective methods of limiting inflation in health care costs must be developed and implemented if health care, including mental health services, is to become more widely available.

NASW Recommendations for Health Care   The NASW has backed a universal approach to health insurance and health care under a **single payer system** (NASW 2003n). Under this system, the federal government would pay for basic health care for all citizens from public revenues. Contrary to popular beliefs, if the United States were to establish a single payer system, citizens would *not* be required to receive their health care at government-run facilities. Rather, as is now the case with Medicare, treatment could be provided privately but reimbursed publicly, with the federal government acting as insurer.

Of course, for such a system to be cost-effective, we would have to implement policies to contain rising costs, which means limiting profits in the powerful health care industry. It would be far too costly for the federal government to simply pay whatever providers decided to charge. As discussed earlier, possible strategies are to implement prospective setting of payment rates and to use the power of the huge buying group created by a single payer system to negotiate lower prices. Further, we could reduce the substantial costs associated with the multiple insurance companies that now oversee health care. Thus far, however, advocates of health care reform have yet to generate sufficient political momentum to make such changes in the U.S. health care system.

Until a universal payer system is implemented, the NASW supports policies that design payment systems so that service providers do not have large financial incentives to either provide or withhold treatment. Rather, providers should base all treatment decisions solely on the best interests of the patient (NASW, 2003n). The NASW also maintains that necessary health and mental health care, including social work services, should be available to all people, regardless of their employment status. Patients' needs should be primary, and legislation to guarantee patients' rights and protection should be passed and enforced. The NASW supports increased public funding for health care education for social workers. It also advocates for all health settings to employ master's-level and baccalaureate-level social workers from accredited schools of social work who are licensed or certified at the appropriate level (NASW, 2003n).

The NASW also supports maintaining Medicare as a defined benefit rather than shifting to a defined contribution approach. In the latter approach, Medicare would allocate a set amount for each older adult, to be used to purchase health care. Once the older adult spent that money, the federal government would have no further responsibility for her or his health care, regardless of the amount of care she or he needs. The NASW is opposed to adopting such an approach.

NASW Recommendations for Mental Health Care   In the area of mental health, the NASW supports full parity of mental health coverage with other health care coverage in public as well as private health insurance systems. Social workers have also voiced concerns about how these insurance systems define mental illness for reimbursement purposes. Mental health policies that provide funding for services specify the definition of mental illness and the basis upon which diagnoses should be made. *The Diagnostic and Statistical Manual of Mental Disorders, Fourth Edition* (DSM-IV-TR), is widely used to classify mental disorders in the United States (American Psychiatric Association, 2000). Social workers have participated in heated debates about the need to view mental illness and mental health in biopsychosocial terms rather than focus so heavily on neurobiological approaches (NASW, 2003o). Definitions and classifications contained in mental health policies would need to be revised if services based on broader definitions of mental health and illness were to be reimbursed through public programs.

Strategies to Promote Recovery, Diversity, and Health   Mental health experts working from the strengths perspective advocate for mental health policies that concentrate on promoting recovery and building resilience (Rapp, 1998). People with serious mental illness often need housing and employment support. Policies should promote full community participation instead of institutionalization, homelessness, and long-term disability. The efforts of people with mental illness to find work should be supported rather than discouraged by negative sanctions such as loss of public benefits. Policies that promote employment of people who have been mentally ill as providers of mental health services should be expanded. For people with mental illness who are in correctional facilities and homeless shelters, policies supporting detection and treatment are critical. The right to treatment as well as the right to refuse treatment should be protected. People with co-occurring conditions, such as mental illness and substance abuse, need integrated services that address both conditions.

In addition, we need to develop policies that support health and mental health training for people from a variety of racial and ethnic backgrounds in order to enhance the provision of culturally competent services. Additional ways of promoting more culturally competent health care include boosting research specific to minorities, tailoring treatment to those from different cultures who speak different languages, integrating mental health care with primary medical care, and increasing mental health services in isolated areas.

Essential social work services should be available in both mental health and health care settings. The expertise of social workers should be recognized. Social work services should be reimbursed at rates comparable to those of other professions.

Social workers must advocate for the financial reforms needed to provide greater access to health care. However, there are additional areas where social workers can play an important part in changing health care policies. For example, although the social work literature has critiqued the medical model, which focuses narrowly on the diagnosis and treatment of illness and pathology by medical experts, it is not enough simply to critique current policies and practice. Rather, promoting health and wellness instead of focusing narrowly on treating illness is central to the strengths perspective. Policies are needed to support new approaches that aren't based on pathology and deficits.

A Health Model   Using the strengths perspective, Weick (1986), a prominent social work scholar, has proposed a "health model" based on a biopsychosocial approach. In contrast to the medical model, Weick's health model urges us to focus on the multiple influences that affect health and health care. Living in unsafe neighborhoods with few health care facilities, dangerous working conditions, and inadequate nutrition are examples of such influences. Weick points out how the environment determines people's health.

The goal of Weick's model is to empower people. Work based on this model encourages holistic approaches that include prevention as well as strategies for maintaining or regaining good health. These strategies should emphasize the capacity of people to heal themselves. Weick's approach encourages practitioners to identify and challenge economic and cultural barriers to health care. It also urges them to advocate for policies that promote assertive outreach and for programs that provide clients with essential health-related information.

Such approaches also reduce the stigma attached to receiving mental health services because they present the act of seeking out services to maintain or regain mental health as a strength. Mental health initiatives based on the health model would be designed to reinforce the positive steps citizens can take to maintain their mental health as well as the benefits of doing so. For example, schools and the broader community could be encouraged to do more to promote strategies for preventing mental health problems and seeking formal treatment if necessary. The initiatives currently under way to encourage positive health habits during pregnancy and the immunization of children provide ideas for developing and implementing such strategies.

A health perspective guides us to consider how we can establish policies that create an environment in which people have the maximum chance for good health and can develop their strengths more fully. Efforts to enact policies that support recovery for people with serious and persistent mental illness illustrate how the strengths perspective can be used in crafting health policy. Employing a health perspective will help you see new possibilities for improving health care in the United States.

CONCLUSION

Health and mental health policies in our country have created a system in which some people who can afford health care get excellent care, but many other people do not have even basic health care. Economic, occupational, social, and environmental policies also influence the state of our health, and the health implications of these policies must be carefully considered if longevity and quality of life are to be maintained. Faced with an aging population and attendant increases in both acute and chronic health care needs, it is critical that we find ways to control health care costs, promote wellness, and ensure adequate health care for people across their life spans. In the final two chapters of this book, we first examine policies and programs for older adults and then turn our attention to strategies for dealing with future policy dilemmas. The health care policy basics covered in this chapter provide the foundation for thinking about how we may begin to address future challenges, including those posed by greater longevity and rapidly increasing health care costs.

MAIN POINTS

- In the United States, approximately 15 percent of the population is uninsured. Most people with insurance are insured through their employers. The United States has the highest per person expenditure for health care, but many health outcomes are not as positive as those in countries that spend far less.

- Cost containment efforts in U.S. health care have resulted in diagnosis-related groups (DRGs) and the introduction of managed care providers to both public and private insurance policies.

- Medicaid provides health insurance to low-income people who fall within the state guidelines for "categorically needy." Medicaid is jointly funded by federal and state governments.

- Medicare provides health insurance for eligible people over age 65, people with certain disabilities, or people with end-stage renal disease. Medicare is administered at the federal level, funded by payroll taxes (Part A) and premium payments and the federal general fund (Part B). The Medicare Prescription Drug Act was passed in 2003 and provides limited coverage for prescription drugs.

- The State Children's Health Insurance Program was established in 1997 to increase the number of children insured in the United States. Children under the age of 19 are eligible for this insurance program.

- Major mental disorders are experienced by one in five people in the United States. These disorders often go untreated owing to barriers such as a fragmented mental health delivery system, inadequate funding, stigma attached to service utilization, and lack of cultural competence.

- The most important next step for health care in the United States is achieving social justice through universal access to health and mental health services. The NASW has backed universal health care and supports full parity of mental health coverage in public and private insurance coverage.

- Promotion of health and wellness rather than a narrow focus on treatment of illness is central to the strengths perspective. The challenge is to develop policies that create an environment in which people have the maximum chance for good health and can develop their strengths more fully.

EXERCISES: PRACTICING SOCIAL WORK

Working with the Sanchez Family

Do you think Joey, the Sanchez family grandchild, would qualify for SCHIP?

1. How would you determine if he was eligible?

2. What other members of the family do you think might qualify for the major health care programs discussed in this chapter?

3. What strategies for overcoming problems in accessing health care for families such as the Sanchez family might prove effective?

Working with the Black Feather Community

1. Examine the information on assessment of elders and young people in the Assess segment of this case study. Pay particular attention to the data on

results of the focus groups. How would you use that information to identify potential areas for policy practice to ameliorate some of the public health risk factors identified in the assessments?

2. Health problems made worse by smoking, alcohol consumption, and poverty are evident in the Black Feather community. Of particular concern is adolescent substance abuse among 12–17 year olds. Based on your knowledge about this issue gained from reviewing the Black Feather case study, what conditions on the reservation contribute to growing health concerns related to adolescent alcohol consumption? What additional resources and strategies do you believe the community will need to develop in order to address this issue?

3. The Muscogee Creek operate three "smoke shops" in the region where relatively low cost tobacco products are sold. As explained in the Black Feather case, one of these shops was found to be selling tobacco products to underage persons in a SYNAR sting operation conducted by the Oklahoma Alcoholic Beverage Laws Enforcement (ABLE) commission. You can read about the regulations resulting from the Synar Amendment in the Tobacco Sales to Minors segment under Resources. This infraction has had a negative effect on the Oklahoma State Department of Mental Health and Substance Abuse Services (OSDMHSAS) whose federal funding is based, in part, on the SAPT Block Grant funds which have been put at risk by poor performance in controlling youth access to tobacco. How do you think the policy linking block grant funding for mental health to compliance with SYNAR will impact tobacco sales to underage youth on the reservation? Do you think this is an effective policy? Why or why not?

3. Indian Health Services has a very high rate of professional staff turnover in the Black Feather community and this contributes to poor health care outcomes. What policy changes can you suggest to increase the quality of health care staff and reduce the rate of health care staff turnover in this community?

EXERCISES: THE SOCIAL WORK LIBRARY

Uninsured Population

Read "The uninsured: A forgotten population" (Galambos, 2005), and do the following:

1. Participate in one of the health care promotion activities suggested by Galambos (2005). Write up a brief summary of what was done and what was learned from the experience.

Influence of Medicare on Discrimination in Health Care

Read "Promoting civil rights through the welfare state: How Medicare integrated southern hospitals" (Quadagno, 2000), and respond to the following questions:

1. Why did federal spending on health care prior to passage of Medicare in 1965 not result in integration of hospitals?

2. What was the role of the Social Security Administration in lessening racial discrimination in health care after Medicare was passed?

3. Why was the federal government able to promote integration in health care more quickly than in areas such as housing, education, and employment?

4. What lessons can we learn from the Medicare example about how future policies initiatives might more effectively be structured to help decrease discrimination?

OTHER EXERCISES

1. What publicly funded health care resources are available for low-income:
   - children
   - older adults
   - families

   How would they find out if they qualified for these resources?

2. Choose a social work agency where you think you might like to work. Find out if they provide health insurance to entry level workers. Is the cost affordable? Are dependents covered? If you have worked previously, how do these health care benefits compare to what you received with previous jobs? What factors do you think account for the differences?

CHAPTER 11

Policies and Programs
for Older Adults

Age is an opportunity, no less than youth itself.

— HENRY WADSWORTH LONGFELLOW

TTAINING THE AGE OF 65, 75, AND INCREASINGLY EVEN 100
is a testament to the strengths of older adults. However, the rewards of
survival should not be poverty and loneliness or premature institutionalization
in a nursing facility. Rather, we need to develop public social policies that support older adults in their quest to age well. To understand the issues associated
with aging from the strengths perspective, we need to broaden our focus from
the deficits and problems associated with aging and consider the resources
necessary to age well.

Kahana and Kahana, prominent scholars in the aging field, define **aging
well** as a "comprehensive and holistic process in which older adults adapt
self and the environment to respond actively to the challenges of aging" (1996).
Aging well becomes possible when we minimize the negative effects of losses
that are often associated with aging—such as those of some physical and mental
capacity, employment, and loved ones—and maximize the benefits that accompany a long life, such as a large network of family and friends, the wisdom
acquired through years of surmounting obstacles, and accumulated assets.

The emphasis on social networks and the social environment in defining
what it means to age well is also supported by the ecological perspective, which
recognizes the influence of relationships and transactions among the older
adult, other individuals, and the older adult's social and physical environments. Carefully crafted public social policies can help older adults overcome
barriers in the social environment that limit autonomy and pose risks to security. Further, by instituting programs that promote economic security, adequate
health care, and social interaction in old age, these policies can support aging

well. The focus on person in environment that is the hallmark of social work places social workers in a key position to press for such policies and programs.

This chapter provides an overview of key policy issues that currently influence older adults. We will examine and evaluate major policies and programs, and we will explore policy strategies that promote economic security, adequate health care, and social interaction.

HISTORY AND BACKGROUND

Prior to the 20th century, most people worked as long as they possibly could and then depended primarily on their families to support them. As we learned in Chapter 2, as far back as the Middle Ages, some guilds and other private organizations developed mutual aid and insurance programs to help their members when they could not work. However, such supports were not available to most people. Poorhouses were the last refuge for older adults who could not work, did not have assets, and had no families who were willing or able to care for them. Keep in mind, however, that in those days, life expectancy was shorter, families typically had more children, and children generally stayed in the same communities as their parents and grandparents. Consequently, there were proportionately fewer elders in need of financial support and health care in relation to the number of children and grandchildren in the community who were available to provide care. Further, most women did not work outside the home and therefore were available to care for elders.

Policy and Program Responses

Before 1870, a majority of U.S. workers were employed on farms. However, in the late 19th and early 20th centuries, industrialization spread rapidly, families became much more mobile, and life expectancy increased. Proportionately fewer people worked as independent farmers, tradesmen, and artisans engaged in family enterprises. Although the traditional supports for people in old age were disappearing at the same time that longevity was increasing, social programs to meet their needs were slow to develop. Private charities, community organizations, and local governments did provide some relief for destitute and disabled older adults. However, prior to the 1930s, there were few public social programs for older adults. In the following sections, we discuss the early public and private retirement programs that were available in the 1800s. We also examine a variety of federal social policies and programs for older adults that were developed beginning in the 1930s.

Private Retirement Programs In the United States, the American Express Company established the first private pension plan in 1875. Within a short time, some banking, utilities, railroads, and manufacturing companies also started offering pensions to their employees (Pension Benefit Guaranty Corporation, 2005). Most of the early pension plans provided defined benefit plans. **Defined benefit plans** pay a specific amount every month if the retired person has worked the required number of years. These early plans were funded entirely by employers (Pension Benefit Guaranty Corporation, 2005). However, only a fraction of U.S employees worked in jobs covered by such plans.

Public Retirement Programs   Recall from our discussion in Chapter 2 that large numbers of veterans, as well as widows and families of veterans, received military pensions after the Civil War. By the early 1900s, many states and municipalities had established retirement programs for their employees. In addition, by that time, many European nations had developed publicly supported retirement systems for the general citizenry. For example, in 1899, Chancellor Otto von Bismarck established a state retirement system in Germany that provided benefits for retired workers age 65 and older.

During the first half of the 20th century, the idea that people should leave the workforce at a certain age and then be subsidized in their retirement through public benefits gained wider support. Industrialization, advances in medicine, and the problem of surplus labor, particularly during economic downturns, contributed to an environment in which retirement policy could be enacted. In the United States, the Great Depression was a particularly hard time for older people. Many elders lost their homes, farms, and life savings. Often, children moved away to pursue opportunities in other parts of the country and therefore could not be counted on to support their parents. Further, jobs were in short supply, which increased public support for policies to get older adults out of the workforce.

Given these conditions, social movements such as the Townsend Movement and the Ham and Eggs Movement gained momentum and exerted strong political pressure on the federal government to enact old age insurance (Axinn & Stern, 2001). Like the Townsend Movement, which we discussed previously, the Ham and Eggs Movement endorsed pensions for unemployed older adults. Specifically, it pressed for weekly pensions for unemployed Californians age 50 and older. The movement's rallying cry was "$30 every Thursday" (Social Security Administration, 2003e). This was the first time in U.S. history that elders organized as a voting bloc to support legislation. It was this confluence of ideology, economics, history, and social movements that made possible the enactment of watershed legislation such as the Social Security Act of 1935, which established Old Age, Survivors, and Disability Insurance (OASDI).

Policies to Provide Health Care and Promote Social Interaction   The other major public programs that aid older adults were established 30 years later. With the passage of Medicare, Medicaid, and the Older Americans Act, 1965 was a

The Social Work Library

If you would like to learn more about the Townsend Movement, the Ham and Eggs Movement, and other social movements in support of public pensions, go to www.mhhe.com/chapin1.

banner year for legislation for older adults. As discussed in the previous chapter, Medicare is the health insurance program for older adults and people with disabilities, and Medicaid is the program for people who are impoverished. Medicare provides eligible older adults with coverage for inpatient hospital care. Optional Medicare coverage for outpatient hospital care and doctors' services may be purchased for an additional premium. Medicaid is the primary payment source for nursing facility care. Many older adults become eligible for Medicaid after they impoverish themselves by paying for long-term care because that care is so costly. Expenditures for OASDI, Medicare, and Medicaid make up the bulk of federal spending directed to older adults.

Congress also passed the **Older Americans Act (OAA)** in 1965. This law was designed to improve the coordination of planning and programs for older adults and to support their efforts to remain in the community even when they needed long-term care. However, it has never been adequately funded. We discuss the Older Americans Act and its subsequent amendments in the following section on major policies and programs. With the passage of OASDI, Medicare, Medicaid, and the Older Americans Act, the nation had established policies to address economic security, health care, and social interaction, three crucial arenas where public support for older adults is needed.

Changes to Job-Specific Pension Programs   Some employment positions in both the public and private sectors offer job-specific pensions. The number of people with job-specific pensions has increased markedly among private sector workers since 1950 (Hooyman & Kiyak, 2002). However, some companies are now eliminating or cutting back on their pension programs. Increasingly, employers are switching from defined benefit pension plans to **defined contribution plans,** whereby employers contribute a certain amount to a retirement account that the employee then invests in company-approved fund options. Unlike defined benefit plans, defined contribution plans don't guarantee a specific amount of retirement income. Further, only 50 percent of people who have job-specific pension programs have worked a sufficient number of years to be fully vested in their plans and hence entitled to their pensions (Hooyman & Kiyak, 2002). In addition, few private pensions provide a replacement rate of income that is adequate for retirement. Instead, the average annual pension income is approximately $5,000 a year, which represents only about 20 percent of the older adult's aggregate income (Hooyman & Kiyak, 2002). Finally, most job-specific pension plans do not provide cost-of-living increases.

The first comprehensive effort to regulate the private pension system is the **Employee Retirement Income Security Act (ERISA),** enacted in 1974. ERISA covers health as well as pension benefits in qualified plans. We examine ERISA in more detail in "Major Policies and Programs."

SSI for Older Adults   In 1974, the Social Security Act was again amended to create the Supplemental Security Income (SSI) program. As explained in Chapter 8, SSI provides income to older adults as well as to other people in poverty. Unlike OASDI, SSI benefits are not dependent on work history or marital status. In December 2002, more than 1.2 million older adults were receiving SSI benefits. Payments to older adults made up 13 percent of all SSI payments (Social Security Administration, 2003d). Women are the majority of beneficiaries for old age assistance under SSI. However, benefits are so low that many beneficiaries continue to live in poverty.

The National Institute on Aging   In 1974, the National Institute on Aging (NIA) was established at the federal level to conduct research and provide training related to the aging process and the problems and diseases associated with an aging population. The NIA's research initiatives focus on improving the health and well-being of older adults in the United States. Recently, the NIA was given primary responsibility for research involving Alzheimer's disease.

 Web Link

To learn more about the NIA's current and past research initiatives, browse the NIA Web site, found at www.mhhe.com/chapin1.

Mental Health Services   The 1975 amendments to the Community Mental Health Act, in combination with Medicare and Medicaid, made it possible for a greater number of older adults to receive mental health services (Tice & Perkins, 1996). In addition, funds provided by the OAA and services made available through some senior centers and some community mental health centers helped increase availability of mental health care. However, inadequate access to mental health services for older adults continues for several reasons, including: (1) reluctance on the part of many community mental health centers to perform outreach; (2) overriding needs of many elders for basic resources such as clothes, food, and shelter; (3) cultural barriers; and (4) elders' negative stereotypes about receiving mental health services.

Mandatory Retirement   In 1986, an amendment to the Age Discrimination in Employment Act of 1967 abolished mandatory retirement for most jobs. We discussed mandatory retirement and other forms of age discrimination in detail in Chapter 7. Ageism continues to create barriers to economic security and well-being for many older adults.

Long-Term Care   Perhaps the most pressing need of older adults is for long-term care (LTC). Long-term care includes many types of medical and social services for people with disabilities or chronic illness. Although a chronic physical or mental disability that necessitates LTC assistance may occur at any age, the older we become, the more likely it is that such a disability will develop or worsen. LTC assistance takes many forms and is provided in many settings, including nursing homes, assisted living facilities, and private homes. LTC also includes home care services and unpaid care from caregivers (Fox-Grage, Folkemer, Burwell, & Horahan, 2001). One component of LTC, **home- and community-based services,** typically is defined as services and supports that assist individuals to continue to live within their homes or a community setting. Personal care, assistance with chores, nutritional programs, night support, and transportation are examples of community-based services (Kane, Kane, & Ladd, 1998).

In the not-too-distant past, the primary option for LTC services was nursing facility care. However, in 1981, the Medicaid Home and Community-Based Services (HCBS) Waiver program was established as part of the Social Security Act. Before the passage of this legislation, Medicaid LTC benefits were limited to home health and personal care services and to institutional facilities such as hospitals, nursing facilities, and intermediate care facilities for persons with mental retardation (ICF/MR). However, the HCBS program now gives states the authority to waive certain Medicaid regulations—for example, living in a nursing facility—in order for Medicaid to cover LTC costs if the recipient requires nursing facility care and has a very low income.

The HCBS legislation made it possible for states to offer additional services not otherwise available through their Medicaid programs. This meant people who met very stringent rules regarding functional limitations and were impoverished could receive long-term care in their own homes and communities. If they received HCBS waivers, states could develop and implement creative alternatives to placing people who are Medicaid-eligible in hospitals, nursing facilities, or ICF/MRs.

 Web Link

If you would like to review a state-level initiative to improve home- and community-based services for older adults, go to the AARP Kansas Web site, found at www.mhhe.com/chapin1.

The HCBS waiver program recognizes that many people at risk of being institutionalized in these facilities can be served in their homes and communities at a cost that is no higher than that of institutional care. However, people who do not have low incomes have few sources to help them pay for home- and community-based services or nursing facility care. Older adults are without access to affordable LTC unless they are impoverished. If they are admitted to nursing facilities, the rates are so high that they often become impoverished. At that point, they become eligible for Medicaid at a cost much higher to the taxpayer than the cost of home- and community-based services.

Nursing facilities are a mainstay of the LTC system. In fact, the vast majority of public spending for LTC still goes to nursing homes. Although there is a constant push for more home- and community-based alternatives, nursing facilities will continue to provide both rehabilitative and long-term care to many older adults. Social workers who are employed in nursing facilities see firsthand the challenges these institutions face. The Nursing Home Reform Act, which was part of the Omnibus Budget Reconciliation Act of 1987, provided for reform in the areas of nurse's aide training, survey and certification procedures, pre-admission screening, and annual reviews for people with mental illness. It also mandated that nursing facility residents have access to ombudsmen when they require protection and advocacy services. Efforts to reform nursing-home care in both the legislative and the agency policy and program arenas continue.

Finally, any discussion of LTC policy would be incomplete without careful attention to the role of family caregivers. Most older adults in need of LTC depend completely on family members and friends to provide that care. Only a little more than 5 percent rely exclusively on paid services (Administration on Aging, 2004). We consider policy strategies to support caregivers later in the chapter.

Prescription Drug Policy   In 2003, Congress passed the Medicare Prescription Drug, Improvement, and Modernization Act. As discussed in Chapter 10, the provisions of the new Medicare prescription drug benefit are complicated, and older adults and their families often have difficulty understanding what is and is not covered. However, the State Health Insurance Assistance Programs (SHIP) can help older adults as well as social workers understand publicly funded health care policies and programs. SHIP is a national program created as part of the Omnibus Budget Reconciliation Act of 1990. The act authorized the Centers for Medicaid and Medicare to make grants to the states to provide Medicare recipients and their families with free counseling and assistance on a wide range of Medicare, Medicaid, and Medigap matters. This program relies heavily on trained volunteers.

 Web Link

Find information on SHIP in your state at the SHIP program locater Web site, found at www.mhhe.com/chapin1.

The Influence of Demographics

During the last 50 years, advances in medicine, technology, and public health policy have contributed to increased life expectancy. This development is changing the demographics of the older-adult population. In 1950, the life expectancy of Americans was 68.2 years at birth, compared to 77.2 years in 2001 (National Center for Health Statistics, 2003). Today, there are approximately 36.5 million adults age 65 or older in the United States. That number will more than double over the next two decades as the baby boomers achieve old age (Administration on Aging, 2003).

Among older adults, people 85 and older are the fastest growing age group. They are projected to increase from 4.9 million in 2004 to 9.6 million in 2030. In addition, elders who are gay, lesbian, transgender, or bisexual; people with developmental disabilities; adults living alone; immigrants and refugees; and older people in prisons will also constitute a larger part of the older-adult population (Council on Social Work Education/SAGE-SW, 2001). Although the number of children in our society will not decline, the ratio of children to older adults will decrease markedly.

Exhibit 11.1 shows how the demographics of our country have changed since 1960 and will continue to change. Note that the population chart for 1960 resembles a pyramid. The baby boom continued from 1946 to 1964, so

EXHIBIT 11.1

*U.S. Residents
Population
Trends by Age,
1960–2030*

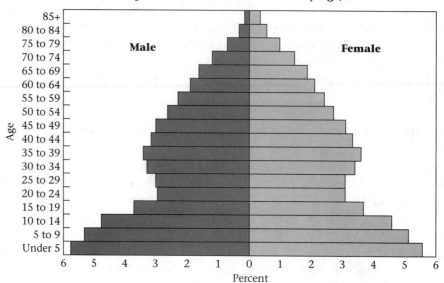

Resident Population of the United States by Age, 1960

Source: Data from Demographic Trends in the 20th Century: Census 2000 Special Reports, by F. Hobbs & N. Stoops, 2002. Washington, D.C.: U.S. Government Printing Office.

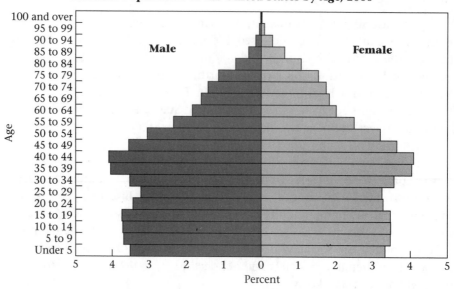

Resident Population of the United States by Age, 2000

Source: Data from Demographic Trends in the 20th Century: Census 2000 Special Reports, by F. Hobbs & N. Stoops, 2002. Washington, D.C.: U.S. Government Printing Office.

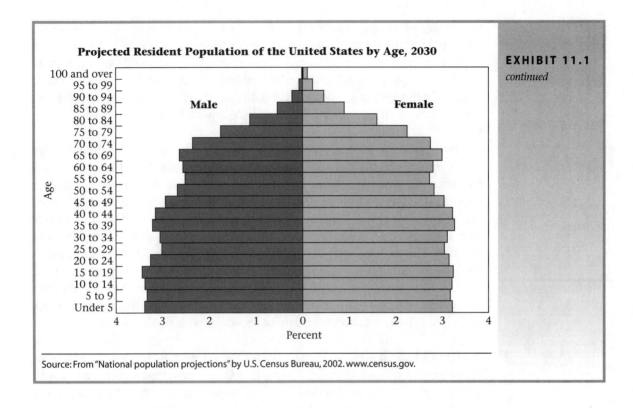

Projected Resident Population of the United States by Age, 2030

Source: From "National population projections" by U.S. Census Bureau, 2002. www.census.gov.

EXHIBIT 11.1
continued

there were many more children than older adults. By 2000, people born during the baby boom were in their middle years. The oldest were in their 50s, and the youngest were in their 30s. Rather than a pyramid, the 2000 population chart is sometimes described as resembling a python that has swallowed an elephant. The elephant is the baby boom generation, and the description is a metaphor for the challenges of digesting such a population swell. The population chart with projections for 2030 is described as a beanpole because the percentages of the older adult and child populations are much closer to that of the population between 18 and 65.

These charts also indicate that women outnumber men in the older-adult population. This disparity becomes even more pronounced after age 85. Furthermore, the percentage of older adults who are members of minority groups will increase from 17.2 percent in 2002 to 26.4 percent by 2030 (Administration on Aging, 2003). Specifically, African American and Hispanic older adults will each represent 11 percent of the elderly population, Asian Americans will represent almost 5 percent, and Native Americans will represent less than 1 percent (U.S. Census Bureau, 2002).

By way of comparison, the percentage of minority children under age 18 in the United States is expected to increase from 36 percent in 2000 to 47 percent in 2030 (U.S. Department of Health and Human Services, 2002). Thus, the percentage of young people from minority groups will continue to be much larger than the percentage of such groups in the elder population. As a result, a growing cohort of younger people from minority groups will be called on to care for an elder population that will be more predominantly white. Becoming familiar with the changes depicted and discussed here will help you understand and anticipate the trends and challenges our society will face in the coming years.

Demographics have a very powerful effect on our lives, including the size of the workforce, the need for health care, the demand for LTC, and societal attitudes. For example, although proportionately more families are caring for older adults than ever before and will undoubtedly continue to do so, in future generations, there will be proportionately fewer children to provide informal care and more adults needing care. Thus, we can expect that the need for formal care will increase. Proposed solutions to LTC problems based on the belief that today's families have somehow deserted their older members and must be pressed harder to care for them are flawed. Demographics are far different today, and relying still more heavily on their families to provide long-term care is not a workable solution for many older adults with disabilities.

Poverty and Aging in Place   Coupled with these trends is the growing emphasis on helping people age in place. **Aging in place** means that an older adult with disabilities is able to maintain residence in the community rather than enter a nursing facility. If older adults are to age in place, issues of poverty and inequities in service delivery, especially to rural communities, will need to be addressed. In 2003, the poverty rate for adults age 65 and older was 10.2 percent, which was lower than the overall poverty rate of 12.5 percent. However, as described in Chapter 8, older women of color are at much greater risk of poverty. In addition, all women age 85 and older are also at higher risk. About 3.7 million older people live below the poverty line. Additionally, 6.7 percent of older adults (2.3 million) were classified as "near poor," meaning that their incomes fell between the poverty level and 125 percent of this level. By way of comparison, 4.5 percent of the entire population fell into this category. Thus, about the same percentage of older adults—16.9 percent—are either poor or near poor as the percentage of poor or near poor in the overall population (U.S. Census Bureau, 2004).

Further, the federal poverty standard for older adults is lower than that for younger adults. In other words, people age 65 and older must have lower incomes than younger people to be considered impoverished. This disparity reflects the assumption that older people spend less money on food and other necessities. Remember, the poverty level is formulated by multiplying the monthly food expense by three. Therefore, when an age group is projected to consume a smaller amount of food, its poverty level is lowered. The major problem with this formula is that older people spend proportionately more money than younger people on housing, transportation, and health care (Hooyman & Kiyak, 2002). If the same standard were used for older adults as for the rest of the population, the poverty rate for older adults would be higher.

Voting Patterns of Older Adults   Although older adults are a minority of eligible voters, they have very high rates of voting and voter registration. For this reason, their political power influences some policy makers to consider their needs. However, the elder population is very heterogeneous and diverse. For example, the young-old, people age 65 to 74, may have very different needs from the old-old, people 85 and older. Currently, people may be lumped into the category of older adults for more that 40 years of their adult lives. The older adult population comprises a great variety of ethnic and cultural groups. It is naive to expect they will all vote as a bloc or support a specific piece of legislation.

MAJOR POLICIES AND PROGRAMS

OASDI, Supplemental Security Income, Medicare, and Medicaid have been examined in detail in other chapters. Later in this chapter, we will discuss these policies and programs in terms of the overall implications the aging of the baby boomers has for public policy. Here, we consider two other major policies that influence the lives of older adults, the Older Americans Act of 1965 and the Employee Retirement Income Security Act of 1974.

The Older Americans Act

Congress passed the Older Americans Act (OAA) (P.L. 89-73) in 1965 to reduce the fragmentation in public services for older adults and generate additional resources to assist them. The OAA created the Administration on Aging (AOA), a federal agency housed in the Department of Health and Human Services (DHSS, formerly Health, Education, and Welfare) that coordinates the implementation of the act and heightens awareness of aging concerns. The OAA also made grants available to states for community planning and services programs as well as for research, demonstration, and training initiatives in aging. In 1972, the OAA was expanded to include a national nutrition program for older adults. In 1973, the OAA Comprehensive Services Amendments established local Area Agencies on Aging. They also created an employment program for older adults with low incomes. In addition, the amendments provided grants to local community agencies for multipurpose senior centers as well as to Area Agencies on Aging, responsible for identifying local needs, planning, and funding services. These services help promote social interaction and enhance independent living.

The OAA provides monies for access services such as case management, in-home services such as limited personal care, nursing services, chore services, and legal assistance. The OAA also funds senior centers, meal programs, and supportive services such as transportation. In addition, it supports health promotion and disease prevention activities, services targeted to low-income minority elders, and advocacy initiatives such as the LTC ombudsman program. Finally, the Older Americans Act Amendments of 2000 created the National Family Caregiver Support Program, which helps sustain caregivers and guards against social isolation. These amendments also extended the programs established by the OAA through FY 2005. State agencies provide oversight for local Area Agencies on Aging. In turn, these agencies either deliver services themselves or contract with private agencies to do so.

The OAA is financed at the federal level by general tax revenues. Programs funded through the OAA are not entitlements. Consequently, money for these programs often runs out, leaving eligible applicants without needed services. The original intent was that OAA-funded services would be available to people 60 years of age and older, regardless of income. However, due to inadequate funding, services have to be directed to people who are most in need. State agencies as well as Area Agencies on Aging conduct outreach to attempt to serve more low-income minority elders and elders located in rural settings. Incremental cutbacks in federal and state funding have resulted in a struggle between a universal service approach and targeted services. Many older people who hover just above the poverty line and therefore are not in the target group still cannot afford the services they need. Area Agencies on Aging try to serve these people as well, when sufficient funds are available. However, because funding to fully implement the OAA is inadequate, many older people who need these services have not been able to obtain them. State and local monies are often used to provide additional funding for these services. As a result, the availability of services varies widely from state to state and community to community. See Box 11.1 for a summary of the OAA.

 Web Link

If you would like to learn more about the work of the Administration on Aging and the Older Americans Act, please visit the AOA Web site, found at www.mhhe.com/chapin1.

The Employee Retirement Income Security Act

The first comprehensive effort to regulate the private pension system is the Employee Retirement Income Security Act (ERISA) (P.L. 93-406), enacted in 1974. The ERISA defines how long a person can be required to work before becoming eligible to participate in a private pension plan, to accumulate benefits, and to be vested, that is, to have a nonforfeitable right to those benefits. It also requires plan sponsors to provide adequate funding for the plan. In addition, it guarantees payment of certain benefits if an insured plan is terminated. In such cases, benefits are paid through a federally chartered corporation, the Pension Benefit Guaranty Corporation (PBGC). The Labor Department's

Policy Goals	To create a comprehensive, coordinated service network for older adults.
Benefits or Services Provided	Planning and coordination as well as services. Access services including transportation, outreach, case management and in-home services, supportive services, legal assistance, and congregate and home delivered meals. National Family Caregiver Support Program.
Eligibility Rules	Age 60 and over. Priority is given to low-income minority elders and older adults living in rural areas.
Service Delivery System	The federal Administration on Aging coordinates overall implementation. State agencies oversee local Area Agencies on Aging, which deliver services directly or through contracts with private agencies.
Financing	Federally funded by general revenue taxes.

BOX 11.1

Older Americans Act, 1965

Source: Adapted from "A layman's guide to the Older Americans Act," by Administration on Aging, 2004. www.aoa.gov.

Employee Benefits Security Administration, together with the Internal Revenue Service (IRS), administer the ERISA.

The PBGC insures certain defined benefit pension plans by guaranteeing benefits up to specified legal limits. To accomplish this task, the PBGC collects insurance premiums from companies with defined benefit pension plans that are protected by the PBGC. The PBGC does not receive tax funds. Rather, income is generated through insurance premiums paid by employers, through investments, and through assets recovered from terminated plans. Weaknesses in some of the pension plans that the PBGC insures have fueled concerns about the corporation's capacity to fund promised benefits. See Box 11.2 for a summary of the act.

EVALUATING POLICIES AND PROGRAMS FOR OLDER ADULTS

The remaining sections of this chapter focus on evaluating current policies and identifying needed policy changes in the areas of economic security, health care, and social interaction. We will begin by examining the social context in which people in our society grow old. This process will help us identify the strengths, needs, and differences of older adults, which should be considered

BOX 11.2 *Employee Retirement Income Security Act, 1974*	Policy Goals	To regulate the private pension system by setting minimum standards and providing limited pension guarantees.
	Benefits or Services Provided	Established minimum standards for participation, vesting, benefit accrual, and funding in qualified programs. Ensures payments to employees who have met the time requirements for nonforfeiture.
	Eligibility Rules	Participants in employer-provided defined benefit pension plans covered by the act who meet time requirements for full participation in the plan.
	Service Delivery System	Benefits paid through the Pension Benefit Guaranty Corporation (PBGC). Federal oversight by the Labor Department's Employee Benefits Security Administration and the Internal Revenue Service.
	Financing	The PBGC is funded by insurance premiums paid by employers, investments, and recovered assets from terminated plans.

Source: Adapted from "Frequently asked questions about pension plans and ERISA," by U.S. Department of Labor, n.d. www.dol.gov.

when evaluating current policy and considering possible policy reforms. The resources of older adults and the supports they need are most clearly understood in the context of their life cycle. Older adults who were poor all of their lives, who were denied educational and employment opportunities, and who received inadequate health care bring that legacy of poverty and discrimination to their later years. Thus, older women and people of color are much more likely to be poor in old age just as they were more likely to be poor earlier in life. Similarly, strong ties to family, friends, church, and community, created and nurtured over a lifetime, may continue to provide them with needed support. Moreover, diversity in life experiences greatly influences the lives of older adults. People who have led very different lives and have had access to varying types and amounts of resources will bring these differences to old age. Age is not the great equalizer. Therefore, any agenda charted must take these individual differences into account.

When we consider needed policy reforms for older adults, we must be careful not to equate strengths with independence. Rather, we should focus more on interdependence among different generations. Indeed, the historic importance of older adults as grandparents providing help to both children and grandchildren creates a base for interdependence later on when grandparents are in need of help. One generation provides reciprocal care for another generation. These systems of interdependence can be a vital source of support when elders are in need of increased care due to chronic illnesses. Discussing this interdependence, particularly the contributions that older adults can and often do make, helps us reframe relationships by emphasizing their reciprocal nature. For example, older women are the repositories of rich historical memories of their families and communities. Local Area Agencies on Aging can help elders find intergenerational programs in which young and old people work together to build historical records of their communities. Our society needs to develop more programs and policies that build links and promote interdependence among generations while highlighting the competencies of both young and old people.

Focusing on reciprocity in relationships will become increasingly important during the next 20–30 years because of changes in family structures and the needs of older adults. Currently, informal sources of support are the backbone of the U.S. system of caring for older adults. This reality will not change in the foreseeable future. Therefore, we will need policies and programs such as elder care at work and training to improve caregivers' abilities.

Although informal caregivers will continue to be the major source of care for elders, owing to lower birth rates and increasing divorce rates, fewer family members are able to provide adequate support (Featherman, Smith, & Peterson, 1990). Additionally, many middle-aged people are caring for small children and aging parents at the same time. These adults are known as the *sandwich generation.* As informal support becomes less available, formal support will increasingly be needed to meet the needs of older adults. This trend will have the greatest impact on low-income older adults who do not have the resources to pay for caregiving, placing increased demands on publicly funded social services. Keeping in mind the insights concerning the social environment of older adults discussed in this section, we will now consider policy issues in the areas of economic security, health care, and social interaction.

Economic Security

The provisions of OASDI, the mainstay of economic security for older adults in this country, were discussed in detail in previous chapters. Popularly known as Social Security, this program is often described as one leg of the three-legged stool that supports retirement. The other two legs are private savings and job-specific pension programs. However, both private savings and job-specific pensions are in short supply among many of the older adults whom social workers serve. In addition, even when older adults have these additional sources of income, that income is often inadequate to sustain them if they don't also receive Social Security and Medicare benefits. Many adults who retire become "unretired" when they realize that the combined income from Social

Copyright © 2004 Jeff Parker. All rights reserved. Used with permission of Cagle Cartoons. www.caglecartoons.com.

Security, job-related pensions, and private savings is not sufficient to sustain them. Of course, returning to work is possible only when severe disabilities, which are more common in old age, have not taken their toll.

Our current focus on reducing the federal deficit has led policy makers to emphasize private sector initiatives such as Individual Retirement Accounts (IRAs) and has eroded some of the support for public sector support of older adults. However, the unexpected, dramatic reduction in the deficit under the Democratic administration of Bill Clinton, succeeded by the precipitous decline in the stock market and the ballooning deficit following the invasion of Iraq during the George W. Bush administration, may have caused many older adults to reconsider the wisdom of relying totally on the private sector to finance their retirement.

In addition, cutting back Social Security will not reduce the current federal deficit. Although this reality is seldom portrayed in the media, because Social Security is financed through a dedicated payroll tax, none of the federal deficit has ever been caused by Social Security. In fact, Social Security is a creditor, not a debtor, of the federal government.

Given the shakiness of the sources of support for older adults other than OASDI, policy makers will be under significant pressure to decide how to keep OASDI financially solvent beyond 2042. The aging of the baby boomers and longer life expectancy will add to these pressures. Policy alternatives include cutting benefits, raising taxes, limiting eligibility, or some combination of all three.

Each of these alternatives will increase the burden on some group of citizens. For example, cutting benefits will negatively impact low-income older adults, particularly very old women. Many people receive small benefits, and even the maximum monthly benefit is only $1,825 for those who retire at full retirement age, which in 2004 was 65 years and 4 months (Social Security Administration, 2004). However, raising taxes on retirement benefits for higher-income older adults could generate additional revenues without destroying the universal, insurance-based approach to public pensions. Of course, payroll taxes (FICA) could also be increased, and high-income taxpayers could be required to pay FICA on all earned income. Another option is to raise the age at which an individual becomes eligible for full benefits to 68, 69, or even 70. Such an approach, however, would further penalize people of color, who have shorter life expectancies.

As explained in Chapter 8, relatively minor adjustments can keep OASDI solvent well beyond the current 2042 projection if they are enacted soon (Social Security Administration, 2003f). However, the longer that reform is delayed, the greater the changes that will be necessary. The key to the future solvency of OASDI is continued economic growth averaging 3 percent or more in the coming years.

Some experts have proposed that the best strategy for improving the economic status of older adults with very low incomes is through changes in SSI (Browne, 1998). For example, raising SSI benefits to 110 percent of the official poverty line and lowering the age of eligibility from 65 to 62 would help a great many older adults escape poverty. However, many older adults who probably are eligible for SSI never apply for it. Therefore, social workers should make certain that older adults are informed about SSI and are aware that they can receive assistance in filling out the complicated application form. Along with the reforms discussed above, the barriers to accessing benefits under the current policy, such as complex forms and insufficient staffing, need to be addressed.

www.ssa.gov/notices/ supplemental-security- income

To learn more about eligibility for Supplemental Security Income, visit the Web site.

Finally, older adults who are able to work should be allowed to do so. To assist older workers, we can enact policies that support their access to employment. One such policy is **phased retirement,** in which an individual reduces the number of hours she or he works during the years leading up to retirement. Other initiatives include creating more part-time positions and strictly enforcing laws that prohibit age discrimination in hiring and layoffs.

The 21st century will be unique in that four or five generations of many families will be alive at the same time. Therefore, we need to evaluate all policies and proposals carefully for their intergenerational impact. Overemphasis on the negative economic impact of population aging threatens to create conflict between young and old. For example, increasing public expenditures on health care and income support for elders that outpace spending on programs for children could be used as evidence of inequitable treatment of young people. Critics may then propose cutbacks in spending on elders as a "remedy" to this alleged injustice. Clearly, the fundamental importance of intergenerational solidarity needs to be underscored in policy decisions.

Significantly, the moral obligation of one generation to another may be combined with enlightened self-interest in crafting policies that support the multigenerational families of the future. Policies to support grandparents as caregivers for grandchildren need to be improved. Intergenerational approaches, such as Foster Grandparents, in which the contributions of elders are clear, help build mutual respect and recognize the older adult's traditional role in fostering alliances among generations. Because the growth of the population age 65 and older has slowed owing to reduced birth rates during the Great Depression, we currently have a window of opportunity to do strategic planning. However, in 2011, the first of the baby boomers will turn 65; by 2031, they will begin turning 85. As this large cohort of older adults becomes more frail, we will need to have effective policies and programs in place to deal with these issues.

Health Care

Rising health care costs create a heavy burden for many older adults. In fact, as a result of copays and deductibles, even those older adults who are eligible for Medicare have very high expenses associated with acute health care. Although Medicare prescription drug legislation was enacted in 2003, it is unclear how much relief for older adults this legislation will actually provide. However, it is in the area of long-term care that older adults are most vulnerable. Although LTC insurance is touted as a private initiative that helps older adults meet these needs, only a small proportion of older adults will be able to afford to pay the premiums over the course of many years before they actually need the service. The average age of nursing facility residents is well over 80. As discussed in previous chapters, Medicaid is the public program that pays for the majority of LTC. However, Medicaid is available only to people who are impoverished. Therefore, we need to enact policies that provide LTC coverage for all older adults.

Long-Term Care Services   Funding LTC is a great challenge, especially given our huge budget deficits and national debt. Nevertheless, the LTC services that older adults receive both in nursing homes and in home and community settings require attention. Experts have asserted that higher minimum standards for nursing staff are needed in order to improve the quality of care provided in nursing facilities and that this increase will raise costs (Harrington et al., 2000).

Going further, the ways in which nursing homes are used is changing. Older adults are increasingly using nursing facilities for short-term rehabilitative care. They then return to their homes and communities if in-home services and alternative care settings are available. The increased availability of community-based services and housing-with-services alternatives such as assisted living has

 Web Links

If you would like to learn more about efforts to improve the quality of life in nursing homes, explore the promising initiatives at the American Society on Aging (Pioneer Network, Eden Alternative) and the Greenhouse Project Web sites, found at www.mhhe.com/chapin1.

expanded the number of older adults who are discharged and diverted from institutional care. However, the system is still not balanced because a disproportionate amount of public LTC expenditures go to nursing home care. Further, cutbacks to home- and community-based services resulting from current state budget shortfalls will increase state LTC costs overall as people no longer have any choice but to enter nursing facilities. There is no doubt that home- and community-based services can be more cost-effective than nursing facility care for some of the current residents of nursing facilities. Moreover, the majority of older adults prefer to remain in their communities even when they have disabilities requiring long-term care. We can develop strategies to provide home- and community-based LTC services more cost-effectively. In addition, we can implement policies to promote cost-effective alternatives so that older adults will be able to remain in their communities.

End-of-Life Planning   Finally, any evaluation of policies that will support adequate health care for older adults must address the end-of-life planning that is necessary if elders are to live out their lives free of unnecessary pain. Studies indicate that older adults often are not adequately treated for pain (Ahronheim, 1997). Policies are needed to ensure that older adults with the cognitive ability to do so retain power over life's end so that humane and compassionate end-of-life care is provided. Policies to help improve end-of-life care both in nursing facilities and in the community are needed. The majority of older people in the United States die outside their homes, in nursing homes or hospitals (Alliance for Aging Research, 1998). One option that has become available to Medicare beneficiaries is hospice care. **Hospice care** is an approach to end-of-life care that focuses on comfort and alleviation of pain rather than treatment of a terminal illness. Although hospice care is available to all Medicare beneficiaries and many adults who carry private insurance, hospice care is used in a small percentage of deaths in the United States.

The right to self-determination needs to be protected at the end of life. Although it is not always honored, all people in the United States have the right to make known their wishes for end-of-life care by signing two basic documents: (1) a living will that states the desired treatment, and (2) a durable power of attorney for health care decisions, which allows a person to designate an individual to make those decisions once she or he can no longer do so.

Web Link

To learn more about planning for end-of-life decisions, visit the Caring Conversations Web link, found at www.mhhe.com/chapin1.

Social Interaction

Positive social interaction is a key element of aging well. Social isolation is a risk factor for deteriorating health status, and it increases the chances of institutionalization for older adults. Social interaction—including opportunities to make choices, set individual goals, and work to attain them—is integral to aging well. We can gain insight into the kinds of policies that are needed to support aging well by examining research that can inform effective policy initiatives in this area. Research on aging well has helped refocus theories of aging so that the emphasis has moved from disengagement and decline to integrating the positive and negative aspects of biopsychosocial aging, thereby providing a more balanced view of aging (Baltes & Baltes, 1990; Chapin, 1995; Kahana & Kahana, 1996; Saleebey, 2002).

These developments call attention to the roles of older adults as key participants in their own processes of aging well based on their competencies, resilience, and life experiences. For example, many women in old age are confronted with the task of taking control of their lives for the first time. Historically, women's strengths and their capacity to control their own lives have not been valued. Nevertheless, due to economic or personal circumstances in later life, women may be abruptly faced with the need to assume control of their lives. Supporting older women in this transition affirms their capacity for self-determination. Women who are so supported may be less likely to allow family members or health care professionals to assume control for them in the future. Although more emphasis on interdependence might be necessary, only older adults can fully understand their interests, hopes, and desires for aging well. Clearly stated and well-publicized policies to protect the right of older adults to self-determination can help change their expectations as well as those of professionals and caregivers.

Clearly, preserving the capacity of elders for self-determination is critical to aging well. At the same time, however, their life conditions may necessitate more emphasis on interdependence. Significantly, self-determination and interdependence are not mutually exclusive. Rather, there is room for self-determination in all social interactions and relationships. For example, an elder could choose to turn to her or his family for advice and care. The family may recommend that the elder consider a nursing facility. However, the elder can still be given a choice to the extent that her or his cognitive abilities allow.

Social exchange theory also helps us understand the importance of social interaction in the lives of older adults (Dowd, 1980). This theory portrays aging as an exchange. In general, people maintain social interaction because they find it to be mutually rewarding. However, aging often involves decreasing social, political, and economic power due to changes in the person's economic, psychological, and employment status. Unfortunately, as social resources are lost, so is the capacity to engage in mutually rewarding social interactions. At the same time, however, a person who has engaged in lifelong caregiving may have additional resources to draw upon. In old age, then, former caregivers may receive care because those people they cared for feel the need to reciprocate.

Theoretical work on social exchange theory sheds light on the relationship between social resources and social interaction. Viewed from this perspective, the loneliness and social isolation of many older adults can not be adequately addressed unless we develop strategies for overcoming barriers to social resources such as economic security, adequate transportation, and meaningful roles that allow elders to continue contributing to the community.

In addition to the loss of social resources, social interaction can be restricted by the widespread cultural belief that women are less valuable than men and that older people are less valuable than younger people. To summarize, then, we know the senior citizen population of the future will be larger, older, and more diverse than it is today. If older adults are to have the opportunity to age well, then social policies will need to recognize and honor this diversity. Policies that address economic security, health care, and opportunities for social interaction will need to be continually evaluated for differences in effectiveness across these diverse groups.

NEXT STEPS

One social work scholar who has examined future trends in aging suggests that older adults are now entering a "third age," defined as a new societal structure, construct, or life stage that is an outgrowth of retirement policies made available through pensions and Social Security income (Fahey, 1996). This third age has both negative and positive aspects. Although there may be more time for leisure and involvement in activities, there is also increased chance of loss and disability. However, our culture has not yet adapted to the reality that many elders are now experiencing prolonged health and productive lives. Therefore, older adults must find meaning and validation without the reassurance of existing societal norms.

Social work has both the value base and the skill set necessary to assist older adults in celebrating the third age. Social work values commit us to working with vulnerable and underserved populations as well as to providing support for client self-determination. Because we experience a heightened possibility of loss and disability as we age, these values are important assets for social workers when working with older adults (Fahey, 1996; Rosen & Zlotnik, 2001). Given social work's holistic approach and its focus on the biopsychosocial and spiritual aspects of individuals in their environment, social workers are well positioned to support policies and programs that allow older adults to maintain positive social interactions as they undergo different biological, social, psychological, and spiritual changes.

Many theories of aging well are used to describe older adults' adaptation and coping based on stress models. For example, Baltes and Baltes (1990) describe aging well in terms of selective optimization with compensation. That is, older adults cope and adapt to changing physical and cognitive limitations by concentrating on high-priority areas. Older adults who are aging well can appraise their psychological well-being in positive terms even if they are experiencing a functional disability (Strawbridge, Wallhagen, & Cohen, 2002). As researchers and policy makers consider the concept of aging well, it is important for them to think in terms of the process of aging well instead of the physical and psychological outcomes of aging. Focusing on aging well will help them understand how older adults minimize losses through adaptation and will enable them to develop policies and programs that support this process (Chiriboga, 1996; Lazarus & Folkman, 1984).

Developing a Strengths-Based Agenda

Web Links

You can view proposals for policy reforms supported by older adults at the OWL and Generations United Web sites, found at www.mhhe.com/chapin1.

How, then, can we chart a policy agenda for the new millennium that helps build on the strengths and resources of older adults so that the years after 65, 85, or even 100 are good years to be alive? Social workers engaged in policy practice can help develop and implement a strengths-based agenda. Strengths perspective policy principles point to the importance of engaging the target group in developing and implementing new policies, determining how best to build on strengths and overcome barriers to implementation, garnering resources, and evaluating outcomes. In order to craft new policies that support aging well for the diverse population of older adults today and in the future, it is important to engage adults and their families across economic and racial groups in defining common interests. Efforts to find consensus must be initiated and supported. For example, information on options for Social Security reform that focuses on potential common interests needs to be widely disseminated and discussed. Strategies to mobilize older people from diverse backgrounds in support of needed policy change must be developed. Younger people also need to understand that public support for older adults enables them to use their resources for themselves and their children rather than taking their parents into their homes as many earlier generations did. If they get involved now, then supportive programs will be in place for them when they become older adults.

Web Link

You can find out about the work of the National Committee to Preserve Social Security and Medicare, a grassroots organization, by visiting its Web site, found at www.mhhe.com/chapin1.

Web Link

You can learn more about the work of the Medicare Rights Center at its Web site, found at www.mhhe.com/chapin1.

Heightening intergenerational conflict is the most destructive and incorrect strategy to use in preparing our future agenda. It is a false dichotomy. If we are lucky, all of us, including young people, will one day be old. Women and children are not impoverished because older adults receive Social Security. Children growing up in poverty disproportionately live in single-parent homes headed by women. These women often receive lower wages than men do. Lower wages provide inadequate support for these young families and will contribute to inadequate income in old age because they inhibit savings and contributions to pension funds. Low income throughout the life span is linked to early death and increased chronic and acute disease. Therefore, policies that diminish the rates of poverty among young people will reduce their health problems in old age. Groups such as the Older Women's League (OWL), as well as groups formed specifically to advocate for Social Security and Medicare Rights, are working to forge coalitions among generations. Generations United is a politically active group that is also working to promote intergenerational policies. Many programs have been established to promote intergenerational connections that are beneficial to all participants. Two examples are the Experience Corps and Connecting Generations.

In Chapter 10, we considered the importance of policies and programs in promoting good health. Policies and programs that address smoking cessation, weight loss, and exercise can help younger adults prepare for a healthier old age and can help older adults prevent the onset of disabilities. Senior centers as well as other community agencies could be much more proactive in getting older adults involved in health and wellness programs.

Creating Needed Infrastructure

In the area of social interaction, efforts are under way at the local, state, and federal levels to create the infrastructure necessary for continued social interaction for older adults with disabilities. For example, communities are now beginning to design age-sensitive community infrastructure so that older adults with impaired mobility can have easy access to places such as churches, restaurants, and public buildings where they have traditionally engaged in social interaction. In some communities, universal housing codes that enhance accessibility in residential construction are receiving greater support. In addition, policies are being passed that require all new construction to conform to these codes.

Area Agencies on Aging and state aging agencies continue to implement promising initiatives such as the National Family Caregiver Support Program, which trains and supports caregivers at all stages of the caregiving experience and also seeks to lessen their social isolation. As the baby boom becomes the elder boom, policies to help caregivers will become even more important. Because men are now living longer, they will increasingly be available to care for their spouses. However, they will need support in assuming a role with which they may be very unfamiliar. In addition, support for caregivers must be increased. As one example, we must develop strategies to more equitably recognize the contributions of younger unpaid caregivers in public pension systems.

Other state agencies are also beginning to realize that preparing for the elder boom is not the job of only the aging agencies. For example, state transportation departments are beginning to test the visibility of road sign paint with 65-year-old drivers rather than 25-year-old men so that older adults may continue driving safely and thus enhance social interaction. Overall, state transportation agencies have long been involved in providing services to older adults, and they are now giving increased attention to policies in that arena. At the federal level, promoting social interaction for older adults is an important goal of programs funded under the Older Americans Act. This essential legislation for older adults needs to be supported and expanded.

 Web Link

You can get more information about the Experience Corps and Connecting Generations at www.mhhe.com/chapin1.

 Web Link

To find out more about caregiver support programs, visit the National Family Caregiver Support Program Resource Room Web site, found at www.mhhe.com/chapin1.

Finally, it is essential that we challenge cultural biases that devalue older adults. For example, we need to focus greater attention on the capacities rather than the deficits of older adults. This new century will provide ample opportunities for social workers who have been educated to be policy practitioners to join with older adults from a variety of backgrounds to help create effective policy. It is clear that supporting older people's strengths, so that they can remain an active and contributing part of the community, rather than narrowly focusing on traditional services will be an important component of planning for the elder boom. Flexibility in policies to accommodate the diversity among older adults, and caution in creating entitlements so expensive that resentment mounts among younger citizens, will be integral to effective planning.

CONCLUSION

Reciprocity between young and old people provides the mutual support on which both groups rely. Policies need to ensure that the generations continue to live in harmony. Exaggerating the economic impact of population aging risks threatening the intergenerational social contract. Positive social interaction among older adults and between young and old people is vital to a continued sense of responsibility and reciprocity. Framing the needs of older adults as competing with the needs of younger people fosters conflict. Alternatively, policies may be crafted to invest in intergenerational approaches that more effectively meet need across the life span.

In the areas of economic security and health care, children are primarily served through means-tested public assistance programs while older adults are primarily served through social insurance programs. Investing in universal income support and health care systems for our children as well as for older adults will help ensure the future for all citizens. A thriving economy is vital to adequately support young as well as older citizens, and healthy children who are well cared for are crucial to economic growth and to securing our future. With the growth in the older population in the United States, more older adults than ever before have the possibility of aging well. The challenge is to craft policies that are equitable and acceptable to young and old alike.

MAIN POINTS

- Policies and programs for older adults should not focus primarily on disability and deficits but rather promote aging well. Aging well is the process of minimizing the negative effects of losses associated with aging by adapting to the challenges and maximizing the benefits of long life.

- Economic security, health care, and social interaction are three critical areas addressed in the passage of key legislation for older adults. The primary legislation affecting older adults are Old Age, Survivors, and Disability Insurance (OASDI), Medicare, Medicaid, and the Older Americans Act.

- Long-term care (LTC) refers to medical and social services provided to people with disabilities or chronic illnesses. LTC occurs in many settings and includes nursing homes, assisted living, unpaid care by informal caregivers, and home- and community-based services.

- The Older Americans Act (OAA) was enacted to support planning and coordinate services for older adults through the provision of access services, in-home services, legal assistance, senior centers, meal programs, and supportive services.

- Older adults are living longer today and compose a larger percentage of the entire population than previous cohorts of older adults. The first cohort of baby boomers will reach the age of 65 in 2011, which will greatly impact the policy arena as the United States decides how to meet the needs of a larger and more diverse aging population.

- The Employee Retirement Income Security Act (ERISA), passed in 1974, was the first federal legislation to regulate the private pension system. The act set minimum standards for participation, vesting, funding, and benefit accrual in qualified job-specific pensions. ERISA established the Pension Benefit Guaranty Corporation to insure certain defined benefit pension plans.

- Economic security of older adults is generally augmented by public support such as Social Security pensions, SSI benefits, or private sources such as job-specific pensions and private savings. Long-term financial solvency of the OASDI needs to be the focus of present political decisions. Making changes now, such as increasing payroll taxes and the taxable income limit, decreasing benefits, or increasing the age of eligibility for retirement benefits, will enable the program to provide benefits beyond 2042.

- Increasing SSI benefits for older adults in poverty is a promising option for addressing the needs of low-income seniors.

- The current push in long-term care is for community tenure with the establishment of home- and community-based services, use of nursing homes for short-term rehabilitation stays, and hospice services that assist people in dying at home.

- Future policy initiatives should take into account outcomes across the life span. Promoting intergenerational programs and policies is preferable to fostering conflict between older adults and younger adults and children.

- Strengths perspective policy principles can be used in charting a policy agenda informed by the needs and goals of an increasingly diverse older-adult population as well as those of younger generations.

EXERCISES: PRACTICING SOCIAL WORK

Working with the Black Feather Community

Explore the Assess portion of the case study and answer these questions.

1. How do you think using information from the Use of Culture and the Medicine Wheel segments (Tools section) to structure the researcher's data gathering with the elders might uniquely influence results of the focus groups for elders?

2. Based on the results of your examination of the data from the elder focus groups that identified perceived needs and issues facing the elder community, what are some potential strategies and resources that can help to address these concerns?

3. What strengths identified in the elder community might potentially be built on when attempting to ameliorate some of the needs of elders as well as those of the rest of the Black Feather community?

4. Read about the Elder Focus Group & Visioning Process described in the Assess segment of the interactive case study. What was learned from this activity that could help guide policy practice initiatives in this community? What are some ways to get elders more involved in helping to change policies and programs? Do you think a similar approach might work with the elders in the communities where you do social work?

EXERCISES: THE SOCIAL WORK LIBRARY

Read "The strengths model with older adults: Critical practice components" (Nelson-Becker, Chapin & Fast, 2006), and respond to the following:

1. How can the stories that social workers hear from older adults in direct practice settings be used to advocate for more effective policies for our clients? Identify three specific steps social workers could take to make this link. What are some cautions to consider when using clients' stories to inform policy?

2. How can social workers use strengths perspective principles to engage older adults in efforts to bring about most just policies?

3. Visit the Administration on Aging's Web site found at www.mhhe.com/chapin1 and read more about the Older Americans Act. Do the programs

and policies outlined by the Older Americans Act support a strengths-based approach to programs for older adults?

OTHER EXERCISES

1. In small groups, discuss the policy implications of the demographic changes this country will undergo between now and 2030. List three positive aspects of these demographic changes and explore how policies could be enacted to build on these positive aspects. List three negative aspects of these changes and explore what policies may be needed to lessen negative outcomes.

2. Visit your local senior center. Find out how the center is funded. Who is eligible for services and what services are provided? How old is the average participant? Do you think the senior center will need to change if it is to attract the baby boomers as they age? What policy and program changes would you suggest?

3. Read the case history of Mrs. M, an 82 year old widow, available at www.mhhe.com/chapin1. After reviewing the case, discuss these questions in small groups. From a policy point of view:

   • What strengths can you identify for Mrs. M?

   • What programs could be available to Mrs. M through her local AAA? Through other agencies?

   • What gaps are there in services for her?

   • What new or expanded policies or programs are needed?

4. In implementing the strengths perspective in social policy analysis, the focus is on giving voice to clients. Although you can not talk to Mrs. M., imagine yourself in her situation and try to answer these questions from her perspective.

   • What would Mrs. M. voice as her needs and concerns?

   • What would Mrs. M say are goals for "aging well?"

   • What would Mrs. M, as a stakeholder, like to see implemented as additional social policies?

5. Given the way our system of social insurance currently is set up, what are the repercussions of the death of the bread-winning spouse (i.e., loss of income)? What alternative policies might help lessen these repercussions?

CHAPTER 12

The Future

An image of the future is at the base of all choice oriented behavior.

We need a vision of the future that energizes our journey.

THIS CHAPTER FOCUSES ON THE FUTURE. BECAUSE NO ONE HAS an accurate crystal ball, it may seem unwise to try to foretell the future, especially in these uncertain times. However, beliefs about the future are central to all the actions we take. For example, when rainy weather is forecast, we grab an umbrella. Similarly, when we hear a friend is having a party on Saturday, we get ready for fun. An interest in prediction and control fuels our attention to the future. People who choose social work as a career generally do so because they want their life's work to be meaningful and rewarding, and they believe that social work will provide those benefits. Because policy and programs are enacted to affect the future and in turn influence the future, you will need to be attuned to what people are predicting about future conditions in order to engage in effective policy practice. As Macarov (1991) has pointed out, without forecasting, there is no freedom of decision.

This chapter, however, is not only about future forecasts. It also identifies strategies for understanding why certain forecasts are made. We will examine a set of guidelines for analyzing forecasts that will help you make sense of the myriad and often conflicting forecasts you will be asked to consider in the coming years. After considering these guidelines, we will explore major trends that are expected to influence future social policy. Finally, you will be challenged to use this information to develop the foresight that can help improve policies and, ultimately, future outcomes for your clients.

FUTURE FORECASTS

Forecasts can be more clearly understood if we consider the motivations of the groups that make the forecasts, the social environment in which the forecasts are made, and the assumptions on which the forecasts are based. Guidelines for exploring factors that shape forecasts are presented below. As you become familiar with these guidelines and begin to use them to analyze forecasts you learn about in the public media, you will be better able to identify which forecasts are not credible and which ones are probably correct and should be heeded.

Guidelines for Understanding Future Forecasts

Listed below is a set of guidelines you can use to understand why forecasts are made, whether they will be accurate, and how they might influence future actions, including policy making. These guidelines are based on analysis of forecasts made by social workers early in the 20th century (Chapin, 1999).

- Analyze the purpose.
- Assess the underlying assumptions and credibility of source information.
- Consider the influence of current socioeconomic conditions.
- Don't expect the numbers to speak for themselves.
- Assess the extent to which surprise events were anticipated.

Analyze the Purpose   When you examine assertions about the future, consider first the background of the person or group making the forecast, including the reasons why this person or group is trying to forecast the future. What is the purpose of this forecast? Among the reasons people make forecasts are the following: (a) social mobilization, (b) system replacement, (c) enhancement of a specific professional group, and (d) collective learning and adaptation (Chapin, 1999). Social mobilization refers to efforts aimed at encouraging large groups of people to take action and prepare themselves for the future being forecast. People pressing for system replacement are trying to demonstrate that unless a system is fundamentally changed or replaced, it will be unable to deal adequately with future conditions. People who believe conditions in the future will make their specific professional group larger or more important will want to publicize that forecast in order to enhance their group. People also make forecasts in order to foster collective learning and adaptation so that groups and society at large are not taken by surprise but rather can learn and adapt to the coming conditions.

For example, one claim about the future is that by 2012 the need for social workers will increase by 30 percent (Bureau of Labor Statistics, 2004). The need for gerontological social workers is expected to increase particularly fast. It is estimated that by 2020, we will need 60,000–70,000 geriatric social workers (Strengthening Aging and Gerontology Education, 2000). When we consider the purpose of these forecasts, we need to be aware that there will be large increases in the number of older adults because of the aging of the baby boomers, a topic we discussed in Chapter 11. Therefore, if social work education does not change so as to prepare more social workers to work with older adults, the profession will not be able to provide the needed services to those who need them. To avoid such a situation, social work educators are being called upon to mobilize and modify the educational system. This example illustrates two purposes of claims: system replacement and social mobilization. People who already are involved in gerontological social work are particularly interested in publicizing this future need in order to garner increased attention to, and resources for, gerontological social work and the aging population with whom they work. Thus, their profession will be enhanced. Clearly, the goals of collective learning and adaptation also motivate the forecasts. By making the need for gerontological social workers well known, those who do so hope the forecasts will lead to adaptation to fill the need.

Try to find forecasts about the future in the popular press. Investigate the backgrounds of the people making these forecasts and consider which of the reasons listed above might have motivated them. Ask yourself, "What is the purpose of this forecast?" A favorite example of mine of a forecast we have already exposed as unlikely to come true is "Social Security will not be there for seniors in the future." As discussed in previous chapters, the Social Security Trust Fund is solvent through 2042. In addition, it can remain solvent well beyond that point if we make certain modest adjustments in benefits and contributions. Consider what purposes people may have for making such a forecast.

Purpose biases such forecasts. Such bias is inevitable. Throughout this text, we have explored many examples of how reality is constructed based on people's points of view. A forecast is such a construction, except that it deals with a possible future reality. Awareness of bias can augment your understanding of the forecast.

Assess Underlying Assumptions and the Credibility of Source Information   After you have analyzed the purposes of the forecasts, carefully consider the sources used to generate them. You should analyze sources for credibility in much the same way that you examine sources appropriate for reference in professional writing.

One prominent example of a credible source on which many forecasts are based is U.S. Census Bureau population projections and estimates. The term **population projection** refers to the number of people who are expected to be in a given group in a specific year. An example is the number of women in the United States who will be age 85 and older in 2030. Population projections are based on a number of underlying assumptions. Demographers who make population projections start with a set of characteristics of interest in a population for a base year (usually a census year). They then apply different assumptions about the amount, direction, and rate of change that could be experienced by that population in ensuing years. For example, to create a population projection of the number of women age 85 and older in 2030, demographers could begin with the number of women age 55 and older in 2000 (a base census year) and then apply assumptions about how many women would either die or migrate in and out of the country over the next 30 years.

The U.S. Census Bureau uses a cohort-component method for developing projections. This method follows each cohort of people of the same age across time. It bases population projections on assumptions about trends in the following areas: (a) mortality—the rate of death for each age group, generally considered separately for men and women; (b) fertility—the rate of births, generally considered separately by age group and race; and (c) net migration—the balance of people entering and leaving a population. For example, when developing projections of the size of the U.S. population for the year 2010, based on data from the 2000 census, the calculation can be thought of as: 2010 population = 2000 population + (births − deaths) + (net migration) + error.

The U.S. Census Bureau has three sets of assumptions that drive the projections. These assumptions reflect differing rates of mortality, fertility, and net migration. Events such as epidemics and wars obviously influence the actual rate of births, deaths, and net migration. For this reason, the agency creates a range of projections labeled *high, middle,* and *low.* Each range is based on different sets of assumptions regarding birth, death, and net migration.

People attempting to develop forecasts based on U.S. Census Bureau projections typically use the Mid-Level Series, or middle assumptions for each component, to inform their work. For example, in 2004, the Mid-Level Series assumptions that drove population projections were (U.S. Census Bureau, 2004a):

- Average life expectancy at birth will increase gradually from 74.1 years for men and 79.8 years for women in 1999 to 81.2 years for men and 86.7 years for women by 2050.

- Total fertility—the average number of lifetime births per 1,000 women— will increase from 2,048 in 1999 to 2,180 in 2025 and 2,186 in 2050.

- Net migration will reach 996,000 in 2025 and 1,097,000 in 2050.

However, when people develop forecasts, they add yet more assumptions based on various factors that we examine below. What you need to remember is that forecasts are built on layers of assumptions. There is nothing inherently wrong with basing analyses on assumptions. In fact, most policy analyses are based on a series of assumptions. However, it is vital that you take time to examine the assumptions made before accepting a forecast as likely to be an accurate portrayal of the future.

Consider the Influence of Current Socioeconomic Conditions   The assumptions on which forecasts are based may be influenced by current socioeconomic conditions. For example, if the economy is in a slump and political efforts are under way to cut social services in order to reduce taxes, the cuts will be easier to justify if people assume that most children in the future will be much better educated and more economically secure than most of us were in our childhood. Forecasts can then be developed that make that point and create that impression. Additionally, current economic constraints may be fueling a push to view future generations of older people as healthy and capable of self-support rather than in need of more public support. In contrast, during the Great Depression, when jobs were scarce and policy makers wanted elders out of the job force, elders were labeled as unable to keep up with the demands of a mechanized workplace. However, just a few years later, when World War II created demand for older adults in the workforce, they were expected to (and in fact did) perform very well in industrialized settings (Chapin, 1999).

Don't Expect the Numbers to Actually Speak for Themselves   Even though people may try to persuade you to the contrary, numbers don't speak for themselves. They must be interpreted. An obvious example is calculating the number of people age 65 and older and then assuming that it represents the number of people incapable of working for the purpose of forecasting dependency. Public policy designed to create opportunity for younger workers and support people in retirement underpins this association. In fact, many people age 65 and older can and do work. In addition, advances in health care will undoubtedly make it possible for many more older adults to do so. Clearly, then, we can emphasize or downplay different interpretations of population projections depending on the future we want to portray. In fact, we can reframe discussions of future public costs associated with retirement to focus initially on issues of choice, the availability of work, the capacity to work, and the willingness of taxpayers to support people in retirement rather than on the numbers of people who are over 65 and therefore assumed to be dependent.

Assess the Extent to Which Surprise Events Were Anticipated   A final consideration is the extent to which the person making the forecast acknowledges and discusses surprise events that may influence the forecast's accuracy. For example, the events of 9/11 helped fuel an economic downturn and contributed to the U.S. decision to invade Iraq. These events significantly affected the accuracy of earlier forecasts about economic trends in the United States during the first decade of the 21st century. Similarly, the baby boom dramatically influenced the accuracy of earlier population projections for 1980 and 2000.

Although nobody can anticipate and consider all future scenarios, the most likely so-called unforeseen events should be anticipated to the extent possible. Possible future breakthroughs in disease prevention are particularly relevant in considering future public social welfare costs and burdens. Current approaches exist for factoring in some of these possibilities. For example, demographers and policy makers attempting to anticipate future costs for Medicare and Medicaid create alternative scenarios based on possible events that will affect future costs of prescriptions and rates of disability. They consider the possible impact of such factors as more stringent antismoking campaigns, greater participation in exercise programs by baby boomers, and possible advances in the treatment of Alzheimer's disease or cancer when developing forecasts of rates of disability and use of medications and, ultimately, Medicaid and Medicare expenditures. In the same way, planners in the private sector also consider the likelihood that such alternative scenarios will come to pass when they make decisions regarding future investments in long-term care facilities. Savvy planners in all areas of the economy make similar calculations.

Medical advances, biological warfare, and major economic downturns are examples of surprise events that may have a great impact on the accuracy of future forecasts. Even if authors do not alert readers that such surprise events may dramatically change the accuracy of their projections, it is incumbent on readers to consider that possibility.

Thinking about the Future: The Strengths Approach

The guidelines discussed above can help us analyze the accuracy and utility of a forecast. However, social workers interested in promoting a strengths approach when considering future social policy initiatives need to conduct additional analysis. From a strengths perspective, forecasts should always be evaluated to gauge whether they are based on a deficit view of the population being discussed. For example, not very long ago, a common prediction was that people with severe disabilities would spend their lives in institutions and certainly would not be joining the workforce. This forecast was based on the assumption that this population was totally dependent on other people.

It is also important to consider the amount of attention given to the current cohort about whom the forecast is being made. Significantly, some forecasts made earlier in the 20th century concerning the social service needs of older adults today failed to take into account the racial and ethnic diversity in the population of children who would become today's elders. When you examine current forecasts, look carefully for similar oversights. For example, people who make forecasts about the future needs of Hispanics or Latinos must pay attention to the life conditions, strengths, and goals of Hispanic families today. If they do so, then they will not overlook such vital information as the rate of entry of Hispanic women into the full-time workforce. This information is an important factor in forecasting the need for formal care of dependent family members. Similarly, lack of attention to the goals and preferences of people in their 40s today will impair our ability to forecast needed resources and social services in 2030 and beyond when that cohort will be over 65.

Engaging and paying close attention to the target population is a central tenet of the strengths perspective. However, although citizen involvement is considered an important component in crafting effective social policy from a strengths perspective, it is only one component. Clearly, there is more to be done. We turn now to additional elements that provide guidance in understanding forecasts and crafting future social policies that reflect the strengths perspective.

Values rooted in the NASW *Code of Ethics* underpin the strengths approach. We are experiencing unprecedented structural change and accompanying uncertainty about the future. Professional values, such as commitment to social justice and the reduction of inequity, offer an anchor that social work professionals can use when considering future policies and programs. Social workers must carefully consider the interplay of professional values, demographics, societal goals, and political realities when they evaluate future scenarios. For example, social service professionals might favor spending more money on children and less on elderly citizens because children experience higher poverty rates. This policy is in keeping with a longstanding commitment to social justice and therefore generational equity. However, as we discussed earlier, forecasts to support such policy changes must be carefully crafted lest we lend unwitting support to those who would dismantle all federal entitlement programs regardless of which age groups they target. The well-being of all generations is interlocked, and future social policies need to be crafted with attention to their intergenerational effects.

Finally, the strengths perspective is based on the insight that our understanding of conditions and events is socially constructed. Social constructions of conditions influence future social policy responses and thus, future realities. For this reason, we can expect forecasts to influence future realities. To the extent that action or inaction by persons with knowledge of the forecasts can shape the future, forecasts have the capacity to become self-fulfilling prophecies. Indeed, basic to many forecasts is a desire to ultimately improve future conditions. An important component of understanding forecasting is the effort to foresee how specific forecasts, added to the weight of other forecasts, may influence the resources and services that are available to our clients. Forecasts that do not take into account the diverse and fluid needs of future generations may compound the problems of providing necessary resources and services.

 Web Links

If you would like a detailed look at the work of futurists— that is, people who study and predict the future based in part on current trends—you can access the Rand Pardee Center (Study of the Future), the Institute for the Future, the World Future Society, and the Millennium Project, at www.mhhe.com/chapin1.

FACTORS THAT WILL SHAPE FUTURE SOCIAL POLICIES

Armed with these insights into understanding future forecasts, we turn now to three major factors that will most likely influence future social policy: increasing diversity, medical and technological advances, and globalization and depletion of natural resources. In this section, we will analyze these factors and consider what their influence on policy may be.

Population Growth and Increasing Diversity

In 2005, the U.S. population exceeded 297 million and the world population exceeded 6.4 billion (U.S. Census Bureau, 2005). Further, the U.S. Census Bureau projects that by 2050, the United States population will exceed 392 million and the world population will exceed 9 billion. The two major factors driving population growth are fertility and net immigration. The crude birth rate—that is, the rate of births per 1,000 people—is predicted to decrease in the United States until 2026 because a smaller percentage of women will be in their childbearing years. However, after 2011, the total number of births each year is expected to exceed the highest annual number of births ever achieved in the United States in the 20th century because a larger overall number (as opposed to percentage) of women will be in their childbearing years. Experts predict that there will be more than 5 million births each year in the United States by 2035, compared to approximately 4.1 million births in 2003 (U.S. Census Bureau, 1996; Hamilton, Martin, & Sutton, 2004).

Another factor affecting population trends is net immigration, which accounts for 40 percent of current U.S. population growth. Estimates are that net immigration will continue to add between 800,000 to 1,000,000 people to the population on a yearly basis through 2050 (Kent & Mather, 2002). This number translates to a total increase of 40–50 million during that period.

Despite these large population increases, the actual *rate* of population growth is projected to decrease by about 50 percent during the next six decades (U.S. Census Bureau, 2001). This decline will be due primarily to the aging of the population, which will lead to a large increase in the number of deaths. Significantly, the future population will be older than is currently the case. In 2005, the median age of the population was 35.2 years. By 2030, it is projected to increase to 38 years (U.S. Census Bureau, 2005).

In addition, the U.S. population will become more racially and ethnically diverse across the life span. The black, Asian and Pacific Islander, Hispanic-origin, and American Indian, Eskimo, and Aleut populations will increase their proportions of the total population; consequently, the non-Hispanic white proportion will decrease. In 2003, the non-Hispanic white population made up 67 percent of the total population. The U.S. Census Bureau projects, however, that by 2030, this proportion will decrease to 57.5 percent (U.S. Census Bureau, 2003; U.S. Census Bureau, 2005). The Hispanic-origin population will be the fastest-growing group. By 2004, this population had increased to more than 41 million (U.S. Census Bureau, 2005). According to U.S. Census Bureau projections, the percentage of Hispanics will nearly double from 12.6 percent of the total population in 2000 to 24.4 percent in 2050 (U.S. Census Bureau, 2004c).

Web Link

*Visit www.mhhe.com/
chapin1 to link to the U.S.
Census Bureau and obtain
the latest statistics on world
population, U.S. population,
and the population of your
state.*

To summarize, then, the future U.S. population will include many more very old people. In addition, a larger proportion of our population will be of African American, Hispanic, Asian and Pacific Islander, and American Indian, Eskimo, and Aleut origin. Examining population projections helps us sketch a broad outline of a future that will clearly require public social policies that can accommodate a population that will be larger, older, and more diverse.

Medical and Technological Advances

Medical advances have contributed to a major increase in life expectancy in the United States. In fact, according to current forecasts, by 2030, there will be more than 71 million older adults in the United States. Of this population, almost 400,000 Americans will be centenarians (100 years of age or older), compared with 71,000 today (U.S. Census Bureau, 2004b). Applications derived from genetic research could lead to major changes in the areas of reproduction, organ replacement, and treatment of what are now devastating diseases.

New medical advances provide more alternatives for controlling reproduction and fertility, but they also create opportunities for exploitation. Poor women in particular may be vulnerable to having their bodies used for unsafe procedures in order to provide children for childless people. Breakthroughs in genetic research may create life-saving opportunities for people suffering from a variety of diseases. However, they also will create a host of ethical dilemmas for people who will have a greater range of choices to consider but still must make decisions in the face of great uncertainty and risk.

Advances in information technology have transformed the ways that many people in the United States communicate, access information and education, investigate medical options, and conduct business. They have also changed the ways in which social workers provide services, educate practitioners, manage agencies, influence policy, and conduct research and evaluation (NASW, 2003m). Online therapy, use of the Internet for community as well as national political organizing, and the ability to rapidly access ideas for policy alternatives from across the country via computerized databases are but a few of the numerous possibilities created by these new technologies.

Advances in technology provide not only opportunities but also challenges for both clients and workers. Issues of privacy and confidentiality are becoming more critical as increasing amounts of personal health and income information are being stored in computer databases. Unauthorized use of data and hackers compromise privacy. In addition, people in poverty and people who face cultural, linguistic, and disability-based barriers often lack access to computers, which limits their ability to participate in an increasingly computerized society. The digital divide is the gap between people who have easy access to the latest technology and people who have little or no access.

This gap is widening, and it will limit the opportunities of less-affluent people to find employment, receive adequate health care, and even receive a thorough education.

Globalization and Environmental Degradation

As discussed in Chapter 4, globalization affects not only economic but also political and social conditions in the United States and around the world. Globalization has created opportunities for economic development and has led to increasing interdependency and closer relations among people from different countries. At the same time, however, both U.S. and foreign workers are competing for jobs that may be transient as employers find workers in other countries who will work for lower wages, accept unsafe working conditions, and expect even fewer benefits. Child labor is a particular concern. Further, the lack of government enforcement of pollution and safety standards in some countries attracts businesses that hope to make a profit at the expense of the citizenry and the environment. Social welfare systems are being restructured in the United States and in many other countries with the stated goal of making the economy more competitive. However, policies that cut back social services and education in order to reduce taxes on businesses often overlook the fact that a healthy and well-educated citizenry is essential to economic competitiveness.

Additionally, as people from very different cultures and religious backgrounds come into close and constant contact, religious conflicts are becoming more visible and are consuming valuable resources that could be used for positive purposes. People in many parts of the world have yet to find ways of accommodating diversity by peaceful means. Global competition for natural resources also fuels violent confrontation. This competition is expected to increase as the world population grows, natural resources are depleted, and globalization becomes even more widespread.

Concerns about environmental degradation and depletion of natural resources cast a shadow over our future. Although social work has always emphasized person in environment, the social environment has been our major concern. Consequently, we have paid much less attention to the influence of the natural environment on human development. Environmental degradation affects all types of social work practice. For example, children exposed to high levels of mercury and lead experience higher rates of developmental disabilities. Similarly, poor air quality contributes to severe respiratory problems for many children and adults, and high levels of pesticides and toxins have been linked to life-threatening health problems. People living in poverty in both inner cities and rural areas are more likely to be victimized by unsafe and unsound environmental practices.

FUTURE POLICY DIRECTIONS

As we have just seen, demographic trends, medical and technological advances, and the economic and social changes that accompany increasing globalization will likely influence future social policies. This text has provided numerous examples of how, in the wake of earlier changes, the government became involved in creating social policies to protect the public at large as well as to protect people deprived of their civil rights. We have also examined instances in which policy making was designed to help quell unrest and preserve the interests of capitalism during periods of rapid change. Compassion has also motivated the creation of social policy. In fact, a variety of changes and motivations may propel the passage of a single piece of legislation. Undoubtedly, these factors will also drive future social policy.

Ideology—the beliefs that guide a group—will also undoubtedly continue to shape social policy in the future. The belief that government contributes to the creation of social problems is often contrasted with the belief that government has a responsibility to act as an ameliorating force in a capitalist society and to promote equality of opportunity (NASW, 2003l). Conservatives are characterized as typically holding the former opinion, while liberals are associated with the latter. However, the examination of social policies and programs in this text has provided ample examples of policies that made problems worse as well as policies that improved social conditions. Armed with the knowledge that government can both help and harm the citizenry and that the forces discussed above will most likely continue to exert great influence on social policy and programs, we can now consider what future public social policy directions and strategies would more effectively support social work's dual mission of enhancing well-being and meeting basic needs. This segment brings together many of the policy and program initiatives discussed in earlier chapters to provide you with a composite picture of promising policy strategies.

Diversity and the Work-Based Safety Net

Given that U.S. public social policies have consistently emphasized individualism, personal responsibility, and the work ethic, particularly for people in poverty, we probably can expect that future policies will also emphasize attachment to the workforce. Thus, if a safety net is to survive, it will quite likely be work based. However, advocates of a work-based safety net have not adequately considered whether the supply of jobs that provide a living wage in the United States is sufficient to support this approach. They also need to ask whether there will be sufficient jobs in the future in the wake of increased mechanization, robotics, and outsourcing.

Nonetheless, unless the public sentiment that propelled the latest welfare reform efforts changes radically in the years to come, future welfare policies will continue to promote work outside the home, even for low-income mothers with very young children. If women are to work, they will need access to either publicly or privately funded high-quality day care in the workplace. Workplace policies that provide the support necessary for mothers to succeed in their dual roles of parent and employee will be vital to the well-being of their families and children and ultimately to societal well-being. Generous family leave, on-site day care, and flexible work schedules will be crucial.

Wages, Jobs, and Retirement Improving women's wages is central to reducing childhood poverty. Women's economic development through micro-enterprises, Individual Development Accounts, and education about economic issues may help them become entrepreneurs. Public social policies need to be designed and funded so that they benefit women and people of color to the same extent that they benefit men.

Globalization has led to reduced job permanency. Therefore, we need to develop policies and programs to help workers transition between jobs. Moreover, as jobs become more transient, the right of workers to transfer retirement programs from one job to another becomes ever more important. Further, because of increases in immigration, whatever programs and services are developed should take into account the needs of people for whom English is a second language.

A new paradigm is developing whereby retirement is considered a process marked by successive decisions, in contrast to the traditional conception of retirement as a single and irreversible event (Hooyman & Kiyak, 2002). People may retire from one job and then very shortly reenter the ranks of non-retired people as they begin new careers. In fact, more companies and individuals are beginning to embrace alternatives to the "30 years of 40-hour workweeks until retirement" conception of work life. As we saw in Chapter 11, such alternatives include part-time positions, job sharing, and phased retirement. Clearly, we need to design policies that support this kind of workplace flexibility while protecting health and retirement benefits. Such policies will also benefit younger men and women who are trying to juggle the responsibilities of work and child rearing when both parents are in the workforce. Currently, the non-portability of pensions and the lack of benefits for part-time work impede the development of alternative work patterns. We will need to craft future employment and retirement policy with careful attention to the needs of both younger workers and workers who are nearing retirement.

Supporting the Intergenerational Family In addition to the reforms proposed above, the intergenerational nature of the family needs to be recognized in the workplace. We need to develop supports for workers who also care for frail elders. Support of these kinds of family-friendly policies in both the public and the private sector will also help employed people provide adequate care for their children. Further, the voices of intergenerational families from diverse ethnic backgrounds must be heard in the development of employment and family policies. Social workers will need to press policy makers and encourage families to make these connections. The impact of future policies on diverse intergenerational families will need careful consideration. Without attention to these issues, policies will inadvertently undercut the functioning and development of the diverse families of the future (NASW, 2003k).

In another family-related development, the sandwich generation will decline as the baby boomers become the generation needing care and their smaller numbers of offspring become the sandwich generation. Members of this smaller sandwich generation will struggle to care for their children and for elders who become more and more frail as they live longer and longer. To support this generation of caregivers, we will need policies that provide for family medical leave, adult day care, and flex time. We also need to find more ways to recognize and honor caring work. Finally, we need to devise methods of compensating unpaid care work, particularly with regard to earning retirement credits.

Social workers need to engage older adults, their children, and their grandchildren in developing a vision upon which we can develop workable policies and programs that respond to increasing diversity and the coming elder boom. Simplistic approaches and characterizations will not suffice. Rather, policies must be crafted based on a complex and diverse vision not only of the older people of 2030 but also of their children and grandchildren. The challenge is to help develop policies that maximize the advantages of an aging society. For example, many older adults will be able to contribute their time and energy to helping our youth meet their basic needs and take advantage of opportunities to improve their quality of life and personal well-being. To accomplish this goal, we could aggressively promote a vision of the future that perceives investments in educating and training the young people who will be future workers as integral to preparing for future population aging (Ozawa, 1997).

Health and the Environment

Advances in medical technology have enabled us to prolong life artificially and have created additional options for reproduction. Ethical dilemmas surrounding the human impact of these advances are the purview of social workers. For example, emerging pressures for cost control and the rationing of health care may tempt health care institutions and insurers to encourage the use of end-of-life practices to control costs (NASW, 2003i). As long as health care is a commodity rather than a social utility, socioeconomic factors will differentially influence access to care, including end-of-life care for clients who have limited ability to pay. Policies to ration basic health care more equitably are needed. Additionally, social workers will need to advocate policies that allow competent people to make informed health care choices. These policies should also address patients' need to be thoroughly informed about options and consequences. Finally, they should protect patients from coercion. Access to adequate heath services for people of all racial and ethnic backgrounds and ages should be a priority for our future.

In addition to the issues we have just considered, our health also depends on the state of our physical environment. For example, low-income people may live in areas where policies to control pollution are not adequate or are not properly enforced. Consequently, social workers need to be alert to cases of "environmental discrimination," such as locating polluting factories and waste-disposal facilities disproportionately in low-income neighborhoods. They also need to consider environmental factors when they assess clients' needs and plan interventions that may include challenging the policies that are damaging clients' physical environment.

One important factor that contributes to environmental degradation is overpopulation. In the area of global population growth, NASW supports:

> The fundamental right of each individual throughout the world to manage his or her fertility and to have access to a full range of safe and legal family plan-ning services regardless of the individual's income, marital status, race, ethnic-ity, sexual orientation, age, national origin, or residence. (NASW, 2003j, 128–129)

Although the profession supports individual rights in access to family planning and reproductive health care services, it will continue to oppose forced steril-ization and all nonvoluntary birth control policies.

Not only does the natural environment affect our health and welfare, but social welfare policies can affect the environment. For instance, housing and transportation policies designed to help low-income people may create further environmental problems if they encourage urban sprawl and travel by automo-bile rather than mass transportation. Social workers appreciate the importance of "person/environmental fit" in the helping process. Policies that will help maintain a healthy environment are critical to attaining and maintaining an adequate quality of life for both our clients and ourselves. However, these policies will be effective only if the public agencies charged with enforcing them are adequately funded.

Information Technology and Privacy

Advances in information technology improve communication and may reduce record keeping. New, innovative ways of providing services via the Internet, in-cluding online therapy, will likely multiply in the future. Social workers can now practice globally. The growing use of computers to store and share client information constitutes a threat to confidentiality, particularly when police authorities and the courts demand access to our records. Therefore, we need to become savvy about ethical and legal issues related to information technology and use of the Internet. In addition, we must research how to use information technology effectively. Finally, we need to advocate for policies that protect clients' privacy when new technology is implemented. The NASW *Code of Ethics* should guide decisions about collecting, storing, retrieving, and sharing electronic client data.

Social workers also need to promote policies that reduce the digital divide that disadvantages many of our clients. Otherwise, groups with little access to modern and widely used information technologies will fall further behind in the competition to secure employment and an adequate education.

The Influence of Pluralism on Future Social Policy

The United States is said to have a pluralistic system of government. As discussed in Chapter 4, in the context of social policy development, *pluralism* refers to a system whereby a variety of interest groups compete to help shape social policies and provide resulting social services. As diversity increases in a society, the variety of interest groups competing to influence the policy process can be expected to multiply. Therefore, pluralism in future social policy and program development will likely increase. Because enacting and implementing major new public social policies typically requires coalitions of a variety of interest groups, policy changes tend to be incremental. Forces that resist change and forces that propel change create checks and balances on each other.

Although most change is incremental, transformative policy changes sometimes do occur, often in response to surprise events. A prominent example is the creation of the Office of Homeland Security in 2001 in the wake of 9/11. The intended and unintended consequences of future transformative changes need to be scrutinized with particular care because the outcomes of such major changes are difficult to foresee and may have very negative impacts on client populations.

Privatization

Although the Radical Right can be expected to continue to argue for the abolition of government social programs, particularly the ones that don't primarily benefit wealthy individuals and corporations, government will continue to be the primary source of funds for social programs. Public and private agencies will likely continue to provide publicly funded social services. Privatization is often sold as a tool for balancing budgets. The state sets an amount that it will pay for a specific service, and the contractor is obligated to provide the service for that amount. However, if the private contractor is unable to provide the necessary services for the set price, state officials don't relish the prospect of having nursing facility residents and children in private foster care deposited on the capitol steps. Consequently, the state often ends up pumping additional appropriations into private coffers. Also, as more private providers, particularly nonprofit voluntary and religious organizations, become increasingly dependent on public funding to function effectively, a very powerful constituency of middle-class voters who are members of those organizations may demand additional funding.

For all these reasons, privatized social services will very likely cost more—rather than less—than services provided directly through the government. Privatization can also be more costly because tax dollars often flow into for-profit private initiatives without the same structural checks and balances that exist in government agencies. For example, if government employees "blow the whistle" to expose unsafe or illegal practices, their positions are protected. In contrast, in private corporations, if complaints surface and the contract is lost, the employee's job disappears. For this reason, employees in private firms may be less likely to report waste and corruption. Finally, privatization often involves declassifying the jobs of direct care providers. As a result, social work education is no longer a requirement for these positions. Consequently, client protection based on adherence to professional ethics is weakened.

Clearly, then, government will increasingly have the role of ensuring that services provided by the private sector are adequate. Even when services are privatized, the state will still be responsible for monitoring inputs and ensuring outcomes. Privatization creates additional layers of service oversight. In addition, it often reduces the wages, qualifications, and career ladder for direct service providers because cutting labor costs is vital to making a profit. Privatization shifts the focus of government involvement toward oversight, while it increases the responsibilities of the private sector to deliver services.

Privatization and decentralization of service provision also can be expected to lead to even greater service fragmentation. **Service fragmentation** means that many organizations will be providing services with less overall coordination or attention to overlapping services and gaps in service. For example, many churches and other charitable organizations are establishing food pantries and other services in a piecemeal fashion in order to serve the needs of low-income families who no longer receive public welfare.

Despite all of these complications, pluralism, as reflected in public-private partnerships, now sustains nonprofit organizations and a commercial welfare industry. Further, privately provided services are often more acceptable to the significant number of people who believe in less government. It is unlikely, then, that we will return to public provision of services even if privatized services do not prove to be more cost-effective or produce more positive outcomes for clients. Therefore, for the foreseeable future, policy makers will focus on making privatized approaches work.

If future public-private partnerships are to work to the benefit of their clients, social workers who understand both the limitations and the potential of such partnerships need to work to ensure adequate public funding and oversight. If the future brings yet more policy initiatives to increase privatization, it will be even more vital to compare the costs of publicly provided services with the costs of privatized services. Policies sold on the basis of cost-effectiveness should be monitored to see if they actually reduce costs. Following the money is always a good idea in understanding and evaluating policies and programs.

Reconsidering Core Values

Although cost-effectiveness is often at the center of the debate about future policy initiatives, value choices also influence the design and oversight of policy and social programs. Work and financial independence are highly valued in our society, as are family care for dependent members and personal freedom to direct one's course in life. Reciprocity is also a core value. Building on these values, U.S. social welfare policy may be viewed from a perspective that focuses on well-being and social responsibility rather than simply on the lessening of deficits such as poverty or even on material well-being (Morris, 2002). For example, a greater focus on well-being could lead to improvements in the food stamp program so that it would promote good health rather than provide food assistance that is barely adequate. A public social policy and program infrastructure could be developed that provides all citizens with access to basic food, housing, and health care and enables them to pursue a range of opportunities in a healthy environment.

Economic efficiency and social justice may be complementary (Morris, 2002). People whose basic needs are met and who have multiple options to enhance their well-being are more likely to fuel economic growth. If policy makers become convinced that tax cuts for wealthy people and spending cuts for low-income people actually impede economic growth, they will be more likely to support socially just policies. One strategy for promoting a more just society is to encourage social capital formation. It includes developing a healthy, well-educated workforce and increased support for the developmental approach to enacting public social welfare policies and programs that bolster economic and community development (Midgley, Tracey, & Livermore, 2000). Policies and programs that focus on enhancing the capacity of people in need to participate in the productive economy rather than rely on social services might receive support from a wider spectrum of voters. Supported employment for people with disabilities, job-training programs for unemployed workers, and Individual Development Accounts that enable low-income people to accumulate assets are examples of initiatives that reflect a developmental approach. These initiatives generally include incentives rather than requirements for participation.

Using a developmental approach, the government redistributes wealth through education, income transfer, and job creation. It also enforces antidiscrimination laws in order to ensure that more people can compete effectively for the benefits of the economy. However, there will never be equality of opportunity because of the individual differences people bring to the competition. People in the target population who are more likely to succeed without new initiatives based on the developmental approach will likely be the ones who benefit most from these initiatives. Helping people who are most likely to succeed is not a bad idea. Certainly, many people who have benefited from policies and programs that emphasize a developmental approach would not actually have succeeded without those opportunities.

Although a developmental approach has great potential, it will not eliminate the need for public income-support and social service programs because many people still won't be able to take advantage of educational and job opportunities. However, because initiatives that reflect a developmental approach are typically oversold so as to gain support, disappointment often ensues when public costs aren't quickly and significantly reduced after these initiatives are enacted. Nevertheless, the emphasis on reciprocal obligation and the importance of work is consistent with the dominant ideologies in the country today. Significantly, ideology often takes precedence over data—even data on costs and expenditures—in the public arena.

Using the Electoral Process

Future social policy will be shaped by electoral realities. Throughout this chapter, we have outlined policy approaches more attuned to the future economic, demographic, and cultural environment that could be expected to contribute to a more equitable future. The key to a more equitable future is participation by people who believe in such a vision of the future. Social workers adhere to the *Code of Ethics*, which supports that vision. Social workers need to participate much more effectively in electoral politics in order to make the vision a reality. The NASW has developed a series of policy statements outlining the organization's support for a wide variety of needed policy changes. These statements are contained in *Social Work Speaks,* a publication frequently referenced in this text. If these policies are to be implemented, then more social workers must engage in electoral politics and help elect candidates who will support needed changes. In the future, the profession must give increased attention and support to the work of the NASW's Political Action for Candidate Election (PACE) as well as other strategies to influence national and state policies.

On a more immediate level, you can register to vote and encourage your friends to vote. Bring up issues of social justice and engage in debate. Think about running for office. Consider doing some policy-related research for your local legislator. For example, a local student who is concerned with low voter turnout among groups other than middle-class white conservatives is research-ing the possibility of reducing the voting age to 16. Such policies have already been adopted in other countries and could also make it possible to do much more meaningful voter education in high schools in the future.

Try to find an issue or a candidate that arouses your passion. If you do get involved, try not to lose heart when a policy you endorse is enacted but does not produce all of the outcomes you had hoped for. Ask yourself, "What in my life actually does work out just as I had planned?" Your answer will probably be, "Very little." In fact, the impulse to oversimplify challenges and identify a single, "fix-all" approach fuels the unrealistic expectation that one policy will change human behavior, reduce structural barriers, and solve all our troubles.

Your voice and your work are important. Your efforts will be even more ef-fective if you band together with other like-minded professionals and work with citizens groups to make your voices heard.

 Web Link

If you are interested in learning more about politi-cal involvement by social workers, visit the Institute for the Advancement of Political Social Work Prac-tice Web site, found at www.mhhe.com/chapin1.

CONCLUSION

An image of the future is at the base of all choice-oriented behavior. We need an image of a future worth going to, a future that can be embraced and enjoyed, not decried. We also need some guidance on how to get there. The synthesis of careful data analysis, citizen involvement, and professional values enables us to help sketch an image of the future that energizes our efforts to craft effective policy and programs. Social workers can help shape our image of the future and implement needed policy changes by becoming involved in electoral politics, publishing articles in professional journals and the popular press, and helping to organize and participating in formal and informal local, state, and national forums. By creating opportunities for policy makers to lis-ten to the target population from the beginning of the policy development process and by explicitly focusing on outcomes that are important to this population, social workers can help policy makers obtain the information nec-essary to craft future strengths-based policy.

The social work profession has deep roots in movements to bring about social change. Since the beginning of the profession, social workers have been instruments of social control as well as social assistance. Undoubtedly, social workers will continue as a profession to fulfill both of these important func-tions. You can also strive to fulfill social work's basic mission of enhancing well-being and meeting basic needs. The involvement of social workers who are attuned to the strengths of all citizens and who are committed to social justice in effective policy practice is critical today. We live in a global village. The pop-ulation of the United States is growing older and becoming more ethnically and racially diverse. The gap between the rich and people in poverty is widening. As the same time, we are witnessing unprecedented efforts to dismantle social policies and programs designed to provide a rudimentary safety net for both young and old people in need. Social workers can develop individual and organizational responses to these policy issues. You can help. It is hard work, but you now have the beginning tools to join the fray. If you decide to act, you may be amazed by what can be accomplished.

MAIN POINTS

- A framework for understanding future forecasts draws attention to the following components: purpose, underlying assumptions and credibility of source, influence of current socioeconomic conditions, interpretation of the numbers or data, and anticipation of surprise events.

- When thinking about the future from the strengths perspective, the following points should be considered. First, life conditions, strengths, and goals of the current cohorts for which predictions are being made should be taken into account. Second, social constructions of conditions influence future social policy responses and future realities. Third, the social work *Code of Ethics* can help anchor our thinking about future policies. Finally, policy implementation should be closely monitored to determine outcomes for clients, with input from the target population.

- The number of people in the United States is expected to increase in the next 50 years because of fertility rates and net immigration. Yet, population growth will decrease owing to the greater age of the population and subsequent number of deaths. As the population grows, it will become more racially diverse, with the percentage of white non-Hispanics decreasing and the Hispanic-origin population increasing fastest.

- In addition to increases in population and diversity, other factors such as medical advances, changes in information technology, globalization, and environmental degradation and depletion of natural resources will shape the future of the United States and the profession of social work.

- Given current U.S. values, it is expected that future public social policy will continue to emphasize attachment to the workforce. The challenges posed by these policies need to be the focus of attention. There will be a need for high-quality day care, improvement in women's wages, assistance with job transitions, implementation of family-friendly policies that take into account families from diverse backgrounds, and changes in the retirement process.

- Future health care policy reforms are needed to increase access to adequate health services, including the opportunity for competent people to make informed choices about health care. Environmental discrimination and the impact of policies on the natural environment also require more attention.

- Pluralism can be expected to increase as the diversity of the population increases.

- Privatization of publicly funded social services needs to be carefully evaluated in terms of both benefits and limitations so that funding and oversight can be tailored to deliver adequate services.

- Future policies will likely focus on both cost-effectiveness and value choices. It is possible to develop public social policies that are economically efficient and also promote social justice.

- Social workers need to participate effectively in electoral politics in order to implement policies consistent with their ethics that promote the well-being of individuals and meet basic needs. This can be done by voting, debating, running for office, campaigning, or conducting policy-related research.

EXERCISES: PRACTICING SOCIAL WORK

Working with the Sanchez Family

1. The Sanchez family is personally experiencing the impact of current immigration policy, and these policies may become even more restrictive in the future. Go to the National Council of La Raza Web site under Relevant Web sites in the Resources folder, and examine the latest immigration policy reforms being proposed. If this legislation is passed, what would be the impact on the Sanchez family?

Working with the Black Feather Community

1. When working cross culturally on policy practice issues, it is essential to understand the unique vision of the target group when considering what kind of future to work toward in their community. In the Black Feather case, what future-shaping issues and policies do you believe would get widespread support in the Native American community and would also be supported by the wider community?

2. What strategies can you suggest for building intergenerational cooperation in crafting policies and programs to address the challenges faced by the Black Feather community now and in the future?

EXERCISES: THE SOCIAL WORK LIBRARY

Trends that Will Influence Social Work

Read "Steering currents for the future of social work" (Sowers & Ellis, 2001), and respond to the following:

1. What were the three currents presented in this article? Have you already encountered these currents in your social work practice?

2. What impact might these currents or trends have on policies in the United States?

3. What impact might these trends have on the profession of social work?

Read "Influencing state policy: Social work arena for the 21st century" (Schneider, 2002), and respond to the following:

1. Does your involvement and interest in political practice focus on federal or state-level policies?

2. With the current political situation, what are the benefits and drawbacks of your level (federal or state) of involvement?

3. Reflecting on the multitude of policies and political issues presented, what issues do you think are the most pressing and in need of your political involvement?

OTHER EXERCISES

1. First, imagine it is 10 years from now and write down a personal goal you hope you will have achieved. Second, write down a goal of a change in social policy you think can be achieved in the next 10 years. Be ready to discuss your social policy ideas in class.

2. What do you think are the benefits and drawbacks of having 16-year-olds vote? Do you think that change would increase voter participation? Do you think we might have more future policies that address the needs of children if younger people could vote? Are you for or against such a policy change? Why?

REFERENCES

Abramovitz, M. (1996). *Regulating the lives of women: Social welfare policy from colonial times to the present* (Rev. ed.). Boston: South End Press.

ACORN Living Wage Resource Center. (2003). Introduction to ACORN's Living Wage Website. Available at www.livingwagecampaign.org/index.php

Adler, L. (2001). The meaning of permanence: A critical analysis of the Adoption and Safe Families Act of 1997. *President and Fellows of Harvard College Harvard Journal on Legislation, 38*(1).

Administration for Children and Families. (2001). *Social services block grant annual report on expenditures and recipients: 2001.* Available at www.acf.hhs.gov/programs/ocs/ssbg/annrpt/index.html

Administration for Children and Families. (2004). *Temporary Assistance for Needy Families (TANF): Sixth annual report to Congress.* Washington, DC: Author. Available at www.acf.hhs.gov//programs/ofa/annualreport6/ar6index.htm

Administration on Aging. (2003). *A profile of older Americans: 2003.* U.S. Department of Health and Human Services. Available at www.aoa.gov/prof/Statistics/profile/2003/2003profile.pdf

Administration on Aging. (2004). *A layman's guide to the Older Americans Act.* Available at www.aoa.gov/about/legbudg/oaa/laymans_guide/laymans_guide.asp

Ahronheim, J. (1997). End-of-life issues for very elderly women: Incurable and terminal illness. *Journal of the American Medical Women's Association, 52,* 147–151.

Ahsan, N. (1996). The Family Preservation and Support Services Programs. *The Future of Children, 6*(3), 157–160.

Allard, P., & Young, M. C. (2002). Prosecuting juveniles in adult court: The practitioner's perspective. *Journal of Forensic Psychology Practice, 2*(2), 65–78.

Alliance for Aging Research. (1998). *One final gift: Humanizing the end of life for women in America.* Washington, DC: Author.

American Psychiatric Association. (2000). *Diagnostic and statistical manual of mental disorders* (4th ed., text revision). Washington, DC: Author.

American Public Human Services Association. (2002). *Bringing systems together.* Available at www.aphsa.org/Policy/Doc/napcwa-bringing.pdf

American-Arab Anti Discrimination Committee. (2002). ADC Fact Sheet: The Condition of Arab Americans Post-9/11. Available at www.adc.org/terror_attack/9-11aftermath.PDF

Americans with Disabilities Act of 1990, Pub. L. No. 101-336,104 Stat. 328. Available at www.usdoj.gov/crt/ada/pubs/ada.txt

Amnesty International. (2002). *United States of America. Indecent and internationally illegal: The death penalty against juvenile offenders.* Available: www.amnestyusa.org/abolish/reports/amr51_144_2002.pdf

Anderson, B. W. (1986). Understanding the Old Testament (4th Ed.). Englewood Cliffs, NJ: Prentice Hall.

Annie E. Casey Foundation. (2003). *Kids count data book.* Baltimore: Annie E. Casey Foundation.

Annie E. Casey Foundation. (2004). *Kids count 2004 data book.* Baltimore: Annie E. Casey Foundation.

Axinn, J., & Stern, M. J. (2001). *Social welfare: A history of the American response to need* (5th ed.). Boston: Allyn and Bacon.

Baltes, P. B., & Baltes, M. M. (1990). Psychological perspectives on successful aging: The model of selective optimization with compensation. In P. B. Baltes & M. M. Baltes (Eds.), *Successful aging: Perspectives from the behavioral sciences* (pp. 1–34). Cambridge: Cambridge University Press.

Banerjee, M. (2002). Voicing realities and recommending reform in PRWORA. *Social Work, 47*(3), 315–358.

Barker, R. (1999). *Milestones in the development of social work and social welfare.* Washington, DC: NASW Press.

Barker, R. L. (2003). *The social work dictionary* (5th ed., p. 357). Washington, DC: NASW Press.

Basch, N. (1998). Family values and 19th-century American politics. *Reviews in American History, 26*(4), 687–692.

Baum, A. C., Crase, S. J., & Crase, K. L. (2001). Influences on the decision to become or not become a foster parent. *Families in Society: The Journal of Contemporary Human Services, 82*(2), 202–213.

Bell, W. (1987). *Contemporary social welfare* (2nd ed.). New York: Macmillan.

Bernstein, I. (1996). *Guns or butter: The presidency of Lyndon Johnson.* New York: Oxford University Press.

Beverly, S. G. (2002). What social workers need to know about the Earned Income Tax Credit. *Social Work, 47*(3), 259–267.

Binstock, R. (1999). Challenges to United States policies on aging in the new millennium. *Hallym International Journal on Aging, 1*(1), 3–13.

Blau, J. (with Abramovitz, M.) (2004). *The dynamics of social welfare policy.* New York: Oxford University Press.

Board of Trustees. (2003). *2003 annual report of the board of trustees of the federal hospital insurance and federal supplementary medical insurance trust funds.* Available at www.cms.hhs.gov/publications/ trusteesreport/2003/tr.pdf

Board of Trustees. (2004). *2004 Annual Report of the Board of Trustees of the Federal Old-Age and Survivors Insurance and Disability Insurance Trust Funds.* Available at www.ssa.gov/OACT/TR/TR04/

Briar Lawson, K., & Drews, J. (2000). Child and family welfare policies and services. In J. Midgley, M. Tracy, & M. Livermore (Eds.). *The handbook of social policy* (pp. 157–173). Thousand Oaks, CA: Sage Publications.

Brissett-Chapman, S. (1995). Child abuse and neglect: Direct practice. In *Encyclopedia of social work* (19th ed., pp. 353–366). Alexandria, VA: National Association of Social Workers.

Browne, C. (1998). *Women, feminism, and aging.* New York: Springer.

Bureau of Labor Statistics, (2002–2003). Social workers. *Occupational Outlook Handbook.* U.S. Department of Labor. Available at www.bls.gov/oco/ oco060.htm.

Bureau of Labor Statistics, U.S. Department of Labor. (2004). *Occupational outlook handbook, 2004–05 edition. Bulletin 2540.* Washington, DC: U.S. Government Printing Office.

Burns, E. M. (1956). *Social security and public policy.* New York: McGraw-Hill.

Cannon, J. (Ed.). (1997). *The Oxford companion to British history.* New York: Oxford University Press.

Carlton-LaNey, I. (1999). African American social work pioneers' response to need. *Social Work, 44*(4), 311–321.

Center for Mental Health Services. (1997). *Addressing the needs of homeless persons with co-occurring mental illness and substance use disorders.* Rockville, MD: Substance Abuse and Mental Health Services Administration, U.S. Department of Health and Human Services.

Center on Aging. (2002). *Kansas elder count.* New York: Milbank Memorial Fund.

Center on Budget and Policy Priorities. (2003). *Number of Americans without health insurance rose in 2002.* Washington, DC: Author.

Centers for Medicare and Medicaid Services. (2003a). *Medicaid: A brief summary.* Baltimore: Department of Health and Human Services. Available at www.cms.hhs.gov/

Centers for Medicare and Medicaid Services. (2003b). *State Children's Health Insurance Program.* Baltimore: Department of Health and Human Services. Available at www.cms.hhs.gov/schip

Centers for Medicare and Medicaid Services. (2003c). *2002 Medicaid Managed Care Enrollment Report.* Available at www.cms.gov/Medicaid/managedcare/ mmcss02.asp

Centers for Medicare and Medicaid Services. (2005). Medicare Trustees report. www.cms.hhs.gov/ publications/trusteesreport/

Chambers, D. E. (2000). *Social policy and social programs: A method for the practical public policy analyst* (3rd ed.). Boston: Allyn and Bacon.

Chapin, R. (1995). Social policy development: The strengths perspective. *Social Work, 40*(4), 506–514.

Chapin, R. (1999). It is expected by the year 2000: Using lessons from the past to plan for the elder boom. *Journal of Gerontological Social Work, 32*(2), 21–40.

Chapin, R. (2001). Building on the strengths of older women. In K. J. Peterson & A. Lieberman (Eds.), *Building on women's strengths: An agenda for the 21st century, revised edition.* Binghamton, NY: Haworth Press.

Chapin, R., & Cox, E. (2001). Changing the paradigm: Strengths-based and empowerment-oriented social work with frail elders. *Journal of Gerontological Social Work, 6*(3/4), 165–180.

Child Abuse Prevention and Treatment Act, 42 U.S.C. 5106 § (1974).

Children's Defense Fund. (2001). *The state of America's children yearbook: 2001.* Washington, DC: Author.

Chiriboga, D. A. (1996). Comments on conceptual and empirical advances in understanding aging well through proactive adaptation. In V. L. Bengtson (Ed.), *Adulthood and aging: Research on continuities and discontinuities* (pp. 41–45). New York: Springer.

Clark, P., & Slack, P. (1976). *English towns in transition: 1500–1700.* New York: Oxford University Press.

Claxton, M., & Hansen, R. (2004, September 26), Working poor suffer under Bush tax cuts. *The Detroit News.*

Coll, B. (1972). Public assistance in the United States: Colonial times to 1860. In E. W. Martin (Ed.), *Comparative development in social welfare* (pp. 128–158). London: Allen & Unwin.

Commager, H. (Ed.). (1958). *Documents of American history* (6th ed.). New York: Appleton-Century-Crofts.

Committee on Ways and Means. (2000). *2000 green book.* U.S. House of Representatives. Washington, DC: U.S. Government Printing Office.

Compensation & Pension Service. (2003). *Veterans' benefits timetable: Information for veterans recently separated from active military service.* Available at www.vba.va.gov/bln/21/Milsvc/benfacts.htm

Congressional Budget Office (2003). *The budget and economic outlook: Fiscal years 2004 to 2013.* Washington, DC: U.S. Government Printing Office.

Congressional Budget Office (2004). *The budget and economic outlook: Fiscal years 2005 to 2014.* Washington, DC: U.S. Government Printing Office.

CongressLink. (N.d.). *Major features of the Civil Rights Act of 1964.* Available at www.congresslink.org/civil/essay.html

Council on Social Work Education/SAGE-SW. (2001). *Strengthening the impact of social work to improve the quality of life for older adults & their families: A blueprint for the new millennium.* Alexandria, VA: Council on Social Work Education.

Cox, R. S. (1998, January 9). Foster care reform. *The CQ Reseacher Online, 8.* Retrieved February 7, 2004, from library.cqpress.com/cqresearcher

Day, P. (1999). *A new history of social welfare* (3rd ed.). Englewood Cliffs, NJ: Prentice Hall.

Day, P. (2000). Social policy from colonial times to the Civil War. In J. Midgley, M. Tracy, and M. Livermore (Eds.), *The handbook of social policy* (pp. 85–96). Thousand Oaks, CA: Sage Publications.

DeLoria, P. J. (1993). The twentieth century and beyond. In B. Ballantine & I. Ballantine (Eds.), *The Native Americans: An illustrated history* (pp. 384–465). Atlanta, GA: Turner Publishing.

DeNavas-Walt, C., Cleveland, R. W., & Webster, B. H., Jr. (2003). *Income in the United States: 2002.* Current Population Reports, P60-221. Washington, DC: U.S. Government Printing Office.

DeNavas-Walt, C., Proctor, B., & Mills, R. (2004). *Income, poverty, and health insurance coverage in the United States: 2003* (P60–226). Washington, DC: U.S. Bureau of the Census.

Department of Veterans' Affairs. (2003). *Facts about the Department of Veterans' Affairs.* Available at www1.va.gov/opa/fact/docs/vafacts.htm

DeWitt, L. (2003). *Brief history.* Social Security Administration Historian's Office. Available at www.ssa.gov/history/briefhistory3.html

Division of Facilities Compliance and Recovery. (2003). *The Hill-Burton Free Care Program.* Available at www.hrsa.gov/osp/dfcr/about/aboutdiv.htm

Dobelstein, A. W. (1996). *Social welfare: Policy and analysis* (2nd ed.). Chicago: Nelson-Hall Publishers.

Dowd, J. (1980). Aging as exchange: A preface to theory. In J. Quadagno (Ed.), *Aging, the individual, and society* (pp. 103–121). New York: St. Martin's Press.

Downs, S. W., Costin, L. B., & McFadden, E. J. (1996). *Child welfare and family services: Policies and practice.* White Plains, NY: Longman.

Drew, E. (1996). *Showdown: The struggle between the Gingrich Congress and the Clinton White House.* New York: Simon & Schuster.

Dripps, D. A. (1996). A new era for gay rights? *Trial 32*(9), 18–21. Retrieved October 3, 2004, from proquest.umi.com

Education for All Handicapped Children Act of 1975, Pub. L. 94-142, S. 6. Available at asclepius.com/angel/special.html

Edwards, K., & Mason, L. M. (2003). *State policy trends for individual development accounts in the United States: 1993–2003.* St. Louis, MO: Center for Social Development.

Elk vs. Wilkins, 112 U.S. 94 (1884). Retrieved December 15, 2004, from http://laws.findlaw.com/us/112/94.html

Ellis, R. (2003). *Impacting social policy: A practitioner's guide to analysis and action.* Pacific Grove, CA: Thomson/Brooks Cole.

Equal Employment Opportunity Commission. (1999). *Milestones in the History of the U.S. Equal Employment Opportunity Commission.* Available at www.eeoc.gov/abouteeoc/35th/milestones/index.html

Fahey, C. (1996). Social work education and the field of aging. *The Gerontologist, 36*(1), 36–41.

Faragher, J. (1990). *The encyclopedia of Colonial and Revolutionary America.* New York: Facts on File.

Featherman, D. L., Smith, J., & Peterson, J. G. (1990). Successful aging in a post-retired society. In P. B. Baltes & M. M. Baltes (Eds.), *Successful aging: Perspectives from the behavioral sciences* (pp. 50–93). Cambridge: Cambridge University Press.

Fischer, G. (1992). The development and history of the poverty thresholds. *Social Security Bulletin, 55*(4), 3–14.

Food and Nutrition Service. (2003). *Women, infants, and children.* USDA. Available at www.fns.usda.gov/wic/

Food and Nutrition Service. (2003a). *Food Stamp Program: Frequently asked questions.* USDA. Available at www.fns.usda.gov/fsp/faqs.htm#1

Food and Nutrition Service. (2003b). *WIC program: About WIC.* USDA. Available at www.fns.usda.gov/wic/aboutwic/default.htm

Food and Nutrition Service. (2005). Food Stamps, Program Data. USDA. Available at www.fns.usda.gov/pd/

Fox-Grage, W., Folkemer, D., Burwell, B., & Horahan, K. (2001). Community-based long-term care. Forum for State Health Policy Leadership. Denver, CO: National Conference of State Legislatures.

Frasch, K. M., & Brooks, D. (2003). Normative development in transracial adoptive families: An integration of the literature and implications for the construction of a theoretical framework. *Families in Society: The Journal of Contemporary Human Services, 84*(2), 201–212.

Geen, R. (2003). Who will adopt the foster care children left behind? *Caring for Children, Brief No. 2.* Available at www.urban.org/url.cfm?ID=310809

Geertz, C. (1973). *The interpretation of cultures.* New York: Basic Books.

Gergen, K. (1999). *An invitation to social construction.* Thousand Oaks, CA: Sage Publications.

Germain, C. (1991). *Human behavior in the social environment: An ecological view.* New York: Columbia University Press.

Gilbert, N., & Terrell, P. (2001). *Dimensions of social welfare policy* (5th ed.). Boston: Allyn and Bacon.

Gilbert, N., Specht, H., & Terrell, P. (1998). *Dimensions of social welfare policy* (4th ed.). Needham Heights, MA: Allyn and Bacon.

Gist, J. R., & Verma, S. (2002). *Entitlement spending and the economy: Past trends and future projections.* Washington, DC: AARP Public Policy Institute.

Goldstein, A. (2004, April 2). Bush signs Unborn Victims Act; federal law establishes 2 crimes against pregnant women. *The Washington Post,* p. A4. Retrieved September 30, 2004, from proquest.umi.com.

Gordon, L. (1998). How welfare became a dirty word. *New Global Development: Journal of International and Comparative Social Welfare, 14,* 1–14.

Greenhouse, L. (2003, June 24). Justices back affirmative action by 5 to 4, but wider vote bans a racial point system. *The New York Times,* p. A1. Retrieved October 3, 2004, from proquest.umi.com

Greenstein, R. (2003). *Statement by Robert Greenstein, Executive Director, Center on Budget and Policy Priorities, regarding the signing of the Medicare prescription drug legislation.* Available at www.cbpp.org/12-8-03health.htm

Guyer, J. (2003). *Implications of the new Medicare prescription drug benefit on state budgets* (Publication No. 4162). Menlo Park, CA: Kaiser Family Foundation. Available at www.kff.org/medicare

Hamilton, B., Martin, J., & Sutton, P. (2004). Births: Preliminary data for 2003. *National Vital Statistics Reports, 53*(9).

Harrington, C., Kovner, C., Mezey, M., Kayser-Jones, J., Burger, S., Mohler, M., Burke, B., & Zimmerman, D. (2000). Experts recommend minimum nurse staffing standards for nursing facilities in the United States. *The Gerontologist, 40,* 5–16.

Hartman, A. (1990). Children in a careless society. *Social Work, 35*(6), 483–484.

Haynes, K. S., & Holmes, D. A. (1994). *Invitation to social work.* White Plains, NY: Longman.

Haynes, K., & Mickelson, J. (2003). *Affecting change: Social workers in the political arena.* New York: Allyn and Bacon.

Hays, E. M. (1989). *Prayers for the planetary pilgrim.* Leavenworth, KS: Forest of Peace Publishing.

Health Care Financing Administration. (2000). *A profile of Medicaid: Chartbook 2000.* Available at www.hcfa.gov/stats/2Tcharbk.pdf

Hine, R., & Faragher, J. (2000). *The American West: A new interpretive history.* New Haven, CT: Yale University Press.

Hobbs, F., & Stoops, N. (2002). *Demographic trends in the 20th century: Census 2000 special reports*. Washington, DC: U.S. Government Printing Office.

Hollinger, J. (1998). *A guide to the Multiethnic Placement Act of 1994 as amended by the Interethnic Adoption Provisions of 1996*. Washington, DC: American Bar Association Center on Children and the Law, National Resource Center on Legal and Court Issues.

Hooyman, N. R. (1994). Diversity and populations at risk: Women. In F. G. Reamer (Ed.), *The foundations of social work knowledge* (pp. 309–345). New York: Columbia University Press.

Hooyman, N. R., & Kiyak, H. A. (2002). *Social gerontology: A multidisciplinary perspective* (6th ed.). Boston: Allyn and Bacon.

Horney, J., Greenstein, R., & Kogan, R. (2005). What the president's budget shows about the administration's priorities. Center on Budget and Policy Priorities. Retrieved February 14, 2005, from www.cbpp.org/2-7-05bud3.htm

Horton, R. (1994). Stormy waters for US health reform. *The Lancet 344*(8921), 533. Retrieved October 2, 2004, from web4.infotrac.galegroup.com

House Budget Committee. Democratic Caucus. (2005). *Summary and analysis of the president's fiscal year 2006 budget*. Retrieved February 15, 2005, from www.house.gov/budget_democrats/analyses/FY06budget_analysis.pdf

Hudson, D. M. (1998). *Along racial lines: Consequences of the 1965 Voting Rights Act*. New York: Peter Lang.

Hymowitz, C., & Weissman, M. (1980). *A history of women in America*. New York: Bantam Books.

Internal Revenue Service. (2003). *Earned Income Credit (EIC): Are you eligible?* Publication 596. Available at www.irs.gov/pub/irs-pub/p596.pdf

Internal Revenue Service. (2004). Earned Income Credit (Publication 596). Washington, DC: Department of the Treasury.

Jansson, B. (1994) *Social policy: From theory to practice*. Pacific Grove, CA: Brooks/Cole.

Jansson, B. (2003). *Becoming an effective policy advocate* (4th ed.). Pacific Grove, CA: Thomson/Brooks Cole.

Jargowsky, P. A. (2003). *Stunning progress, hidden problems: The dramatic decline of concentrated poverty in the 1990s*. Washington, DC: Brookings Institute. Available at www.brookings.edu/es/urban/publications/jargowskypoverty.html

Jouzaitis, C. (1993, February 19). Working poor benefit from tax credit plan. *Chicago Tribune*, p. 17. Retrieved September 30, 2004, from proquest.umi.com.

Kahana, E., & Kahana, B. (1996). Conceptual and empirical advances in understanding aging well through proactive adaptation. In V. L. Bengtson (Ed.), *Adulthood and aging: Research on continuities and discontinuities* (pp. 18–40). New York: Springer.

Kaiser Family Foundation. (2005). *The Medicare prescription drug benefit—September 2005*. Available at www.kff.org/medicare/upload/7044-02.pdf

Kansas Action for Children. (2001). *The Kansas child welfare system: Where are we? Where should be we going?* Topeka: Author.

Kane, R., Kane, R., & Ladd, R. (1998). *The heart of long-term care*. New York: Oxford University Press.

Kao, G., & Thompson, J. S. (2003). Racial and ethnic stratification in educational achievement and attainment. *Annual Review of Sociology, 29*(4), 417–243.

Kaplan, D. H., Wheeler, J. O., & Holloway, S. R. (2004). *Urban geography*. Hoboken, NJ: John Wiley & Sons.

Karger, H. J., and Stoesz, D. (2002). *American social welfare policy: A pluralist approach* (4th ed.). Boston: Allyn and Bacon.

Kenney, C. (1981, August 30). New look to grants. *Boston Globe*, p. 1. Retrieved October 2, 2004, from proquest.umi.com

Kent, M. M., & Mather, M. (2002). What drives U.S. population growth? *Population Bulletin, 57*(4). Washington, DC: Population Reference Bureau.

Kingdon, J. (2003). *Agendas, alternative, and public policies*, (2nd ed.). New York: Addison-Wesley Educational Publishers.

Knappman, E., Christianson, S., & Paddock, L. (Eds.). (2002). *Great American trials* (2nd ed., Vols. 1–2). Detroit: Gale Group.

Kogan, R., & Kamin, D. (2004). *President's budget contains large cuts in domestic discretionary programs: Documents not made widely available show domestic discretionary programs to be cut $45 billion a year by 2009*. Washington, DC: Center on Budget and Policy Priorities.

Kretzmann, J., & McKnight, J. (1993). *Building communities from the inside out: A path toward finding and mobilizing a community's assets*. Evanston, IL: Institute for Policy Research, Northwestern University.

Ku, L. (2003). *CDC data show Medicaid and SCHIP played a critical counter-cyclical role in strengthening health insurance coverage during the economic downturn.* Center on Budget and Policy Priorities. Available at www.cbpp.org/9-23-03health.htm

Kutler, S. I. (Ed.). (2003). *Dictionary of American history* (3rd ed., Vols. 1–10). New York: Charles Scribner's Sons.

Lazarus, R. S., & Folkman, S. (1984). *Stress, appraisal, and coping.* New York: Springer.

Lazere, E., Fremstad, S., & Goldberg, H. (2002). States and counties are taking steps to help low-income working families make ends meet and move up the economic ladder. Center on Budget and Policy Priorities. Available at http://cbpp.org

Leiby, J. (1978). *A history of social welfare and social work in the United States.* New York: Columbia University Press.

Levit, K., Smith, C., Cowan, C., Sensenig, A., Catlin, A., & The Health Accounts Team. (2004). Health spending rebound continues in 2002. *Health Affairs, 23*(1), 147–159.

Lindsey, D. (1994). *The welfare of children.* New York: Oxford University Press.

Link, A., & Catton, W. (1967). *American epoch: A history of the United States since the 1890s.* Vol. 1: 1897–1920. (3rd ed.). New York: Alfred A. Knopf.

Loeske, D. (1995). Writing rights: The "homeless mentally ill" and involuntary hospitalization. In J. Best (Ed.), *Images of issues* (pp. 261–286). New York: Aldine De Gruyter.

Macarov, D. (1991). *Certain change: Social work practice in the future.* Silver Spring, MD: NASW.

MacEarchern, D. (1994). *Enough is enough: A hellraiser's guide to community activism.* New York: Avon Books.

Marsh, J. (2002). What knowledge is relevant to social work practice? The case of TANF reauthorization. *Social Work, 47*(3), 197–200.

Marshall, T. H. (1950). *Citizenship and social class, and other essays.* Cambridge, UK: Cambridge University Press.

Martin, J. A., Hamilton, B. E., Ventura, S. J., Menacker, F., & Park, M. M. (2002). Births: Final data for 2000. *National Vital Statistics Report, 50,* 5. Available at www.cdc.gov/nchs/data/nvsr/nvsr50/nvsr50_0.pdf

Marty, D., & Chapin, R. (2000). The legislative tenets of client's right to treatment in the least restrictive environment and freedom from harm: Implications for community providers. *Community Mental Health Journal, 36*(6), 545–556.

Matheson, L. (1996). The politics of the Indian Child Welfare Act. *Social Work, 41*(2), 232–235.

McDonald, W. R., & Associates. (2004). *Child maltreatment 2002.* Washington, DC: U.S. Government Printing Office. Available at nccanch.acf.hhs.gov/pubs/factsheets/canstats.cfm

McInnis-Dittrich, K. (1994). *Integrating social welfare policy and social work practice.* Pacific Grove, CA: Brooks/Cole.

McKinney-Vento Homeless Assistance Act, 42 U.S.C. § 11301 *et seq.* (1987).

Midgely, J. (2000). The institutional approach to social policy. In J. Midgley, M. Tracy, and M. Livermore (Eds.), *The handbook of social policy,* (pp. 365–375). Thousand Oaks, CA: Sage Publications.

Midgley, J. (1998). The American welfare state in international perspective. In H. J. Karger and D. Stoesz, *American social welfare policy: A pluralist approach* (3rd ed., pp. 434–452). New York: Longman.

Midgley, J. (1999). Growth, redistribution, and welfare: Toward social investment. *Social Service Review, 73*(1), 3–16.

Midgley, J., Tracey, M., & Livermore, M. (Eds.). (2000). The future of social policy. In *The handbook of social policy* (pp. 493–502). Thousand Oaks, CA: Sage Publications.

Mills, R. J., & Bhandari, S. (2003). *Health insurance coverage in the United States: 2002* (pp. 60–223). Washington, DC: U.S. Government Printing Office.

Monitz, C., & Gorin, S. (2003). *Health and heath care policy: A social work perspective.* Boston: Allyn and Bacon.

Moon, M. (2001). Medicare. *New England Journal of Medicine, 344*(12), 928–931.

Moriarty, L. (2003). *The center of everything.* New York: Hyperion.

Morris, P. M. (2002). The capabilities perspective: A framework for social justice. *Families in Society, The Journal of Contemporary Human Services, 83(3),* 365–373.

Moynihan, D. P. (1973). *The politics of a guaranteed income: The Nixon administration and the family assistance plan.* New York: Vintage Books.

Nabokov, P. (1993). Long threads. In B. Ballantine and I. Ballantine (Eds.), *Native Americans: An illustrated history* (pp. 301–383). Atlanta, GA: Turner Publishing.

Nash, G. B., Jeffrey, R. J., Howe, J. R., Frederick, P. J., Davis, A. D., & Winkler, A. M. (2004). *The American people: Creating a nation and a society* (6th ed.) New York: Pearson/Longman.

National Association of Social Workers. (1973). *Standards for social service manpower.* Washington, DC: NASW Press.

National Association of Social Workers. (1999). *Code of Ethics of the National Association of Social Workers.* Washington, DC: NASW Press.

National Association of Social Workers. (2003). *Social work speaks: National Association of Social Workers policy statements, 2003–2006* (6th ed.). Washington, DC: NASW Press.

National Association of Social Workers. (2003a). Affirmative action. In *Social work speaks: National Association of Social Workers policy statements, 2003–2006* (6th ed., pp. 16–19). Washington, DC: NASW Press.

National Association of Social Workers. (2003b). Gender-, ethnic-, and race-based workplace discrimination. In *Social work speaks: National Association of Social Workers policy statements, 2003–2006* (6th ed., pp. 152–160). Washington, DC: NASW Press.

National Association of Social Workers. (2003c). Immigrants and refugees. In *Social work speaks: National Association of Social Workers policy statements, 2003–2006* (6th ed., pp. 201–208). Washington, DC: NASW Press.

National Association of Social Workers. (2003d). Lesbian, gay, and bisexual issues. In *Social work speaks: National Association of Social Workers policy statements, 2003–2006* (6th ed., pp. 224–235). Washington, DC: NASW Press.

National Association of Social Workers. (2003e). People with disabilities. In *Social work speaks: National Association of Social Workers policy statements, 2003–2006* (6th ed., pp. 224–235). Washington, DC: NASW Press.

National Association of Social Workers. (2003f). Child abuse and neglect. In *Social work speaks: National Association of Social Workers policy statements, 2003–2006* (6th ed.). Washington, DC: NASW Press.

National Association of Social Workers. (2003g). Juvenile justice and delinquency prevention. In *Social work speaks: National Association of Social Workers policy statements, 2003–2006* (6th ed.) Washington, DC: NASW Press.

National Association of Social Workers. (2003h). Public child welfare. In *Social work speaks: National Association of Social Workers policy statements, 2003–2006* (6th ed.). Washington, DC: NASW Press.

National Association of Social Workers. (2003i). Client self-determination in end-of-life decisions. In *Social work speaks: National Association of Social Workers policy statements, 2003–2006* (6th ed., pp. 16–19). Washington, DC: NASW Press.

National Association of Social Workers. (2003j). Environmental policy. In *Social work speaks: National Association of Social Workers policy statements, 2003–2006* (6th ed., pp. 116–123). Washington, DC: NASW Press.

National Association of Social Workers. (2003k). Family planning and reproductive choice. In *Social work speaks: National Association of Social Workers policy statements, 2003–2006* (6th ed., pp. 124–131). Washington, DC: NASW Press.

National Association of Social Workers. (2003l). Role of government, social policy, and social work. In *Social work speaks: National Association of Social Workers policy statements, 2003–2006* (6th ed., pp. 293–303). Washington, DC: NASW Press.

National Association of Social Workers. (2003m). Technology and social work. In *Social work speaks: National Association of Social Workers policy statements, 2003–2006* (6th ed., pp. 337–340). Washington, DC: NASW Press.

National Association of Social Workers. (2003n). Health care. In *Social work speaks* (6th ed.). Washington, DC: NASW Press.

National Association of Social Workers. (2003o). Mental health. In *Social work speaks* (6th ed.). Washington, DC: NASW Press.

National Center for Health Statistics. (2003). *Health, United States 2003.* Hyattsville, MD: Author. Available at www.cdc.gov/nchs/hus.htm

National Clearinghouse on Child Abuse and Neglect. (2003). *How does the child welfare system work?* Available at http://nccanch.acf.hhs.gov/pubs/factsheets/cpswork.cfm

National Commission on Working Women (1986, Spring/Summer). *Women at work, 3.2.*

National Urban League. (2004). *The state of Black America 2004: The complexity of Black progress.* New York: National Urban League.

O'Connor, J. (1973). *The fiscal crisis of the state.* New York: Saint Martin's Press.

Office of Family Assistance. (2003). TANF federal five-year time limit (Table 9). *Caseload estimated from*

TDR–Section One, disaggregated data. ACF/OFA: 06-29-2004. Available at www.acf.dhhs.gov/programs/ofa/timelimit/2003/timelimitindex.htm

Office of Family Assistance. (2004). *Fact sheet.* Washington, DC: Author. Available at www.acf.hhs.gov/opa/fact_sheets/tanf_factsheet.html

Office of Juvenile Justice and Delinquency Prevention. (2002). *Guidance manual for monitoring facilities under the JJDP Act.* Available at betasites.aspensys.com/ojjdp/funding/jjact2002.html

Office of Management and Budget. (2000). *A citizen's guide to the federal budget: Budget of the United States government fiscal year 2001.* Washington, DC: U.S. Government Printing Office.

Office of Management and Budget. (2005). *Overview of the president's 2006 budget.* Retrieved February 14, 2005, from www.whitehouse.gov/omb/budget/fy2006/overview.html

Older Women's League. (1998). *Women, work, and pensions: Improving the odds for a secure retirement.* Washington, DC: Author.

Olsen, K. (1999). *Daily life in 18th-century England.* Westport, CT: Greenwood Press.

Oltmanns, T. F., & Emery, R. E. (1995). *Abnormal psychology.* Englewood Cliffs, NJ: Prentice Hall.

Organisation for Economic Co-operation and Development. (2001). *1980–1998: 20 years of social expenditure.* The OECD Database. Paris: OECD.

Organisation for Economic Co-operation and Development. (2003). *Health at a glance: OECD indicators 2003.* Paris: OECD Publications.

Organisation for Economic Co-operation and Development. (2004). *OECD health data 2004.* Paris: OECD Publications.

Ozawa, M. (1997). Demographic changes and their implications. In M. Reisch & E. Gambrill (Eds.), *Social work in the 21st century* (pp. 8–27). Thousand Oaks, CA: Pine Forge Press.

Patterson, J. T. (1996). *Great expectations: The United States, 1945–1974.* New York: Oxford University Press.

Pear, R. (2005, February 8). Subject to Bush's knife: Aid for food and heating. *New York Times,* p. A22.

Peller, J., & Shaner, H. (1998). *Medicaid eligibility standards for low-income families and children: State implementation of the Personal Responsibility and Work Opportunity Reconciliation Act of 1996.* Available at www.nasmd.org/pubs/tanfmedicaid2.htm

Pelton, L. H. (1989). *For reasons of poverty: A critical analysis of the public child welfare system in the United States.* New York: Praeger.

Pension Benefit Guaranty Corporation. (2005). *History of Pension Benefit Guaranty Corporation.* Available at www.pbgc.gov/about/hptext.htm

Peterson, J. (2002). *Feminist perspectives on TANF reauthorization: An introduction to key issues for the future of welfare reform.* Institute for Women's Policy Research. Available at www.iwpr.org

Peterson, K. (2003, February 25). *Gay marriage a complex political, legal issue.* Available at www.stateline.org

Peterson, K. (2004, October 6). 50-state rundown on gay marriage laws. Available at www.stateline.org

Petr, C. G. (2004). *Social work with children and their families: Pragmatic foundations* (2nd ed.). New York: Oxford University Press.

Piven, F. F., & Cloward, R. A. (1971). *Regulating the poor: The functions of public welfare.* New York: Pantheon.

Pollard, W. L. (1995). Civil rights. In R. L. Edwards & J. G. Hopps (Eds.), *Encyclopedia of social work* (19th ed., pp. 494–502). New York: NASW Press.

Popple, P. (1995). Social work profession: History. In R. L. Edwards, *Encyclopedia of social work* (19th edition, pp. 2282–2292). Washington DC: NASW Press.

Popple, P. R., & Leighninger, L. (1998). The policy-based profession: An introduction to social welfare policy analysis for social workers (1st ed.). Boston: Allyn and Bacon.

Postrel, V. I. (1988, May 20). Religious rights: A matter of property. *Wall Street Journal,* p. 1. Retrieved October 3, 2004, from http://proquest.umi.com

President's New Freedom Commission on Mental Health. (2003). *Achieving the promise: Transforming mental health care in America. Final Report.* (DHHS Pub. No. SMA-03-3832). Rockville, MD.

Provost, C., & Hughes, P. (2000). Medicaid: 35 years of service. *Health Care Financing Review, 22*(1), 141–174.

Quadagno, J. (1999). *Aging and the life course: An introduction to social gerontology.* Boston: McGraw-Hill.

Quadagno, J. (2000). Promoting civil rights through the welfare state: How Medicare integrated southern hospitals. *Social Problems, 47*(1), 68–69.

Quigley, W. (1996a). Five hundred years of English Poor Laws, 1349–1834: Regulating the working and nonworking poor. *Akron Law Review, 30*(1), 73–128.

Quigley, W. (1996b). Work or starve: Regulation of the poor in colonial America. *University of San Francisco Law Review, 31,* 35–83.

Rapp, C. (1998). *The strengths model: Case management with people suffering from severe and persistent mental illness.* New York: Oxford University Press.

Rapp, C., & Chamberlain, R. (1985). Case management services to the chronically mentally ill. *Social Work, 30,* 417–422.

Rapp, C., Pettus, C., & Goscha, R. (in press). The principles of strengths-based policy. *The Social Policy Journal.*

Rappaport, J., Davidson, W., Wilson, M., & Mitchell, A. (1975). Alternatives to blaming the victim or the environment: Our places to stand have not moved the earth. *American Psychologist, 30*(4), 525–528.

Reid, P. N. (1995). Social welfare history. In R. L. Edwards (Ed.), *Encyclopedia of social work* (19th ed., pp. 2006–2225). Washington, DC: NASW Press.

Reisch, M. (2000). *Social policy and the Great Society.* Social Policy Handbook. In J. Midgley, M. Tracy, & M. Livermore. (Eds.) *The handbook of social policy* (pp. 127–142). Thousand Oaks, CA: Sage Publications.

Rennison, C. M., & Rand, M. R. (2003). *Criminal victimization, 2002* (NCJ 199994). Washington, DC: Bureau of Justice Statistics. Available at www. rainn.org/ncvs_2002.pdf

Richmond, M. (1917). *Social diagnosis.* New York: Russell Sage Foundation.

Roberts, C. R. (1988). Supply-side economics—Theory and results. *Public Interest, 93*(Fall), 16ff. Retrieved September 21, 2004, from http://proquest.umi.com

Rosen, A., & Zlotnik, J. (2001). Demographics and reality: The "disconnect" in social work education. *Journal of Gerontological Social Work, 36*(3/4), 81–98.

Rowse, A. L. (1950). *The England of Elizabeth.* New York: Macmillan.

Saleebey, D. (1992). Power in the people. In D. Saleebey (Ed.), *The strengths perspective in social work practice* (pp. 3–17). New York: Longman.

Saleebey, D. (Ed.). (2002). *The strengths perspective in social work practice* (3rd ed.). Boston: Allyn and Bacon.

Schick, A. (with LoStracco, F.). (2000). *The federal budget: Politics, policy, process* (Rev. ed.). Washington, DC: Brookings Institution Press.

Schneider, R., & Lester, L. (2001). *Social work advocates: A new framework for action.* Belmont, CA.: Wadsworth.

Schreiner, M., Clancy, M., & Sherraden, M. (2002). *Saving performance in the American Dream Demonstration: A national demonstration of individual development accounts.* St. Louis, MO: Center for Social Development. Available at http://gwbweb.wustl.edu/csd/Publications/2002/ADDreport2002.pdf

Segal, C., & Stineback, D. (1977). *Puritans, Indians, and manifest destiny.* New York: Putnam.

Segal, E., & Brzuzy, S. (1998). *Social welfare policy, programs, and practice.* Itasca, IL: F. E. Peacock.

Sentencing Project. (2003). *Juveniles in adult criminal courts.* Available at www.sentencingproject.org/pubs_07.cfm

Shapiro, I., & Kamin, D. (2004). *Concentrating on the wrong target: Bush cuts would reduce domestic discretionary spending, as a share of GDP, to its lowest level in 46 years.* Washington, DC: Center on Budget and Policy Priorities.

Sherraden, M. (1991). *Assets and the poor: A new American welfare policy.* Armonk, NY: M. E. Sharpe.

Sherraden, M. (2000). From research to policy: Lessons from Individual Development Accounts. *Journal of Consumer Affairs, 34*(2), 159–181.

Sherraden, M. S., Slosar, B., Sherraden, M. (2002). Innovation in social policy: Collaborative policy advocacy. *Social Work, 47*(3), 209–223.

Sickmund, M. (1994). *OJJDP update on statistics: How juveniles get to criminal court.* Washington, DC: Office of Juvenile Justice and Delinquency Prevention.

Sickmund, M. (2004). *Juvenile offenders and victims national reporting series: Juveniles in corrections.* Washington, DC: Office of Juvenile Justice and Delinquency Prevention.

Singman, J. (1995). *Daily life in Elizabethan England.* Westport, CT: Greenwood Press.

Skocpol, T. (1993). American's first social security system: The expansion of benefits for Civil War veterans. *Political Science Quarterly, 108*(1), 85–116.

Smith, C., Cowan, C., Sensenig, A., Catlin, A., & The Health Accounts Team. (2005). Trends: Health spending growth slows in 2003. *Health Affairs, 24*(1), 185–194.

Snyder, H. (2004). *Juvenile justice bulletin: Juvenile arrests 2002.* Washington, DC: Office of Juvenile Justice and Delinquency Prevention.

Social Security Administration. (2000). *A brief history of social security.* SSA Publication No. 21-059. Retrieved October 2, 2004, from www.ssa.gov

Social Security Administration (2002). *Social Security benefit: Annual statistical bulletin.* Available at www.ssa.gov/policy

Social Security Administration. (2003a). *Annual report of the Supplemental Security Income Program.* www.ssa.gov/OACT/SSIR/SSI03/index.html

Social Security Administration. (2003b). *Understanding Supplemental Security Income (SSI).* Available at www.ssa.gov/notices/supplemental-security-income/text-understanding-ssi.htm

Social Security Administration. (2003c). *Understanding the benefits.* SSA Publication No. 05-10024. Available at www.ssa.gov/pubs/10024.html

Social Security Administration. (2003d). *Annual report of the Supplemental Security Income program.* Available at www.ssa.gov/OACT/SSIR/SSI03/index.html

Social Security Administration. (2003e). *Brief history.* Available at www.ssa.gov/history/early.html

Social Security Administration. (2003f). *2003 annual report of the Board of Trustees of the Federal Old-Age and Survivors Insurance and Disability Insurance Trust Funds.* Available at www.ssa.gov/OACT/TR/TR03/index.html

Social Security Administration. (2004). *Fact sheet Social Security: 2004 Social Security changes.* Available at www.ssa.gov/pressoffice/colafacts-alt.htm

Social Security Administration. (2004a). *Annual statistical supplement, 2003.* Washington, DC: U.S. Government Printing Office.

Social Security Administration. (2004b). *Fast facts and figures about Social Security, 2004.* Washington, DC: U.S. Government Printing Office.

Social Security Administration. (2005). *History.* Retrieved January, 2005, from www.ssa.gov

Spano, R. (2000). Creating the context for the analysis of social policies: Understanding the historical context. In D. Chambers, *Social policy and social programs: A method for the practical public policy analyst* (pp. 31–45). Boston: Allyn and Bacon.

Staudt, M., Howard, M. O., & Drake, B. (2001). The operational, implementation, and effectiveness of the strengths perspective: A review of empirical studies. *Journal of Social Service Research, 27*(3), 1–21.

Stevenson, R. W. (2005, February 8). President offers budget proposal with broad cuts. *New York Times.* Retrieved February 15, 2005, from http://proquest.umi.com

Stoddard, S., Jans, L., Ripple, J. M., & Kraus, L. (1998). *Chartbook on work and disability in the United States, 1998.* Washington, DC: U.S. National Institute on Disability and Rehabilitation Research.

Strawbridge, W. J., Wallhagen, M. I., & Cohen, R. D. (2002). Successful aging and well-being: Self-rated compared with Rowe and Kahn. *The Gerontologist, 42*(6), 727–733.

Strengthening Aging and Gerontology Education. (2000). *Social work with older adults* (2nd ed.) [Brochure]. Alexandria, VA: Council on Social Work Education.

Substance Abuse and Mental Health Services Administration. (2003). *About SAMSHA.* Available at www.samhsa.gov/about/about.html

Substance Abuse and Mental Health Services Administration. (2004). *Results from the 2003 National Survey on Drug Use and Health: National findings* (Office of Applied Studies, NSDUH Series H-25, DHHS Publication No. SMA 04-3964). Rockville, MD: National Clearinghouse for Alcohol and Drug Information.

Swatos, W. (Ed.). (1998). *Encyclopedia of religion and society.* Walnut Creek, CA: AltaMira Press.

Tanne, J. H. (2003). US ban on "partial birth" abortions could outlaw other forms as well. *British Medical Journal 327*(7422), 1009. Retrieved September 30, 2004, from http://proquest.umi.com

Taylor, J. (1997). Niches and practice: Extending the ecological perspective. In D. Saleebey (Ed.), *The strengths perspective in social work practice* (2nd ed.), (pp. 217–227). New York: Longman.

Tice, C. J., & Perkins, K. (1996). *Faces of social policy: A strengths perspective.* Pacific Grove, CA: Wadsworth Publishing.

Tice, C., & Perkins, K. (1996). *Mental health issues and aging.* Pacific Grove, CA: Brooks/Cole.

Tice, C., & Perkins, K. (2002). *The faces of social policy: A strengths perspective.* Pacific Grove, CA: Wadsworth Group, Brooks/Cole.

Title IX Education Amendments, 20 U.S.C. Section 1681–1688. (1972). Available at www.dol.gov/oasam/regs/statues/titleix.htm

Titmuss, R. M. (1974). *Social policy: An introduction.* New York: Pantheon Books.

Towle, C. (1945/1987). *Common human needs.* Silver Spring, MD: National Association of Social Workers. (Original work published 1945.)

Trattner, W. (1989). *From poor law to welfare state: A history of social welfare in America* (4th ed.). New York: The Free Press.

Trattner, W. (1999). *From poor law to welfare state: A history of social welfare in America* (6th ed.). New York: The Free Press.

U.S. Census Bureau. (1996). *Population projections of the United States by age, sex, race, and Hispanic origin: 1995 to 2050.* Current Population Reports, P25-1130. Washington, DC: U.S. Government Printing Office.

U.S. Census Bureau. (2001). *National population projections.* Available at www.census.gov/population/www/pop-profile/natproj.html

U.S. Census Bureau. (2002). *National population projections*. Available at www.census.gov/population/www/projections/natproj.html

U.S. Census Bureau. (2003). *2003 American community survey*. Available at http://factfinder.census.gov

U.S. Census Bureau. (2003). Age and sex of all people, family members and unrelated individuals iterated by income-to-poverty ratio and race. *Annual Social and Economic Supplement*. Available at ferret.bls.census.gov/macro/032003/pov/toc.htm

U.S. Census Bureau. (2003). *Children's living arrangements and characteristics: March 2002*. Washington, DC: U.S. Government Printing Office.

U.S. Census Bureau. (2003). *How the Census Bureau measures poverty*. Available at www.census.gov/hhes/poverty/povdef.html

U.S. Census Bureau. (2004). 2004 health insurance. *Annual Social and Economic Supplement*. Available at http://pubdb3.census.gov/macro/032004/health/toc.htm

U.S. Census Bureau. (2004). *CPS 2004 annual social and economic supplement*. Washington, DC: Author.

U.S. Census Bureau. (2004). *Poverty thresholds for 2004 by size of family and number of related children under 18 years*. Washington, DC: U.S. Government Printing Office. Available at www.census.gov/hhes/poverty/threshld/thresh04.html

U.S. Census Bureau. (2004a). *Interim projections of the U.S. population by age, sex, race, and Hispanic origin: Summary methodology and assumptions*. Washington, DC: Author. Available at www.census.gov/ipc/www/usinterimproj/idbsummeth.html

U.S. Census Bureau. (2004b). *Statistical abstract of the United States: 2004–2005*. Washington, DC: U.S. Government Printing Office.

U.S. Census Bureau. (2004c). *U.S. interim projections by age, sex, race and Hispanic origin*. Available at www.census.gov/ipc/www/usinterimproj/

U.S. Census Bureau. (2004). *Population estimates*. Washington, DC: U.S. Government Printing Office.

U.S. Census Bureau. (2005a). *Age and sex of all people, family members and unrelated individuals iterated by income-to-poverty ratio and race (Table number POV01)*. Washington, DC: U.S. Government Printing Office. Available at http//pubdb3.census.gov/macro/032005/pov/new02_100.htm

U.S. Census Bureau. (2005b). *Income, poverty, and health insurance coverage in the United States: 2004*. Washington, DC: U.S. Government Printing Office. Available at http://pubdb3.census.gov/macro/032005/pov/new01_100_04.htm

U.S. Department of Education, National Center for Education Statistics. (2003). *The condition of education 2003*. NCES 2003-067. Washington, DC: Author.

U.S. Department of Health and Human Services. (2001). *Delivering on the promise: Preliminary report of federal agencies' actions to elimination barriers and promote community integration*. Available at www.hhs.gov/newfreedom/prelim/fullrpt.html

U.S. Department of Health and Human Services. (2002a). *Child Support Enforcement Program*. Available at www.acf.dhhs.gov/news/facts/csenew.htm

U.S. Department of Health and Human Services. (2002b). *HHS role in child support enforcement*. Available at www.hhs.gov/news/press/2002pres/cse.html

U.S. Department of Health and Human Services. (2002c). *Trends in the well-being of America's children and youth 2002*. Available at http://aspe.hhs.gov/hsp/02trends/index.htm

U.S. Department of Health and Human Services. (2003). *2003 CMS statistics* (CMS Pub. No. 03445). Available at www.cms.hhs.gov/researchers/pubs/03cmsstats.pdf

U.S. Department of Health and Human Services. (2003). *Summary of immigrant eligibility restrictions under current law*. Available at aspe.hhs.gov/hsp/immigration/restrictions

U.S. Department of Health and Human Services. (2003a). *Major federal legislation concerned with child protection, child welfare, and adoption*. Available at nccanch.acf.hhs.gov/pubs/otherpubs/fedlegis.pdf

U.S. Department of Health and Human Services. (2003b). *National adoption and foster care statistics*. Available at www.acf.hhs.gov/programs/cb/dis/afcars/publications/afcars.htm

U.S. Department of Health and Human Services. (2004). *Medicare & you: 2004*. Available at www.medicare.gov/Publications/Pubs/pdf/10050.pdf

U.S. Department of Health and Human Services. (2004). *National adoption and foster care statistics*. Available at www.acf.hhs.gov/programs/cb/dis/index.htm

U.S. Department of Health and Human Services. (2005). *Federal Register, 70*(33), 8373–8375.

U.S. Department of Housing and Urban Development. (2000). *HUD's public housing program*. Available at www.hud.gov/offices/pih/programs/hcv/index.cfm

U.S. Department of Housing and Urban Development. (2001). *Tenant-based housing*. Available at www.hud.gov/offices/pih/programs/hcv/index.cfm

U.S. Department of Justice. (2000). *Introduction to federal voting rights laws.* Available at www.usdoj.gov/crt/voting/intro/intro_b.htm

U.S. Department of Justice. (2004). *ADA homepage.* Available at www.ada.gov

U.S. Department of Labor. (2004). *Unemployment compensation: Federal-state partnership.* Washington, DC: Author. Available at http://workforcesecurity.doleta.gov/unemploy/pdf/partnership2004.pdf

U.S. Department of Labor. (N.d.). Frequently asked questions about pension plans and ERISA. Available at www.dol.gov/ebsa/FAQs/faq_compliance_pension.html

U.S. Public Health Service Office of the Surgeon General. (2001). *Mental health: Culture, race, and ethnicity: A supplement to* Mental health: A report of the Surgeon General. Rockville, MD: Department of Health and Human Services, U.S. Public Health Service.

United Nations. (2004). Indicators on health. Available at http://unstats.un.org/unsd/demographic/social/health.htm#srce

Waldfogel, J. (2000). Economic dimensions of social welfare policy. In J. Midgley, M. Tracy, and M. Livermore (Eds.), *The handbook of social policy* (pp. 27–40). Thousand Oaks, CA: Sage Publications.

Wan, L. (1999). Parents killing parents: Creating a presumption of unfitness. *Albany Law Review, 63*(1), 333–359.

Washburn, L. (1999, December 18). For disabled, new federal law provides a ticket to work. *The Record (Bergen County, NJ)*, p. A18. Retrieved October 2, 2004, from http://web4.infotrac.galegroup.com

Weick, A. (1986). The philosophical context of a health model of social work. *Social Casework 67*(9), 551–559.

Weick, A., Rapp, C., Sullivan, P., & Kisthardt, W. (1989). A strengths perspective for social work practice. *Social Work, 37*, 350–354.

Weimer, D., & Vining, A. R. (1999). *Policy analysis: Concepts and practice* (3rd ed.). Upper Saddle River, NJ: Prentice Hall.

Weiss, R. J. (1997). *"We want jobs": A history of affirmative action.* New York: Garland Press.

Wilensky, H. L., & Lebeaux, C. N. (1965). *Industrial society and social welfare: The impact of industrialization on the supply and organization of social welfare services in the United States.* New York: The Free Press.

Wilson, J. Q., & DiIulio, J. J., Jr. (2004). *American government* (9th ed). Boston: Houghton Mifflin.

Zerbe, R., & McCurdy, H. (2000). The end of market failure. *Regulation, 23*(2), 10–14.

Zhan, M. (2003). *Saving outcomes of single mothers in Individual Development Accounts.* St. Louis, MO: Center for Social Development.

GLOSSARY/INDEX